WYOMING PLACE NAMES

Mae Urbanek

MOUNTAIN PRESS PUBLISHING COMPANY
Missoula

Library of Congress Cataloging-in-Publication Data

Urbanek, Mae Bobb.
  Wyoming place names.

  Reprint. Originally published: Boulder, Colo.:
Johnson Pub. Co., c1974.
  1. Names, Geographical — Wyoming — Dictionaries.
2. Wyoming — History, Local. I. Title.
(F759.U72   1978)   978.7   87-5755
ISBN 0-87842-204-8 (pbk.)

PRINTED IN THE UNITED STATES

Mountain Press Publishing Company
P. O. Box 2399 • Missoula, MT 59806
406-728-1900

One of the greatest wonders of Wyoming's Teton Mountain Range is that of noticing the way the many peaks change in shape and form as the viewer moves past their face. From the area near Jenny Lake, three peaks of varying configuration and height fall into a symmetrical pattern known as the "Cathedral Group" offering an evenly pointed, triple summit to the sky. From the left, the peaks are 12,325 foot Mt. Teewinot, 13,770 foot Grand Teton (highest in the range), and 12,928 foot Mt. Owen. Courtesy Wyoming Travel Commission

DEVILS TOWER

The nation's first national monument and its most spectacular volcanic neck, the Devils Tower is a photographer's dream. The awesome landmark rises abruptly 1280 feet above the valley of the Belle Fourche River and changes moods with each passing hour. The Tower area (including Missouri Buttes, Keyhole State Park, Black Hills National Forest) is open year around and features fishing, camping, picnicking, hunting, boating, and rockhounding.

Courtesy Wyoming Travel Commission

Preface

"There is no place like this place anywhere near this place, so this must be the place." So said Sagebrush Sam, and I started on my long search how "this place" got its appellation. The result is *Wyoming Place Names*.

The romance of Wyoming is included in the names of its rivers and mountains, in the titles of its cities and counties. I have gathered my information from a thousand sources: books, newspapers, private letters, pamphlets, and interviews. Listing source material for each name is not practical, since information for one name may come from a dozen sources.

There may be mistakes and misinformation. This book is only as accurate as possible. Obvious names suggested by topography, circumstance, or vegetation, such as Cottonwood Creek, are not listed, unless there is an historic bit of information concerning them. Names whose origins I do not know are omitted.

I owe special recognition for research started on Wyoming place names to Grace Raymond Hebard, University of Wyoming; to extensive information obtained from *Guide to the Wyoming Mountains and Wilderness Areas* by Orrin H. and Lorraine Bonney; to records kept by Wyoming State Archives and Historical Department, Cheyenne; to Coe Library, University of Wyoming, Laramie; to United States Geological Survey for official names in Yellowstone Park; and to many individuals who helped me find the sources of names in their counties.

Abbreviations used in *Wyoming Place Names* are: YNP, Yellowstone National Park; UP railroad, Union Pacific railroad; USGS, United States Geological Survey; BLM, Bureau of Land Management.

Following each name is the county in which the place is located. If the name is that of a peak or mountain, it is followed by its altitude in feet; ca means calculated.

If we waited until we were sure,
Not anything would exist to endure.

May you find the name in which you are interested.

Mae Urbanek,
Lusk, Wyoming 82225

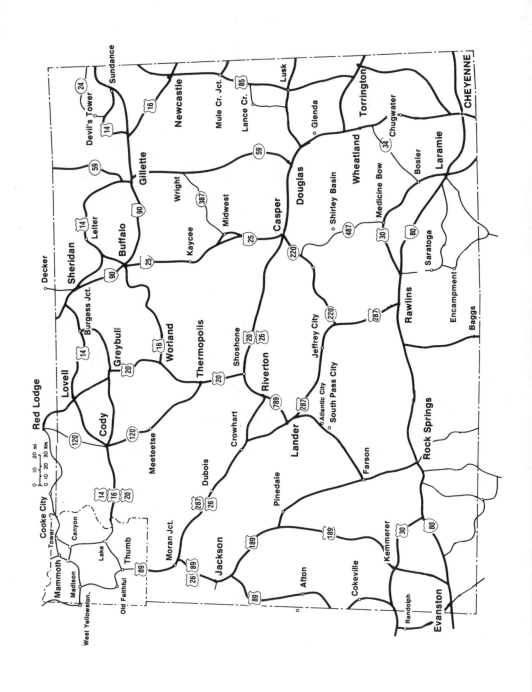

A

Abiathar Peak, 10,800, YNP: named by USGS for Charles Abiathar White, paleontologist in 1885; has been climbed following a ridge path made by bighorn sheep.

Absaroka Mountains (Ab-sa'-ro-ka), Fremont, Park, Teton, YNP: named by USGS in 1885 for Crow or Absaroka Indians, whose home base was east and south of these mountains; first known to trappers as Yellowstone Mountains; in 1873 rechristened by Captain Jones as Sierra Shoshone.

Absaroka Mountains were piled up by volcanic eruptions, partly eroded away, then piled up again and again. Their rough breccias and basaltic overflows have eroded into dramatic figures and spires, as seen along Highway 20 from Cody to Yellowstone Park; this stretch is called the most dramatic fifty miles in the United States. Absaroka Mountains are "the greatest slag pile on earth."

Absaroka Range, Lincoln: named for Indian tribe.

Absaroka Reservoir, Fremont: named for the mountains.

Abuse Spring, YNP: named because of the large amount of debris thrown into its hot water. Erupted first time after the 1959 earthquake.

Acme, Sheridan: coal mine camp, post office, and station on Burlington railroad; acme means prime, or best coal.

Alderville, Lincoln: early coal mine camp with many nationalities; founded in the 1870s; moved to new town of Kemmerer in 1897; black scars on sage-covered knolls, adobe piles, and several stone piles mark this ghost town.

Adon, Campbell: post office, discontinued in 1944.

Africa Geyser, YNP: first erupted in 1971 from a crater shaped like the African continent; roars.

Afton, Lincoln: settled in 1879; William Bedge, official in Church of Latter Day Saints, and a native of Scotland, watched the rapidly flowing waters of Swift Creek, on which Afton is located, and remarked that poet Burns could not have sung "Flow gently, Sweet Afton" about this turbulent stream. His companions then decided to call their new town Afton.

Mormon immigrants surveyed the site using a carpenter's square and a long rope, taking bearings from the North Star. An official survey later proved the streets only five feet out of true.

Afton is the largest town in Star Valley; an elkhorn arch across main street contains more than 3,000 elk antlers. Reuel Call and brothers started an airplane factory here and built their first plane in 1939. It produces agricultural planes. The Calls also invented an air-driven sled called a "snow car," and skis for airplanes.

An experiment station in Afton specializes in studies of irrigated crops. Afton is noted for cheese.

Aladdin, Crook: on Hay Creek; successor to Hay Creek and Barrett post offices. Established in 1898 when Burlington railroad was being built to reach Wyoming coal fields. The California capitalist who was backing the railroad laid out the town, and named it for Aladdin of *Arabian Nights*,

1

suggesting good luck and riches.

Fossil cycads, petrified tree trunks, and footprints of small reptiles were once found in this vicinity. To the north is a triangular basin with the lowest elevation in the state, 3,125.

Alamo, Big Horn: named by J. W. Shaffer, postmaster and rancher, for the Texas Alamo; means poplar; there was a ferry here once; town is now Manderson.

Alaska Basin, Teton: cold and snowy.

Albany, Albany: post office and railroad station established in 1900, and named by railroad officials for the county.

Albany County: created in 1868 by Dakota legislature from larger Laramie County; extended the full width of Wyoming Territory. Charles D. Bradley, a member of the Dakota legislature from Wyoming, worked for the new county, and named it for the capital city of New York, his native state; the county was organized in 1869. County seat is Laramie.

Albany County in 1910 elected Mary G. Bellamy as the first woman to serve in a state legislature. She went to Washington, D.C. in 1917 to represent Wyoming women in the national suffrage drive that ended with passage of the Nineteenth Amendment. This law originated by action of Esther Morris at South Pass City, and in half a century spread across the nation.

The University of Wyoming is located in Albany County. Lumbering, livestock raising, and manufacture of cement are chief county industries; Snowy Range attracts tourists, and offers much in winter and summer recreation.

Albany Peak, Albany: named for county.

Albin, Laramie: post office established in 1905 by John Albin Anderson, first postmaster, on his father's ranch; has been moved several times.

Alcova, Natrona: town near site of hot springs flowing from solid rock walls of a canyon. An eastern syndicate planned a health resort here in 1891, and named it Alcova because the springs were in a nest of coves. Project did not develop, even though the water had exceptional medicinal quality. Promoters decided that in Wyoming people took baths only on Saturday nights.

Alcova Dam, Natrona: named for the town; started in 1935, and completed in 1938; has capacity of 190,500 acre-feet; is one of the largest dams in the Kendrick project on North Platte River for water control and irrigation. Alcova Power Plant was built in 1955. A state park is here for recreation.

Alger, Sheridan: a Burlington railroad station named for Horace C. Alger, one of two men who first mined coal here for commercial purposes.

Alkali, Sweetwater: old stage station named for alkali in water; Walter Scott Davis, shotgun guard for Cheyenne-Deadwood stage line, tracked horse thieves here through snow from Lance Creek, Niobrara County; told by a woman at Alkali stage station that two men were sleeping in a haystack, he captured his men in a gun fight, and recovered eight stolen horses; he had ridden 375 miles across unmarked, snow-covered prairies.

Alki, Sheridan: railroad station named for alkaline content of water; name later changed to Ulm.

2

Allen, Carbon: railroad station named for William Allen, engineer.

Allyn, Albany: discontinued post office named for John J. Allyn, postmaster in 1876.

Almond, Sweetwater: stage and relay station in 1862; now railroad station; for name of community; post office was renamed Point of Rocks.

Almy, Uinta: coal town estalished in 1868; named for James T. Almy, bookkeeper for Rocky Mountain Coal and Iron Company that headquartered here. Chinese were being imported as miners in 1870, and racial feeling ran high. Explosive dust and firedamp plagued the miners, 87 of whom were killed in an explosion; mines were abandoned, and buildings moved in 1900. Black scars mark the ghost town today, and millions of tons of coal remain there unmined.

Alpine, Lincoln: hamlet with half of its streets in Wyoming, and half in Idaho; established in 1900, and named for the alpine beauty surrounding it. Robert Stuart and his party camped in this vicinity in the fall of 1812 trying to avoid harassing the Indians.

Alpine Lakes, Fremont: named by a group of surveyors for their beauty; a virtually unexplored region on the east side of the continental divide between Fremont Peak and Angel Pass.

Alta, Fremont: see Hudson.

Altamont, Uinta: railroad station and post office named as a high point on top of hills; railroad station name has been changed to Akwenesa.

Altus, Laramie: means high; point was one of highest on railroad; once a shipping point for limestone from nearby quarries; abandoned in 1931.

Altvan, Laramie: combination of names Altma and McUlvan, men who organized famous Hereford ranch on Crow Creek, largest pure Hereford ranch in the world; railroad station on the ranch.

Alva, Crook: for Alva S. Bender, first postmaster in 1891; original post office was located in a dugout.

Ames Monument, Albany: 65-foot pyramid of native granite constructed in 1881-82 at the highest point on UP railroad in honor of Olive and Oakes Ames, whose financial assistance made possible the construction of the railroad. They were eastern shovel and tool manufacturers. When railroad ran out of money, Oakes wrote officials to "go ahead; the work shall not stop even if it takes the shovel shop," which it did.

Monument is now a mile from the railroad which was moved in 1902. It was erected by UP at a cost of $75,000, and serves as a marker for the ghost town of Sherman.

Amesville, Lincoln: small settlement near junction of Willow Creek and Salt River; named for a family living there.

Amethyst Creek, YNP: named for the mountain on which it rises.

Amethyst Mountain, 9,423, YNP: named for amethysts found on it.

Amphitheater Lake, Teton: named for the peak; set in a glacier cirque which forms an amphitheater on three sides.

Amphitheater Peak, 10,847, Teton: named for its massive shape which forms an amphitheater around the head of a creek by that name.

Amsden Creek, Sheridan: for Bemis Amsden, pioneer of 1880; he was the first surveyor in the county; mapped the townsite of Big Horn with a vial of water fixed on a block of wood for a transit.

Anchor, Hot Springs: named for brand of C. E. Blonde, postmaster and rancher; post office discontinued.

Anchor Dam, Hot Springs: on south fork of Owl Creek; has the first trajectory spillway in the nation; water hurtles downstream over a projecting lip, and leaps like a skier; finished in 1960; for irrigation.

Anderson, Fremont: discontinued post office named for Laura Anderson.

Anderson Creek, Park: named for A. A. Anderson, once superintendent of national forests.

Andersonville, Hot Springs: founded in the 1870s on what Indians called Po-pa-da (Owl) Creek; named for Anderson brothers from Illinois; having heard of the Bighorn Basin as a garden spot, they came intending to raise beans, but started a town instead. It became a hangout for gunmen such as Butch Cassidy, and Kid Curry's Hole-in-the-Wall gang. When Thermopolis started across the river, Andersonville was abandoned.

Anemony Geyser, YNP: basin lined with pearly beads of cinder that glow pinkish or yellow—hence the name.

Angel Lake Pass, Sublette: named by one of many tourists; no one knows who or why, but the name stuck; this is true of many names for mountains, peaks, lakes, and trails.

Angel Terraces, YNP: at Mammoth Hot Springs, named for delicate and beautiful formations of white color tinted with pink.

Angels Lakes, 10,958, Fremont: excellent fishing.

Antelope, Uinta: railroad station named for wild game in region. These are not true antelopes, but "pronghorns"—the fastest of all four-footed animals. They have been clocked at a mile a minute for short distances.

Antelope Butte, 9,965, Big Horn: good skiing.

Antelope Gap, Platte: named for Antelope Gap Grange No. 60.

Ant Hill, 10,958, Johnson: in Cloud Peak Primitive Area; this peak, named for its shape, obscures the view of Cloud Peak for residents of Buffalo.

Ant Hills, Niobrara: three knolls shaped like ant hills; in an oil producing district.

Antler Creek, Sheridan: many deer and elk once ranged along this stream, and shed their antlers here.

Apollinaris Spring, YNP: a sparkling mineral beverage which mountains distill; named for god Apollo of sunshine and music. Nearby mountain has very strong and unusual acoustics. Jim Bridger liked to camp here, and said that on retiring he shouted "Jim! Six o'clock! Time to get up!" At six in the morning, the echo came back, and awoke him—no need for an alarm clock.

Arapaho, Fremont: post office established in 1880 by Indian Service, and named for the tribe by John Burnet, postmaster; also a railroad station. Arapaho is a Crow Indian word meaning "tattooed," given that tribe because they tattooed their chests; the Arapahos could not pronounce the word until they learned English, as they have no sound for R and H in their language.

Arapaho Creek, Albany: named by early settlers in the 1860s for Indians who passed through. Arapahos called themselves He-nau-ana-nan-wan, the chosen people. Their traditions tell of creation and a deluge similar to those of the Bible. Another meaning of their name is "he who buys and trades."

Arch Creek, Crook: named for natural arch of rocks.

Archer, Laramie: railroad station named for William Archer, member of an engineer corps that was attacked by Indians when surveying for UP railroad in 1867; Archer was wounded but escaped.

Archer Field Station, Laramie: named for nearby Archer railroad station; an agriculture substation organized in 1912 by Wyoming Farm Board of Commissioners in cooperation with U.S. Department of Agriculture; the station specializes in dry farming and highland grain growing; the average precipitation is 11.97 inches, average frost-free period 127 days.

Arcola, Laramie: post office named around 1898 by Mrs. Bertha C. Miller for an ancient city in Italy; discontinued.

Arizona Creek and Lake, Teton: named for "Arizona George" who had no other name; he was a trapper on Jackson Lake from 1888-89.

Arizona Island, Teton: named for Arizona George, trapper in 1880.

Arkansas Creek, Sheridan: named for a settler from Arkansas who homesteaded near head of creek.

Arland,, Park: founded in 1884 by cattleman Victor Arland; town became a "Saturday-nighter" for shootin' cowboys. After a pot shot killed Victor, his village was moved to Meeteetse in 1896.

Arlington, Carbon: founded about 1860 by Joe Bush as Rockdale at the crossing of Rock Creek; when the post office was established, it was changed to Arlington—no one knows why Arlington; it was a log store and dance hall with a school room upstairs. Here in 1865 Indians attacked a train of 75 wagons; they captured two young girls, Mary and Lizzie Fletcher, after killing their mother. After months with the Indians, Mary was bought by a white trader, and returned to her father in Salt Lake City. Thirty-five years later, a white woman who was raised as an Arapaho came to Casper with Indians from Wind River Reservation. Mary, reading about her, returned to Wyoming, and identified the woman as her sister Lizzie. Lizzie Brokenhorn refused to leave the reservation, where she enjoyed the superiority her white skin gave her over other Indian women.

Arminto, Natrona: post office named for Manuel Armenta who owned the "Jack Pot" ranch near the railroad station, whose officials changed the spelling to Arminto. This was the second incorporated town in Natrona County, and once hoped to rival Casper as a business center. Armenta was accused of being a horse thief, but there were many stories of his kindness to people in trouble.

Arno, Sheridan: railroad station named by a railroad worker for Arno River, Italy.

Arnold, Converse: named for Stephen Arnold; now part of a ranch.

Arpha, Converse: post office named for Mrs. Arpha Grace Tracy.

Arraster Creek and Lake, Carbon: named for an arrastre, a crude dragstone mill for pulverizing ore; such a mill was erected by the lake in early times.

Arrow Canyon and Creek, YNP: canyon is shaped like an arrow shaft.

Arrowhead Lake, Sublette: named by Toler party for its shape.

Arrowhead Mountain, 12,600, Sublette: named by K. A. Henderson for its resemblance to an arrowhead when seen either from north or from south.

Arrowhead Pool, Teton: in Hanging Canyon; named for its shape.

Artemisia Geyser, YNP: color of its pool resembles blue-green sagebrush.

Arthur Peak, 10,428, YNP: named for President Chester A. Arthur, in 1883 the first president to visit Yellowstone National Park during his term in office.

Artists Paintpots, YNP: small basins of colored, boiling mud.

Artists Point, YNP: spectacular view from here of the Falls and Grand Canyon of Yellowstone River. Here the roar of Lower Falls may be distinctly heard, although they are nearly a mile away.

Arvada, Sheridan: known as Suggs in 1891, but the name was changed by Burlington railroad officials. Here natural gas once flowed from an artesian well with water; brave citizens lighted the gas, and drank burning water.

Ashenfelder Creek, Albany: also called Asherfeld; named before 1900 for pioneer Ashenfelder.

Ashley Creek and Mountain, Albany and Platte: three versions of name: for William Ashley, trapper from 1822-23; for John Ashley, early miner; for General Ashley Fowkes.

Aspen, Uinta: this old, now extinct, boom town sprang up ahead of graders for UP railroad in 1867. Frontier Index had an office here, and printed editorials against lawlessness. A mob of graders armed with picks and shovels burned the jail, releasing the prisoners; then started for the printing office. Freeman, the editor, fled. Mob destroyed the press and type, and burned the building; was named for aspen trees.

Aspen Hill, Uinta: in 1901 UP railroad blasted a 5,900-foot tunnel through this hill to shorten its route ten miles. The tunnel cost $12,000,000, and was difficult to construct because of gas and crumbling earth.

Aspentunnel, Uinta: railroad station; post office discontinued.

Astoria Cabin, Natrona: first cabin built in state by known builders. In 1811 Wilson Price Hunt led the first group of white men to traverse what is now Wyoming westward to build Fort Astoria at the mouth of Columbia River. A returning group led by Robert Stuart on November 2, 1812, reached what is now known as Bessemer Bend on Platte River west

6

of Casper. Here they built a cabin, eight feet wide and eighteen feet long, covered with buffalo hides, and a fireplace in the center. Disturbed by a band of Arapaho Indians, they moved down the Platte, deserting their cabin.

Astoria Mineral Springs, Teton: see Counts.

Astoria Peak, Teton: named for the Astorian party under Hunt who traveled through Jackson Hole in 1811.

Atherton Creek, Teton: named for Atherton, settler in 1890 who wanted to get away from people.

Atkins Peak, 12,700, YNP: named for John Atkins, Indian commissioner.

Atlantic City, Fremont: founded in 1868 by gold miners from nearby South Pass City. One story says the name comes from the fact it is on the Atlantic side of the continental divide; another tale says that five residents from Atlantic City, New Jersey, named it.

In its heyday in the 1870s Atlantic City had a population of more than 2,000; it boasted an opera house, and the first beer garden and brewery in Wyoming. Flinging golden nuggets under dancers' feet, and tipping up bottles, miners squandered their hard-won gains. Here was the site of St. Mary's stage station; here Willie's Company of Mormons perished in a blizzard in 1857.

The granddaddy of grand pianos came overland by ox team to Atlantic City 100 years ago. Now its weathered buildings house a museum with relics of its famous past.

Atlantic Creek, Teton: heads at Two Ocean Pass, and flows to the Atlantic Ocean via Yellowstone, Missouri, and Mississippi rivers.

Atlantic Lake, Fremont: on Atlantic side of the continental divide.

Atlantic Peak, 12,734, Fremont: was originally called Stambaugh Peak for Lt. Stambaugh by members of the Hayden survey; renamed by mountain climbers because it is entirely on Atlantic side of the divide.

Auburn, Lincoln: in 1879 site of second settlement of Mormons in Star Valley, but was soon abandoned. When the settlement was revived a few years later, a Mormon woman looking at deserted buildings which reminded her of Goldsmith's "Deserted Village" suggested the name Auburn. The church here was the only rock building in Star Valley in 1900; people came to it on snowshoes.

Augur Hill, Laramie: this hill in Cheyenne was named for General C. C. Augur who established Fort D. A. Russell in 1867.

Aurum Geyser, YNP: named for yellow iron oxide on its cone. Aurum is Latin for gold.

Austin Reservoir, Uinta: named for Austin family who owned land where it was built.

Avalanche Canyon, Teton: avalanches frequently occur here. It is a beautiful canyon, glacially carved with tall peaks on both sides.

Ayres Crags, Teton: ascended by F. Ayres and J. Oberlin in 1946.

Ayres Natural Bridge, Converse: LaPrele River wore its way through red sandstone, creating a natural stone bridge 30 feet high, with a span of 90 feet. This arch supports several hundred tons of sandstone. It is located in an amphitheater of red sandstone, with a small crystal cave above it.

Dr. F. V. Hayden, USGS, and William H. Jackson, famous photographer, visited this beautiful spot in 1870. It was named by early residents for Alva Ayres, who owned land here. His brother, Curly Ayres, was a freighter on the Cheyenne-Deadwood trail. Mr. and Mrs. A. C. Ayres donated land around the bridge to Converse County in 1921 for a public park.

Azusa, Sweetwater: railroad station named for the manager of a Chinese store in Rock Springs.

B

Babione Creek, Sheridan: named for W. H. Babione, who operated a sawmill on it.

Bacon Creek, Teton: pioneers with heavy-ladened wagons followed a trail along this creek; still visible in places are ruts on what is now a jeep road; creek named for the chief food of these pioneers.

Bacon Ridge, 10,033, Teton: a red-topped ridge resembling bacon, about five miles long; a high point in the Gros Ventre-Green divide.

Bacon Rind Creek, YNP: probably named by early campers.

Badger, Converse: named for the animal; a stopping place in the late 1880s; mail, passengers, and freight were hauled here from Douglas to connect with the Colorado and Southern railroad.

Badger, Platte: railroad station where iron ore from Glory Hole was hauled in the 1890s. Had post office named for postmaster General George Badger.

Badger Basin, Park: post office discontinued in 1935.

Bad Medicine Butte, Fremont: named by Shoshone Indians because of the unexplained death of one of their scouts who climbed the butte to scan for enemies. They found him there, dead, with his face on his folded arms. No Shoshone will go to the top of the butte.

Badwater Creek, Fremont: usually dry in summer, but it floods quickly with heavy rains. Name appears on Colton's map of 1869; an Indian name. In 1923 Badwater Creek washed out several miles of railroad, and for weeks disrupted train service between Basin and Casper.

Badwater Creek, Natrona: Indians named this creek because it was often flooded with heavy rains; once their entire encampment was washed away by a cloudburst.

Baggott Rocks, Carbon: named for Amos Baggott, homesteader in 1878.

Baggs, Carbon: town on Little Snake River established about 1876; originally called Dixon for Bob Dixon, trapper; renamed Baggs for George and Maggie Baggs, large ranchers. Because of its isolation, in the 1880s and 1890s Baggs was a rendezvous for gangs of bad men who had a rock fortress in the hills, and held their celebrations in town.

Bailey Bar on Bailey Creek, Lincoln: place where sluice boxes and placer flumes were built, and gold washed in the early 1900s.

Bailey Creek and Bailey Lake, Lincoln: named for Bailey who built a cabin at the mouth of the creek; he worked the creek as a hunter and trapper; was first to pan for gold here.

Bairoil, Sweetwater: a company town of the Bair Oil Company; named for Charles Bair, a sheepman who promoted the first oil development in this area in 1916.

Bair Peak, 2,335, Fremont: named for Jack Bair, early trail blazer and ranger in the area; occasionally called Big Chief Mountain.

Baker Cabin, Laramie: in Frontier Park, Cheyenne, where it was moved from its original site near Dixon, Carbon County. Jim Baker, famous trapper, scout, and guide to John Charles Fremont, built this cabin in 1873 from hewn logs, dovetailed at the corners. Originally it was three stories high, with cupola and loopholes. Later the cupola was removed, leaving a small, two-story blockhouse which was moved to Cheyenne in 1917.

Jim Baker, born in Illinois, came west; trapped with Jim Bridger; operated a ferry over Green River on the Oregon Trail; prospected in Sierra Madre Mountains, and settled down with two Indian wives to tend his traps; he had ten children; he died in 1898. A canoe, "Mauritania," that he carved from a cottonwood tree, is on display in Wyoming State Museum, Cheyenne.

Baker Peak, Carbon: named for Jim Baker; his grave is in Savery.

Baker Springs, Crook: once a placer mining camp on Sand Creek, where large nuggets of gold were found; named for Baker who built a mill and cabins there in 1916.

Bald City, or Bald Mountain City, Sheridan: a gold mining ghost town on Old Baldy, built in 1892. Several million dollars of eastern capital were sunk into this venture. A huge amalgamator was dragged by 24 bull teams up a 65-mile treacherous trail. Once in place, it was powered by three steam engines to extract gold from crushed rock. Gold was not found in any paying quantities; the costly venture of the Fortunatus Mining Company ended in 1895; has been called City of Broken Hearts.

Bald Mountain, Albany: so named because the mountain has no vegetation on top; named about 1880.

Bald Mountain, Sheridan: bare of timber. An eastern company dug a five-foot tunnel here looking for gold in the late 1880s. They found no gold.

Baldwin Creek, Fremont: named for N. B. Baldwin, a pioneer, and a bold, courageous friend.

Baldy, 11,859, Sublette: named for its bare top; ascended in 1877 by members of Hayden survey, who first thought it the peak Fremont had climbed, but later concluded it was not.

Ball, Sublette: early post office, now discontinued, named for Charles Ball, on whose ranch it was at the foot of Ball Butte.

Ballistic Missile Launching Site, Laramie: the first intercontinental launching site under Strategic Air Command; started in 1958. Missiles are buried in underground silos; near Cheyenne which is also near the famed Lindenmeier prehistoric campsite, judged by scientists to be more than ten thousand years old. Here ancient nomads left a collection of their stone knives, hammers, and hide scrapers, and Folsom points with bones of slaughtered animals. The Lindenmeier site is just across the line in Colorado, and is named for the man who owns land there.

Bamforth Lakes, Albany: named for Fred Bamforth, rancher here in 1900. A federal migratory bird refuge was located here in 1930.

Banks, Goshen: an old ranch building here in 1863 had portholes on all sides; a haven of rest for weary travelers on the Oregon Trail that offered protection from Indians. John Owens, first sheriff of Weston County, took part in an Indian battle here in winter of 1867-68. Three white men killed were buried at the ranch and 17 Indians on an island in Platte River. A post office was established here in 1899, then the Rock ranch owned by Swan Land and Cattle Company. Mrs. Mattie Smith was postmaster. Named for Ed Banks, ranch foreman. Post office now discontinued.

Banner, Johnson: post office established in 1884.

Banner, Sheridan: post office; its first postmaster had a flag as a cattle brand; early settlers called it a "banner," hence the name of the post office which was in the dining room of the ranch house.

Bannock Falls, Teton: named for the western Indian tribe who once roamed here in Gallatin Range, but was finally placed on a reservation in Idaho.

Bannock Peak, 10,323, YNP: named for Bannock Indians who entered Yellowstone Park in 1877.

Baptiste Lake, Fremont: probably named for son of Sacajawea, carried on her back as a child when she guided the Lewis and Clark expedition westward from 1804-05. Baptiste was called Pomp, the dancer, by Clark who later placed him in school in St. Louis. He is buried beside his mother in Wind River cemetery.

Baptiste's Fork, Goshen: a relay station on Cheyenne-Deadwood trail. Named for Baptiste Pourier, "Little Bat," a guide and Indian fighter. John Hunton's road ranch at Bordeaux was home for Little Bat in his early boyhood; later he lived many places in the area.

Bar B C, Teton: second dude ranch in Jackson Hole; started about 1912 by Struthers Burt and Dr. Horace Cornoress.

Barber, Johnson: named for Amos Barber, acting governor from 1890-93.

Bargee, Fremont: post office established at Marcus ranch, and named for their brand Bar G; post office discontinued in 1933.

Bargee Reservoir, Fremont: named for Bar G, Marcus brand.

Barlow Peak, 9,800, YNP: named for Capt. J. W. Barlow, leader of military expedition of 1871 which traveled with Hayden party of USGS; Barlow mapped the headwaters of Snake River, and made many photographs which were later destroyed in the Chicago fire.

Bar-M Creek, Albany: named in 1878 for the Bar-M ranch brand.

Barnes, Goshen: railroad siding between Lingle and Fort Laramie. Named for John Barnes, an early settler. Section house and beet dump were once located here.

Barnum, Johnson: early post office named for Thomas F. Barnum, homesteader who had a way station and post office in his home in 1897; discontinued.

Baronett Peak, 10,404, YNP: named by USGS in 1878 for C. J. Baronett, "Yellowstone Jack," a famous scout and guide who built the first bridge across Yellowstone River near Tower Falls in 1871.

Barquin Mines, Fremont: when opened, these mines were on land of the Barquin family.

Barrel Springs, Uinta: stage station on Overland route. In the vast expanse of sagebrush was this crystal-clear spring, ice-cold, and much prized by early emigrants who had to use mostly bitter alkali water. The stationkeeper knocked the ends out of a 50-gallon whiskey barrel, and set it around the springs.

Barrett, Crook: post office on Hay Creek established in 1889 as a successor to Hay Creek post office; named for John M. Barrett, coal miner; discontinued.

Barrett Ridge Winter Sports Area, Carbon: in western part of Medicine Bow National Forest; has ski and slalom runs; source of name unknown.

Barron Creek, Park: named for guide and prospector Barron.

Bartlett, Laramie: discontinued post office, established in 1892; named for Frank W. Bartlett.

Basin, Big Horn: county seat; was established in 1896, and named for Bighorn Basin. In 1897 a hot county seat fight raged between Otto, Basin, and Cody, which was then in Big Horn County. Cody split the vote, and Basin won by 38 votes over Otto.

Basin and Greybull were the first towns in whole Northwest to have natural gas for lighting and heating. Basin, the lilac city, is in an irrigated bean growing area.

Bastard Peak, Sweetwater: so named because it stands alone.

Bates Battleground, Washakie: named for Capt. Alfred Bates who in 1874 led a cavalry troop with about 100 Shoshones under Chief Washakie in pursuit of Arapaho raiders, who were defeated.

Bates Creek, Campbell, Natrona, Washakie: named for Capt. Bates. Explorer Fremont named it Carson Creek for his guide Kit Carson, but after Capt. Bates skirmished with Indians here, it became Bates Creek.

Bates Creek Reservoir, Natrona: named for Capt. Alfred E. Bates.

Bates Hole, Carbon, Natrona: named for Capt. Bates; is bounded on south by Laramie Plains; on east by Muddy Mountains; on west by Platte River; and on north by Casper Mountain.

Bath House, Laramie: Henry Bath built a stone house with walls two feet thick on Laramie Plains in 1875.

Bat's Creek and Canyon, Converse: named for French-Canadian trapper Baptiste, known as "Little Bat."

Battle, Carbon: ghost town and discontinued post office near top of

Sierra Madre Mountains; in 1898 an overnight stop for freight wagons en route to Ferris-Haggarty Mine; once had forty houses, a sawmill, newspaper, five saloons in false-front buildings; named for several battles; in early days two Indian tribes battled near the mouth of the creek; Jim Baker and companions were later surrounded by Arapaho and Ute Indians between Battle Creek and Little Snake River, where they dug pits and stood off the Indians for two days. The Indians, tired of the fight, left without killing any whites. Another story says Henry Fraeb and four companies of Rocky Mountain Fur Company were killed here by Indians about 1841.

Battle Butte, Sheridan: named for battle from 1876-77 between troops under Col. Nelson Miles and Indians who were finally driven from the heights of the butte by two cannons concealed in wagons.

Battle Lake, Carbon: a deep crater lake just below the continental divide. Here Thomas A. Edison, a member of the Henry Draper expedition that came to view the solar eclipse in 1878, went fishing. In liberating his bamboo fishing pole from an evergreen tree, Edison noted how tough bamboo fibers were. Here in the silence of spruce-spired forests he found the answer he had sought in a thousand experiments—a suitable filament for his incandescent electric light bulb that revolutionized all industry. Fittingly, nearby Cheyenne was the first city in the world to be lighted by incandescent street lamps in 1882.

Battle Mountain, Carbon: see Battle.

Battle Mountain, Teton: scene of skirmish between Shoshone and Bannock Indians and a posse of officers and settlers sent to enforce game laws in Jackson Hole in 1895; posse rounded up a group of Indians for trial. They made a dash for freedom; one Indian was killed; the others escaped; the result of disagreement over treaty rights of Indians.

Battlement Mountain, 11,800, Park: a triple-ridged peak with many pinnacles; named for its shape.

Baxter, Sweetwater: railroad station named for Robert W. Baxter, who worked his way up, step by step, from a Laramie telegrapher to superintendent of UP railroad.

Baxter Pinnacle, Teton: a 60-foot spire first climbed by A. Baxter in 1948. Now a popular climb because of accessibility and good rock.

B-Bar-B Ranch, Campbell: buffalo ranch of D. C. Basolo, Jr.; more than 2,000 buffalo on 100 square miles of ranch south of Gillette. In 1967 Basolo herded buffalo with jeeps; sold roasts and robes clipped to make fancy furs; also sold buffalo skulls.

Bead Geyser, YNP: named by Prof. E. B. Comstock, geologist on the Jones expedition of 1873, to describe its beautifully beaded tubes.

Bear Canyon, Weston: Hank Mason, pioneer, killed a bear here.

Bear Creek, Converse: discontinued post office.

Bear Creek and Gulch, YNP: prospectors under Austin in 1863 found a hairless bear cub here.

Bear Head Mountain, Albany: named before 1900 for its resemblance to a bear's head.

Bear Lake and River, Uinta: first called Quee-yaw-pah by Indians for tobacco root that grew there; then named Miller by McKenzie for Joseph Miller, ex-soldier and Astorian partner who accompanied Wilson Price Hunt on his trek from St. Louis to Astoria. Miller quit the company, and joined John Hoback's trappers; he was among the first white men to see the lake and river. Miller guided Robert Stuart's returning Astorians in 1812 along this river, which was later given its present name for many bears along its course. The oldest water right in Wyoming was given from Bear River to Meyers Land and Livestock Company in 1862.

Bear Lodge, Big Horn: Pioneers killed a bear here.

Bear Lodge Mountains, Crook: many bear dens once here; site of battle between Captain Reynolds and Indians in 1865.

Bear Mountain, Goshen: named for wind-carved sandstone statue that looks like a bear, or a pioneer woman with sunbonnet; can be seen from Highway 85.

Bear River, Uinta: longest river in the world that does not flow to an ocean; wanders in Idaho, Wyoming and Utah before it finally ends up in Salt Lake.

Bear Springs Road Ranch, Laramie: in 1875 Joseph Armijo opened this stop for travelers with hay, grain, meals, and liquor. Later he sold it to his brother Miguel who was slow with payments; in a drunken quarrel Miguel shot Joseph.

Bear Tooth Mountains and Plateau, Park: named for Bears Tooth Peak; once an ocean bed, before it was raised by volcanic action; limestone formations are now at 11,000 feet elevations; oldest rocks were formed by heat and pressure deep within the earth; granite, hornblende, gneiss, mica, schist, and quartzite have been exposed to the weathering action of glaciers, wind, and water, for more than a million years.

A good highway is now built between mountain peaks, passes, and innumerable blue lakes; many switchbacks; lakes have good fishing; rocks are good for climbers; scenery little marked by people.

Bear Town, Uinta: named for Bear River. Originally called Gilmer. Founded in 1867 before the UP tracklayers arrived. A rowdy town that died after the railroad builders passed on. A ghost town without any ruins left.

Bear Trap Creek, Johnson: named for bear traps that were built near its source by early settlers.

Bearpaw Lake, Teton: resembles a bear's paw in shape.

Bears Ears Peak, 11,841, Fremont: landmark for hikers; name obvious.

Bears Gulch, Washakie: named for George B. McClellan who was known as "The Bear."

Bears Tooth Lake and Pass, Park: named for Bears Tooth Peak.

Bears Tooth Peak, 12,200, Park: a black cone, shaped like a tooth, that shows up dramatically against the white of Grasshopper and Downs glaciers.

Beat-The-Hell-Out-Of-Me Creek, Sublette, Teton: a Dr. Binns was processing fish to study when a companion asked the creek's name. Dr. Binns answered "Beats the hell out of me."

Beatty Creek and Gulch, Sheridan: named for James Beatty, an early cowboy who was thrown from his horse here. Joking cowboys said he took up a homestead where he lit.

Beauvais Springs, Goshen: in the late 1840s G. P. Beauvais established a trading post on the south side of Platte River, and carried on brisk trade with Indians.

Beaver Dick Lake, Teton: named for famous scout and hunter "Beaver Dick" Leigh. His protruding teeth gave him the appearance of a beaver. Beaver Dick Lake was once known as String Lake.

Beaver Rim, Fremont: name obvious; good jade hunting country.

Bechler River, Teton, YNP: named for G. B. Bechler, a leader in the 1877 Hayden expedition; he partly mapped area in 1872. This southwest corner of Yellowstone National Park where Bechler River runs is a wilderness of cascades and waterfalls; abundant with wildlife; home of trumpeter swans.

Beckton Junction, Sheridan: named for pioneer George W. Beck who built a flour mill here. A post office was established here in 1883; discontinued.

Beckwith, Lincoln: station on Oregon Short Line railroad; named for A. C. Beckwith, original owner of extensive Beckwith and Quinn ranch.

Beckwith Formation, Teton: named for I. C. Beckwith, homesteader.

Bedford, Lincoln: town named by Mormon Bishop Preston for Bedford, England, his former home; a sheltered farming valley settled in the 1880s. Post office discontinued.

Bed Tick, Converse: Pony Express station named for Bed Tick Creek.

Bed Tick Creek, Converse: named by pioneers for the condition of their beds.

Beehive Geyser, YNP: named by Washburn party in 1870, for the symmetry of its cone.

Beer Mug Mountain, Carbon: named for the brand of "Missouri John," pioneer; his brand was a beer mug.

Belknap Creek, Park: named for Henry Belknap, English rancher who brought some of the first cattle into Bighorn Basin about 1880.

Belknap Creek, Teton: named for Captain Henry Belknap, rancher in 1883.

Bell, Carbon: named for Albert Hiram Bell.

Bell, Converse: discontinued post office at the Bell ranch.

Bell Creek and Bell Hill, Albany: named for A. H. Bell, rancher here about 1888.

Bell Springs, Carbon: a bell-shaped formation; in early days only place where water could be found between Muddy Gap and Rawlins.

Belle, Crook: post office established in 1907; Thomas M.Coffey first postmaster; named for Belle Fourche River, on which it was located; discontinued.

Belle Fourche River, Campbell, Crook, Weston: pronounced "bell foosh"; named by French trappers before 1870; meaning "beautiful fork;" known to Indians as Bear Lodge River; runs over lowest spot in Wyoming, 3,100 feet, two miles lower than the highest point, Gannett Peak, 13,785.

Bellewood, Platte: stage station and post office from 1887-92. Post office moved when railroad connecting Wendover and Orin Junction was built; relocated on flats, and renamed Glendo because of the glen where railroad construction crew camped.

Bench Creek, Fremont: runs on top of a bench; an early road followed it.

Bennett Creek, Park: named for pioneer rancher Bennett.

Bennett Mountains, Carbon: named for Ed Bennett, rancher; these are granite mountains with red bands on cliffs at base.

Benton, Carbon: named for Thomas Hart Benton, western promoter; once a station on Overland stage route; for a few months in 1868 an end-of-the-track town, with dusty streets echoing the curses of men seeking solace from hard labor, bawdy laughter of women after easy money, and too often the sharp crack of a gun ending a dispute. Brawling Benton grew in a day, and vanished in a night when carted away to Rawlins.

Bernard Peak, 12,193, Fremont, Sublette: of rusty steel-colored granite which rings when walked on; has been climbed three times.

Bertha, Campbell: post office in 1904, named for Mrs. Bertha Poole, first postmaster; discontinued in 1934.

Berthaton, Natrona: see Johnstown.

Bess, Uinta: discontinued post office and settlement, named for James L. Bess, rancher.

Bessemer, Natrona: ghost town and site of first cabin built in Wyoming by Robert Stuart's returning Astorians in 1812. Bessemer was once "Queen City of the Plains," when it vied with Casper for county seat of Natrona County in 1889, and lost; at this time Bessemer had a space platted for the capitol of Wyoming. This once ambitious town is now a field of alfalfa. It was named by Wyoming Improvement Company for Sir Henry Bessemer, an Englishman, who in 1854 invented a process for making steel from cast iron.

Bessemer Bend, Natrona: a fertile valley in a bend of Platte River; named for town Bessemer, which folded when in 1891 the bridge across the river was seized by the county for unpaid taxes.

Bessemer Mountain, Natrona: see Bessemer.

Bettelyoun Flats, Platte: named for Isaac Bettelyoun, a trapper who built a cabin here in 1867.

Betty Creek, Park: named for Betty, daughter of A. A. Anderson.

Beulah, Crook: post office established in 1883 in a corner of a saloon; many of the first settlers here had attended school at Exira, Iowa, as pupils of Mrs. Beulah Sylvester, so they named their post office in her honor. Later she came to Crook County to teach.

Once a grindstone mill operated here; later it was replaced by a roller mill, turned by water power of Cold Spring Creek; teams and wagons waited their turn to have their loads of wheat turned into flour and bran.

Beulah Lake, Natrona: site of an early skirmish between Indians and emigrants from Iowa; probably named for Beulah Belle, early settler.

Big Baldy, Goshen: one of the three Rawhide Buttes; named for its rounded, bare top.

Big Chief Mountain, Fremont: see Bair Peak.

Big Creek, Carbon: rises in Sierra Madre Mountains; named from earliest times for large volume of water it carries.

Big Cub Geyser, YNP: named by Supt. Norris in 1881, when he named others in the trinity Lion and Lioness.

Big Game Ridge, Teton, YNP: has always been a favorite summer range for elk and other big game animals; its highest summit, Mount Hancock, 10,100, is inside Yellowstone National Park.

Big Goose Creek, Sheridan: rises in Big Horn Mountains, flows through a picturesque canyon, and is joined by Little Goose Creek in the heart of the city of Sheridan; named by early emigrants who found wild geese nesting along its banks.

Big Hollow, Albany: large, wind-eroded valley which appears as if it were scooped, or hollowed out; on 1862 and 1869 maps it was called "The Sinks"; by 1873 it was known as Big Hollow.

Big Horn, Sheridan: a town named for the mountains; a log cabin and two-horse log barn, left by outlaws, were found here when O. P. Hanna, first settler, came in 1878; site was on Bozeman road in the 1860s; by 1881 Big Horn became the first village in what is now Sheridan County.

In 1894 a building of bricks, baked by W. E. Jackson in a nearby kiln, housed the first college in the area, Wyoming College and Normal School started by Congregational Missionary Society; however, it closed in 1898 because it could not get enough students to pay tuition of $100. Bradford Brinton Memorial Museum is now near Big Horn. Bill Eaton Day, named for pioneer guide, is a professional rodeo packed with action, held in Big Horn every August.

Big Horn Canyon, Big Horn: the Grand Canyon of Wyoming; one of the famous deep-cut gorges of the West; the Clark expedition in 1806, camped at the mouth of Big Horn Canyon; fur traders used this water route; now a national recreation area around the canyon, which is flooded by water from Yellowtail Dam in Montana.

Big Horn County, named for mountains on its eastern boundary; authorized by an act of the legislature in 1890; was not organized until 1896, with Basin as county seat; took in all of Bighorn basin until Hot Springs, Park, and Washakie counties were sliced off. Livestock raising, irrigated farming, oil industry, and processing bentonite are principal industries.

Big Horn Mountains, Big Horn, Johnson, Natrona, Sheridan, Washakie: named from Bighorn River. (The river, basin, and forest are correctly written as one word; town, county, and range are spelled with two words). They were called "The Shining Mountains" by early explorers

16

because of glistening snow on their peaks. They rise in a long, low curve, like the horn of the animal for which they were named; this high plateau is about 120 miles long, and 30 to 50 miles wide, has high, level alpine plains of grass, broken with granite peaks of 13,000 feet elevation. Glacial cirques make many lakes, waterfalls, and meandering streams, creating unusual beauty; also good hunting and fishing; home of Eaton dude ranch, first in the nation.

Big Medicine Road, name given to Oregon Trail by Indians who watched with suspicion and fear, as white men's caravans streamed across their hunting grounds.

Big Muddy, Converse: translated from name given by early French trappers and traders, "Grande Riviere Vaseuse," Great Muddy River.

Big Muddy Oil Field, Converse: named for the unusually dry creek that flows through it; oil discovered here in 1916; reached peak production in 1919, with an average of 8,000 barrels per day from 200 wells; still producing.

Big Piney, Sublette: established as a post office on Mule Shoe ranch of A. W. Smith in 1888; moved to ranch of Dan Budd, Sr., who named it for the creek, Big Piney; however, no native trees in town; often reported as the coldest spot in nation, when mercury drops through bottom of thermometer in winter; altitude 6,780.

Big Piney Creek, Sublette: named for pines along its course; often called North Piney. Three Piney Creeks flow into Green River at nearly the same place. First cattle brought in 1878 by Ed Swan and Otto Leifer.

Big Pond Stage Station, Sweetwater: erected in 1862 of sandstone and limestone rocks embedded with shells; line abandoned in 1868.

Big Sandy, Sweetwater: Pony Express station and post office, discontinued; named for Big Sandy Creek nearby. Pony Express station burned by Indians in 1862. Now there is a Big Sandy State Park near Farson for recreation.

Big Sandy Mountain, Sublette: probably so named because it overlooks the drainage of 17 lakes by Big Sandy Creek.

Big Sandy Reservoir, Sweetwater: for irrigation and recreation; 2,500 acre-feet. A state park created here in 1952.

Big Sheep Mountain, 11,500, Sublette: excellent view of divide peaks and cirques from top.

Big Timber, Sweetwater: Pony Express station.

Big Trails, Washakie: post office first called Red Bank, but changed to avoid mail confusion; four main Indian trails lead to site from four points of compass, hence the name; discontinued in 1940.

Big Warm Springs Creek, Fremont: when President Chester A. Arthur with a military guard, and with Togwotee as guide, traveled this valley in 1883, they tried to camp on Clark's place near mouth of DuNoir Creek. Clark ordered them off. Gen. Sheridan called him down saying, "This is the President of the United States." Clark answered, "I don't care what he is president of; he's camping on my property without permission. I want him off." Camp was moved.

17

Bighorn Basin, Big Horn, Fremont, Hot Springs, Park, Washakie: largest fertile basin in state, about 80 miles wide, and 100 miles long; John Colter was the first white man to enter the basin in 1807; Edward Rose was the first white resident about 1808; he joined the Crow Indians, and lived with them. Bridger's Trail ran through the basin to Montana. First cattle came in 1879; J. D. Woodruff brought the first sheep in 1876; first oil well was drilled at Bonanza in 1887.

When President and Mrs. Calvin Coolidge left Cody by train in 1927, they were served a dinner completely grown in Bighorn Basin, even to salt and pepper. Menu was: bean soup, sage hen, corn on cob, honey, ice cream; his comment, "Rather unusual."

Bighorn National Forest, Big Horn, Sheridan, Johnson, Washakie: 11,113,000 acres; was set aside by government proclamations of 1897 and 1904. Bighorn sheep, native here, are extremely surefooted; the bottom of each foot is concave, enabling them to walk, run, and jump on steep rocks.

Bighorn Pass, 8,900, YNP: over the Gallatin Range; named for bighorn sheep.

Bighorn Peak, 9,930, YNP: a very steep and crumbly peak.

Bighorn River, Big Horn, Washakie: named by Lewis and Clark on their expedition of 1803 as a translation of Indian name Ah-sah-ta for the great droves of these bighorn sheep at the mouth of the river. The Wind River rises in Wind River Range, Fremont County, and flows north into Wind River Canyon. In this canyon at a place called "Wedding of the Waters" its name is changed to Bighorn River. The river flows through the deep Wind River Canyon; no stream joins it at the Wedding of the Waters.

Bill, Converse: post office named for four men with given names of Bill, whose homesteads cornered here.

Billy Creek and Billy Creek Oil Field, Johnson: named for Billy Doyle, pioneer who lived on the creek.

Billy Creek, Teton: named for Billy Bierers, homesteader.

Billy Flats, Washakie: named for Uncle Bill Robinson, early settler.

Binford, Albany: discontinued post office named for Binford family who lived here in 1899.

Binford, Platte: post office located on the Binford ranch.

Bingham, Sheridan: discontinued post office named for John A. Bingham, Jr., who was superintendent of stage line run by the Patrick brothers in 1879.

Birdseye Creek and Pass, Fremont: named by Indians for Charlie Fogg's brand: a dot in a circle, that looked like a bird's eye.

Birdseye Stage Station, Fremont: used in the 1880s; crumbling away.

Birthday Cake Peak, 10,238, Teton: looks like a birthday cake with candles, when approached from west ridge.

Biscuit Geyser Basin, YNP: named for geyserite knobs or forms that look like biscuits.

Bishop, Natrona: railroad station and post office established in 1913; named by patrons for Marvin L. Bishop, president of Natrona County Woolgrowers Association, who had his sheepshearing pens here; post office discontinued.

Bitch Creek, Teton: corruption of French word "biche" meaning deer.

Bitter Creek Stage Station, Sweetwater: on Overland stage route; also a railroad grading camp in 1868; named for creek with high alkali content in water that gives a bitter taste.

Bivouac Peak, 10,600, Teton: climbed by F. Fryxell and Kovens in 1930; named by them because they were benighted here, and had to bivouac, cold and hungry.

Black Buttes, Sweetwater: stage and railroad station named for nearby buttes that stand large and dark against the sky.

Black Canyon, Lincoln: named for Daniel Black of Ashley party.

Black Hills, Crook, Weston: from Indian name Paha Sapa, hills black; from a distance their evergreen forested slopes make them appear black; they were sacred land to Sioux Indians who fought fiercely to keep out gold seekers and settlers.

Black Hills, eastern Wyoming: now known as Laramie Range; was called the Black Hills by early trappers and explorers; this makes history confusing to present-day readers.

Black Hills National Forest, Crook, Weston: extends into Wyoming from South Dakota; lumber is harvested under Bureau of Land Management.

Black Mountain, Big Horn: formerly known as Cookesley's Peak, but renamed when a number of oil wells on its north slope produced heavy, black oil. Indians thought it "Land of Souls," and hung offerings to gods on trees.

Black Mountain, 11,562, Park: large peak in Sunlight mining region; consists of many minor summits and pinnacled ridges, whose timbered slopes appear black from a distance.

Black Tail Butte, Teton: extensive flats on its summit are feeding grounds for blacktail deer; a conspicuous landmark.

Black Tail Buttes and Ponds, Teton: named for blacktail deer.

Black Thunder Creek, Weston: in early days when wild horses roamed the range, a handsome, black stallion had a herd here. Sheriff Johnny Owens and friends were out riding, when this stallion swept past them like the wind. Owens exclaimed, "There goes Black Thunder." So the horse and the creek were named.

Black Tooth Peak, 13,014, Divide, Big Horn, Johnson: second highest peak in Big Horn Mountains; impressive black basaltic dike, shaped like a huge tooth; contrasts with grey granite of range; has a small glacier and snowfields on north side.

Blackhall Mountain, 10,990, Carbon: named for James Blackhall, one time supervisor of Hayden National Forest; now part of Medicine Bow.

Black's Fork, Lincoln, Sweetwater, Uinta: creek that empties into

Green River; named for Daniel Black, member of Ashley party. Uncle Jack Robinson, a squaw man, built a cabin on this creek in 1834; earliest permanent settler in region.

Blackwater Burn, Park: denuded slopes left by big forest fire of 1937, in which 15 men lost their lives fighting it; burned 1,250 acres.

Blair Meadows, Albany: picnic grounds named for Dave Blair, pioneer rancher.

Blair's Stockade, Sweetwater: Archie and Duncan Blair built a trading post near the springs, for which the town Rock Springs is named, in 1866, and furnished travelers with venison steaks and coffee. Becky Thomas, station master, charged ten cents a head for watering horses. Back of the station rise rocks on which emigrants carved their names.

Blairtown, Sweetwater: when the UP railroad came through, Archibald and Duncan Blair opened a coal mine, and employed miners. They built a dwelling and restaurant, and called them Blairtown; all was moved to Rock Springs in 1875.

Blaurock Pass, 12,500, Fremont: named for Carl Blaurock, prominent mountaineer, active in several mountain climbing organizations; member of the first party using this pass.

Bliss Creek, Park: named for horse thief Bliss, captured and shot near mouth of creek by posse about 1894.

Block Tower Peak, 12,000, Fremont, Sublette: almost hidden and very inaccessible; named for shape.

Blonde's Pass, Hot Springs: named for C. E. Blonde; post office was an important stop for mail stage before railroad came; pass was so steep that an extra team was put on to pull stage to top. Gen. Merritt and his forces crossed this pass in 1877 to head off Nez Perce under Chief Joseph.

Bloody Lake, Carbon: named for a battle between Indians and wood cutters for the UP railroad; wood choppers were killed before relief came from Fort Halleck.

Blue Creek, Fremont: named for color; falls in terraces and cascades.

Blue Creek, Sheridan: deep, swift-flowing stream; blue in color.

Blue Holes, Fremont: extinct geysers; depth of craters gives water a deep azure hue, hence the name. Indian pictographs are on nearby ledges; very scenic country.

Bluejay Peak, Albany: named in 1878 for bluejays who frequented a mining camp on the peak at that time.

Boar's Tusk, Sweetwater: a volcanic neck or leucite monolith rising in Red Desert 400 feet above the floor of Killpecker Valley; has the appearance of a great tooth; noted landmark in early days; can now be seen from Highway 187.

Bob's Creek, Fremont: named for the father of Toorey and Alvin Roberts, a rancher on the reservation known as "Indian Bob."

Boedeker Butte, Fremont: named for Henry Elmer Boedeker. In 1885 he was a stage driver from Crazy Woman station to Buffalo. Later he was marshall and deputy sheriff in Lander for 20 years. During that time he took Butch Cassidy as a prisoner from Lander to Fort Laramie in a wagon. The first state prison was at Fort Laramie. Boedeker homesteaded north of Dubois.

Boles Canyon, Weston: named for a rancher who lived there many years.

Bollinger Peak, 12,232, Fremont, Sublette: for Karl Bollinger who made his last successful climb here in 1953; he met his death next day, climbing War Bonnet summit; Bollinger was a member of Chicago Mountaineers; climbing was his life and inspiration.

Bolton Creek and Bolton Creek Oil Field, Natrona: named for oil promoter Bolton.

Bomber Mountain, 12,887, Big Horn, Johnson: a B17 bomber crashed here in 1943; named by Sheridan chapter of American War Dads.

Bona, Big Horn: railroad station; the name is short for Bonanza.

Bonanza, Big Horn: so named because oil was discovered seeping from a spring here in 1887; oil was so good it could be burned in lamps without refining; promoters thought they had found a "bonanza"; did not prove so, and rigs pulled out in 1890; deeper drilling has now brought back the Bonanza oil field; town is a ghost town.

Bondurant, Sublette: a ranch post office named for B. F. Bondurant, pioneer and first postmaster.

Bondurant Creek, Sublette: a ranch post office named for B. F. Bondurant, pioneer and first postmaster.

Bone Cabin Quarry, Albany: one of the most famous dinosaur beds in the world. A sheepherder used the plentiful dinosaur bones to build part of his cabin. Sixty complete skeletons were removed from the quarry, both large and small species. Dinosaurs roamed here in the Mesozoic era about 200 million years ago.

Bonneville, Fremont: post office and railroad station named for Captain B. L. E. Bonneville, who in 1832 led an expedition of 110 men, and a train of 20 wagons west along Platte River, up the Sweetwater, and westward; his were the first wagons through South Pass.

Bonneville Cabins, Fremont: built by Capt. Bonneville in 1835 to hold his trade goods. These five cabins were the first mercantile establishment in central Wyoming. Major Noyes Baldwin used the cabins for trading in 1866; vacated them in 1867; located a trading post on Baldwin Creek, near present Lander, in 1876; moved to site of Baldwin store in Lander same year.

Bonneville Lake and Mountain, 12,570, Sublette: a triple-topped peak named for Capt. Bonneville, a restless wanderer who made careful maps, recorded much that did not interest unschooled trappers, and so furnished Washington Irving with many descriptions and facts for his writings.

Bonneville Pass, Fremont: connects Brooks Lake with DuNoir Valley; named for Capt. Bonneville.

Bonneville's Folly or Fort Nonsense, Lincoln: in 1832 Captain Bonneville built cabins here for protection, then realizing that the place was wrong for spending a hard winter, evacuated it.

21

Bonney Pass, 12,700, Sublette: named for Orrin H. Bonney, mountain climber and author of *Guide to Wyoming Mountains and Wilderness Areas*, a detailed and accurate book on trails and climbing routes.

Bonney Pinnacle, 12,000 Teton: named for Orrin H. Bonney and his wife Lorraine, also a climber and author.

Boone Creek, Teton: in memory of Daniel Boone, famous trapper.

Bordeaux, Platte: stage relay station and post office established in 1877. This was the second post office in Wyoming Territory. The first was in Cheyenne. Bordeaux was named for Frenchman James Bordeaux who had a road house here that was the scene of many brawls; supplies were freighted through here from Cheyenne to Fort Fetterman; Gen. Fremont passed through here in 1842; Francis Parkman in 1846; Gen. Crook in 1875; near site of Grattan massacre; not in existence now.

Border, Lincoln: railroad station and discontinued post office on Idaho-Wyoming border, hence the name.

Borie, Laramie: railroad station named for Andy Borie, who was station agent at Buford, mayor, postmaster, justice of peace, and fire warden; a man Mark Twain would call a "concentrated inhabitant."

Borner's Garden, Lander, Fremont: named for Johnis Borner who homesteaded here. He married Lena Canary, sister of Martha Jane Canary (Calamity Jane) about 1869 or earlier.

Bosler, Albany: village and post office named for Frank Bosler, owner of Diamond Ranch which was once headquarters of Tom Horn, hired killer for big stockmen; he was finally hanged in Cheyenne, after he had killed a boy instead of his father.

Bosom Peak, Fremont: named for resemblance to female figure when seen from Dinwoody area.

Boswell Creek and Springs, Albany: named by Forest Service about 1880 for Nathaniel K. Boswell, early-day sheriff of Albany County; he captured a party of horse thieves near these springs; was once called Beaver Creek and Springs; post office discontinued.

Bothwell, Natrona: in 1889 cattle barons started a trading post here; it and post office named for J. R. and A. J. Bothwell, ranchers. Jim Averill started a saloon here. Homestead of Cattle Kate Maxwell or Ella Watson was about a mile away. She was believed to have added to her cattle herd by persuading cowboys to put her brand on calves for personal favors allowed them.

Ranchers ordered Cattle Kate and Averill, her friend, to leave; they refused; a posse hung them to a cottonwood tree. Members of the posse were known, but never punished; was end of Bothwell.

Bothwell, Sweetwater: named for J. R. and A. J. Bothwell, ranchers; heads of Sweetwater Land and Improvement Company.

Bottle Pinnacle, 11,500, Sublette: a bottle-shaped peak.

Boughton Canal, Albany: named for Boughton, a rancher in 1884.

Boughton Lane, Albany: named for an early rancher.

Boulder, Sublette: town and post office named for Boulder Creek, so named because of the large boulder in it from cliff above.

22

Boulder Creek, Albany: named for the boulders in and around it.

Boulder Ridge, Albany: a mountainous ridge named for boulders in old wagon road, used to haul ties in early construction days.

Boundary Creek, YNP: flows along Idaho-Wyoming line.

Boundary Lake, Carbon: near northern boundary of twenty-mile land sections granted to UP railroad by U.S. government.

Bow Mountain, 13,000, Sublette: named by K. A. Henderson, climber and mountaineer author, because of its circular shape surrounding a glacier at its base.

Boxelder, Converse: Pony Express station and post office, discontinued in 1943; named for trees on nearby Boxelder Creek.

Bowie Bluff, Platte: named for Al Bowie, manager of T Y ranch, Swan Land and Cattle Co. in 1887. This bluff in Chugwater Valley resembles the profile of a man with a very high nose. Locally it is known as Bowie's Nose.

Bowie's Nose, Platte: picturesque bluff named for Al Bowie, pioneer.

Boyd, Weston: discontinued post office; named for Boyd, first postmaster; was in log store building; home of Armfield, postmaster in the 1890s; also known as Elroy and Wrighter; owned by Mabel E. Brown, editor of *Bits and Pieces*, an historic magazine.

Boyd Creek, Fremont: named for William Boyd, pioneer who lived in an adobe house.

Boysen Reservoir, Fremont: first dam built in 1903 by Eramus Boysen, rich rancher. Caused water to back up over Burlington railroad which brought suit and had the dam blasted out. New dam was built about one and a half miles above old dam in 1948. Old dam site now marked by hanging bridge.

Bozeman Trail, Campbell, Converse, Johnson, Sheridan: following the discovery of gold in Montana, John M. Bozeman in 1863, against the advice of Jim Bridger, laid out a new route from Platte River near Fort Fetterman up Powder River, and north into Montana east of the Big Horn Mountains. When heavy traffic started in 1864, Indians fought fiercely to protect their invaded hunting lands.

Bozeman Trail was laid out in violation of the treaty of 1851 with Indians; still the U.S. government built protecting forts along it, and many were the bloody battles. The northern forts were abandoned, and the trail closed in 1868, in order to satisfy Indians, and keep them north of Platte River, so the UP railroad could be built; the trail became known as "The Bloody Bozeman."

Nelson Story of Ohio brought the first big trail herd of 1,000 cows with calves up the Bozeman Trail to Livingston, Montana, in 1866. Cows were then worth $10 a head with calves thrown in.

Braae, Converse: post office named for Andrew Braae, homesteader who lived in a log cabin. Post office opened February 4, 1926, and closed September 30, 1939.

Braae Mountain, Converse: named for Andrew Braae.

Bradford Brinton Memorial Museum, Sheridan: named for Bradford Brinton, eastern industrialist, who bought Quarter Circle A ranch, raised fine horses; collected western art and Indian relics. Willed by his sister, Helen Brinton, to the county as a museum in 1960; near Big Horn; open to the public in summer.

Bradley Creek and Lake, Teton: named for Dr. Frank H. Bradley, geologist in party of Capt. Reynolds of Army Engineers exploring Jackson Hole in 1960. Bradley drowned looking for a ford to cross Snake River.

Bradley Spur, Laramie: named for stone mason Bradley from Cheyenne.

Brees Field, Albany: airfield at Laramie named for Major-General Herbert Jay Brees, an early-day resident.

Breitenbach Pinnacle, Teton: named for John Breitenbach, former Exum school guide who was killed on 1963 American expedition to Mt. Everest.

Brent Creek, Fremont: named for George Brent, homesteader with a long, white beard.

Breteche Creek, Park: named for early settler Paul Breteche, Frenchman.

Brewster Springs, Uinta: named for Dr. William Brewster, surgeon, U.S. Army.

Bridge Bay and Creek, YNP: named by Hayden in 1871 for a natural bridge of trachyte which crosses the creek.

Bridger, Uinta: railroad station named for Jim Bridger, the Daniel Boone of the Rockies; town was a trading place for trappers and Indians as early as 1843; made a military post by Gen. Johnston in 1857.

Jim Bridger, "Old Gabe," who told his tales of fact and fancy over 10,000 camp fires, spent 49 years roaming the west; all of what is now Wyoming was mapped in his mind. A squaw man whom the Indians liked, he built Fort Bridger, the first motel west of Missouri River.

More than 20 places are named for him in Wyoming: a basin, a butte, and a bench, Carbon; a butte and a mountain saddle, Big Horn; a Pony Express station and ferry, Converse; a bottom or valley, Sweetwater; a lake, Teton; mountains, Hot Springs, Washakie, Fremont, and Natrona; a national forest and a wilderness area, and a valley in western Wyoming.

After tramping through what is now Yellowstone National Park, Jim Bridger told of petrified trees on which sat petrified birds singing petrified songs.

Bridger Butte, Uinta: named for Jim Bridger.

Bridger Creek, Fremont: named for Jim Bridger.

Bridger Lake, Teton: Jim Bridger camped here in 1830; he loved this region which is now in the Teton Wilderness Area.

Bridger National Forest, Lincoln, Sublette: has gone through many changes since it was set aside as part of Yellowstone Forest Reserve in 1891; in 1907 it became Wyoming National Forest; in 1923 the Bonneville National Forest to the east was added; in 1941 the name was changed to Bridger National Forest to honor Jim Bridger, early explorer; now contains 1,711,804 acres.

Bridger Pass, Carbon: discovered by Jim Bridger; where Ben Holladay in 1862 re-routed his stage line because of Indian troubles farther

24

north; called new route Overland route; it was later paralleled by UP railroad. A stage station was at the pass, from 1862-68; first mail went through in 1862; a sawmill here furnished lumber for building Rawlins, and logs for woodburning engines on UP railroad.

Bridger Peak, 11,007, Carbon: named by Captain Howard Stansbury for his scout Jim Bridger, who was guiding his exploring expedition through in 1850. A rock building on top of the peak was once used as a fire lookout by the Forest Service.

Bridger Road, Big Horn and Washakie: road developed and used by Jim Bridger in 1859.

Bridger Trail, west from Fort Caspar to where Lysite now is, up Bridger Creek, through Bighorn Basin west of Big Horn Mountains, and joined Bozeman Trail east of present town of Bozeman, Montana. Jim Bridger went this way to avoid trespassing on Indian hunting lands south and east of Big Horn Mountains.

Bridger Wilderness Area, Sublette: 383,300 acres, remote and scenic; a cherished wild region left as the Indians and Jim Bridger knew it in 1824. Trails are maintained by Forest Service; people can walk, or join pack outfits to enter this magic wonderland, with everything but their own personal items furnished. Pinedale is one starting place.

Bridger's Ferry, Converse: near present Platte River bridge southeast of Orin Junction; operated in 1857 with scale and pulleys; made a round trip over Platte River in 11 minutes.

Bright, Niobrara: used to be Warren; post office established in 1898 at ULA ranch which was named for owner's daughter Eula Wulfjen; this discontinued post office was named for Joe Bright, postmaster.

Brilliant, Lincoln: a coal mining camp that took its name from the brilliant, black quality of coal mined here.

Brimmer's Point, Platte: a high cliff overlooking Guernsey Lake; named for George Brimmer, a prominent citizen of Cheyenne.

Brimstone Basin, YNP: named for its smell of sulphur.

Brimstone Mountain, 12,700, Sublette: named by R. L. M. Underwood who climbed the peak in 1930, because of the strong smell of sulphur that accompanied any rock fall.

Britannia Mountain, Albany: named by Frank Banner in 1905 for a mountain similar in appearance to one which he had lived near in England.

Brokenback Creek, Big Horn, Washakie: in 1880 W. P. Noble and party tried to cross this creek; after a wagon broke down, they blocked it up for repairs, and it fell on a man who had crawled underneath it. Although his back was not broken, the creek was named for an accident that almost occurred.

Broken Egg Spring, YNP: so named because spring is shaped like an egg set on end, with its top broken off.

Broken Falls, Teton: so named because the plunge of water is broken by a shelf of rocks.

Bronx, Sublette: discontinued post office at Cox ranch, named by Mrs.

William Pape, early settler, for Bronx, New York.

Brooklyn Lake, Albany: named about 1880 for Brooklyn mine located nearby; at one time called Range Lake. A snowfield here is used by a college climbing club for snow and ice craft construction.

Brooks Lake and Brooks Lake Creek, Fremont: named for Bryant B. Brooks, the cowboy governor of Wyoming from 1905-11.

Broom Creek, Goshen: named for John McBroom who built a cabin where the emigrant road crossed the creek in the 1850s.

Brownlee Reservoir, Carbon: built by John Brownlee, pioneer, who secured one of the oldest reservoir rights in state.

Brown Park, Albany: a large park on top of Pole Mountain; named for road agent Brown who had his hangout in this place in early days before the railroad.

Brown Peak, Albany: named for Judge M. C. Brown who was interested in mining in this region in the early 1880s.

Brown's Hill, Carbon: named for Henry Breckmere who was known as "Bible Brown."

Brown's Hole, Sweetwater: named for Baptiste Brown, French-Canadian squaw man and trapper who lived here about 1835.

Brown's Spring, Converse: named for Lt. Brown who was wounded and died here in a fight with Indians in 1876; he was buried by the spring.

Brownsville, Carbon: named by Gen. G. M. Dodge in the spring of 1868; tent town of railroad builders on an alkali flat; occupied while building a railroad bridge across Platte River; vigilantes from Cheyenne tried to enforce law and order; they were known as "The Gunny Sack Brigade." Town was soon deserted; moved to Benton.

Brownsville, Fremont: discontinued post office named for James Brown.

Bruce, Fremont: named for Ed and Lewis Bruce, old-time ranchers.

Bruce Creek, Sheridan: named for Eugene Bruce, lumberman in Forest Service.

Bryan, Sweetwater: at first a stage stop; in 1868 a railroad center with roundhouse; vast supplies for South Pass were shipped from here during gold boom; men died in Bryan with their boots on in fierce fights in the days of its fleeting glory; named for Lt. Francis Theodore Bryan, surveyor. Now only a cemetery marks site of this ghost town.

Buchtel Peak, Sublette: named for Henry Buchtel, mountaineer; member of American Alpine Club; he ascended this peak in 1930.

Buck Mountain, 11,400, Teton: farthest south of high Teton peaks; probably named for the animal; attempts have been made to change name to Alpenglow. One of first major peaks to be climbed in 1898 by Bannion of the U.S. Geological Survey party.

Buckboard Bottom, Sweetwater: place where Thomas Fitzpatrick of William Ashley fur expedition had his first cache.

Buckeye, Albany: discontinued post office on Laramie, Foxpark, and Pacific railroad, whose officials named it for the Buckeye ranch about

1904. Ranch was named by its owner, a native of Ohio, the Buckeye state.

Buckeye Creek, Albany: named for Buckeye ranch.

Buckhorn, Weston: discontinued post office; named for mountain sheep by Isaac F. Sawyer, first postmaster.

Buckland Draw, Albany: named for landowners George and Frank Buckland about 1900.

Bucklin Reservoir, Carbon: named for landowners here, the Bucklin family.

Buckman, Natrona: named for Charles K. Buckman, fur trapper and trader who served with Gen. Nelson A. Miles.

Bud Kimbel Creek, Washakie: named for a pioneer who lived here.

Buffalo, Johnson: county seat; although its main street is said to follow an old buffalo trail, the town was named by five early residents who each put a name on a slip of paper, and dropped it in a hat; the name drawn out was Buffalo, put in by Alvin J. McCray, native of Buffalo, New York.

Buffalo has the distinction of being the only place in the United States where a motorist can make a legal U-turn on a bridge on a US highway. This can be done on the bridge over Clear Creek almost in the center of the town.

Buffalo was founded in 1879 by cattlemen, homesteaders, and miners, after the Sioux country was opened; claims the oldest county fair in the state in 1887, with a large premium list, and $5,000 in purses for horse races. Jim Gatchell Memorial Museum here has historic and archeological displays.

Buffalo Back, 12,200, Big Horn: a massive ridge named for its shape; climbed by Willcox party in 1933.

Buffalo Bill Dam, Park: known as Shoshone Reservoir; completed in 1910; 328 feet high, then the highest dam in the world; is between granite wall of Cedar Mountain on south, and Rattlesnake Mountain on north; has 6,690 acre-feet of water; for power, irrigation, and recreation.

Dam was named for William Cody, "Buffalo Bill," a Pony Express rider at 15; buffalo hunter for railroad construction crews, where he earned the name "Buffalo Bill," supplying tons of meat with his rifle "Lucretia Borgia," and his pony "Old Brigham"; estimated he killed more than 4,280 buffalo.

In this, his favorite county, he helped found Cody, and promoted irrigation; he organized a famous Wild West show; toured eastern states and Europe with Indians and cowboys, and publicized Wyoming; show started about 1883, and lasted more than 25 years.

He died in Denver in 1917, and is buried on Lookout Mountain near Denver, although he definitely wished to be buried at Cody.

Buffalo Bill Museum, Park: in Cody; contains many mementos from the colorful and romantic life of William "Buffalo Bill" Cody; opened in 1927; has more than 50,000 items of historical memorabilia.

Buffalo Bill State Park, Park: west of Cody; for recreation.

Buffalo Bill Statue, Park: in Cody; this bronze statue of Buffalo Bill on horseback is silhouetted against the mountains he loved; created and donated by Gertrude Vanderbilt Whitney; dedicated in 1924.

Buffalo River Ranch, Teton: old homestead and store buildings of Charles "Beaver Tooth" Neil; a character, over six feet in height, weighing 200 pounds; was the homeliest man in country; wore a derby hat, long black coat, and carried a cane; he came in 1908; was a good story teller. No trace of buildings now.

Buford, Albany: post office, railroad station named for Gen. John Buford in 1867. A military fort was established in 1866 to protect the Overland Trail and UP railroad from Indians; fort soon renamed Fort Sanders. Post office remained Buford.

Bug Creek, Fremont: tributary of Wiggins Fork; known for agatized and petrified wood branches.

Bull Creek, Albany: a branch of Cow Creek; named about 1878 by Jack Newell who shot a bull elk here.

Bull Creek, Washakie: named for Frank Bull, pioneer in the 1890s.

Bull Lake, Fremont: a Shoshone Indian legend says that a white buffalo bull was chased into the lake by Indians coveting his sacred, white hide. The bull drowned; in winter, the ice covering of the lake rises and falls with a moaning sound; Indians say the bull's spirit is roaring in anger; hence their name for the lake.

A Wind River medicine man used to have to sleep near Bull Lake as an endurance test that caused many young Indians to give up their ideas of becoming medicine men, most elevated position in the tribe.

Bull Lake Creek and Reservoir, Fremont: named for the lake; dam supplies water for Riverton irrigation project; 3,186 acre-feet; a recreation area.

Bull Peal, Albany: so named because bulls used to haul freight from Rock Creek Station were wintered here in early days.

Bull-of-the-Woods, Teton: annual snow slide in Hoback Canyon, named by Al Austin, forest ranger who was once caught in the slide. The avalanche of snow rushes down a gulch, across a frozen river, and then up the opposite hillside for a distance of more than 300 yards; it then slides back down to the river, giving the appearance of two slides.

Bull's Bend, Platte: so named because the Platte River in vicinity of old post office, Cassa, twists in shape of an ox yoke. Another explanation of the name is that the protected valley here was a wintering place for pioneer work cattle.

Bumpus Butte, YNP: named for Hermon C. Bumpus, once educational chairman for National Park Service; he supervised the building and equipping of park museums at Norris, Madison Junction, Old Faithful, and Fishing Bridge.

Bunker Hill, Crook: named for Solomon Bunker, once postmaster at Beulah and editor of a newspaper, probably the first in the country.

Bunsen Peak, 8,100, YNP: named by Geodetic Survey in 1872 for Robert W. Bunsen, prominent chemist and physicist who investigated the action of geysers, and first explained those phenomena. He invented the Bunsen burner.

Burke, Sheridan: discontinued post office, named for Rebecca Burke.

Burlington, Big Horn: town named by a colony of Mormons in 1893 for Burlington railroad which they hoped would make a large town; another story says it was named for Walter Burlington in 1887.

Burlington Railroad, short for Chicago, Burlington and Quincy, a merger of several lines in Wyoming; in 1886 a branch was built from Alliance, Nebraska, to important coal fields at Cambria, Gillette, and Sheridan, and on to Billings, Montana. Two branches were built from Montana into Bighorn Basin: to Cody in 1901; to Thermopolis in 1911.

Colorado and Southern railroad was acquired by the Burlington in 1908; tracks were extended through Casper to join the Bighorn Basin with Cheyenne in 1914. In 1943 the parallel tracks of the Burlington, and Chicago and Northwestern railroads west of Casper were consolidated, eliminating 87 miles of Northwestern tracks.

In 1900 the Burlington built a branch from Nebraska to Guernsey; this then joined with the Colorado and Southern, which ran from Denver to Orin Junction, joining the Chicago and Northwestern railroad there.

Burned Cabin Creek, Teton: so named because early settlers found a trapper's burned cabin on this creek.

Burned or Burnt Ridge, Teton: named for forest fire.

Burnett Pond, Weston: named for Charles D. Burnett who built the pond.

Burns, The, Fremont: just south of South Pass City; an old fireplace and small spring probably used by early trappers. A forest fire once started here, hence the name.

Burns, Laramie: town established in 1907 as Luther by Iowa people planning to have a German Lutheran colony here. UP railroad officials called its station here Burns for one of its division engineers. When the post office Burns, Uinta County, was discontinued in 1910, the railroad won the dispute, and Luther became Burns.

Burntfork, Sweetwater: named for the stream that runs nearby, and gets its name from burned timber along its course. Here in 1825 Gen. William Ashley held his first rendezvous with trappers, free traders, and Indians; post office discontinued.

Burnt Ranch or Burnt Fork, Fremont: old Pony Express and telegraph station, and stage stop near where the Lander cut-off took off to the north; started by Col. W. F. Lander in 1858; shortened old Oregon Trail about 200 miles.

Burris, Fremont: post office on Wind River; named by postmaster Mrs. Morrison for her first husband.

Burro Flats, Johnson: once a pasture for burros owned by EK outfit.

Buttressed Mountain, 12,200, Fremont, Sublette: named by W. Buckingham and W. Robinson, mountaineers, in 1961, for its shape.

Byran, Sweetwater: end-of-track town on UP in 1868; existence brief.

Byrne Creek, Uinta: named for Moses Byrne, early rancher.

Byron, Big Horn: town named for Byron Sessions, early Mormon settler who was influential in building Sidon Canal for irrigation. Soon after Mormons settled here, a farmer saw gas escaping from a fence post hole;

ignited, the gas burned for several years. In 1906 a test hole found gas sands at 700 feet, with a heavy gas flow. Byron gas field was developed to supply surrounding towns.

C

C Y Ranch, Natrona: Judge Joseph M. Carey built a log cabin here in 1876, and started collecting his vast holdings; named for his brand. Carey later bought the Goose Egg ranch. C Y Avenue in Casper is named for the ranch on which part of Casper is built.

Cabin Creek, Lincoln, Park, YNP: named for old cabins on banks.

Cache Creek, Park, Teton, YNP: so named because early trappers used to cache their furs and supplies near these creeks.

Cache Mountain, 9,596, YNP: takes name from creek where Indians surprised prospectors, and stole their horses, except two mules; men had to "cache" what mules could not pack.

Cactus, Campbell: post office discontinued in 1933; named for cactus on the prairies.

Cadiz, Sheridan: discontinued post office; station on railroad named by a railroad builder for Cadiz, a city and a province in Spain; mail put off here for Leiter.

Cadoma, Natrona: railroad station established in 1903; named for Indian word meaning to hide.

Cairn Peak, 12,100, Sublette: a square-topped peak with a cairn.

Caldwell Lake, Albany: named for Judge I. P. Caldwell, rancher in 1878.

Calfee Creek, YNP: named for H. B. Calfee, noted photographer of Yellowstone National Park.

California Trail, another name for Oregon Trail, which see.

Calpet, Sublette: discontinued post office for California Petroleum Oil Company.

Calvin, Carbon: named for Calvin, station agent here in 1870.

Cambria, Weston: ghost town that can be reached only with a jeep; named for Cambria, or Wales, where there were lots of coal and mountains. Frank W. Mondell discovered coal here in 1887; this made possible the building of the Burlington railroad into northeastern Wyoming; coal was hard, and made fine coke.

At peak of development 400,000 tons of coal were mined yearly; 24 coke ovens burned; a company town filled the steep canyons; miners were mostly Austrians, Italians, and Swedes. Long stairways led up hillsides to their homes, and to a school, opera house, bathhouse, and gymnasium, all company-built. Liquor was forbidden.

The end came suddenly in 1929 when the coal pinched out; miners left the company houses with unwashed supper dishes on tables; buildings were moved, or have crumbled away; only a cemetery, high on a hill, is left, grass-grown and neglected.

Cameahwait Lake, Fremont: named for a Shoshone Indian Chief, Cameahwait, brother of Sacajawea; he smoked a pipe of peace with explorer Meriwether Lewis in 1805. Cameahwait removed his moccasins and pointed the pipe stem to the four cardinal points of the heaven, starting in the east, in reverence for the earth, all before the long smoke began.

Camel Back Mountain, Albany: named before 1900 for a series of humps resembling those of a camel; also known as Camel Rock, Sitting Hen, and Sand Creek Sphinx; interesting for climbers who need ropes and pitons to conquer its crumbly sandstone.

Camels Head, Teton: a 60-foot pinnacle; named for shape.

Cameron Pass, Albany: named about 1900 for James Cameron, rancher.

Camp Brown, Fremont: when Chief Washakie asked for protection, Gen. Christopher C. Augur built Camp Augur on present site of Lander in 1869; in 1870 the camp was moved to Little Wind River, and name changed to Camp Brown for Capt. Frederick Brown, who was killed in the Fetterman Massacre in 1866. This was renamed Fort Washakie in 1878; is now center of reservation activities for Shoshone Indians.

Camp Bruce, Fremont: named for John Bruce.

Camp Carey, Converse: named for Senator Robert D. Carey who gave Boy Scouts 40 acres for their camp on Boxelder Creek.

Camp Carlin, Laramie: in 1867, after Fort D. A. Russell was established, Col. E. B. Carling built an army supply depot nearby, with warehouses, blacksmith, and repair shops; in records it was misspelled Carlin, although named for its builder; soon became known as Cheyenne Depot; was second largest supply post in West, caring for 12 army posts; had in its corrals 1,000 mules for transportation; also supplied annuity goods to Indian tribes.

Camp Colter, Park: named for John Colter; see Powell.

Camp Connor, Johnson: named for Gen. P. E. Connor; later Fort Reno, which see.

Camp Creek, Albany: named for an old timber camp on creek in the 1860s.

Camp Creek, Sheridan: rises on top of Big Horn Mountains, and empties into Fool's Creek; afforded a fine campground for early travelers.

Camp Davis, Teton: named for Prof. J. B. Davis; a Michigan summer school for civil engineers, founded in 1874; oldest school of its kind; discontinued.

Camp Marshall, Converse: early camp destroyed by government to prevent its selling liquor to the Indians.

Camp McGraw, Fremont: surveyors from Ft. Kearney, Nebraska, spent the winter of 1857-58 in Popo Agie valley, and built a house here known as Camp McGraw for William M. McGraw, leader and contractor for building the government road to Oregon. He was relieved of his command by Col. F. W. Lander in the spring of 1858.

Camp Medicine Bluff, Uinta: destroyed by government in 1872 to prevent its selling liquor to the Indians.

Camp Menace, Park: named for Prince Albert of Menace, guest of Buffalo Bill in 1913; first ruling prince to visit the United States.

Camp Pilot Butte, Sweetwater: an army camp set up at Pilot Butte after white miners massacred and ran Chinese miners off in 1885. UP railroad brought Chinese back, and lodged them in boxcars in Rock Springs; Chinese had been brought in as strike breakers, and were hated by white miners; barracks of camp are used as apartment houses.

Camp Platte, Natrona: see Casper.

Camp Scott, Uinta: a makeshift winter camp erected near present site of Fort Bridger by Col. Albert Johnston in his campaign against Mormons, who had burned Fort Supply and Fort Bridger in 1857. Camp Scott was named for Gen. Winfield Scott.

Camp Sheridan, YNP: constructed in 1886 near Mammoth Hot Springs by Capt. Harris, and named for Gen. Philip H. Sheridan. See Fort Yellowstone.

Camp Stambaugh, Fremont: established in 1870 on Oregon Trail to protect miners from Indians; consisted of four large log barracks; named for Lt. George B. Stambaugh who was killed by Indians in 1870.

Camp Stool, Laramie: discontinued post office named for Campstool cattle ranch whose brand was a campstool.

Camp Walbach, Laramie: established in 1858 to protect emigrants through Cheyenne Pass; branch roads from here went north to Fort Laramie, and south to Denver; named for Gen. J. B. Walbach; abandoned in 1859.

Camp Winnifield, Uinta: established in 1857 by Capt. Van Fleet when army came to enforce laws among Mormons.

Campanula, YNP: named for a wild flower, a bluebell, of that name.

Campanula Creek, YNP: named for the wild bluebell which grows here.

Campbell County, created in 1911, with Gillette as county seat; named for John A. Campbell, first Territorial Governor; another version: for Robert Campbell, early fur trapper here, one of Ashley's men. County is rich in coal and oil deposits; also has bentonite and uranium; good livestock country.

Campbell Lake, Carbon: named for Arch and Jack Campbell, sheepmen.

Campground Pinnacles, 10,200, Johnson: so named for a group of peaks that appear to be camping together.

Canon Creek, Albany: canon is Spanish for canyon; like a number of other Canyon Creeks, it was so named because it flows in a canyon.

Cantonment Conner, Johnson: named for General Conner who established it. A Powder River crossing on Bozeman Trail in 1865. Rebuilt by Colonel Henry Carrington in 1866 and renamed Fort Reno.

Cantonment Reno, Johnson: established in the fall of 1867 as army supply base by Captain Pollock, three miles from old Fort Reno. Renamed Fort McKinney on the Powder in 1877; abandoned in 1892.

Canyon Ranche, Lincoln: post office discontinued in 1933.

Canyon Springs Stage Station, Weston: on Cheyenne-Deadwood route. A famous robbery occurred here in 1878; three men were riding "shotgun" protecting the stage, when it pulled into the log station; bandits fired from the stable; guard Scott Davis escaped, running for help; when reinforcements came in two hours, they found the bust-proof treasure box broken open, and more than $20,000 in gold gone. The loot was believed to have been buried in the vicinity. This was known as the Cold Springs Robbery.

Years later a man digging potatoes near Red Butte suddenly dumped his potatoes, picked up something, and left the country and his family for good.

Capitol Hill, 6,420, YNP: a glacial moraine; on top of it in 1879 the first administration building for Yellowstone National Park was built. It had a bullet-proof cupola; a fort seemed necessary because of incursions into the park by Nez Perce and Bannock Indians in 1877 and 1878. See Mammoth Hot Springs.

Carbon, Carbon: named for coal deposits; the UP railroad opened its first coal mine here in 1868; wild frontier life and Indian troubles made people sometimes spend the night in the mine with guards at the entrance; mining ended in 1902 when the Hanna cutoff put Carbon off main track; it became a ghost town.

Carbon County, created in 1868 by Dakota legislature, and extended the whole width of Wyoming Territory; name suggested by Charley Bradley for vast deposits of coal within its boundaries; cut down in 1875 as Johnson County was formed, and in 1888 by Natrona County. Present size finally adjusted in 1924. Rawlins is county seat; a rich mining, livestock, and recreation area.

Careyhurst, Converse: named for Hon. Joseph M. Carey, one of first U.S. senators from Wyoming. He was a rancher who owned large tracts of land in central Wyoming, and who worked diligently for statehood; author of the bill admitting Wyoming to statehood. Post office Careyhurst, named for his ranch, was discontinued in 1945.

Caribou National Forest, Lincoln: 9,415 acres of this forest extend into Wyoming from Idaho; the headquarters are at Pocatello, Idaho; named for the animal.

Carissa Mine, Fremont: one of the richest gold mines near South Pass City; discovered in 1867; produced millions in gold.

Carlile, Crook: discontinued post office established on Cabin Creek in 1887; Cecil S. Handcock, first postmaster, named it for a relative; also a railroad station.

Carlson Creek, Carbon: named for an old timber worker whose cabin was on this creek.

Carneyville, Sheridan: a mining camp and post office, discontinued; founded by Carney brothers on Burlington railroad.

Carpenter, Laramie: town named for J. Ross Carpenter, a real estate promoter from 1906-08; he brought in settlers from Iowa to homestead 160-acre plots.

Carrington Island, YNP: in Yellowstone Lake; named for Campbell Carrington, zoologist.

Carroll, Sheridan: discontinued post office named in 1904 for Minnie Carroll, first and only postmaster; discontinued in 1922.

Carroll Lake, Albany: named for Thomas Carroll, early settler.

Carson Creek, Washakie: see Bates Creek.

Carter, Uinta: railroad station named for Judge William A. Carter, from Iowa, first merchant at Fort Bridger; in 1871 he became 5th vice president of Wyoming Stockgrowers Association.

Carter County, South Pass City, county seat; miners at South Pass City in 1867 feeling the need of local government, organized Carter County which was recognized as official by the Dakota legislature; it was named for Judge W. A. Carter of Fort Bridger. A South Pass attorney, Parley L. Williams, wrote: "We did not know the laws of Dakota, and paid no attention to them. We lived the life of primitive men, paid little attention to law, and really got along very well."

Wyoming territorial legislature renamed the county Sweetwater for Sweetwater River in 1869.

Carter Creek, Big Horn, Fremont: named for Charles Carter, pioneer who founded the famous Bug ranch on its banks in 1880; in 1879 he trailed the first cattle into Bighorn Basin from Oregon.

Carter Creek, Park: named for Dr. Carter, foster brother of Buffalo Bill.

Carter Mountain, 12,000, Park: named for Judge William A. Carter of T E ranch, who brought the first herd of cattle into the basin in 1879.

Cascade Canyon and Creek, Teton: is reached by boat across Jenny Lake; one of most beautiful trails in Wyoming winds along it; grazing ground for moose.

Cascade Corner, YNP: so many streams in the southwestern part of the park tumble and cascade over ragged escarpments of lava, that W. C. Gregg called this Cascade Corner.

Casebier Hill or Hills, Park: named for William Casebier, pioneer.

Casper, Natrona: named for Fort Caspar which was first known as Camp Platte; when the railroad station was named in 1888, its officials adopted the spelling Casper.

Rapid growth followed the discovery of oil in nearby Salt Creek field. In early days women did not walk on the west side of Center Street, which was mostly saloons. The second state fair, Wyoming Industrial Convention, was held in Casper in 1904.

Casper is the second largest city in Wyoming; three major oil refineries, Mobiloil, Texaco, and American Oil process oil here. Fort Caspar Museum and Natrona County Museum with many pioneer and Indian relics are in Casper, county seat of Natrona County.

Casper Junior College, Natrona: started in 1945 with enrollment of 75; now more than 2,500 students fill its many buildings; more than 100 come from out of state; college offers many cultural and technical courses, and has a good sports program.

Casper Mountain, Natrona: named for Fort Caspar: 500-acre park on top of the mountain is threaded with hard-surfaced roads; for all types of recreation; Hogadon Ski Area has tows and ski patrol.

Cassa, Platte: post office and railroad station named for a Spaniard who worked on the railroad.

Castle, Johnson: named for a rock formation.

Castle Gardens, Fremont: Indian pictographs of stone-age type, believed to be more than 3,000 years old, are on red and yellow cliffs; also old Indian fire pots. Sandstone cones and minarets in long valley give the name.

Castle Gardens, Washakie: red spires and giant toadstools; a burlesque in stone caricatures of castles, animals, cannon balls, and even salted peanuts.

Castle Geyser, YNP: named by Lt. Doane of Washburn party in 1870 because its cone resembles a partially ruined feudal castle.

Castle Rock, Fremont: a rocky structure that resembles a castle.

Castle Rock, Park: also called Colter Rock because John Colter probably passed here from 1807-08; an intriguing volcanic plug, castle-shaped.

Castle Rock, Sweetwater: a great, beetling rock, guardian to town of Green River; has the names of early emigrants carved on it; its sandstone cliffs rise 1,000 feet above Green River, the town.

Castor Peak, 10,854, YNP: named for Greek mythological character.

Cathedral Group Mountains, Teton: spire-pointed mountains that can be seen through the window of the Chapel of Transfiguration near Moose.

Cathedral Spire, 13,300, Fremont, Sublette: a spire-like peak just north of Fremont's summit. It juts out of a glacier; was ascended by Goodwin and Shane in 1948.

Cave Springs, Weston: north of Newcastle; named for beautiful natural caves from which springs bubble.

Cedar, Washakie: first post office in region; discontinued.

Cedar Mountain, Park: named for great number of cedars growing on it, west of Cody. William "Buffalo Bill" Cody's last wish was to be buried here, but it was not fulfilled. He is buried on Lookout Mountain, Colorado.

Cellers, Weston: discontinued post office named for Bessie Cellers.

Centennial, Albany: S. W. Downey discovered a quartz gold mine here in 1876, and named the town for the centennial year; United States declared independence in 1776.

Centennial Ridge, Albany: named for town and Downey's Centennial Mine.

Chalcedony Creek, YNP: named for water-formed rock. When water-carrying silica gel dries slowly, it forms chalcedony, or layers of agate; minerals give them color.

Chapel of Transfiguration, Teton: a rustic chapel built in 1924; services every Sunday during summer; window back of the altar frames the Tetons.

Chapman Draw, Carbon: where Mrs. Chapman lost her life in a blizzard in the early 1880s; near Medicine Bow.

Charcoal Kilns, Uinta: built by Moses Byrne in 1869 to supply pioneer smelters in Utah valley.

Chatham, Washakie: post office; was Winchester, but Mr. Winchester, postmaster, would not give the Burlington railroad consent to use his name on the boxcar that served as a station; they named their station Chatham.

Chauvenet Mountain, 12,280, Fremont: named for Louis Chauvenet, topographer in 1877.

Cheeseman, Park: discontinued post office named for Harris Cheeseman, pioneer.

Chelsea, Uinta: railroad station named by an Englishman for the borough Chelsea in London.

Cheney, Teton: discontinued post office started by Selar Cheney.

Cherokee, Sweetwater: railroad station named for Cherokee Indian tribe who were originally from Georgia, but were constantly driven west by white settlers; returning from California, they trailed through what is now Carbon County over Cherokee Pass, and back to Arkansas.

Cherokee Creek, Peak, and Trail, Carbon: named for the Indian tribe; their trail was used by emigrants and cattlemen; Overland Stage Route followed it part of way.

Cherry Creek, Goshen: named for many chokecherries on its tributaries.

Cheyenne, Laramie: capital of Wyoming and largest city in the state; had first post office in Wyoming. In 1867 Gen. Grenville Dodge laid out a construction camp for UP railroad, and called it Cheyenne for Cheyenne Pass to the west. Because of its rapid growth, Cheyenne was known as "the Magic City of the Plains." First it was a rip-roaring end-of-the-track town; later stage coaches left from here for the gold fields of Deadwood, South Dakota, and brought back gold for shipment.

In 1868 Cheyenne jail was in a tent; in 1882 Cheyenne was the first town in the world to be lighted with incandescent street lights; first county library in the United States was established here in 1886.

The dawn of a new era was marked in 1920 when Buck Heffron bumped a DeHavilland biplane off a buffalo grass runway and headed west with 400 pounds of mail out of Cheyenne on Transcontinental Air Mail Service.

First US missile launching site was started near here in 1958; missiles, launched from underground silos, can speed 5,000 miles at 15,000 miles per hour.

Cheyenne and Northern Railroad, became Colorado and Southern railroad, which see.

Cheyenne Club, Laramie: a romantic old club house built in Cheyenne in 1881 at the cost of more than $25,000; membership limited to 200 cattle kings, the richest cattle barons in the world.

Cheyenne-Deadwood Trail, Laramie, Goshen, Niobrana, Weston: bull teams with freight, stagecoaches with passengers, treasures, and mail followed this trail to the gold fields of South Dakota and back. The first coach left Cheyenne January of 1876; by 1877 Luke Voorhees, superintendent, was using 600 horses and 30 Concord coaches to carry the traffic. These coaches were made in Concord, New Hampshire, shipped around South America to the west coast, and brought to Cheyenne from there. They were huge, swinging on straps of leather known as thorough braces, and drawn by six horses, hitched tandem, in three teams.

First class tickets, Cheyenne to Custer, $20, third class $10, but this class often had to walk up hills. The route was divided into 40-mile stretches; average speed 8 miles an hour; traveled night and day; protected by armed guards who rode "shotgun" beside the driver, or on horseback.

In 1883 Russell Thorp, Sr. purchased the line, and made Rawhide Buttes Station, Goshen County, his home station. Last coach left Cheyenne in February of 1887, with George Lathrop on the ribbons—reins.

Cheyenne Depot, Laramie: see Camp Carlin.

Cheyenne Frontier Days, Laramie: in 1896 a group of Cheyenne business men coming home from Denver on a train decided Cheyenne should have an annual celebration. They started this "show of shows" in 1897, and it has been going continuously ever since; a rodeo "The Daddy of 'Em All" is now held the last full week in July, with street parades and Sioux Indians to add to the excitement.

Cheyenne Horticultural Field and Research Station, Laramie: established in 1928; researches on plant hardiness and adaptability for the Rocky Mountain area; located on probably the first ranch site in the state, where Judge W. L. Kuykendall built his claim shack.

Cheyenne Pass, Laramie: named before 1860 for Cheyenne Indians; Cheyenne is a corruption of the name given them by Sioux Indians; meaning "aliens," or "people of a foreign language"; on the maps of 1860, the Shyenne River, Cheyenne Pass. Cheyennes called themselves Dzitsistes.

Another version of the word Cheyenne is that it comes from the French word "chienne," which means "female dog," and is pronounced the same way.

Cheyenne Pass Road, Laramie, Albany: an old stage road that ran from Cheyenne to Laramie through Cheyenne Pass, west of Laramie it crossed Laramie Plains, and joined the Overland road.

Cheyenne Reservoir, Albany: water supply for Cheyenne.

Cheyenne River, Niobrara, Weston: named for Indian tribe; rises in these counties.

Chicago & Northwestern Railroad, Converse, Fremont, Natrona, Niobrara: in 1886 the Fremont, Elkhorn, and Missouri Valley railroad extended its lines westward from Chadron, Nebraska, entering Wyoming, spawning towns along its tracks, and reaching Douglas in 1886; this line was also known as the Wyoming Central railroad. The Chicago & Northwestern then acquired this line, and pushed tracks on to Casper by 1888. Rails to Lander were completed in 1906, but this service is now discontinued.

Chicago, Burlington & Quincy Railroad, see Burlington railroad.

Chicago Mine, Platte: huge, open-pit iron mine developed by eastern capital from 1899 to the 1900s; located near Hartville; iron ore shipped via Colorado and Southern railroad to Colorado for processing. Indians once camped here, and used iron ore for war and beautification paint.

Chimney Creek, Fremont: tributary of Sweetwater; named for an old stone chimney, all that's left of a house.

Chimney Park, Albany: named about 1905; a prospector's cabin burned here; native rock chimney remained standing.

Chimney Rock, Niobrara: about nine miles north of Lusk, east of US Highway 85; near Hat Rock; both named for their shapes.

Chinaman Thermal Spring, YNP: normally dormant; in the early days of the park, an enterprising man put in soap, and proceeded to wash clothes in its warm waters; by chance it erupted 40 feet high, as it sometimes does, throwing clothes and soap skyward; hence the name.

Chinatown, Uinta: north of the tracks in Evanston; a huddled group of shanties built on railroad land; rich in early history of Chinese workers. A Joss House, one of three in United States, was here in the 1870s and 1880s; thousands came here to worship on Chinese New Year about February 10; bursts of firecrackers welcomed each new trainload; a great 200-foot-long dragon, covered with gaudy embroidery, was in the parade; legs of 50 or 60 men were the dragon's feet, sticking down below its gay covering; explosion of a large rocket ended the day. In 1922 Joss House burned.

Chinese Wall, Park: a weathered wall of basalt above the road from Cody to Yellowstone National Park. The Absaroka Mountains along this road have been eroded into many fantastic shapes, making this 50-mile stretch one of the most picturesque roads in the United States. The road is in the Shoshone River canyon.

Chinook winds, makers of Wyoming history; warm winds from southwest that come as by magic in the cold of winter, melting snow and uncovering grass for grazing; named for Chinook Indians, once a powerful tribe on Columbia River.

Pioneers thought the wind brought its warmth from the Japanese current; scientists have decided that chinook winds derive their snow-melting power from their extreme dryness; rising over the Rocky Mountains, these winds from the west lose their moisture, and descending on the east side of the mountains are warmed by compression, one degree for each 180 feet of descent. In the winter of 1886-87 there were no chinook winds to uncover the grass; hundreds of thousands of cattle perished, ending the regime of cattle barons grazing free government land, without winter protection, or hay for feed.

Chittenden Memorial Bridge and Mountain, 10,181, YNP: named by USGS in 1878 for George B. Chittenden, a member of the Hayden survey.

Chocolate Pots, YNP: so named for thermal springs with small cones, coated with algae and iron, which make them look like chocolate.

Chouteau Trading Post, Goshen: early-day trading post built by Auguste and Pierre Chouteau; near where Fort Laramie was built.

Christian Pond, Teton: named for Tex Christian, homesteader.

Christina Lake and Pass, Fremont: said to have been named for the wife of a Swedish prospector there in mining days.

Chrystal, Big Horn: a Burlington railroad station named for the crystal clearness of Chrystal Stream.

Chug Springs, Platte: an Indian chief called "The Dreamer" was too lazy to hunt buffalo the hard way; he is supposed to have thought up the idea of stampeding them over chalk cliffs that break abruptly away; because of the sound of falling waters, it was known as "water at the place where the buffalo chug." Whites adopted the Indian name.

Patten built a log cabin here in 1871 as a stopping place for travelers from Fort Russell to Fort Laramie; it was also a station of the Cheyenne-Deadwood stage route until 1882.

Chugwater, Platte: named from Chugwater Creek which was named for Chug Springs; was once home of huge Swan Land and Cattle Company.

Chugwater Creek, Albany, Platte: see Chug Springs.

Chugwater Formation, a geological term for "Red Beds" of Triassic period; what is now red gypsum and shale, was laid down by water action in ancient times; probably named by N. H. Darton, USGS, when he studied the strata near Chugwater Creek; it is a time mark for geologists wherever found.

Chugwater Stage Station, Platte: sometimes called Chug Springs; Robert Campbell spent the winter of 1834 in this pleasant valley on his way to Green River rendezvous with four cows and two bulls; much later Portugee Phillips served meals, had a bar, and kept stock here.

Church Buttes, Uinta: a railroad station and gas field named for Church Buttes formation.

Weathered, rocky spires and cathedral shapes on old Oregon and Mormon trails; a company of Mormons held religious services here one July Sunday in 1847; hence the name.

Church Draw, Campbell: so named because it is near the home of a young, homesteading couple by name of Church, who were murdered here by Slim Clifton, their supposed friend, for their few possessions; Mrs. Church was pregnant. He buried their bodies in a sheep corral, and thought he had committed a perfect crime; was caught because he mailed a diamond ring; he confessed, showed where the bodies were buried, was taken from a Newcastle jail by a posse, and given a "long drop" from a bridge in 1903; the necktie party said the law was too slow. State Highway 59 now goes right by the former location of the house of the murdered couple.

Cinnabar Mountain, YNP: named for color of its rocks, mercuric sulphide, which were mistaken for cinnabar; color is due to iron.

Cinnabar Park, Albany: named for the red ore cinnabar, from which mercury is extracted; unsuccessful cinnabar mine nearby in the 1880s.

Circle, Fremont: discontinued post office named for Circle ranch brand.

Circle Ridge and Circle Ridge Oil Field, Fremont: named for shape of ridge.

Cirque of Towers Region, Fremont, Sublette: an amphitheatral recess surrounded by high peaks and mountains.

Citadel Mountain, 12,100, Park: named for shape; an impressive mass of cliff-banded ridges.

Clagett Butte, YNP: east of Mammoth Hot Springs; named for Judge William H. Clagett, who drafted original bill to create Yellowstone National Park, embodying the famous expression "for the benefit and enjoyment of all people, " carved on the north gateway arch.

Clare, Laramie: discontinued post office named for William St. Clare.

Clareton, Weston: town named for an early rancher, Clareton.

Clarissa Mine, Fremont: famous gold mine near South Pass City; named for Clarissa Whitney, probably first white child born in Wyoming.

Clark, Park: town and post office named for Len Clark, early rancher.

Clark Draw, Albany: mountain valley named for Clark, a homesteader.

Clarkelen, Campbell: discontinued post office; railroad station.

Clark's Fork, Park: a river that flows into Montana; named for Capt. William Clark, leader and explorer on the Lewis and Clark Expedition from 1804-05.

Clarkson, Natrona: post office on Clarkson ranch; discontinued in 1901.

Class Lake, Albany: named for Billy Class, a prospector who located on Libby Flats about 1900.

Clay Spur, Weston: railroad station named for bentonite clay deposits; first bentonite processing plant in the world built here; near Osage.

Clearmont, Sheridan: named for Clear Creek where it is located; good farming lands here, with some irrigation; livestock shipping center.

Clepsydra Geyser, YNP: named by T. B. Comstock in 1873, because, like the ancient water clock, it marked the passage of time.

Clifton, Weston: discontinued post office; railroad station once called "Whoop-up," but renamed by railroad officials for R. C. Clifton, prospector and pioneer of 1890; some say it was named for nearby cliff, on which are numerous Indian pictographs; once a stage station on Cheyenne-Deadwood route which diverged here, one branch going via Indian Creek to avoid road agents and Indians; old route went directly south to Hat Creek station.

Clocktower Creek, Park: named for a large rock resembling a clocktower.

Cloud Peak, 13,165, Big Horn, Johnson: name appears on 1859 maps; named for its summit which attracts clouds; highest mountain in Big Horns, and seventh highest in Wyoming; it has a glacier.

Cloud Peak Primitive Area, Big Horn, Johnson: 137,000 acres of wilderness, excellent for pack trips, hiking, and fishing; glacier-formed lake. Area was set aside in 1932.

Cloud Veil Dome, 12,016, Teton: dome shaped and often cloud covered.

Cloverly, Big Horn: discontinued post office named by Jack Copman for the wonderful growth of clover he raised on his ranch, on which post office was located.

Club Sandwich, Johnson: an eccentric rock formation on Rock Creek that resembles a sandwich.

Coachy Creek, Johnson: named for early settler, "Coachy," English cab driver.

Coad Mountain, Carbon: named for John and Mark Coad who cut and hauled wood from this mountain to Fort Steele. John Coad was a member of the territorial legislature in 1872.

Coburn, Big Horn: discontinued post office named for Edwin Coburn, postmaster.

Cody, Park: county seat; first post office here known as Richland; townsite platted in 1895 by George T. Beck; incorporated in 1901; named for William "Buffalo Bill" Cody, its famous promoter.

Burlington railroad came to "Cowboy Town" in 1901; growth and development of irrigation was rapid; 50 scenic miles from east gateway to Yellowstone National Park, Buffalo Bill Museum and Whitney Galley of Western Art are in Cody.

Cody Peak, 10,267, Park: named for Buffalo Bill Cody who spent much time hunting here.

Coffee Siding, Converse: named for Charles F. Coffee, rancher, banker.

Cokeville, Lincoln: established in 1874 as Smith's Fork, for the river; early settlers found good coal for coke in the vicinity and renamed the town; cattle raising district; ski runs nearby.

Cold Springs, Albany: discontinued post office; named for nearby cold springs.

Cold Springs, Converse: discontinued post office; good campgrounds here now; fishing and recreation off paved highway.

Cold Springs, Goshen: site of old Pony Express station, and stage station from 1859-62. Much later, the construction of a ditch destroyed the springs.

Cold Springs Robbery, Weston: see Canyon Springs stage station.

Cole Creek, Converse: originally named Coal Creek for nearby coal mine; the spelling was changed later.

Collins, Hot Springs: discontinued post office on old Thermopolis-Meeteetse stage line; named for W. S. Collins, pioneer newspaperman.

Collins Creek and Peak, Albany: named for an early settler, Thomas J. Collins.

Collins Mountain, Albany: named for Martin Collins, gold miner in the 1890s.

Colony, Crook: discontinued post office; named by group of settlers who hoped to have retired school teachers from East come here, homestead, and form a colony; no colony was ever formed.

Colorado and Southern Railroad, Laramie: also known as Cheyenne and Northern; spur from Denver that joined UP railroad four miles west of Cheyenne in 1877; never built on north. See Burlington railroad.

Colores, Albany: railroad station named for highly colored red rocks and buttes nearby. Colores is related to Spanish verb colorear.

Colter, Washakie: railroad station named for famous John Colter, first white man in Wyoming, who with undaunted courage and incredible endurance in the winter of 1807-08, with a 30-pound pack on his back made a 500-mile journey on snowshoes from, and back to Fort Lisa, Montana, to contact Indians, and induce them to come to Fort Lisa, and trade their furs. Colter was the first white man to see the wonders of Yellowstone National Park, and the grandeur of the Tetons. He later returned to St. Louis, married, settled on a farm, and there lived and died. Colter was a hunter for the Lewis and Clark Expedition of 1804-06.

Colter Bay, Teton: named for John Colter; a tourist center was built here with modern log cabins; also a tent village with ice boxes and grills; all of the lure and the lore of the West, with the nation's best scenery.

Colter Canyon, Teton: named for John Colter; a long canyon best reached by boat across Jackson Lake; scenic wilderness.

Colter Pass, Park: Chief Joseph and his Nez Perce Indians fleeing from United States troops crossed here in 1877.

Colter Peak, 10,359, YNP: named for John Colter, first white man to see the wonders of Yellowstone National Park from 1807-08.

Colter's Hell, YNP: when John Colter returned from his winter trip in 1808, he told of steam vents shooting water hundreds of feet into the air; of boiling springs; and thundering falls that did not freeze; he became known as a colossal liar, and the region he so vividly described became known as "Colter's Hell." Not until the Washburn exploratory party of 1870 entered the region were these wonders verified, and the tales of John Colter confirmed. The story of the discovery of Yellowstone National Park is well described in *Colter's Hell* by Grace Johnson.

Columbus Creek, Sheridan: named for Christopher Columbus Eller, early cowboy.

Commissary Ridge, Lincoln: stockmen grazed sheep here in the late 1880s, and pulled their commissary or supply wagons up here, hence the name.

Como, Carbon: railroad station; at original station in 1870 Dr. O. C. Marsh, professor of geology at Yale University, saw a large fossil vertebra holding open the door. His investigation led to the discovery of a huge bed of dinosaur bones laid down in the Cretaceous period. Station takes name from Como Bluff.

Como Bluff, Albany: takes name from Como Lake; here is the oldest house in the world built of dinosaur bones; 5,796 bones make up the walls weighing more than 102,000 pounds; bones are one to two million years old; taken from "Dinosaur Graveyard" on Como Ridge.

Como Lake, Carbon: once known as Aurora Lake; was renamed Como for a mountain lake in Italy.

Como Ridge, Albany: after dinosaur bones were discovered by Dr. Marsh, 14 complete skeletons were removed for museums; one was 70 feet

42

long; also skeletons and bones of other early mammals were unearthed and shipped to museums in the 1880s.

Conant Basin Creek, Pass, and Trail, Teton: named for Al Conant who nearly lost his life in the creek in 1865; named by Richard Leigh; made famous in the book *The Virginian* by Owen Wister.

Coney Ridge, Albany: named for coneys or rabbits.

Congress Springs, Uinta: 12 mineral springs, circular in form, with dome-like craters; named by Dr. Hayden, USGS, because of their similarity of water to Congress Springs, Saratoga, New York.

Conner Springs, Johnson: named for General Conner.

Connor Battlefield, Sheridan: Gen. P. E. Connor's soldiers from Ft. Laramie attacked a large party of Arapahos here, and destroyed more than 250 lodges; women and children were killed or captured in 1865. Now a state park with picnic benches.

Continental Divide, across entire state, south central from the Colorado Rockies, northwest into Yellowstone National Park.

Converse County, created in 1888 and named for A. R. Converse, Cheyenne banker who with F. E. Warren established a large ranch in the eastern part of the county; first newspaper was Bill Barlow's *Budget* issued at Ft. Fetterman in 1886; later moved to Douglas; newspaper became nationally famous for its brilliant writing and philosophy of "Fair, Faithful and Fearless."

Douglas is county seat; state fair is held here every August. Agriculture, stock raising, mining, and lumbering are chief industries.

Cook Lakes, Sublette: named for John Cook, trapper here in the early 1900s; in Bridger Wilderness Area; good fishing for California golden trout here.

Cook Peak, 9,742, YNP: named for Charles W. Cook, prospector and explorer in 1869 expedition.

Cookesby Peak, Crook or Weston: named for retired Captain Cookesby of English army.

Cookesley Park and Peak, Big Horn: see Black Mountain.

Coolidge Canal, Fremont: named for Sherman Coolidge, an Arapaho who was adopted and educated by Capt. Coolidge of US Army.

Coon Creek, Park: named for Negro cook, Dick Sparks, who came to area in 1879, and died in a blizzard in 1887.

Coon Hollow, Sweetwater: on Wyoming-Utah line; so named because a Negro, Tunner, built a cabin and hunted for a cache of gold supposed to have been buried here by bandits.

Cooper Creek, Albany, Carbon: named for Cooper Lake.

Cooper Lake, Albany: discontinued post office; railroad station; named for Cooper Lake. Here on the Laramie Plains in the blizzards of 1868-69 six trains were stalled for more than a week. Men came from Laramie on showshoes to bring plenty of food. On one train was a group of opera singers on their way to California; their entertaining helped pass the time until the tracks were finally opened.

Named for Arthur Francis Thomas Cooper, Englishman, member of USGS Hayden party in 1859; he developed a ranch on Rock Creek in early 1868.

Cooper Spring, Albany: named for Mrs. Esther Cooper, homesteader in the 1890s.

Copeman's Tomb, Mountain, Big Horn: named for early settler and sheepman who requested his ashes be scattered over the mountain. •

Copper Mountain, Hot Springs: Peb Williams hunting on Little Rattlesnake Mountain shot a deer; it rolled down the mountain, and he followed it on horseback; a bunch of wild horses joined in the race, and knocked down a ledge or lead revealing copper; mining claims were quickly staked; much work done, but not profitable; changed name of mountain from Little Rattlesnake to Copper.

Copperton, Carbon: discontinued post office; ghost of a ghost town; once a stopping place for freighting outfits, supply camp for sheep and cattlemen; named by prospectors in hope of copper in surrounding mountains.

Cora, Sublette: post office established in the 1890s on Elmer ranch; mail came twice a week by horse stage from Big Piney; named for Cora House, an old maid cowgirl. About 1900 it was moved three miles to the ranch of Mrs. Minerva Westphall who had a store and bootlegged whiskey. She carried mail from Big Piney, about 70 miles, on a gray stallion; during high water she had to swim Green River twice a trip. About 1902 the Cora post office moved to the ranch and store of James Noble. Town, Cora, served the tie camp; it had blacksmith shop, saloon, newspaper, and dance hall. Last move was to a paved road, 8,000 feet altitude. Post office now in the original building. Store serves cattle and dude ranchers. Cora population: three.

Corbett, Park: railroad station on old stage line between Cody and Red Lodge, Montana; named for James Corbett, early rancher.

Corbett Diversion Dam, Park: named for James Corbett; finished in 1908; furnished irrigation water for Powell and Deaver areas.

Corduroy Creek, Albany: named for an early crossing lined with poles which gave a corduroy effect to those crossing.

Corlett, Laramie: railroad station named for William Corlett, a prominent attorney for UP railroad from 1867-90.

Corlett Junction, Laramie: named for William Corlett; the rails from Denver join the main UP railroad track here.

Corner Mountain, Albany: named before 1890; because the road makes an L-curve around the mountain.

Corrals, Sweetwater; volcanic in origin, a gigantic mass of rocks takes the shape of corrals; once a retreat of outlaws and horse thieves; caverns under the rocks contain tons of unmelted ice.

Cosgriff, Lincoln: railroad station named for Cosgriff brothers who had a large sheep business, and owned banks in several towns.

Cotant Creek, Johnson: named for Major Bill Cotant, round-up foreman in 1882.

44

Cottier, Goshen: discontinued post office; railroad station named for Robert Cottier, pioneer.

Cottonwood, chosen as Wyoming's state tree by the legislature in 1947. The model tree for emblem grew on the Clyde Cover homestead near Thermopolis. It was 77 feet tall, and 29 feet in circumference.
Cottonwoods grow along nearly every creek and river in the state.

Coulter Creek, Teton, YNP: named for John M. Coulter, botanist who published a manual of Rocky Mountain Wild Flowers in 1909; was a member of Hayden Expedition in 1872.

Counter Image, 10,550, Teton: a peak named for its reflection in Hanging Lake.

Countryman Peak, Natrona: named for the Countryman family.

Counts, Teton: hot springs named for John Counts, pioneer and settler on Snake River; now called Astoria Mineral Springs. Herds of deer used to winter on Counts land, where the warmth of the springs kept snow off.

Coutant Creek, Sheridan: named for C. H. Coutant, author of *The History of Wyoming*.

Cover Cut, Hot Springs: named for J. M. Cover, owner of the land where the railroad made a cut through a stony hill in 1907.

Coverdale Basin, Albany: named for landowner Coverdale; on some maps the name is misspelled Cloverdale.

Cow Creek, Carbon: discontinued post office; railroad station.

Cowley, Big Horn: the town was established in 1901; named for Mathias F. Cowley, Mormon apostle. Mormons brought irrigation to Bighorn Basin and this region; vegetables are grown here for a canning cooperative.

Coxcomb Ridge and Mountain, 12,150, Fremont, Sublette: jumbled ridge of large rocks that resembles a coxcomb; highest peak, Wolf's Head.

Craig Pass, YNP: named for Mrs. Ida Craig Wilcox, the first tourist to cross the pass in 1891.

Crandall Creek, Big Horn, Park: named for prospector Marvin Jack Crandall who with companion T. Doughety found traces of gold in Clark's Fork meadows; found killed by Indians in 1870; remains of his log cabin were still standing in 1967.

Crandall Creek Fire, Park: burned nearly 14,000 acres of timber in 1935. Clay Butte lookout station was built after this fire; a scenic view from it.

Crandall Lake and Pass, Park: named for Crandall Creek.

Crater Lake, Carbon: located at the bottom of very steep slopes in Medicine Bow Mountains.

Crater Mountain, 12,000, Park: has an extinct crater in its top.

Crazy Creek, Park: runs mostly on high ground, not in a canyon; tumbles over rocky bed in a crazy fashion.

Crazy Woman Creek and Hill, Johnson: two legends: a trader bought whiskey or "fire water" to gain favor with the Indians; when it was gone, the Indians demanded more which he could not supply; Indians then killed him in the presence of his young wife who made her escape, and wandered up and down the stream, demented. Second version: a squaw left alone after an attack on an Indian camp, lost her mind, and lived in a squalid wickiup until her death; she could be seen on moonlit nights leaping the creek. Crow Indians thought she brought them good luck in 1850.

Crazy Woman Creek, Niobrara: see legends above.

Cream and Sugar Bowl Formations, Sweetwater: a picture of these made by W. H. Jackson won him the contract to be official photographer for the UP railroad.

Creighton, Johnson: discontinued post office named for Tom Creighton, postmaster and stage station agent in 1878.

Creighton Lake, Albany: named for Edward T. Creighton, rancher and builder of the telegraph line through Albany County about 1860.

Creston, Sweetwater: railroad station so named because it is on the crest of the continental divide.

Crevice Creek, YNP: Lou Anderson and party in 1867 found gold at the mouth of this stream and called it Crevis Gulch; later called creek.

Cripes Butte, Fremont: named for pioneer Doc Curry whose favorite expression was "by cripes." He was with a posse who rode this butte hunting horses stolen by Indians. Exhausted, he exclaimed, "By cripes, what's a cayuse. Let's go home."

Crisman Bench, Lincoln: named for James Crisman, rancher and banker who grazed cattle here.

Crompton Reservoir, Uinta: built by Lester Crompton; 90 acre-feet.

Crook County, established in 1875; then it included Campbell and Weston counties; not organized until 1885; named for General George H. Crook, famous soldier and Indian fighter. Crook was called "Grey Fox" by Shoshones.

Sundance is county seat of Crook County, a livestock land with lumbering and farming. Devils Tower is a great tourist attraction.

Crooks Gap, Fremont: gap in Green Mountains named for General George Crook.

Crosby, Hot Springs: named for Jesse W. Crosby, Mormon pioneer; town started by Dad Jones, prospector and miner, who supplied Thermopolis with coal from here in the early 1890s.

Croton, Campbell: discontinued post office; railroad station; so named because it is located on Wild Horse Creek, where water affects those who drink it like croton oil.

Crow Creek, Laramie: Walter D. Pease filed on the first homestead in Wyoming Territory on Crow Creek.

Crowheart, Fremont: named for Crowheart Butte.

Crowheart Butte, Fremont: Chief Washakie was always anxious to preserve peace, and prevent loss of life in fighting. When he led Shoshones and Bannocks against Crows led by Big Robber near here in 1866,

Washakie asked that he and Big Robber fight alone on top of this butte, and that the winner eat the other's heart; Washakie won. Later when asked if he actually ate the heart, he replied that "youth does foolish things." The peak became Crowheart Butte.

Cruse Creek, Sheridan: named for James Cruse (sometimes spelled Kruse) who homesteaded in this valley.

Crystal Peak, 10,954, Teton: so named because calcite crystals can be found on this and adjoining peaks.

Cumberland, Lincoln: coal mining camp of UP railroad established in 1903; first known as Little Muddy from the stream, but the name was changed to Cumberland for the mines; these were named by Frank McCarthy, camp boss who was homesick for his native Blue Ridge country.

Cummins City, Albany: named for John Cummins, a mining prospector in 1879; after he salted the area with copper ore samples, a Denver company paid $10,000 for mining rights; a city of 170 blocks was laid out. After Cummins absconded to Texas, the name was changed to Helm; a tie camp; all is gone now.

Cunningham Cabin, Teton: historic site for small, dynamic J. Pierce Cunningham, a trapper in 1885, and later homesteader. A posse from Jackson killed several horse thieves holed up here in 1892.

Cuny Hills, Platte: named for Adolph Cuny who was killed in 1877 by Clark Pelton, alias Billy Webster, a road agent. Cuny was an early sheriff of Albany County and a squaw man; he once ran a saloon and gambling den near Ft. Laramie.

Cupric Caldron, YNP: has a green, algal deposit which accounts for its name.

Curtis, Platte: railroad station named for Curtis Templin, pioneer rancher.

Curtis Canyon, Teton: named for "Slow-up" and "Flare-up" Curtis, brothers, both powerful men; pioneers.

Curtis Gulch, Albany: a mountain valley named about 1894 for Fred Curtis who lived there.

Cusp Peak, 12,266, Lincoln: named for the converging lines of its cusp-like summit.

Custard's Hill, Natrona: named by soldiers from Ft. Caspar for Sgt. Amos Custard and 18 of his men who were killed by Indians near Platte River bridge in 1865. Caspar Collins had been killed a few hours earlier.

Cutler Creek and Pass, Sheridan: named for H. E. Cutler whose cattle once ranged along this heavily timbered and scenic stream.

Cutoff Peak, 10,638, YNP: a steep-sided ridge, so named because the north park boundary cuts it off.

D

Dad, Carbon: named for A. T. "Dad" Corlett, rancher; others say for Stephen Adams, also "Dad," who ran a post office and stage station here for freighters between Baggs and Wamsutter in 1900; sheep country and large shearing pens here now.

Daisy Geyser, YNP: small and dainty, hence the name.

Dakoming, Weston: oil field railroad siding named for its location on Dakota-Wyoming border.

Dale, Niobrara: discontinued post office at the mouth of Alkali Creek. So named because Fred Dale was instrumental in starting it about 1900.

Dale City, Albany: town in the late 1860s named for workers building Dale Creek bridge; 45 log cabins, dance hall, court room, three hotels, and cemetery; brief, but rowdy existence.

Dale Creek, Albany: named for Virginia Dale Slade in 1862, wife of the notorious outlaw Joseph A. Slade, who managed the Dale Creek station of the Denver-Salt Lake road; first known as Clear Creek because of its clear water.

Virginia Dale Slade made one of the great rides in western history in Montana on Billy Bay, her thoroughbred, to save Jack Slade from hanging by Vigilantes, but she lost the race.

Dale Creek Bridge, Albany: said to be the world's highest railroad bridge when it was built across a deep canyon in 1868; made entirely of timber trestles, 36 feet high, and 650 feet long. It was replaced nine years later with a spider-web steel bridge; abandoned when UP tracks were moved in 1900-01; only the stone foundations are left.

Daley Basin, Carbon: named for Hon. William W. Daley, rancher.

Daly Gap and Spring, Natrona: named for John Daly, early prominent sheepman.

Damfino Creek, coloquial for "Damned if I know"; reply of some pioneer when asked if he knew the name of the creek. (Damfino where it is in Wyoming—author).

Dana, Carbon: once a tent town and mining camp, abandoned by Negro miners who froze out; white miners had a gay time, hunting and fishing on Elk Mountain, and dancing in the haylofts of ranches. Named for Col. Dana, railroad clerk at Laramie.

Ex-convict Lovett tried to rob the Portland Rose, overland limited, here in 1934. He detailed the engine and two coaches but found the train filled wth Marines; Lovett fled; was later captured.

Daniel, Sublette: named for T. P. Daniel, who had a post office in his store in 1904. The post office was once "Burns," when located on the Slate ranch.

Two miles below the town is the site of the famous Green River rendezvous, held as early as 1833 for trappers, traders, and Indians. Here Father DeSmet held the first mass in what is now Wyoming on July 5, 1840; called "Prairie de la Messe"; the altar is made of cottonwood branches covered with wild flowers. A monument for Father DeSmet was erected here in 1925.

Darby Mountain, Lincoln: named for Darby fault, caused by an upheaval of the earth's surface ages ago.

Dave Creek, Albany: named in the 1870s for an old miner Charley Bellamy, called "Dave."

Dave Johnston Power Plant, Converse: named for Dave Johnston, a retired Pacific Power & Light Co. executive; on the Platte River and the old Oregon Trail; largest plant creating electricity from steam and coal in the Rocky Mountain region in 1967; see Pacific Power and Light Company.

Davidson, discontinued post office, established in 1899 in what was then Laramie County; named for Nora W. Davidson, postmaster.

Davis, Carbon: railroad siding named for Captain Lou Davis, on whose ranch it was located.

Davis Creek and Pass, Fremont: named for a Davis who prospected with Jim Lysaght; both were killed by Indians.

Days, Carbon: railroad siding named for Robert Day, land owner.

Day's River, Lincoln: named for John Day, pioneer.

Dayton, Sheridan: named for Joseph Dayton Thorn, Sheridan banker; established in 1882; it gained fame in 1911 by electing Susan Whissler mayor; known as the first woman mayor in the nation.

Dayton held the first rodeo in Wyoming in the 1890s with bronco riding, hurdle jumping, trick roping and tying; had no corrals; held a five-day rodeo the following year.

Dead Head Creek, Platte: near Mule Creek; name was given by early-day soldiers who rode mules. When the mules grazed on Mule Creek, they were okay; when grazed or watered on Dead Head Creek, the mules sometimes died; hence the name.

Dead Horse Creek, Campbell: so named because Frank Lavering had a valuable stallion that fell over the bank of this creek and broke its neck.

Dead Horse Gulch, Fremont, Hot Springs: named by Indians who lost three horses here in the heavy snows of 1884.

Dead Indian Creek, Hill, Pass, Peak, Summit, 8,000, Park: one version: in the early days prospectors were attacked by Indians on this huge hill, and one Indian was killed; the prospectors propped him up on the rocks near the top of the hills as a warning to other war parties, and the place became known as "the hill with the dead Indian on it."

Another version is that Gen. Miles in 1878 attacked a party of Bannock Indians here, and one Indian was killed; the next day Crow Indians found and scalped him. Third version: from one place the peak looks like the profile of an Indian.

Through this portal or break in the mountains, great herds of wild game once migrated from the mountains to the plains, and back again. Countless Indian hunting and war parties used this pass. In 1877 Chief Joseph led his Nez Perce Indians this way in their strategic retreat, pursued by soldiers of the United States Army.

The first road improvement was done here by the settlers of Sunlight Basin in 1909; the road was very dangerous, and wagons going down had to be rough-locked. The road is improved now, but still steep and winding; exotic scenery.

Dead Line, Sweetwater: established by cattlemen in 1902, when they thought sheep outfits were crowding their ranges. The year before, several sheepherders had been wounded in fights at sheep camps by cattlemen. The line followed the creek along the south boundary of Horse ranch, about 42 miles southwest of Green River City. All land south of this line extending to the mountains was cattle range, on which sheepmen were warned not to venture.

Dead Man Creek, Albany, Carbon: named about 1868, when the body of Jack Hockins was found buried in the gravel of the creekbed. Hockins had assaulted and killed a girl in the East. His body was found after the brother of the dead girl learned where Hockins lived on this ranch.

Dead Man Mountain, Lincoln: an early resident encountered a bear here; he fired and wounded the bear who also died. His picketed horse starved to death. All three skeletons were found later, hence the name.

Dead Man Mountain, Pass and Creek, Lincoln: two trappers built a cabin here in the early days. In the spring, after they had gathered their winter's take of furs, one partner returned unexpectedly to the cabin after checking his traps; he found the partner gone with the best furs; he trailed the partner to the pass, stuck his hat on a stick and raised it; two bullets hit the hat; Broadbent then shot his escaping partner, hence the name.

Dead Man's Bar, Teton: in 1886 four Germans prospected for gold on the Snake River. John Tonnar later showed up alone, and worked for a rancher haying. A fisherman found three bodies covered with piles of boulders by the river.

Tonnar was arrested; tried in Evanston, then the county seat; Tonnar claimed he had acted in self-defense, and was set free. The place has since been known as Dead Man's Bar; it was the scene of the movies "Three Bad Men," and "The Big Trail."

Dead Man's Canyon, Weston: so named because Thomas Waggoner was seized at his homestead by three unknown men in 1892, and hanged in this canyon—one of the acts that made homesteaders and small cattlemen fight the big stockmen in the Johnson County War.

Dead Man's Creek, Lincoln: an early trapper was setting a heavy bear trap here; the trap sprang shut, catching him. The creek was named when his body was found.

Deadman's Cut, Albany: about a mile from Albany town two men were loading a hole with dynamite; they used an iron bar to tamp down the charge; what was left of them was loaded into a car in a gunny sack, hence the name.

Dead Man's Gulch, Fremont: a traveler killed his partner here and buried him in a shallow grave; then he stole a team and wagon; the man was caught at Twin Creek, confessed at Lander, and was sent to the penitentiary about 1870.

Dead Man's Gulch, Platte: so named because in the early days a skeleton was found at the mouth of this gulch, with leather boots still on the feet; an enormous pair of solid silver spurs was attached to the boots; the body was never identified.

Dead Man's Gulch or Suicide Gulch, Sheridan: so named because a dead man was once found here; also several suicides have taken place here.

Dead Man's Point, Sheridan: so named because in 1900 a rock slide here killed three men who were blasting through a granite cliff to make a tie flue for McShane Tie Company.

Dearth Draw, Lincoln: named for Del Dearth, a government trapper who had his headquarters in this draw.

Death Canyon, Teton: famed for its scenic beauty; made famous in Wister's *The Virginian*.

Death Canyon Creek, Teton: sheer precipices, thousands of feet high, give this canyon its name; it seems certain death to travel here; it may be part of the story in *The Virginian*. A member of the 1903 Thomas Bannon survey party wandered into this canyon, and was never again seen.

Death Gulch, YNP: gas from vents in this gulch once caused the suffocation of many animals, hence the name.

Death Valley, Teton: in 1896 cowboys killed two sheepherders and more than 200 sheep here, hence the name.

Deaver, Big Horn: town named for D. Clem Deaver, immigrant agent for Burlington railroad; he was greatly interested in developing the Bighorn basin; tent town in 1917.

Deaver Dam, Park: named for the town; completed in 1928; for irrigation.

Deckleman Ridge, Crook: an imposing rimrock half a mile long, and about 300 yards wide at the head of a canyon; Indians and early hunters drove deer into this natural corral, and shot them; edges of the rimrock drop straight down to Sand Creek.

Deer Creek, Converse: Owen Wister, author of *The Virginian* spent his first summer in Wyoming in 1885, at Wolcott's V R ranch on Deer Creek; he slept in a tent and took his morning bath in Deer Creek.

Deerwood, Albany: abandoned station on Laramie and Hahns Peak railroad; named for the nearby Deerwood ranch of Fred W. Geddes.

Defenbach Hill, Crook: named for Defenbach, a cowboy killed by Indians.

Deitz, Sheridan: once a coal camp of the Burlington railroad; named for A. N. Deitz, mine operator.

DeLacy Creek, YNP: named by Supt. Norris in 1880 for Walter DeLacy leader of a party of mineral prospectors who in 1863 discovered the Shoshone Geyser Basin.

Delunon Lake, YNP: so named because it was once believed to be an arm of Yellowstone Lake.

DeMaris Springs, Park: named for Charles DeMaris who homesteaded here in 1885; warm sulphur-flavored water fizzes out of the springs; many tepee rings are nearby. Legends tell that all Indians laid down their arms and bathed together here. John Colter passed by in 1807, and drew a map of "Boiling Springs"; also called Needle Plunger.

Demmon Hill, Goshen: named for O. J. Demmon, rancher.

Dempsey Ridge, Lincoln: named for Robert D. Dempsey, trapper and trail maker.

Dempsey Trail, Lincoln: an old sheep trail named for the Dempsey sheep outfit; about four miles north of the Sublette Trail, and at one time part of the Oregon Trail.

Dennis Triangulation Station, 11,286, Sublette: named by surveyors for Dennis Mitchell of Pinedale.

Dennison, Fremont: discontinued post office; once on the dude ranch of R. V. Dennison.

Depot McKinney, Crook: named for Lt. McKinney killed in Dull Knife battle on the Powder River in 1876.

Derby, Fremont: old stage and freighting stop; the army was stationed here to protect travelers in the 1870s.

Derby Dome, Fremont: named for its shape; oil fields are here. Bonneville discovered "tar springs" here about 1833; greased his wagon.

Desolation Peak, 13,100, Sublette; named by Theodore Kovena, mountain climber, for its location in a wild and forbidding cirque of Wells Creek.

Devil's Basin, Fremont: badly eroded place named by old timers.

Devil's Causeway, Big Horn: a narrow canyon that divides Medicine Mountain on which Medicine Wheel is located; causeway or canyon walls run sheer to the valley below; once well worn with travois trails.

Devil's Elbow, Park: a dramatically eroded rock on volcanic basalt; on the scenic road from Cody to Yellowstone National Park.

Devil's Gate, Natrona: beyond Independence Rock the Sweetwater River makes an abrupt turn, and flows through a granite ridge, through which it has cut a chasm 330 feet deep; 400 feet wide at the top, and only 30 feet wide at the bottom. In 1812 the returning Stuart party noted the chasm, which may have been cleft by a convulsion of nature, and then widened by the river.

Near here in 1856 Capt. Edward Martin's handcart company of 576 Mormons found shelter in a November blizzard. They had left Iowa City in the spring, pushing and pulling their handcarts across the prairies; the handcarts made of green lumber warped, and often fell apart; more than a third of the company died on the way; they were rescued at Devil's Gate by a party from Salt Lake City, coming with food and supplies.

Devil's Gate was on the Oregon Trail; once a Pony Express stop.

Devil's Gate Creek, Albany: named about 1880 for an imaginary devil's face in a cliff overhanging the creek.

Devil's Kitchen, Big Horn: badland formation of weird shapes molded by wind and water erosion.

Devil's Kitchen, Natrona: group of crazy forms in Hell's Half Acre, which was first known as Devil's Kitchen.

Devil's Kitchen, YNP: interior of an extinct hot spring, 35 feet deep and 75 feet long; the home of bats who escape the carbon dioxide gas which rises here.

Devil's Pass, Albany: named about 1900 for the difficulty of crossing here.

Devil's Playground, Albany: a mountainous region of disheveled granite boulders; named in 1929 by Cheyenne businessmen who were promoting it as a place for outings.

Devil's Punchbowl, Hot Springs: near Thermopolis; once a large spring with a bowl 60 feet deep and 300 feet across; minerals built a circular rim around it. Indians called the spot Thunder Ground, because the rocks give a hollow sound when struck.

Devil's Slide on Bird's Eye Pass, Fremont: treacherous ground covered with loose rocks which tested the skill of stage drivers and freighters in the early days; one freight wagon plunged over, and slid down into a deep canyon; nothing was ever salvaged.

Devils Tower, Crook: an 865-foot monolith resembling a colossal petrified tree stump; formed in the earth of molten lava about 50 million years ago; cooling slowly in the earth formed the columns; the earth eroded away from around it, leaving a unique landmark.

Indians called it Bad God's Tower; also Mateo Tepee, Grizzly Bear Lodge, for the legend which stated it was raised to save several little Indian girls from a bear. Richard I. Dodge, while escorting a USGS party in 1875, named it Devils Tower, Bad God's Tower.

Local ranchers, Willard Ripley and Will Rogers, drove wooden pegs in a crack, and fashioned a wooden ladder on which they climbed the tower, July 4, 1893; it is now tourists' delight and a climbers' mecca.

Devils Tower rises 1,280 feet above Belle Fourche River, and is estimated to contain enough material to surface a road nine times around the world at the equator. Capt. W. F. Reynolds and members of his expedition of 1859 were probably the first white men to see it.

Devils Tower National Monument, Crook: became the first national monument in the United States in 1906; it has a museum, a tourist campground, administration buildings, and an amphitheater where nightly lectures are given during the tourist season on the origin, history, and climbing routes of Devils Tower.

Prairie dogs inside the monument are protected, and beg for handouts from interested visitors.

Dexter Peak, Carbon: named for Dexter, a rancher who lived below the peak.

Dexterville, Carbon: named for Dexter, owner of a ranch stopping place with a blacksmith shop and saloon for the stage between Rawlins and Dillon.

Diamond, Platte: discontinued post office and railroad siding named for Diamond ranch, established in 1882 by George R. Rainsford, a famous breeder of horses. The ranch buildings are now used as a recreation center; ranch probably was named for a brand.

Diamond G. Ranch, Fremont: discontinued post office.

Diamond Mountain, Sweetwater: once a hideout of an outlaw gang that robbed UP trains and gambled in their spare time. Salisbury, an English member, got badly in debt to others, and wrote checks on an English bank. When the checks bounced, Salisbury was told to make them good or be killed. He wrote to an English friend that he had found a mountain filled with diamonds, and asked for money to develop it. His friend deposited the money, and the checks were made good. Salisbury, freed, rode away.

The English friend came to see the diamonds, discovered the fraud, and spent his life chasing Salisbury; when both were old men, he finally found Salisbury in England and shot him.

Diamondville, Lincoln: in 1868 Harrison Church, a prospector, found a vein of coal here; Eastern capital developed it in 1894; it was a town for years; the buildings are now a suburb of Kemmerer.

Dick Creek, Park: named for an Indian Dick, who lived here until 1890.

Dickie, Hot Springs:, discontinued post office named for David Dickie, rancher.

Dietz, Sheridan: discontinued post office named for C. N. Dietz, president of the Sheridan Coal Company, and one of the founders of the Dome Lake Club.

Difficulty, Carbon: settlement named for the creek.

Difficulty Creek, Carbon: settlers here in 1879 were pursuing Indians who had stolen their horses. The settlers became mired in the creek, and got out with great difficulty, hence the name.

Dike Mountain, Park: so named because it has steep walls and dikes.

Dike Needle, Teton: slender summit of the middle Teton; named for its black dike.

Dillinger, Campbell: discontinued post office named for Della C. Dillinger, postmaster.

Dillon, Carbon: a miners' town; founded when saloons were forbidden in Rudefeha by the company; named for Malachi W. Dillon, saloon owner. The town became notorious because of Grant Jones, newspaper editor of Dillon *Doublejack*; he wrote syndicated columns for the Eastern newspapers, portraying life in a mining town, and publicizing legendary creatures like six-legged Coogly Woo, and one-eyed Screaming Emu. Dillon, now a ghost town, is hard to find.

Dillon, Weston: named for rancher Dillon.

Dines, Sweetwater: named for Courtland Dines, one of the original owners of the Colony Coal Company.

Dinwoody Caves and Lakes, Fremont: named for Dinwoody Creek; low cliffs surround the three lakes; caves in the cliffs are nearly filled and may contain ancient artifacts. On the cliffs by the second lake are petroglyphs thousands of years old.

Dinwoody Creek, Fremont: once called Campbell's Fork; the name was changed by USGS in 1911 to Dinwoody for Lt. William A. Dinwoody, member of United States cavalry stationed at Ft. Washakie.

Dinwoody Glaciers, Fremont: named for Dinwoody Creek; these ice fields are the largest in the United States outside Alaska.

Dinwoody Pass, Fremont: renamed Bonney Pass in 1983 to honor Orin H. Bonney, author, by United States Board of Geographical Names.

Dipper Lake, Carbon: so named because the shape was originally like a dipper; a stockman has recently altered its shape.

Dirty Man Creek, Carbon: named for a homesteader who lived here, and left much to be desired in the way of cleanliness.

Dirty Man Mountain, Albany: named for an early careless housekeeper who lived here.

Disappointment Peak, 11,616, Teton: named by a climbing party after a day of disappointments; a popular one-day climb, with an excellent view from the summit.

Ditch Creek, Teton: named for ditches dug in 1870 to divert water for placer mining.

Diversion Dam, Fremont: built in 1921-23 to divert water from the Bighorn River into Wyoming Canal; cost $9,000,000; part of Riverton Reclamation Project. A road was built across the dam in 1924.

Divide, Laramie: discontinued post office; named Divide because it was on the divide between Lodge Pole Creek and Horse Creek.

Divide, Niobrara: also known as "the Breaks"; a pine-covered break in the land running northwest from Crawford, Nebraska. Prairie on the south side of the divide is some of the best dry, sandy-loam farming land in Wyoming, with heavy winter snow cover. The land breaks down a thousand feet or more to gumbo prairies, mostly devoid of snow; good winter grazing.

Dixon, Laramie: named for Robert Dixon, a trapper who lived to an old age. He said he wanted to live to see a railroad train cross the Laramie Plains, but he was killed by Arapahoe Indians a year before the UP railroad came; near the original site of the Jim Baker cabin now in Frontier Park, Cheyenne.

Doane Mountain, 10,656, YNP: named in 1870 by the Washburn party for Lt. Gustavus C. Doane, commander of their military escort. He wrote the first official report of the wonders of Yellowstone National Park.

Doane Peak, Carbon: named for George Doane, prospector.

Doane Peak, 11,354, Teton: named for Lt. Gustavus C. Doane who took a boat down the Snake River in mid-winter of 1876, attempting to explore it. Doane Peak is also called Cairn Peak for the cairn on the summit, built by surveyor E. M. Buckingham, who made the first ascent of the peak in 1931.

Dodge, Big Horn: discontinued post office named for Charles H. Dodge, postmaster.

Dodge Butte, Sublette: named for pioneer Dodge who shot a black bear here. When the wounded animal charged him, Dodge stuck his fist down the bear's throat, choking and knifing it to death. Dodge later wore a beard to cover the scars on his face made by the bear's claws.

Dogie, Niobrara: discontinued post office. Mrs. Reta A. Butler, first postmaster, wanted the name "Eureka" because she liked the country. The Post Office Department said no, so she chose "Dogie" for a motherless calf.

Dog Springs, Uinta: many years ago Carter Cattle Company was camped at these springs during their spring roundup. A train stopped; some of the passengers got off and walked around. Among them was an elderly lady walking her dog. He ran away to the roundup camp, and off with the cowboys' dogs. The lady had to go on without her dog. Cowboys called the place Dog Springs; listed on soil maps as Oasis Springs.

Dome Lake, Sheridan: named for Dome Rock which was named for its shape.

Dome Lake Recreation Area, Sheridan: a club creating the area was formed in 1895; the land was secured before Bighorn National Forest was formed.

Donald, Crook: discontinued post office named for James O. McDonald, postmaster.

Donkey Creek, Campbell: named by early settler for a runaway donkey; a post office was here for one year, while it was headquarters for the engineers constructing Burlington railroad.

Donohue Point, Teton: after Jackson Dam was built, this became an island point.

Donovar, Sweetwater: railroad siding, incorrectly spelled, named for General Doniphan of Mexican War fame.

Doty Mountain, Carbon: named for A. H. Doty, rancher.

Doublet Peak, 13,600, Fremont, Sublette: named by Kenneth Henderson for the mountain's appearance from Dinwoody Peak.

Dougherty, Albany: in 1890; discontinued; named for James Dougherty, postmaster.

Douglas, Converse: county seat; named for Stephen A. Douglas, United States senator from Illinois, and Lincoln's opponent in the famous debate; a tent town in 1886, where the first church services were held in a saloon with a card table for an altar.

Douglas was the home of Bill Barlow's pithy newspaper, *The Budget*; it was also claimed as home by Red Fenwick, noted columnist. It was also the home of Shannon Garst, author; Wyoming State Fair; and the Jackalope, a unique animal that looks like a jackrabbit, has horns, and sings before a thunderstorm.

The state fair was located in Douglas with a $50,000 appropriation by the legislature when Joseph Carey was governor. The first fair was held in 1905 on land given by Chicago and Northwestern railroad. An old Burlington railroad engine, a UP chair car, and a Chicago and Northwestern caboose have been donated and placed on the fair grounds. Also on the grounds is Pioneer Museum with relics of the early days, and an early school house, dating from about 1885.

Douglas Creek, Albany: named for Capt. Douglas who discovered gold on its banks about 1857.

56

Dover, Albany: discontinued post office on the Dover ranch, hence the name.

Downey, Albany: discontinued post office; named for S. W. Downey, pioneer statesman.

Downey Lakes, Albany: named for S. W. Downey.

Downing, Crook: discontinued post office named for Mrs. Mary Downing, postmaster.

Downs Lake and Mountain, 13,344, Fremont: named for John Downs, Lander, who hunted in this region. The mountain was climbed by USGS in 1906; F. Mitchell built a cairn on its top in 1961.

Dow Prong Creek, Sheridan: named for A. P. Dow, early rancher.

Dragons Mouth, YNP: thermal spring named for its deep, gurgling roar.

Dream Creek and Lake, Sublette: named by Sadie Hall, wife of a forest supervisor about 1910; she thought it was so beautiful, it looked like a dream.

Drizzlepuss, Teton: a pinnacle where it always seems to rain or hail when a climbing party is taken there by the Exum Mountaineering School, hence the name.

Dry Medicine Lodge Creek, Big Horn: named by Indians because when the creek was dry, they could hear water running underground.

Dry Sandy, Sublette: a Pony Express station named for the nearby creek. Located six miles southeast of where the Sublette cutoff left the Oregon Trail. (See Wyoming Annals, spring 1973).

Dubois, Fremont: Mrs. John Burlingham, pioneer, called area "Never Sweat," while kidding the men for not working too hard. When a post office started about 1886, the name Never Sweat was applied for, but postal officials didn't want that name, and chose Dubois for U.S. Senator Dubois of Idaho, who was on the Senate committee for post offices at that time. The local residents liked this choice because Senator Dubois worked for bills that favored small homesteaders.

The first mail was brought on snowshoes from Fort Washakie. Now it is a favorite town of sportsmen and rockhounds.

Duck Lake Stage Station, Carbon: in 1860 several lakes were here; emigrants looked forward to reaching this station in desolate Indian country.

Dull Center, Converse: discontinued post office named for Walter Dull.

Dull Knife Battleground, Johnson: in 1876 Col. Mackenzie surrounded the Cheyenne Indian camp of Chief Dull Knife at dawn, and drove them from their lodges into the hills; this left the whites in control of the Big Horn Mountains.

Dull Knife Pass, Johnson: where old Chief Dull Knife and his braves slipped through in sub-zero weather, while being pursued by Col. Mackenzie.

Dumbell, Park: discontinued post office named for the dumbbell brand of Philip Vetter.

Dunbar Meadows, Fremont: named for pioneer Dunbar.

Duncam, Fremont: discontinued post office; named for Duncan family.

Duncom Mountain, Sheridan: named for Duncom who first discovered gold in the Bald Mountain area.

DuNoir Creek, Fremont: probably named for French "black" because of black rock formations in the region; once a timber dump and the headquarters of Wyoming Tie and Timber Company.

Dunraven Pass and Peak, 9,000, YNP: named by Henry Gannett, USGS, in 1878 for Earl of Dunraven, who visited Yellowstone National Park in 1874, and wrote "The Great Divide," an article that made the park wonderland known to the people of Europe.

Durham, Laramie: railroad station named for old settler Durham.

Durkee, Washakie: named for Durkee, an early-day booster for the community and a railroad worker.

Durkee Community, Washakie: named for a pioneer settler.

Duroc, Goshen: railroad siding named for the Duroc hogs raised on the Davis ranch, where the siding was located.

Durrance Ridge, Teton: named for J. Durrance, mountain climber.

Durrance Route on Devils Tower, Crook: named for Jack Durrance who pioneered this route via the Leaning Column; the most popular and safest route for climbing Devils Tower.

Dutch Creek, Sheridan: first called Hungarian Creek for a Hungarian who homesteaded there; the word was too long for settlers who shortened it to "Dutch."

Dutton Creek, Albany: named for Ben Dutton, pioneer in the 1870s.

Dwyer, Platte: old-timers called this settlement Buckhorn, for it was on the Buckhorn Flats. Homesteaders renamed it Dwyer for J. E. Dwyer, once superintendent of the Colorado and Southern railroad. Farmers here struggled with drought and blowing dust, and thought it a good "next year country,"—next year when they hoped to raise a crop.

Dwyer Flats, Platte: also known as Buckhorn flats.

E

E K Mountain, Johnson: named for Plunkett, Roche and Company horse brand.

E Plane, Sweetwater: once a small mining town named for a plane or level in coal mine.

Eadsville, Natrona: a ghost mining camp on top of Casper Mountain; named for Charles W. Eads, who surveyed and platted a town here around spring in 1891; many ore mines were opened, and a stamp mill planned; log cabins were built; the population grew to almost 5,000. The boom collapsed in 1897.

Eagle, Albany: discontinued post office named for a nearby peak.

58

Eagle Peak, Albany: named in 1878 by Jack Newell who killed a golden eagle there that year.

Eagle's Nest Gap, Platte: some wagon trains on the Oregon Trail went south through Eagle's Nest Gap in the 1870s to avoid the difficult North Platte River canyon; this was known as Fetterman Cut-off. The pass took its name from a high, eroded formation resembling an eagle's nest; many names were carved on the sandstone cliffs by emigrants; road agents used the gap for holdups.

Eagle's Nest Stage Station, Park: established in the 1890s by Tom Lanchberry on Fort Washakie to Red Lodge, Montana, route; stout four- and six-horse teams under salty drivers, pulling heavy wagons, were changed every 15 to 20 miles. The charge at this station to dust-covered passengers was one dollar for supper, bed, and breakfast.

Eagles Rest Peak, 11,257, Teton: the name was suggested by the sight of a bald eagle perched on a tree.

Early Creek, Sheridan: named for John Early, stockman in 1882.

Earthquake Geyser, YNP: started in 1959 by an earthquake, hence the name.

Easy Day Peak, 11,600, Sublette: named in 1955 by an ascent party who spent a rest day planning a hair-raising route to the summit.

Eaton, Sheridan: the first real dude ranch in Wyoming established in 1904 by the Eaton brothers; they moved to this ideal country from Medora, North Dakota. Their many guests insisted on paying, and so on this large, scenic ranch in the Big Horn Mountains, the brothers made paying guests a business; it had a post office, store, and individual cabins. The ranch was featured in the writings of Mary Roberts Rinehart.

Bill Eaton Day is now an annual rodeo held in the Kelly Howie arena at Big Horn, with the proceeds going to the Gottsche Rehabilitation Center in Thermopolis.

Eaton Trail, YNP: named for Howard Eaton, famous horseman and guide who also had a dude ranch in the Big Horn Mountains. The trail in the park is about 150 miles long, and follows a scenic route close to Grand Loop road. The trail was named by Sam T. Woodring, chief ranger, for Howard Eaton, who had guided more than 100 horseback parties through the park.

Echeta, Campbell: discontinued post office; named by Mr. Wilson who saw a wild pony running along the creek. Echeta is an Indian name for horse.

Echinus Geyser, YNP: named for Greek "spiny molding"; large and beautiful; a favorite in the Norris Geyser Basin.

Echo Peak, YNP: according to Jim Bridger, he used this distant peak as an alarm clock; when he crawled into his sugans at night, he hollered, "Time to get up, Jim!" At daybreak the echo came back: "Time to get up, Jim!"

Economic Geyser, YNP: fitting name for a quiescent geyser.

Edelman Creek and Pass, Johnson: named for W. H. Edelman, Sheridan business man.

Edelman Creek, Sheridan: named for W. H. Edelman, local business man.

Eden, Sweetwater: named by the Mennonites who settled here considering it "a land of promise"; an irrigated agricultural district; State Agricultural Experiment Station is located here.

Eden Valley, Sweetwater: named by the Mennonites. This rich valley has become famous for its artifacts and petrified wood. A Mr. Finley found very old stone tools and weapons here in a blowout; archeologists named the Finley Site in 1940, when they uncovered ancient arrowheads they called Eden Valley Yumas; these are now known as Eden points. Petrified wood, also found here, has a white rind, with a jet-black interior that takes a high polish.

Edgerton, Natrona: town in the oil field named for being on the edge of the famous Salt Creek oil field.

Edson, Carbon: railroad siding named for J. A. Edson, train dispatcher.

Ega Ditch, Fremont: the Shoshone word for new is ega; so the new ditch in the ceded portion of the Wind River Reservation is Ega Ditch.

Egan Draw, Fremont: named for Egan Nonatsie, an Army captain on the Oregon Trail; he had so many narrow escapes that the Indians became superstitious about him, and admired him.

Egbert, Laramie: named for Dan and Augustus Egbert, railroad workers who selected this site for a station in 1868.

Eleanor Creek, Park: named for a daughter of A. A. Anderson.

Electric Peak, 11,155, YNP: named in 1872 by Henry Gannett, a surveyor who was ascending the peak when an electric storm came up causing his hair to stand on end and his fingers to tingle painfully.

Elephant Back, 8,600, YNP: named by Hayden in 1871 because of its rounded form at the summit, and almost vertical sides.

Elgin Park, Johnson: named for Walter Elgin.

Elk, Teton: named for the animal; its true name is wapiti; when the English came to Virginia, they named this animal "elk," the name for European moose. Wapiti is an Asiatic deer. Elk belong to the deer family.

The largest elk herd in the world winters in Jackson Hole. They were originally plains animals, but were driven to the mountains by civilization. They have large hooves, and cannot paw through the snow for feed. They come down out of summer ranges in the mountains, and are fed hay on their winter refuge.

Elk Creek, Albany: named for elk that lived here in the 1880s.

Elk Horn Prairie, Crook: named for a huge pile of elk horns evidently left here by the Gore party of 1854.

Elk Mountain, 11,162, Carbon: an outstanding landmark in Medicine Bow Range; named for Chief Standing Elk, Sioux warrior; another version says it was named for the animal. First ties for the UP railroad were cut here in 1866, hand-hewn, and floated down streams. Portable saw mills and huge trucks now speed lumbering, the fourth largest industry in Wyoming.

Elk Mountain, Carbon: post office named for the nearby mountain; once a stage station; near the Medicine Bow elk wintering range.

Elk Refuge, Teton: insures the yearly survival of 15,000 elk on land once taken from them by early settlers; started in 1914; now 23,648 acres; a winter refuge.

Elkhorn, Platte: a Pony Express station; the name is obvious.

Elkhorn, Sublette: discontinued post office; named for the creek.

Elkhurst, Uinta: railroad station for elk who were plentiful here when the UP railroad was built in 1869.

Elkol, Lincoln: a coal mining town established in 1908; the name was derived from nearby Elk Mountain. Utah Power and Light Company has a large plant here producing electricity, using local coal.

Ellingwood Peak, 13,000, Sublette: named for Albert R. Ellingwood, a mountain climber who made a solo ascent of this peak in 1926.

Ellison Pass, Albany: named for Frank Ellison, a land owner about 1904.

Ellsburg Divide, Crook: named for Mert Ellsburg.

Ellwood Spring, Carbon: a watering place in the early days, where there was a grove of aspens and willows; named for the trees.

Elmo, Carbon: a small village started by a group of Finlanders; the community grew up around a store on a homestead; named for Elmo, who was killed by Indians.

Elsa Lake, Johnson: an almost circular body of sparkling blue water named for Elsa Spear Byron, daughter of a pioneer sawmill owner.

Elwood, Carbon: once a busy transfer point in the days of Encampment copper boom; freight, mail, and passengers bound for higher altitudes in the winter changed to sleds here; heavy loads coming down shifted from sleds to wagons. A renowned freighter was Southpaw who even banked under that name; he handled teams on the mountain slopes with great dexterity. Elwood is now a ghost town.

Embar, Hot Springs: post office in 1885 on the huge ranch of Capt. Robert A. Torrey, who later recruited troops for the Rough Riders during the Spanish-American War; named for his brand M—; discontinued. Here Woodruff built the first cabin in the basin in 1871.

Embar Formation, named for the Embar post office; a limestone with shales of various colors; found in most of Wyoming; lower than the Chugwater Formation.

Emblem, Big Horn: formerly Germania because the country was settled by mostly German people; the name was changed during World War I; probably Emblem was chosen for the flag. It was once known as "Liberty Bench."

Emigh, Campbell: discontinued post office named for George Emigh, first postmaster.

Emigrant Gap, Natrona: about 12 miles west of Fort Caspar the Oregon Trail went through a gap or draw, at the bottom of which flows Poison Spider Creek; many stopped for night at this landmark from 1840-69, hence the name.

61

Emigrant Gulch, YNP: named for early emigrants; deep canyon that terminates in a long rocky slope. A stream in the canyon yields placer gold.

Emigrant Peak, YNP: towers over Emigrant Gulch with stunted timber below its naked granite peak.

Emigrants Laundry Tub, Platte: a spring that flows 70-degree water the year around; emigrants on the Oregon Trail stopped here to do their laundry, and wash off the dust of the trail, hence the name.

Emigrants Springs, Lincoln: a pioneer campsite on Sublette Cutoff to Fort Hall, Idaho; this route reduced the distance by 53 miles, but was unpopular because of a 30-mile waterless stretch between Big Sandy and Green River.

Emma Matilda Lake, Teton: named for Emma Matilda Owen, the wife of Uncle Billy Owen who was the first to make a public survey in Jackson Hole; also the first to lead a party in an ascent of Grand Teton.

Emmons Mesa, Sweetwater: an extinct crater.

Empire, Goshen: a Negro settlement named for Mr. Empire; a post office, now discontinued, was established in 1912; had a school with a Negro teacher who, at that time, was the only college graduate teaching in Goshen County; no Negroes live in the area now.

Encampment, Carbon: named for Encampment River; the town developed in 1898 with the discovery and mining of copper in nearby mountains. An aerial tramway, 16 miles long, the longest tramway in the world, brought ore to the town's smelter. A branch of the UP railroad was built to here from Walcott. After the copper mines were exhausted in 1908, lumbering, livestock raising, and dude ranching became the main industries in the area.

Judge Charles E. Winter lived in Encampment in 1903, and went east to promote mining interests; in three weeks he became so homesick for Wyoming, that while riding a train through Pennsylvania he wrote a poem: set to music by G. E. Knapp of Laramie and Mrs. Harold Vaughan of Casper, it became the state song "Wyoming."

Four books have been written about the romance of copper mining near Encampment: *Grandon of Sierra, Ben Warman* and *Gold of Freedom* by Charles E. Winter; and *The Treasure of Hidden Valley* by Willis George Emerson.

Reconstructed buildings now form a museum center with many old-time relics.

Encampment River, Carbon: here Indians held their yearly encampment by a warm spring, when they were hunting; Jim Bridger, Bill Sublette, Jim Fitzpatrick, Kit Carson, and Jim Baker traded furs and goods with Indians here, and called it "Camp le Grande," which became grand Encampment.

Enga Creek, Fremont: a Shoshone word meaning "red"; creek flows though red clay.

Enos Creek and Lake, Teton: named for Chief Enos, an Indian exhibited at San Francisco Exposition in 1915; Enos was then 102 years old; he lived 4 more years; he served as a guide for Gen. John Fremont; this region was his favorite hunting ground.

62

Eothen, Crook: discontinued post office; at the ranch and sawmill of John Pearson in 1887; he named it for a friend.

Ervay, Natrona: discontinued post office on the stage line from Casper to Lander; established in 1882 by Jake E. Ervay.

Eslick, Weston: discontinued post office named for Lovina Eslick, postmaster.

Esterbrook, Converse: village at the site of an old copper mine near Laramie Peak; named for Esterbrook Creek; a rustic log church here has an inspirational setting; its window frames Laramie Peak; good campground.

Esterbrook Creek, Converse: named for Mrs. Ester Cooper, pioneer in 1897.

Ethete, Fremont: pronounced E-the-tee; town on the Wind River Reservation; when Arapahoes learned there was to be a mission, they named the railroad station and post office Ethete, meaning "good." St. Michael's Mission, Episcopal, here for Araphoes.

Etna, Lincoln: a farming community, mostly Mormon. Bishop Carl Cook met with a group to choose a name for the town. He read names from an insurance book. When he came to the name Etna, someone suggested it was short and easy to pronounce and spell. The group voted for the name.

Euarye, Fremont: word in Shoshone language means "warm valley"; mountain lakes lie crystalline and quiet here.

Eureka Canyon, Platte: an early party of pioneers found they could not cross the Platte River here, but found this canyon where they made a good camp, and called it Eureka; it was an old Indian campground.

Evans Pass, Albany, Laramie: Gen. Grenville M. Dodge and a party were out looking for a railroad pass over mountains west of Cheyenne in 1865; chased by Indians, they fled past a lone pine, growing out of the rocks, and down a draw on Sherman Hill, thus accidentally finding the best route for railroad. Dodge named the pass for James A. Evans, a UP surveyor. It is also known as Lone Tree Pass and Sherman Pass for Sherman Hill.

Evanston, Uinta: county seat; established by UP railroad officials in 1869; named for James A. Evans, surveyor and civil engineer. Actress Sarah Bernhardt was delayed here in 1884 by a landslide on the railroad; Shoshone braves entertained her and other passengers with their riding, stunting, and lassoing to the great delight of the Madame.

Ranching, dairying, and lumbering are the basic industries of the region. The State Hospital for the Insane is located in Evanston.

Evansville, Natrona: oil refinery town east of Casper; named for W. T. Evans, blacksmith, who homesteaded here. The old Platte River crossing was used here as early as 1834. Reshaw or Richard Bridge was built here in 1851-53.

Everts Mountain, 7,900, YNP: named by the Washburn party in 1870 for Truman C. Everts, a member of the party who became lost, and wandered for 37 days around Mount Sheridan living on roots and berries; he was found, weak but alive. Fossil-bearing marine deposits are on Everts Mountain.

Expedition Island, Sweetwater: in the town of Green River, where John Wesley Powell and ten men in four wooden boats set out to float down the Green and Colorado rivers in 1869 and 1871 on their expedition.

Exum Mountaineering School, Teton: operated by Glenn Exum, Jackson; it provides basic training, also advanced courses, in climbing; practice courses are on Storm Point, Rockchuck, Fryell, and Disappointment peaks; the final climb is made on Grand Teton, the Matterhorn of America. All climbers in the Tetons must clear with the Jenny Lake Ranger Station before climbing; no solo climbs are permitted.

F

Fackler Pass, Albany: named about 1908 for Dan Fackler, a sheep man who discovered this mountain pass, and brought his sheep wagon through it.

Factory Hill, 9,607, YNP: named for its resemblance on a frosty morning to an active factory; a northern foothill of Mount Sheridan.

Fairbanks, Platte: ghost town; named for N. K. Fairbanks, eastern capitalist who with G. N. Pullman built a smelter here after copper was discovered; a busy smelter town in the late 1880s. Wagon trains drawn by mules brought coke here from Cheyenne, 110 miles away, and hauled back metal; more than $200,000 worth of copper was smelted here; once it had log cabins, dance halls, and saloons for miners.

Wyoming historian I. S. Bartlett, who lived here, was caught by a summer cloudburst and flood which swept through his home; he had to air and dry his soppy notes. Now it is a picnic ground known as Kelly's Park.

Fairview, Lincoln: town settled in 1885; named by Heber Grant for the fair view it gives of Crow Creek valley; once a freighters' stop with their caravans of wagons and sleds.

Fairy Falls, YNP: named by Capt. J. W. Barlow in 1871 for their appearance.

Faler Lake and Tower, Sublette: named for Vint Faler, old time freighter, trapper, and dude ranch operator. Ralph Faler froze to death in devotion to duty with a 1st class mail sack under his arm in 1921 between Dry Sandy Stage Station and South Pass City. Mary Faler, daughter-in-law of Vint, is a well-known lady packer and guide into Bridger Wilderness. Faler Lake is noted for its golden trout. It is one of the few natural lakes in Wyoming that have an island.

Fall Creek, Albany: named about 1900 for the falls in the creek.

Fall Creek, Teton: named for the swiftness of its current.

Fallen City, Sheridan: a geological phenomenon; a jumble of huge oblong boulders, deposited on a hillside by a prehistoric glacier, suggesting a city tumbled by an earthquake, hence the name.

Fall River, Sublette: named for its many cascades.

Fanny's Peak, Weston: so named because, according to legend, a pioneer girl, Fanny, threw herself from its ledge to escape a party of Indians; now known as Red Butte.

Farrall, Crook: discontinued post office, established in 1894 with William Farrall Smith as first postmaster, hence the name.

Farson, Sweetwater: named for John Farson, Chicago broker who started a reclamation and irrigation project here; near the site where Jim Bridger and Brigham Young met in 1847, and conferred about the route west and the fertility of the Great Salt Lake valley. Bridger is said to have offered Young $1,000 for the first bushel of corn he could grow there. Farson is the site of the Big Sandy Pony Express Station burned by Indians in 1862.

Farthing, Laramie: a railroad station named for Charles Farthing, who donated the land for the station; he settled here in 1904. Nearby post office, Iron Mountain.

Faye Lake, Albany: named for Faye Donnell.

Fayette, Sublette: discontinued post office named by Mrs. Fred Fisher for nearby lake.

Fayette Lake, Sublette: named by Fred Fisher, homesteader, for Fayette, Arkansas, where he came from.

Febbas Mountain, 13,488, Fremont: named for Febbas who guided English lords during 1898 from Wells dude ranch, an early dude ranch on Green River.

Federal, Laramie: named by J. Ross Carpenter for the Federal Land and Securities Company that gave the land for the town site.

Felix, Campbell: named for Felix, the first telegraph agent at this railroad station.

Felix Creek, Albany: named for a pole fence constructed by two miners near the source of the creek in 1888.

Ferric Geyser, YNP: its waters are stained red-brown by ferric (iron) oxides, hence the name.

Ferris-Haggarty Mine, Carbon: named for George Ferris and sheepherder Ed Haggarty. Grubstaked by James Rumsey, Robert Deal, and George Ferris in 1897, Ed Haggarty found tons of red copper ore and staked a 20-acre claim, calling it Ru-de-fe-ha, using the first two letters of their four names.

Expensive mine equipment was freighted high into the rugged mountains; the longest aerial tramway in the world, 16 miles long, was built over the mountain to carry buckets of ore to Encampment to smelt and ship; highest tram altitude 10,700.

The towns of Copperton, Battle, Rambler, and Dillon sprang up, filled with freighters and miners; now their crumbling remains are barely visible. Mining ceased in 1908 when the Ferris-Haggarty Company was indicted for fraudulent stock sales. More than two million dollars in ore had been taken out, and more remains. It was too costly to freight the machinery down, so the remains of the old mine and deserted cabins lie scattered over the mountainside, with only a jeep trail leading to them. Now in the National Register of Historic Places.

Ferris Mountain, Carbon: spiny, timber-covered ridge that from a distance looks like the backbone of a prehistoric beast. Named for George Ferris, early settler who promoted development of Ferris-Haggarty copper mine. He was killed by a runaway team when he was thrown from the wagon, and landed on his head, in 1900 near Snow Slide Hill.

Festo Lake, Platte: in 1948 the Wyoming Industrial Company deeded 78 acres including this lake to Platte County to be known and maintained as Joseph A. Elliott Memorial Park. Elliott was a civil engineer who served the Wheatland Flats irrigation project for many years. The lake is now a wild game bird refuge; only rowboats may be used for fishing; bass and blue gills are here.

Fetterman, Converse: a railroad station named for Col. W. J. Fetterman.

Fetterman Creek, Converse: named for Col. Fetterman; see Ft. Fetterman.

Fiddler Creek, Weston: so named because a fiddling cowboy lived at head of creek.

Fiddler Creek Oil Field, Weston: first oil well was drilled here in 1948.

Fiddlers Lake, Fremont.

Fiery Narrows, Natrona: named by Robert Stuart in 1812 for the swiftly running rapids and whirlpools between the red walls; also known as the Grand Canyon of the Platte, and Pathfinder Canyon.

In 1824 Fitzpatrick's boats were wrecked here, and his cargoes of furs lost. Gen. John C. Fremont's rubber boat overturned here in 1842; Fremont, Kit Carson, and others got wet and cold, before they rescued the scientific equipment from the river in several hours of effort, hence the name Pathfinder Canyon. Fremont was known as "The Pathfinder."

Fifteen Mile Creek, Johnson: fifteen miles from old Fort Reno, hence the name.

Fillmore, Albany: discontinued post office; railroad station named for Luther Fillmore, pioneer railroad superintendent and rancher about 1904.

Finley Site, Sweetwater: see Eden Valley.

Firehole Canyon, Sweetwater: so named for brilliant coloring of buttes and eroded formations; contrast with green junipers.

Firehole Lakes, Johnson: named for a forest fire in canyon.

Firehole Lake, YNP: under favorable atmospheric conditions, rising globular masses of mixed air and superheated steam below water surface, give an optical illusion of fire in the water; the name dates back to 1832.

Firehole River, YNP: numerous vents in the banks, from which light-colored flames gleam and seem to be constantly extinguished by water; caused by escaping gas reflected in the water. Jim Bridger said water ran downhill so fast, it heated the rocks which gave off ghostly flames.

Fish Cut, Lincoln: named for fossil fish found here.

Fish Cut, Sweetwater: named for a fossil formation through which a cut was made by UP railroad; once it was a prehistoric ocean bed; skeletons of fish are well preserved in layers of shale.

Fish Cut, Teton: named for fossil fish found here.

Fisher, Converse: old railroad station named for F. H. Fisher, owner of the XH cattle ranch in the vicinity.

Fisherville, Sweetwater: discontinued post office established in 1889; named for Mrs. Helen Fisher, postmaster.

Fish Hook Creek, Sheridan: creek makes a sharp hook, hence the name.

Fishing Bridge, YNP: an institution in tourist life; a bridge across the Yellowstone River, lined in tourist season with people of all ages from all states, with all types of trolling and casting rods, fishing for native cutthroat trout; no license is required; they stand elbow to elbow from dawn to dusk. A bridge was built in 1930 to replace the narrow structure used by stagecoaches; the first automobile entered the park in 1916.

Five Fingers, Johnson: rock pinnacles near Cloud Peak, rising like an upthrust hand, hence the name.

Five Mile Creek, Sheridan: five miles from Dayton, hence the name.

Flag Butte, Crook: first known as Water Butte. A United States surveyor placed a flag on it for surveying purposes, hence the name.

Flagstaff Area, Washakie: so named because homesteaders found a tall, straight tree which they felled, peeled, and hauled to their community for a flagstaff.

Flagstone Peak, 13,200, Fremont: named by Phil Smith for the flagstones he found on its summit in 1946; also known as Philsmith Peak for this noted mountain climber.

Flaming Gorge Recreation Area, Sweetwater: the water is the Green River backed up by Flaming Gorge Dam, Utah; now a large fishing and boating area where rattlesnakes, desert lizards, and cactus once thrived.

Flaming Gorge Reservoir, Sweetwater: lake 91 miles long; 43,000 acres of clear water; scenic with a canyon along the shores; it was named for the brilliant red of cliffs.

Flat Creek, Teton: flows through the open, flat part of Hoback valley; it takes its name from the character of the country.

Flattop, Platte: discontinued post office; railroad siding named for a nearby flat-topped butte.

Flattop Creek, Albany: named for nearby Flattop Mountain.

Fletcher Park, Albany: discontinued post office; named for Robert Fletcher who homesteaded here and developed a summer resort.

Fletcher Park, Albany: named for Robert Fletcher.

Floral Valley, Weston: named by Gen. George Custer in 1874, who in violation of the United States treaty with the Indians, was sent by the United States government to explore the Black Hills; members of his Seventh Cavalry found so many flowers, they decorated the manes and bridles of their horses with them, hence the name.

Florence Lake and Pass, 11,000, Johnson: named by an early settler for his daughter Florence.

Flying V Ranch, Weston: probably named for the brand of the Driscolls, ranchers here. The main building, the Casino, was erected as a memorial to those who discovered and developed the anthracite coal beds at nearby Cambria; it is old English in style; great beams, many of them mine timbers, support the ceilings; it has collection of pioneer relics and fossils. Now it is a recreation center and dude ranch.

Folsom Peak, 9,326, YNP: named for David E. Folsom, leader of the 1869 expedition of the USGS.

Fontenelle, Lincoln: post office named by first postmaster, Justin Pomeroy in 1878 for Lucien Fontenelle, outfitter for the American Fur Company, fur trader, and squaw man in the 1830s.

Fontenelle Creek and Peak, Lincoln: named for Lucien Fontenelle.

Fontenelle Reservoir, Lincoln: completed in 1963 for power, irrigation, and recreation; contains 345,000 acre-feet.

Fool's Creek, Sheridan: so named because of its deceiving bends; it "fools" people who think they are at its head, only to find another bend. Another story is that mica in its sand was thought to be gold, and created false excitement.

Foote Creek, Albany, Carbon: named in 1866 for Robert Foote who furnished hay for Fort Halleck.

Forest, Crook: discontinued post office that took its name in 1896 from the forested region in which it was located.

Forks, Crook: discontinued post office established in 1883 at the confluence of two forks of Hay Creek, hence the name.

Fort Augur, Fremont: named for Gen. Christopher C. Augur of Civil War fame. The site is marked with a block of granite on Main Street near 3rd Street in Lander; in 1869 it had log buildings with dirt roofs and was surrounded by a ditch; name was changed to Camp Brown.

Fort Bernard, Goshen: a crudely constructed log building when Francis Parkman stopped there in 1846; owned and operated by two Richard brothers who traded for furs; burned in 1846; was 7 or 8 miles below Fort Laramie on the bank of the Platte River.

Fort Bonneville, Sublette: built in 1832 by Capt. Bonneville about 6 miles west of present Daniel; first fur fort in Wyoming; before it was completed, Capt. Bonneville realized the location was impractical because of high elevation and winter snow, and he abandoned it; it was also known as Fort Nonsense or Bonneville's Folly; near the famous Green River Rendezvous of trappers and Indians, held yearly from 1824-39.

Fort Bridger, Uinta: Jim Bridger, realizing the need for a stopping place, established this log trading post and blacksmith shop in 1843 (first motel in Wyoming). It was then in Mexican territory. Bridger was one of America's greatest frontiersmen and scouts; see Bridger; he said he came when Laramie Peak was a hole in the ground.

Fort Bridger was taken and improved by the Mormons in 1853 (Jim Bridger claims he never sold it), then burned by them when they were fleeing from Johnston's United States Army in 1857; later that year it was reconstructed by the United States Army and remained a military post until 1878. It was a Pony Express station in 1860.

Fort Bridger has several Wyoming firsts: the first piano was freighted here by ox team from the Missouri River in 1864; the first schoolhouse in Wyoming was built here by Judge W. A. Carter in 1866—it is still standing; the first printing press and newspaper was at the fort in 1863. Martha Jane "Calamity Jane" Canary washed dishes here as a girl, before she commenced her famous bull-whacking career. A treaty with the Shoshones was made here in 1869.

Fort Bridger State Park, Uinta: buildings of the famous old fort are now preserved, including Pony Express stables; they house many relics of pioneer life.

Fort Brown, Fremont: see Camp Brown.

Fort Buford, Albany: named for Gen. John Burford, Civil War general; established in 1866 to protect UP railroad workers from Indians; renamed Fort Sanders later that year.

Fort Carrington, Johnson: see Fort Phil Kearny.

Fort Caspar, Natrona: first known as Camp Platte; erected in 1858 to protect the Platte River bridge on the Oregon Trail; renamed Fort Caspar for Lt. Caspar Collins who was killed by Indians when he went to the aid of travelers near the bridge in 1865. The fort was abandoned by troops; it was burned by Indians in 1867; now it is reconstructed and open to visitors.

Fort Connor, Johnson: founded in 1865 by Gen. P. E. Connor as a supply base for his Powder River expedition. Connor was a red-headed Irishman who gruffly ordered troops to kill any Indian over 12 years old on sight. The fort existed only a year; it was moved a mile upriver and became Fort Reno. Connor was recalled in partial disgrace.

Fort D. A. Russell, Laramie: site picked by Gen. John D. Stevenson as camp for soldiers protecting UP railroad builders in 1867; the fort was named for Union General David A. Russell; it was enlarged and was one of the largest military posts in the nation during World War I; it was renamed Fort Francis A. Warren by Congress in 1930. Warren served as United States Senator from Wyoming for 37 years. Now it is Warren Air Force Base.

Fort Davy Crockett, Sweetwater: named by a friend for a friend killed in the Texas battle of the Alamo. A fur trading post in 1836, it was in ruins in 1844.

Fort Fetterman, Converse: built in 1867 for the protection of Oregon and Bozeman trails; named for Col. William J. Fetterman who disobeyed orders and lost his life and those of a company of 81 men following Indians into a trap near Fort Phil Kearny in 1866.

Fort Fetterman was built on a windy eminence, and was considered a disciplinary assignment by troops. After the Fort Laramie treaty of 1868, it was the last Army outpost along the Indian border of the Platte River; it was important as a trading post and supply depot.

From here Gen. Crook launched his Powder River expedition against the Sioux in 1876, which ended in his defeat on the Rosebud; one of his teamsters was Calamity Jane. Cattlemen took over the fort after it was discontinued as a military post in 1882 and made it a hell-roaring frontier town; it was deserted after Douglas was founded in 1886; buildings are now being restored and repaired as a historic park.

Fort Fetterman Road, an old stage and freighting route beginning in Albany County and connecting southern trails with the Oregon and Bozeman routes at Fort Fetterman.

Fort Francis E. Warren, Laramie: see Fort D. A. Russell.

Fort Fred Steele, Carbon: was established on June 30, 1868, by Gen. G. M. Dodge to guard the UP railroad workers and the bridge over the Platte River; it was named for Gen. Frederick Steele, Civil War hero; the fort was an important trading center and shipping point until it was abandoned as a military post in 1886.

Fort Halleck, Carbon: established in 1862 as a strategic post on the Overland Stage route; named for Gen. H. W. Halleck; logs for the buildings were hauled from Elk Mountain; abandoned in 1866.

Fort Hat Creek, Niobrara: after gold was discovered in the Black Hills in 1874, Capt. Egan and a force of cavalry were sent out from Fort Laramie to establish a fort on Hat Creek in Nebraska. Wandering in unmarked wilderness they came to Sage Creek, and thinking it was Hat Creek, they built a fort close to water and wood in 1875. The fort passed into private ownership in 1876; it became an important stage stop on the Cheyenne-Deadwood route.

Fort John, Goshen: in 1834 Robert Campbell and William Sublette built a small trading post on Laramie River, and called it Fort William; in 1835 they sold it to the American Fur Company. It was renamed Fort John for John B. Sarpy, a fur trader and partner. It was enlarged and fortified with bastions, blockhouses, and loopholes; Indians were encouraged to come and trade furs for trinkets, tobacco, and whiskey.

A shipping clerk in St. Louis, instead of writing "Fort John on the Laramie," simply wrote Fort Laramie on freight boxes, and thus it became known.

The Laramie River was named by early trappers for Jacques La Ramie, a French-Canadian trapper who according to Jim Bridger set out to look after his traps and did not return in the spring of 1818; it is said he was killed by Indians. La Ramie has his name perpetuated in Wyoming by having a county, a city, a town, three rivers, a peak, plains, a fort, and a national monument using the anglicized version of his name.

Fort John Buford, Albany: see Fort Sanders.

Fort LaClede, Sweetwater: an old stage station on the Overland Trail built about 1862 after Indian raids; the rocky remains still mark the site; it was named for LaClede, a St. Louis fur trader.

Fort Laramie, Goshen: see Fort John for the name. This was the most important post in the settlement of the West; all travelers on the Oregon Trail stopped here for supplies and repairs; Indians camped nearby for trade, treaty making, and annuities. On the recommendation of Gen. J. C. Fremont, the United States government bought the fort in 1849, and made it a military post.

In 1836 Dr. Marcus Whitman and Rev. H. H. Spalding arrived at Fort Laramie with their brides, Narcissa and Eliza, the first white women to enter and cross Wyoming. With the discovery of gold in California in 1848, a flood of emigrants and Mormons fleeing persecution for their religion, came up the Oregon Trail.

70

Fort Laramie was the first permanent settlement of white men in Wyoming; it was a Pony Express station in 1860 and an important stage and telegraph station. Mrs. Susan Luman, born here in 1836 when the fort was in Missouri Territory, lived here 54 years, and was in Missouri, Idaho, Dakota, and Wyoming territories before Wyoming became a state.

The iron bridge across the Platte River near the fort was built in 1875, and is the oldest iron bridge in Wyoming, also the oldest existing military bridge west of the Mississippi River; it was used by the Cheyenne-Deadwood stage line, and even by heavy trucks until 1958, when a new concrete structure was built.

A famous treaty with Indians, "inscrutable as granite rocks," was signed at Fort Laramie in 1868, promising them the land north of the Platte River inviolate "so long as grass shall grow and water flow." This was to keep them away from construction crews building the UP railroad. By government order General Custer and the Seventh Cavalry marched through these Indian lands in 1874, and discovered gold in the Black Hills of South Dakota, breaking the treaty with the Indians.

The first school in Wyoming opened at Fort Laramie in 1852. The first Wyoming book was *Dictionary of Sioux Language*, compiled by Charles Guerren, and printed at the fort.

This famous historic site was abandoned as a military post in 1890. Buildings were auctioned off to homesteaders at bargain prices, dismantled, and hauled away. Not until 1937 did the State of Wyoming buy 214 acres, on which the remaining ruins of some buildings stood, and give them to the nation. Fort Laramie was declared a national monument in 1938. Twenty-one of the original structures remain—some as ruins, many, repaired and restored. They are being used as museums with military, Oregon Trail, and pioneer displays.

FORT LARAMIE

Two hundred years ago this was
La-no-wa, Land of Paradise;
Land of the grass-clothed plains and blue
Majestic mountains capped with ice.
Here Indians, camping by the bend
Of the river, dried their buffalo meat;
And in the smoke of campfires danced
To the boom, ta ta boom of the tom-tom beat.

Then to this red man's paradise
Came change, as bearded men explored
The streams, or climbed the mountain heights;
Blazed trails; and marked the river ford.
Sometimes with Indians they smoked
A pipe of peace, and promised wealth
In stocks of glittering ornaments;
Their frauds provoked the native stealth.

Here LaRamie explored and trapped—
And, massacred, he left his name
To dot Wyoming's map. And here
The long, grass-covered mounds acclaim

71

The last of those first buildings made
In this vast wilderness, where trade
And treaty with the Indians
Brought need for force and armed brigade.

In eighteen forty-nine The Stars
And Stripes were raised above a fort
That stood where rivers blend and flow
Together; in seas of grass a port,
Half way to California
And Oregon, where tired and worn,
The weary caravans could rest,
And resting find their dreams reborn.

To eastward lay the dusty miles,
The heat and hunger, broken wheels;
The stone-marked graves along the trail,
The disappointments life reveals.
To westward rose the dim, blue peak
Of Laramie, lone mountain scout,
That promised them the gold they sought,
And freedom for the more devout.

The plodding caravans are gone.
In rocks their tracks may still be seen.
Some of the palisade's old walls
Still stand, although they seem to lean
And crumble with a century's weight.
Bare rivers now are edged with trees,
While homes surround an ancient Fort,
Immortalized with memories.

Mae Urbanek

Fort Laramie, Goshen: a town named for the nearby old fort.

Fort Mackenzie, Sheridan: an Army post established in 1897 to protect citizens from hostile Indians on the nearby reservation; named for Gen. Ronald Mackenzie, Indian fighter; discontinued as a military post in 1914; left deserted until designated as a U.S. Health Service hospital in 1920, which opened in 1922. It covers 342 acres, including a farm unit, vegetable and flower gardens, picnic ground, and ball field.

Fort McGraw, Fremont: see Camp McGraw.

Fort McKinney, Johnson: first located on the Powder River, then moved to Clear Creek for better protection and water in 1877; named for Lt. J. A. McKinney, killed in Dull Knife Battle of 1876.
 The fort became a supply depot, and finally was donated to the state of Wyoming for a soldiers' and sailors' home in 1903.

Fort Nonsense, Sublette: see Fort Bonneville.

Fort Phil Kearny, Johnson: first called Fort Carrington, but re-named for Gen. Philip Kearny, Civil War general; a cavalry post with the bloodiest history of any fort in the West; established in 1866 in the heart of

Indian country. Indians stood on nearby bluffs and watched white men move into their beloved hunting grounds, pledged to them by treaties. Indians called it "the Hated Fort."

On a bitter winter day in 1866 Col. Henry B. Carrington, the commander, sent Capt. Wm. Fetterman and 81 men in pursuit of Indians who had attacked a wood-cutting crew. Carrington warned Fetterman not to follow the Indians over the ridge. Fetterman, who had boasted that with 80 men he could ride through the whole Sioux nation, was led on into ambush, and all 82 men were killed

That night John "Portugee" Phillips started on the greatest ride in Wyoming history, 236 miles to Fort Laramie, for reinforcements. Mounted on Carrington's thoroughbred horse, he fought a blizzard and sub-zero temperatures for three days and three nights, until he reached Fort Laramie on Christmas Eve. The horse dropped dead in front of Old Bedlam. Portugee Phillips, a civilian, was never paid for his service, and never fully recovered from the ordeal.

In the spring of 1867 another wood-hauling crew was attacked near Fort Phil Kearny. They used their overturned wagons for protection, and with new, breech-loading rifles routed the Indians. This was the Wagon Box fight.

In March after the Fort Laramie treaty of 1868, Fort Reno and Fort Phil Kearny were abandoned, and immediately burned by Indians. Fort Phil Kearny is now partly restored, and opened to visitors as an historic site.

Fort Platte, Goshen: built by Lancaster P. Lupton in 1841 to compete with Fort John (Fort Laramie) in trade with Indians; located near an iron bridge; abandoned in 1845.

Fort Reno, Johnson: built in 1866 by Col. H. B. Carrington near a spring on the Powder River about a mile from the abandoned Fort Connor; had good log blockhouses; never attacked by Indians; named for Gen. Jesse L. Reno, Civil War hero; abandoned in 1868.

Fort Sanders, Albany: established in 1866 as Fort John Buford to protect railroad builders from Indians; renamed that fall for William P. Sanders, Civil War general; famed "Hell on Wheels" newspaper, *Frontier Index*, was published here in a boxcar; its publisher began the demand that the new territory be named Wyoming. President U. S. Grant stopped here in 1869 to confer with UP railroad officials; the fort was abandoned in 1882.

Fort Stambaugh, Fremont: built for the protection of South Pass miners in 1870; named for Lt. Charles B. Stambaugh, who was killed nearby earlier that year fighting Indians; had four large log barracks; abandoned in 1878.

Fort Stand Off, Teton: a point of rocks northeast of Jackson used by Cal Thompson and other outlaws to resist arrest by U.S. marshalls.

Fort Supply, Uinta: built about 12 miles southwest of Fort Bridger by the Mormons in 1853 to protect their agricultural workers in that valley from Indians; supplied emigrants with grain; burned by the Mormons fleeing Col. Johnston's army in 1857.

Fort Thompson, Fremont: built on Popo Agie River; of brief duration from 1857-58.

Fort Walbach, Laramie: see Camp Walbach.

Fort Warren, Laramie: see Fort D. A. Russell.

Fort Washakie, Fremont: Camp Brown was renamed Fort Washakie in 1878 in recognition of Chief Washakie's leadership of the Shoshone Indians, and his friendship for the white men. When President U. S. Grant presented him with a silver-trimmed saddle in Washington, the chief was asked for a word of appreciation. Washakie answered: "Do a kindness to a white man; he feels it in his head, and his tongue speaks. Do a kindness to an Indian, he feels it in his heart; the heart has no tongue."

Chief Washakie is buried in a nearby soldiers' cemetery. Sacajawea, the famous Shoshone woman guide for Lewis and Clark, is buried in a Shoshone cemetery near Fort Washakie. She was personally known to Dr. John Roberts who buried her here in the land of her fathers.

Fort Washakie was a military post until 1909. It is now the headquarters of the U.S. Indian Service on the Wind River Reservation.

Fort William, Goshen: see Fort John.

Fort Yellowstone, YNP: administration of Yellowstone National Park was vested in the military from 1886-1916; their headquarters were at Mammoth Hot Springs and were called Fort Yellowstone; it was first known as Camp Sheridan.

Fortification Creek, Campbell: named because of the heavy flow of water from tributaries in the spring, or after heavy rains.

Fortification Creek, Johnson: named for its rocky walls.

Fortunatus, Sheridan: named for a European legendary hero, who received an inexhaustible supply of gold from Fortune; see Bald City.

Forty Mile Creek, Albany: named by stage drivers on the old Fort Fetterman Road because this watering place was 40 miles from the Rock Creek station.

Forty Mile Peak, Albany: named for Forty Mile Creek.

Forty Rod, Sublette: a stream that has never been known to freeze over. The state fish hatchery is here.

Fossil, Lincoln: named for nearby fossil beds; post office discontinued in 1945.

Fossil Butte and Ridge, Lincoln: rocks were laid down about 50 million years ago; lower red rocks are of Knight formation; upper shales were laid down when a huge lake covered what is now western Wyoming. In its mud fish were trapped, and their skeletons perfectly preserved. Fossil fish in this Green River formation include herring, perch, catfish, and sting rays, as well as insects, birds, and bats. This is one of the world's largest and most noted fossil fish beds. Now it is a national monument that preserves about 8,000 acres. There are digging beds outside the monument.

Fossil Mountain, 10,912, Teton: a huge limestone ice cave in the mountain has 800 feet of known passages; the 30-degree temperature transforms dripping water into sparkling icicles, columns, and larger formations. Explorer Vic Schmidt believes the frozen stream is a 10,000-year-old remnant of a glacier.

74

Four Bear Creek, Park: this mountain stream was first called Rose Creek for the great number of rose bushes on its banks. In the early 1880s Col. Pickett killed four bears on its banks in one morning, hence the name. An early post office in the vicinity was called Four Bear.

Four Corners, Weston: post office and store where Highway 585 comes into Highway 85, and a road leads east to Mallo Canyon, thus making four corners.

Four Horse, Weston: railroad station; post office discontinued in 1935.

Four Mile Creek, Albany: named in the days of the Overland stage for the distance from Rockdale station, now Arlington.

Four Mile Creek, Johnson: four miles from old Fort Reno.

Fourlog Park, Albany: a prospector started a cabin here in the 1870s and quit after he had laid up four logs, hence the name.

Fourt Glacier, Fremont: named for E. H. Fourt, leader of the first party to visit this glacier; considered one of Dinwoody Glaciers.

Fowkes Formation, Uinta: for Reuben Fowkes, homesteader and one-time foreman of Almy mines.

Fowler, Crook: for B. F. Fowler who came about 1884 to practice law and later served as attorney-general of Wyoming.

Fox Creek, Goshen, Platte: named for a pioneer named Fox who trapped on this creek for several years and then mysteriously disappeared.

Foxpark, Albany: railroad station named by officials for wild foxes here in the early days. A post office was established in 1906; it is in the midst of good lumbering country. Many railroad ties came from here in the early days.

Foxton, Platte: a railroad station named for trapper Fox, for whom Fox Creek was named.

Fraeb's Post, Carbon: American Fur Company trading post; named for Henry Fraeb, trapper, who with four companions was killed here in 1841.

Franc Peak, Sheridan: named for Otto Franc, German nobleman and hunter who established the Pitchfork ranch in Bighorn Basin.

Francell, Goshen: discontinued ranch post office named for Francell, ranch owner.

Francis, Weston: discontinued post office named for Francis M. Jenkins, postmaster.

Francis E. Warren Air Force Base, Laramie: see Fort D. A. Russell.

Franc's Peak, 13,140, Park: named for Otto Franc; see Franc Peak. An early battle between Indian tribes took place here. A tribe on top of the peak was being starved out by tribe below. An Indian took a buffalo paunch and, stealing down at night, filled it with water and carried it back up to his companions. This short reprieve did not help; those on top were defeated.

Frank, Sweetwater: discontinued post office named for Otto Frank.

Frank Island, YNP: largest island in Yellowstone Lake; named in 1871 for Frank, the brother of Henry Elliott, a member of Hayden expedition.

Frannie, Big Horn: a railroad junction and oil field supply town; named by railroad officials for Frannie, daughter of Mrs. Jack Morris, pioneer. Frannie is the home of pungent sagebrush candles.

Frederick, Goshen: discontinued post office named for Charles Frederick who settled here about 1889.

Frederick Creek, Goshen: named for a very early settler, Frederick, who built a cabin where the emigrant trail crossed the creek; he was no relation to Charles Frederick who came later.

Fred's Mountain, Teton: named for Fred Clark who worked with G. B. Bechler mapping Jackson Hole for the Hayden Survey in 1878.

Freedom, Lincoln: oldest settlement in Star Valley; located on the state line; settled by the Mormons in 1879. Arthur Clark stated: "Here we shall find freedom," and the town was named.

In 1890 when Idaho was a territory under government rule, and officials were trying to ban polygamy, the step across the state line to Freedom was important. Wyoming, wishing to encourage settlement, did not bother the Mormons. Later inhabitants stepped as easily over state lines, when liquor prices were lower in Idaho.

Freeland, Natrona: discontinued post office; railroad station named for Bill Freeland, rancher in Bates Hole.

Freezeout Mountain, Carbon: two stories about this name: a mail carrier was caught in a storm, and wrote "froze out" on a rock; a bunch of hunters from England went into these mountains in the early 1870s, and froze out.

Freezeout Point, Sheridan: a point named for its exposed, cold location.

Freezeout Saloon, Fremont: on the site of the present-day Timberline ranch where early-timers played freezeout poker; they were out when they lost all their chips.

Fremont Canyon, Natrona: named for Gen. J. C. Fremont, the "Pathfinder" who in 1842, attempting to descend this canyon, lost his boat and most of his equipment. Granite pinnacles along the canyon make good climbing.

Fremont County, Lander, county seat: named for Gen. John Charles Fremont, surveyor and explorer searching for a route to the Pacific Ocean with a company of 20 men in 1842; Kit Carson and Enos, a Shoshone Indian, acted as guides.

Fremont County was created in 1884; it then included Park, Big Horn, and Hot Springs counties, which were split off in 1890. With wide open ranges and high mountains, Fremont County has mineral, oil, and livestock wealth. Uranium from Gas Hills is refined into yellow cake at five processing mills. Wyoming ranks second among the states in uranium production; more than half of it is in Fremont County.

Black, olive, and apple-green jade, the finest in the world, is found in all directions from Jeffrey City, which is also near the Sweetwater agate beds, where polished jewels lie on the sagebrush prairies. Jade was voted the gem stone of Wyoming by the 1967 state legislature.

The geographical center of Wyoming is 58 miles northeast of Lander.

Fremont, Elkhorn, and Missouri Valley Railroad, see Chicago and Northwestern railroad.

Fremont Island, Natrona: in the Platte River where Gen. Fremont camped in 1842.

Fremont Lake, Sublette: named for Gen. Fremont. Probably Wyoming's deepest body of water with 22 miles of shore line; good mackinaw trout water. First named Stewart Lake for English adventurer, Sir William Drummond Stewart, by his hunting party in 1837.

Fremont Peak, 13,730, Fremont, Sublette: supposed to be the peak which Gen. Fremont climbed in 1842, and on which he unfurled the first U.S. flag to fly in what is now Wyoming.

However, from a detailed description of the peak he climbed, having a snow field, it is believed by authorities that he climbed Mount Woodrow Wilson. Fremont's story of this climb and the fascinating view of the Wind River Range is a classic to be found in *The Immortal Wife* by Irving Stone. This book also tells of Fremont's great adventures in the West, and of his part in saving California for the United States.

Fremont Peak was probably first climbed by the Hayden party in 1878, and photographed by William Jackson who was with them. Jackson used glass plates on which he spread solution, and which were developed in the darkness of a tent. Photography was very difficult in those early days, yet Jackson made photographs which have never been surpassed.

Fremont Sheep Driveway, Sublette: each year about 160,000 sheep move up this trail to grazing grounds in Bridger National Forest and Wilderness Area. The ranger at Dutch Joe Station counts them in; 60 days grazing is allowed; the sheep are moved out in August, and peace again returns to the forests.

Fremont's Monument Mountain, Uinta: see Medicine Butte.

French, Carbon: discontinued post office; railroad station named for French Creek.

French Creek, Carbon: named for French tie cutters here in the early railroad-building days.

Frenchy Draw, Albany: a mountain valley named in 1894 for R. A. Ring, known as "Frenchy"; a rancher.

Freuds Castle, Johnson: large sandstone butte on the south fork of the Powder River; named for Freud, a gunsmith who hunted here.

Frewen, Sweetwater: railroad station named for Moreton Frewen.

Frewen Castle, Johnson: built by Moreton and Richard Frewen, Englishmen. After they came to hunt big game in 1878, they were so intrigued with the beauty of the Big Horn Mountains, they stayed and founded the Powder River Cattle Company.

They built a two-story log mansion, with fireplaces and a winding stairway. Imported furnishings were brought by mule teams from Rock Creek, the nearest railroad station, on the UP railroad more than 200 miles away. This spacious home, built like an English castle, was the scene of many gay parties, with lords and ladies attending, including Sir

Randolph and Lady Churchill, parents of Winston Churchill who later became the British prime minister. The castle was torn down in the 1900s.

The Powder River Cattle Company controlled more than 100,000 acres with 70,000 cattle and employed 75 cowboys.

Friend Creek and Park, Albany: named about 1888 for D. L. Friend, rancher.

Frontier, Lincoln: town near Kemmerer: one of the oldest coal mining camps; named in 1897 by P. J. Quearly for its location on the frontier. An explosion here in 1919 killed 98 men.

Frontier Creek, Fremont: named for the primitive area through which it flows. Up this creek in the Restratified Wilderness Area is one of the largest standing petrified forests in Wyoming. About 40 million years ago pines and cedars covered the area; they were buried under hundreds of feet of volcanic debris and petrified; today the remains of some of these giants still stand—one is 15 feet in diameter.

Frontier Days, Laramie: see Cheyenne Frontier Days.

Frost Cave, Park: see Spirit Mountain caverns.

Frost Lake, YNP: named for Ned Frost, naturalist and explorer.

Fry, Natrona: railroad siding named for Fry, father of Mrs. Howard Geary. Many years ago the Natrona County Pioneer Association held its annual picnic at the Geary ranch; the members made the trip of about 10 miles in a special train that stopped at the ranch.

Frye Lake, Fremont: named for Jacob Frye, who has a sawmill here; on the scenic loop drive to South Pass City.

Frying Pan Thermal Spring, YNP: a small spring that stews continuously like a frying pan on a hot stove.

Fryxell Mountain, 11,266, Teton: at the head of Paintbrush Canyon; named for Fritiof Fryxell, a climber who has made many first major climbs in Teton Range; he was once a park ranger and author. He made the first ascent of this peak in 1929.

Fun Valley, Sheridan: ski area below Granite Pass.

G

Gallatin Lake and River, YNP: the river was named by Lewis and Clark for Albert Gallatin, Secretary of the Treasury under President Thomas Jefferson.

Gallatin Range, YNP: named for the Gallatin River; the range is volcanic breccia and granite.

Gallio, Laramie: discontinued post office named for Gallio C. Connolly, early-day minister.

Gangplank, Laramie: here the granite rocks to the west are Precambrian, more than a billion years old. The sedimentary rocks to the east are only 10 million years old and have been deposited against the granite. A person can stand here with this dramatic difference in the age of the ground between his two feet.

Gannett Peak, 13,785, Fremont, Sublette: gilded with glaciers, this highest point in Wyoming was named in 1906 for Henry Gannett, a great geographer and a member of Hayden surveys and USGS from 1882-1914. He wrote a newspaper account of the first climbing of the peak: "View from here sublime; can see the whole Teton Range to the west. The Grand First View."

Gap Lakes, Albany: located in a gap of the Snowy Range, hence the name.

Garden of the Gods, Weston: so named for the eroded formations which appear like fantastic figures of gods.

Gardiner Canyon and River, YNP: named for Johnson Gardiner, trapper for the American Fur Company in 1832.

Gardiner Mountain, Johnson: named for Tom Gardiner, pioneer settler.

Garfield Peak, Natrona: undergoing survey by government men on the day President James Garfield was shot, July 2, 1881; it is the highest peak in the Rattlesnake Mountains.

Gargoyle Pinnacle, Johnson: so named because it is a small needle, crowned by a fantastic rock which leans into space like one of the monsters on Notre Dame Cathedral, Paris, France; named by the Wilcox party; excellent climbing.

Garland, Park: named in 1901 for John Garland, forest ranger.

Garland Gulch, Sheridan: named for John Garland.

Garland Oil Field, Big Horn: named for John Garland.

Garnet Canyon, Teton: named for the garnets found at the head of the canyon.

Garnicks Needles, 12,600, Sublette: named for Notsie and Frank Garnick, early climbers and explorers.

Garrett, Albany: established in 1903 with Mary A. Garrett, first postmaster; Mary A. Garrett was the first woman in the world to be elected Justice of the Peace in 1902. She served in that office for more than twenty years.

Gas Hills, Fremont: in 1953 Neil and Maxine NcNeice checked the land here on a knoll now called Discovery Hill with a Geiger counter; its wild clicking told them they had made a find in uranium; probably one-third of the nation's reserves, or an estimated 13 million tons, lie in this bleak, desolate country.

Now huge earth movers scrape up 30 tons of uranium-rich soil in one pass, mills crush the rocks, and sulphuric acid leeches out uranium salts which are pressed into yellow cake. Uranium eroded out of the surrounding mountains, as they wore down during the centuries, and was attracted by carbonaceous matter into seeps and boggy sumps. There are three uranium mills at Gas Hills, one at Jeffrey city, and one at Riverton which process the uranium.

Gatchell Museum, Johnson: this museum in Buffalo was named for Jim Gatchell, cowboy and friend of Indians; he collected Indian relics, frontier firearms, and pioneer souvenirs.

Gebo, Hot Springs: discontinued post office; railroad station in bituminous coal district; named in 1908 for Samuel W. Gebo, developer of the coal mines in the 1890s.

Gebo Oil Field, Hot Springs: named for Samuel W. Gebo.

Geddes Lake, Johnson: named for Judge Geddes of Toledo, Ohio, who owned a summer cabin at Dome Lake. Barbara Bel Geddes, movie star, is his granddaughter.

Geers Point, 11,207, Park: named for William C. Geers, a guest at Sunlight ranch and head of the metallographic department at Cornell University.

Geezer Geyser, YNP: joke name; irregular performance.

Geikie Mountain, 12,378, Sublette: named in 1877 for Sir Archibald Geikie, a noted Scottish geologist; first ascended in 1890 by William O Owen.

Gem City, Albany: see Laramie.

Geographical center of Wyoming is fifty-eight miles northeast of Lander.

Germania, Big Horn: see Emblem.

Ghost Creek, Converse: a rancher was hauling home a new mowing machine on a wagon. He forded a creek and looked back to see if all was O.K. On the seat of the wagon he saw the ghost of his sheepherder friend, Vedeer, who had been murdered by another sheepherder. So it became Ghost Creek.

Ghost Creek, Park: named for an old ghost story.

Giant Geyser, YNP: named by the Washburn party in 1870; sends steaming water 250 feet into the air.

Gibbon Canyon, Falls, Hills, Meadow, River, YNP: named by Hayden in 1872 for Gen. John Gibbon who first explored the river.

Gibbon Geyser Basin, YNP: named for Gen. John Gibbon.

Gift of the Waters, Hot Springs: pageant written by Marie Horton and performed annually by the Shoshone Indians at Thermopolis. In ritualistic ceremonies Chief Washakie presents white men with the magic waters of Hot Springs.

In 1896 Chief Washakie by treaty ceded to the United States a tract of land ten miles square from the Wind River Reservation which included Hot Springs, the largest mineral springs in the world, flowing 18,600,000 gallons of water at 135 degrees Fahrenheit every 24 hours. The treaty requested that a portion of this healing water be reserved for free public use forever.

Hot Springs were called by Shoshones Bah-guewana, smoking water. The United States government gave the land to Wyoming; Hot Springs State Park was created.

Gilbert Creek, Park: named for Gilbert, an early settler.

Gilkey Tower, Teton: named for Art Gilkey, climber, who lost his life climbing in 1953.

Gillespie, Albany: discontinued post office named for Samuel Gillespie, who came here in 1878.

Gillette, county seat, Campbell: named for Weston E. Gillette, surveyor and civil engineer who directed the building of the railroad here. Gillette was once called Donkey Town after Donkey Creek, on which it was first located. After being moved to its present location, it was Rocky Pile for the rocky draw; when the Burlington railroad arrived in 1891, the town was renamed Gillette.

The first airplane flight over Wyoming took place at Gillette on July 4, 1911. Daredevil George Thompson was paid $3,500 to make the flight in a plane that was shipped to Gillette in a boxcar, and assembled there.

Charles A. Lindbergh landed a plane on the flats east of Gillette about 1916, and rode in on a pony borrowed from a boy.

A state-operated experiment farm is east of Gillette, testing the best types of trees, grain, and livestock feed to grow in the region. Gillette lies in a rich oil and coal district which has made it a boom town with greatly expanded population.

Gillis Creek, Crook: named by Captain W. S. Stanton in 1877 for Captain James Gillis who led an expedition for observation in the Black Hills.

Gilmer, Uinta: see Bear River City.

Girl Scout National Center West, Washakie: six miles from Tensleep, on Canyon Creek. Girls from all over the world gather here yearly for wilderness experience and knowledge.

Glacier Creek, Teton: named by Supt. Woodring because of its milky color, characteristic of streams originating from ice fields.

Glacier Lake, Albany: named because of a large snowbank on an adjacent mountain.

Glacier Primitive Area, Fremont: 177,000 acres on the Wind River Reservation.

Glazon, Lincoln: railroad station for the Glazon coal mining camp.

Gleason, Laramie: village named for the Gleason family in 1911.

Glencoe, Lincoln: coal mining camp established in 1902; named by Thomas Sneddon, Supt. of Diamond Coal Company, for Glencoe, Scotland.

Glencoe Spire, 12,200, Teton: named by J. Lewis and H. Smith, climbers, for their home town, Glencoe, Scotland.

Glendevey, Albany: discontinued post office; was on the ranch of Captain Thomas E. Davy who liked the country so much he named his ranch Glendevey; was a ranger station.

Glendo, Platte: named by a young engineer for the pretty glen it nestled in when the railroad reached here in 1887; the Mormons had developed one of the first irrigation systems in the state here in the early times. This is the former site of the Horseshoe stage station. The post office was moved here from Bellewood.

Glendo Reservoir, Platte: named for the town; completed in 1958 with 12,500 acre-feet surface, and a 78-mile shore line; built for storage of water released by other dams for power. It also has generators; a recreation area.

Glendo State Park, Platte: the large surface of the Glendo Reservoir allows water skiing, boating, and fishing; camping and rock hunting.

Glenrock, Converse: first known as Mercedes, then Nuttell (or Nuttall) for William Nuttell, discoverer and developer of coal deposits; also as Deer Creek stage station, which see. Officially named Glenrock for the "Rock in the Glen," now by the railroad station; a favorite campground of emigrants from 1843-87; the Mormons built a way station here in 1850; now it is near the Big Muddy oil field.

A "buffalo jump" (place where Indians drove buffalo herds over a high cliff for slaughter) was discovered west of Glenrock and excavated from 1968-69. Many artifacts and bones revealing the history of 1,000 years uncovered.

Glenys, Laramie: discontinued post office; named for Glenys, daughter of Mrs. W. J. Hixenbaugh, early rancher.

Glory Mountain, 10,000, Teton: named by Orestes St. John of the Hayden survey; a topographic station; liking the mountain, they named it Glory.

Glover Peak, 11,000, Sublette: named for George M. Glover, forest ranger and game warden at Pinedale in 1904. On a clear day the Tetons are visible from the top of the peak.

Goat Flat, Fremont: an amazing sight, with many square miles of weathered stone lying flat as a pool table at 12,000 feet, with glaciers and Gannett Peak rising behind. The wind sometimes blows so hard it is almost impossible to stand.

Goff Creek, Park: named for John Goff, an early hunter.

Gold Creek, Big Horn: log cabins stood here in the gold strike of 1898.

Gold Hill, Albany: railroad station and mining town where prospectors found gold; promoted by the Union Mining Company in the 1890s.

Gold Run Creek, Albany: a gold placer mine was here in the 1870s. Particles of gold ore silted down the creek, causing it to "run gold."

Golden Gate, YNP: south of Mammoth Hot Springs; the road lies at an altitude of 7,256 feet; this is a portal into Yellowstone National Park through rocky walls that gleam golden in sunlight, due to the growth of lichen on the rocks; it could also be called Golden Gate because the government spent considerable money here for road construction. A concrete viaduct at the lower end of the canyon has support arches fitted into the cliff; it is the only one of this type in the world.

Golden Lake, Johnson: named for the golden trout planted here.

Goldie, Crook: discontinued post office; named for Goldie, daughter of Edward W. Jolley, first postmaster.

Goldie Divide, Crook: named for Goldie Jolley.

Goldsmith, Laramie: discontinued post office established in 1866 on the ranch of Peter Goldsmith; moved to the McCarty ranch in 1897.

Gomm Creek, Lincoln: named for the Gomm family who lived here.

Goodland, Goshen: railroad station that describes the country.

Goodwin Peak, Lincoln: named for Goodwin, an early settler.

Goose Creek, Johnson: lots of geese were here in the early days. To the Indians it was the Tongue River; their sign for it was touching the tongue, and motioning with the hand as if going away.

82

Goose Creeks, Big and Little, Sheridan: a large number of geese rest here in migratory flights.

Goose Egg, Natrona: discontinued post office named for the ranch.

Goose Egg Ranch, Natrona: the Searight brothers trailed in 27,000 head of cattle from Texas, and established a ranch on Poison Spider Creek in 1877. Cowboys found a nest of wild goose eggs, and brought them to the cook; this gave the owners an idea for a brand and a ranch name. Fearing an attack by Indians, the cowboys quarried stone on Casper Mountain and built a two-story stone house.

Here cowboys exchanged babies at a Saturday night dance, according to Owen Wister in *The Virginian*. The Searights sold their cattle, more than 20,000 head, to the Carey brothers before the big "die-out" winter of 1886. So they had the goose that laid the golden egg—they sold just in time.

The old stone house became unsafe for the many curious sightseers, and was torn down in the 1960s—a famous landmark lost.

Gose Butte, Weston: named for Gose family, early settlers.

Goshen, Goshen: discontinued post office named for the county.

Goshen County, Torrington, county seat; created in 1911, organized in 1913; named for Goshen Hole; a rich, irrigated farming country; livestock raising; oil wells.

Goshen Hole, Goshen: there are four versions of the name for this rich valley; Goshe, an Assiniboine Indian trapper, had a cabin on Cherry Creek in the early days, and was found dead there, probably killed by Arapahoes; was called Goshe's Hole in 1846, before it appeared on the map in 1888 as Goshen Hole.

Another version: a French-Canadian trapper started a trading post here. His prices were so exorbitant that traders called him "cochon," which is French for hog; the land surrounding his post was called "Cochon." When the Americans came, they pronounced the word "Goshen," thinking it originated in the Bible, meaning "land of plenty."

A third version is that Gouche, a French trader, was a crafty and deceitful man; Indians called him "co-han," because that was his favorite expression, meaning "Hurry up!"

The fourth version: when the county was formed in 1911, it was named for Goshen Hale, a cowboy who worked for the Union Cattle Company, an English outfit with huge headquarters on Bear Creek.

Gosling Creek, Sheridan: since there were Big and Little Goose creeks, cowboys thought there should be a Gosling Creek.

Gottfried Lake, Sublette: named for an old mountaineer and trapper, Gottfried Rahm; he laid out and supervised the construction of trails on the upper Green River. Gottfried means "peace of God."

Gottsche Rehabilitation Center, Hot Springs: an institution at Thermopolis for the cure of crippling and deforming diseases by using warm water from the springs for baths; named for William and Carrie Gottshe, and endowed by them; their daughter's life was claimed by poliomyelitis.

This is a non-profit institution for people of all ages, races, and creeds.

Government Farm Stage Station, Goshen: log buildings sheltered by a rocky ledge. Vegetables were cultivated here by Fort Laramie soldiers. The place was said to be inhabited by the ghost of Updike, an early sheepherder who froze his feet and died here.

Governor's Mansion, Laramie: built of red brick in the Georgian colonial style for $37,000. First occupied by Gov. and Mrs. Bryant B. Brooks from 1905-11. It was remodeled in 1937 and last occupied by Gov. and Mrs. Stan Hathaway. A new governor's mansion was built in 1973-74. The old mansion is now a museum and is kept as it was.

Gowdy Park, between Cheyenne and Laramie: named for Curt Gowdy, sports broadcaster by Gov. Stan Hathaway.

Grace Lake, Goshen: named for Grace Emery.

Graham, Uinta: discontinued post office named for Kate E. Graham, first postmaster.

Gramm, Albany: discontinued post office; railroad station named by railroad officials for Otto Gramm, pioneer and president of the Foxpark Timber Company that furnished ties for the railroad.

Grand Canyon of the Platte, Natrona: see Fiery Narrows.

Grand Canyon of the Yellowstone, YNP: a picturesque gorge cut by the Yellowstone River; the colorful part is about three miles long, with an average depth of 750 feet, and an average width of 1,500 feet from rim to rim; the colors, due to traces of iron and other metallic oxides, vary through all the shades of red and yellow, with yellow predominating.

The canyon was first painted by Thomas Moran of Hayden expedition; the newspapers of 1872 called the members of this expedition "bug hunters."

Grand Encampment, Carbon: see Encampment.

Grand Geyser, YNP: erupts to a height of 200 feet; named by the Hayden party in 1871.

Grand Loop Road, YNP: named by Harry Franz in 1923; he said: "This is the path of pilgrims seeking God of the open air . . . footprints, hoof marks, and tire prints of countless travelers are required to make a great road which must lead to some mecca."

Grand Prismatic Thermal Spring, YNP: in the lower Geyser Basin; noted for its prismatic coloring.

Grand Teton, 13,766, Teton: see Teton Range for the name; known as Mount Hayden by the Doane expedition of 1870; second highest mountain in Wyoming—only 19 feet lower than Gannett Peak; the first notable ascent of Grand Teton was made by N. P. Langford, Supt. of Yellowstone National Park, and James Stevenson of the Hayden survey in 1872. In 1898 the William Owen and Bishop Spalding party reached the summit, and claimed that Langford never had reached it. In 1929 the Wyoming legislature ruled in favor of Owen; a plaque proclaiming Owen's party as the first climbers of the peak was placed on the summit.

Later Owen's own papers revealed that Capt. Charles H. Kieffer and two soldiers reached the top in 1893, and described the route taken by Owen, who never revealed this.

Paul Petzoldt was so thrilled by his climb of Grand Teton that he started the Petzoldt-Exum school of mountaineering in 1923. More than 2,000 people, veterans and novices alike, have now scaled Grand Teton, and registered their names on its summit.

84

Petzoldt and a party of climbers try to scale Grand Teton every New Year's Day. They made their ninth attempt in 1974. Three attempts were successful out of the first eight tries. Why do people struggle so hard to climb a mountain? "Because it's there," said Sir Edmund Hillary, the first man to conquer Mount Everest. Of the 1974 Grand Teton try: 7 reached the top; the first woman on New Year's: Mrs. Helen Highby.

Grand Teton National Park, Teton: named for the Teton Range. John D. Rockefeller, wife and three sons visited Yellowstone National Park and Jackson Hole in 1926. They were profoundly impressed with the view of the Tetons; Rockefeller was greatly disturbed by a telephone line being strung between the road and the Tetons; he foresaw that commercial refreshment stands, motels, etc. along the road would destroy the grandeur of the mountains.

Rockefeller organized the Snake River Land Company in 1927, and bought 35,310 acres of land for $1,400,310. The government then withdrew public lands in the area from further settlement. In 1929 the Grand Teton National Park was created by Congress, but it included only the Tetons and a fringe of lakes. Ranchers fought to hold their private lands, and political storms raged in Teton County.

In 1943 President Franklin D. Roosevelt set aside 221,000 acres east of the Tetons as the Jackson Hole National Monument; establishment of a national park required action by Congress. In 1949 Rockefeller deeded his land to the federal government; in 1950 Congress established the present-day Grand Teton National Park, including the monument, which was abolished.

Laurance Rockefeller, son of John, is continuing to preserve this natural beauty, and develop it for maximum tourist enjoyment. He has built Jackson Lake Lodge, a deluxe resort with lounge windows framing the Tetons. It is run as a non-profit organization. Numerous log cabins have been built by the lodge, and in several places around the lakes, bordering the Tetons; thus there will be more rooms at low prices for all to enjoy the exotic beauty, saved by Rockefeller foresight, initiative, and money, for posterity.

This is the only national park where annual big game hunting is sometimes allowed. The elk herd, largest in the world, must be kept within the limit of the food supply.

Grand Teton National Park had 2,673,000 visitors in 1966—more than Yellowstone National Park which had 2,130,312 during the same year.

Grange, Sweetwater: first this was a stage stop garrisoned by Col. Connor to protect passengers from Indians; it was named for Gen. Gordon Granger; it was also a Pony Express station. In 1868 it became a UP railroad camp; in the 1880s it was an important railroad junction with the Oregon Short Line—three boxcars on a siding provided the depot and waiting rooms.

Ties were floated down Ham's Fork to Granger. It was on the main travel route west, from the days of Elijah White's wagon train in 1842, until U.S. Highway 30 was moved farther south, and Little America became Granger's rival; now it is left, quiet, on the sagebrush prairies.

Granier Ditch and Meadows, Fremont: named for Emile Granier, engineer who organized the Rock Creek Ditch Company about 1884.

Granite Canyon, Laramie: a railroad station and post office named for ridges of granite. Here Mary O'Hara came for her mail while living on a nearby ranch. This country is the setting for her books *Wyoming Summer, My Friend Flicka, Thunderhead*, and *Green Grass of Wyoming*.

Granite Mountains, Fremont: also known as Sweetwater Rocks or Knobs; near sage-covered flats where Sweetwater agates, prairie jewels, are found.

Grant, Platte: discontinued post office named for Grant, postmaster.

Grass Creek, Hot Springs: village named for Grass Creek.

Grass Creek Oil Field, Hot Springs: when first developed in 1917, pipe and equipment were hauled in with 20- and 24-horse teams.

Grassy Lake, Teton: covers more than 300 acres; name obvious.

Grattan Massacre, site of, Goshen: in 1854 a Mormon emigrant lost a lame cow which the Indians killed. When Mormons reported it at Fort Laramie, Lt. L. Grattan and 29 men went to the Indian camp, demanding the surrender of the Indian who killed the cow.

The Brule chief refused to give up the Miniconjou Sioux, his guest, but offered to bring him to the fort, saying, "If you shoot, you will all be killed." Grattan ordered his men to fire and they were all killed; also Brave Bear, the Brule chief. Some blame a drunken white interpreter for the incident. When Indians won, it was recorded in history as a massacre; when white men won, it was called a victory.

Grave Lake, Fremont: Bill Hobbs, while prospecting in 1905, found a grave by this lake; suspecting foul play, surveyors and prospectors dug up the grave, and found a dead dog that some sheepherder had buried.

Gravel Mountain, 9,645, Teton: piles of gravel and boulders at the base of the mountain give it its name.

Graves Creek, Sheridan: for Henry S. Graves, chief of Forest Service, 1910-19.

Gravy Springs, Weston: springs flow through a thick, white clay, making the water like gravy.

Gray Reef Reservoir, Natrona: completed in 1961; stabilizes the flow of water in the Platte River from fluctuation releases from Alcova Power Plant; steady water flow is necessary for the maintenance of fish. The reservoir, built for irrigation and recreation, has 181 acre-feet of surface.

Grayling Creek, YNP: named in 1885 by USGS for this edible fish.

Grayrocks, Platte: William Atchison and his wife built a two-sory house of rocks here in the early 1900s; they called the post office and store that grew up here Grayrocks. All are gone now. The name was given to a reservoir on the Laramie River.

Great Arrow, Park: on a hogback east of Meeteetse is the Great Arrow, 58 feet long, and about 5½ feet wide; it points toward Medicine Wheel on top of the Big Horn Mountains. Made of piled stones, it is believed to have been made by the prehistoric people who made Medicine Wheel.

Great Falls of Yellowstone River, YNP: have a dramatic drop of

86

308 feet; the roar of the water can be heard a mile; also known as Lower Falls.

Great Medicine Road, the Indian name for the Oregon Trail; when they saw so many people passing through, they thought a great void must exist in the land of the rising sun; 1840 marked the transition from the fur trapping and trading era to the migration period.

Great Tar Springs, Fremont: Capt. Bonneville in 1832 found an oil seep in the bluffs east of where Lander is now. This thick fluid had the color and consistency of tar, and was used to grease wagon wheels; its medicinal quality also helped heal sores on horses. Mike Murphy drilled three oil wells here in 1884; one was known as Murphy No. 3. It was just off U.S. Highway 287.

Green Lakes, Sublette: a dazzling green in contrast to surrounding grey rocks.

Green Mountains, 7,000-9,025, Fremont: named for heavy growth of evergreens. They funnelled early travel westward through South Pass. Now they furnish good hunting for uranium prospectors and jade seekers. Unusual petrified wood is also found here.

Green River, Sublette, Lincoln, Sweetwater: called Seeds-ke-dee (Crow Indian for sage hen) by Indians and some early trappers. Other trappers called it Rio Verde, also Spanish River. Gen. William Ashley in 1823 named it Green River because of its color. In places it has green soapstone banks which water wears away, and which impregnate the water with a bright green color.

Another version says that Gen. Ashley named it for Green, his associate in the fur trading business. The Green River flows into the Colorado River, and helps cut the Grand Canyon of the Colorado.

Green River, Sweetwater: town named for Green River; settled in 1868; was an Overland stage station 1861-68; also a Pony Express station. With the buildup of the UP Railroad more than 300,000 ties were floated down the Green River to here.

Castle Rock, a picturesque sandstone cliff, guards the town, which is county seat of Sweetwater County. William Hutton's private museum is here with pioneer relics and Indian artifacts; open on appointment.

Green River Ordinance: started in Green River to protect the sleep of its railroad men from daytime disturbances by salesmen; the law passed in 1931 prohibiting door-to-door selling. The ordinance is now used by more than 3,000 towns and cities.

Green River Rendezvous, Sublette: as early as 1825 trappers, traders, and Indians met in the Green River valley for an annual get-together, trading session, and celebration. Fur companies packed in supplies and whiskey to trade for the winter's take of pelts. Rendezvous is French for "get-together."

Missionaries came to pray. Mountain men and Indians both thrilled at the presence of two white women, wives of Dr. Whitman and Rev. Spalding in 1836. The last rendezvous was held here in 1840, with corn meal $1 a pint; coffee beans, cocoa beans and sugar $2 a pint; diluted alcohol $4 a pint; chewing tobacco, which also smoked, $2 a twist.

Sublette County Historical Society now presents a colorful pageant of a rendezvous each year on the second Sunday in July where the early ones took place, at the junction of today's U.S. Highways 187 and 189. Costumes used are authentic.

Gregory Lake, Albany: also called Towner Lake; named for Gregory who worked gold mine in the Snowy Range in the 1880s.

Grenville, Carbon: a railroad station named for Gen. Grenville Dodge, surveyor for UP railroad; later named Parco.

Grenville Dome, Carbon: named for Grenville.

Greub, Johnson: discontinued post office that was on ranch of J. E. Greub.

Greybull, Big Horn: named for the river; hub of the Bighorn Basin; founded in 1909 in a farming district; the first gas well was brought in by Phil Minor, prospector, in 1908; many oil wells were drilled in Grass Creek Field in 1915. Two refineries were built in Greybull.

The town was flooded by an ice jam on the Bighorn River in 1923, and was flooded again in 1929; it is located in cattle country; it is near bentonite deposits as well as near fossils of dinosaur bones, ammonites, and cycads, which make for good rock hunting. A complete skeleton of Eohippus (dawn horse) was found near here by Iowa geologists.

Greybull River, Big Horn and Park: named by Indians for an albino buffalo bull who once roamed here, and was held sacred by them. Indian pictographs on a cliff overhanging the river show a buffalo bull with an arrow through his body.

Greyrocks, Platte: discontinued post office named for rocks.

Greys River, Lincoln: first called John Day's River for a member of Astorian party. Lt. Doane's group, stranded in region in winter of 1877, lunched on rose seed hips along river; renamed for John Gray or Grey, trapper, who stabbed Milton Sublette for an indignity to Grey's daughter.

Griffy Hill, Fremont: named for Griffy who owned land around the Riverton airport; he lived in a bleak log cabin, and raised goats that ranged the hills, and could often be seen from U.S. Highway 26.

Grigg, Johnson: discontinued post office for Alfred Grigg, the first postmaster who also sold chewing and smoking tobacco; he made the post office a gathering and information place; one of Tom Horn's hangouts.

Grizzly Buttes, Uinta: extensive chain of fossil-bearing buttes; the name was given by F. V. Hayden on hearing story of Jack Robertson that told of finding a petrified grizzly bear here.

Gros Ventre Canyon and River, Teton: pronounced Gro-vont in French; rhymes with want; named for Gros Ventre Mountains. Has trail for hiking and bird watching.

Gros Ventre Mountains, Teton: faulted at same time as the Tetons and eroded down; steep, timbered slopes with good grazing and protection for elk, deer, bear, and mountain sheep; scenic wilderness.

The mountains were named for the Indian tribe of Arapahoes, or Gros Ventres, French for "big bellies"; originated from their sign of passing both hands in front of their stomachs, saying they were always hungry.

Gros Ventre Slide, Teton: side of mountain, loosened by rain, slid down in 1925, forming Slide Lake, which see.

88

Grotto Geyser, YNP: named by Washburn party of 1870 for weird formation of enclosing rock.

Grover, Lincoln: named for Jacob Grove, Mormon pioneer; settled in 1891.

Grovont, Teton: discontinued post office; the name is a phonetic rendering of Gros Ventre.

Guernsey, Platte: incorporated in 1902; named for Charles A. Guernsey, rancher, mine promoter, and author of *Wyoming Cowboy Days*; his favorite quotation: "A dreamer lives forever; a toiler but a day."

Guernsey is on Oregon Trail. In Guernsey Hotel is Lester Robinson collection of geological specimens, Indian artifacts and beadwork, and pioneer relics. National Guard camp is held here every year.

Guernsey Reservoir, Platte: named for Charles A. Guernsey, whose dreams and determination brought it into being. He started working for the government as a private individual to build a power dam.

He kidnapped a group of U.S. Senators bound for Denver in 1909 by having the train detoured to Hartville, where he showed them the iron mines, and proposed the dam site. He won their approval of the project; the dam was started in 1925, and finished in 1927, impounding 2,382 acre-feet of water. After 40 years, Guernsey had finally crystallized his dream into a reality of stone and mortar for regional power, irrigation, and recreation; it is now a state park.

Guffy Peak, Hot Springs: named for John Guffy, rancher.

Guffy's Peak, Carbon: known as Bridger's Peak until John Guffy located a ranch here.

Gunbarrel Creek, Park: an old, rusty gunbarrel of very early make was found here. Mildred Albert Martin wrote a story of the region in *The Martins of Gunbarrel*. Another version: the creek flows through a canyon, straight and narrow as a gunbarrel.

Gunn, Sweetwater: the village started in 1908 and was named for George E. Gunn, first president of Gunn-Quealy Coal Company.

Gunst Reservoir, Carbon: built by Louis Gunst on Antelope Creek.

H

H. E. Ranch, Hot Springs: owner, Tom McCoy, actor, was a friend of the Indians who named him "High Eagle" or Nee Hee Chaoot.

Hadsell, Carbon: railroad station named for Frank A. Hadsell; he started a horse ranch in 1880 at Elk Mountain; served as sheriff, cooperating with UP railroad officials in trying to stop train robberies by outlaws. These officials changed the station name from Salon to Hadsell in appreciation of his efforts. Hadsell was also warden of the penitentiary at Rawlins, and U.S marshall.

Haggarty Creek and Gulch, Carbon: named for Edward Haggarty, the prospector who found outcroppings of copper ore near Bridger Peak, and helped develop the Ferris-Haggarty Mine and Rudefeha.

Hagie, Goshen: discontinued post office named for C. E. Hagie, pioneer.

Hague Mountain, YNP: named for Dr. Arnold Hague, USGS, an authority on thermal activity.

Hahn's Peak Railroad, Albany: also known as the Colorado, Wyoming and Eastern railroad; runs from Laramie through Centennial Valley and Medicine Bow National Forest; named for Colorado's Hahn's Peak.

Hailey, Fremont: discontinued post office for Ora Hailey; a stage and freighting stop on the old trail to Rawlins.

Hailey Pass, 11,165, Fremont, Sublette: named for Ora Hailey who is reputed to have first used the pass for crossing with sheep when fleeing from cattlemen who objected to his sheep in Sublette County in 1903. Hailey was a senator in the first Wyoming state legislature.

Halfmoon Lake and Mountain, Sublette: the shape of the mountain suggests the name; formed by an immense glacial moraine.

Halfway, Sublette: discontinued post office that was half way from Big Piney to Merna.

Haliburton Hill, Johnson: a Haliburton truck went off the road here, upset and went into the ditch.

Hall Creek, Fremont: named for Robert Hall, blacksmith and wagon maker.

Halleck Ridge, Carbon: named for Fort Halleck.

Hallelujah Peak, 12,600, Johnson: named by W. B. and A. W. Willcox for their expression of awe at the sight of it. The peak cleaves the sky like a knife blade; it is narrow with almost vertical sides; a challenge to climbers.

Halls Creek, Lake, and Mountain, 12,470, Sublette: named for Harry Hall who arrived with a team in the Pinedale area in 1900. A sawmill in Hall's Basin supplied logs and lumber to build many early homes.

Hallville, Sweetwater: a railroad station named for Milton Hall who started a coal mine near here when the railroad came in 1868.

Hamilton, Johnson: named for Milo Hamilton, rancher.

Hamilton, Laramie: discontinued post office named for William F. Hamilton.

Hamilton, Sheridan: discontinued post office named for Hamilton Ranch on which it was located.

Hamilton City, Fremont: see Miner's Delight.

Hamilton Dome, Hot Springs: post office named for Dr. Hamilton.

Hamilton Dome Oil Field, Hot Springs: named for Dr. Hamilton.

Hammond, Converse: discontinued post office named for Sarah Hammond.

Hampton, Uinta: railroad station named for Hampton, early rancher.

Hams Fork, Lincoln: name dates from 1824, the time of Ashley; named for the creek; one of the oldest settlements in the region; was a Pony

Express station and home stage station on overland route. A garden was grown so there would be fresh vegetables in the summer; the village was known as North Kemmerer.

Hams Fork Creek, Lincoln: probably named for one of Ashley's trappers.

Hancock Mountain, 10,214, YNP: once sucked a handkerchief down its throat, and returned it laundered by boiling water; became clogged with tourist-tossed trash.

Hanging Canyon, Teton: a photogenic valley; heavily timbered sides give a canyon appearance of hanging.

Hanging Woman Creek, Sheridan: so named because a Cheyenne Indian girl was found hanging on a tree near the creek, sometime prior to 1879. She was a sister of Bob-tail Horse and Hollow Wood.

Hanna, Carbon: once a stage station and coal mining town named for Mark A. Hanna in 1886. Mark Hanna was a financier and a politician who was on the board of directors of the UP Railroad.

A mine explosion in 1903 killed 169 men; another explosion in 1908 killed 59 men; the mine was closed.

Now a revived ghost town with black blood pumping through its veins. The demand for coal was so great that 3,000 tons were shipped out daily in 1973; there is a large housing development for workmen; this is also true of nearby Elmo.

Hanna Creek, Sheridan: for Oliver P. Hanna; scout and buffalo hunter in 1870s who built a cabin and 20-horse stable on this creek. He was the first permanent settler in Sheridan County; supplied Fort McKinney with fresh game meat; this place is said to have been used by the James gang.

Hans Creek, Albany: named about 1900 for a tie hack whose first name was Hans.

Happy Jack Creek and Sports Area, Albany: for "Happy Jack" Hollingsworth, who took up a ranch in the foothills of Laramie Range in 1884. He was always singing and whistling at his work hauling wood from the mountains to sell in Cheyenne. This route through Cheyenne Pass was much used in the early days. A skiing area down Sherman Hill developed in 1935 by the Forest Service; one of the first areas in Wyoming.

Hardee Cabin, Park: mining settlement named for Hardee, miner.

Harding Geyser, YNP: first erupted in 1923, the year President Warren G. Harding visited the park; doesn't erupt very often.

Harding Ranch, Niobrara: stage stop on Cheyenne-Deadwood trail; a dugout fort in a clay bank; it had a log roof and portholes; a dugout stable for horses; station owner Harding served meals; also known as Indian Creek stage stop.

Captain Egan and his "Grays" camped here in 1876 to protect stages from Indians and road agents.

Hard Luck Mountains, 11,788, Park: very rough country.

Hargraves, Goshen: discontinued post office for William Hargraves. See Jay Em.

Harmony Church, Albany: this church was built on the plains between Sheep Mountain and Laramie in 1907, in an effort to establish harmonious relations between several church denominations.

Harney, Albany: railroad station named for Harney Creek.

Harney Creek, Albany: named by army officials at Fort Sanders for Gen. William S. Harney, Indian fighter.

Harper, Albany: section house on the railroad named in 1868 for George Harper, stockman; mayor of Laramie in 1895.

Harriman, Laramie: UP station for Edward H. Harriman, who reorganized the railroad in 1898 and had the poor track rebuilt.

Harris Park, Albany: a mountain park named about 1900 for Harris who homesteaded here.

Harrison Creek, Carbon: named for Harrison Cut.

Harrison Cut, Carbon: named by railroad officials for a contractor who made the cut for the railroad.

Harrower Glacier and Peak, Sublette: named for James King Harrower, forest ranger, game warden, historian.

Hart Mountain, Park: named for early homesteader on mountain.

Hartman, Big Horn: discontinued post office named for the Hartman family who lived on Crooked Creek.

Hartville, Platte: named for Major Virling K. Hart who once owned a copper mine here; this rich copper deposit occurred as a replacement in the Guernsey limestone formation.

One of the largest pure iron deposits in the nation is located here, first used by Indians as ceremonial and war paint. Colorado Fuel and Iron Company operates the mine and ships ore to a steel mill in Pueblo, Colorado. Mining has been continuous since 1887; first open pit mining that dug "Glory Hole," or Chicago Mine, 650 feet deep, or deep enough to hide the Washington Monument, 550 feet; also deeper than the height of the United Nations building; one of the largest open pit mines in the world. In 1941 underground mining started. Production reached a million tons in 1942, but has since declined.

Italian and Greek miners thronged to Hartville when the mine opened; they made Hartville a cultural center, with a Dante Alighieri Society; operas were sung, and Italian food enjoyed.

Hartville Uplift, Platte: a geological formation that takes its name from the town.

Harvard, Washakie: discontinued post office named for William Harvard, pioneer.

Harvey Trail Draw, Albany: named for James Harvey who traveled the draw to his homestead in 1910.

Hat Creek, Carbon: ditch constructed in 1883 to irrigate the Swan hay meadows; named for Hat brand of William F. Swan.

Hat Creek, Niobrara: for name see Fort Hat Creek; one of the main stations on the Cheyenne-Deadwood stage line. In 1877 Jack Bowman advertised he would "furnish accommodations to the traveling public at reasonable rates"; blacksmith shop, brewery, bakery, hotel; post office and later telegraph station. Buffalo were killed here as late as 1878.

John Storrie and Tom Swan erected a two-story store in the 1880s that was popular with cowboys and as a stage stop.

The route to the north of Hat Creek station was the most dangerous section due to Indians and road agent robbers; the route divided here, one way going by Indian Creek, another directly north to the Cheyenne River. The main building then, a large log structure, is still in use as a ranch home. A post office was established in 1877 according to postal records.

Hat Creek Oil Field, Carbon: named for Hat Creek.

Hatchet Lake, Fremont: named for its shape.

Hattie Lake, Albany: named by surveyor M. N. Grant for Hattie Andrews, Mrs. Charles Phillips, wife of a railroad conductor; Lake artificially enlarged in 1911.

Hauf, Platte: named for C. Hauf and sons, ranchers, who raised some of the best shorthorn cattle in Wyoming in 1925.

Havely Rock Garden, Fremont: a long ridge and plateau, broken by many couloirs; ragged.

Hawk Springs, Goshen: a town and a reservoir named for "Black" Hawk, saloon keeper. The springs are now covered by the reservoir.

Hay Creek, Crook: post office established, and townsite laid out in 1888 in connection with coal mines in the vicinty. The post office name changed to Barrett in 1889, which see.

Hayden Arch Bridge, Park: named for Dr. F. V. Hayden, noted geologist; highest bridge in Wyoming, 141 feet above the waters of the North Fork of Shoshone River; completed in 1966; 594 feet long.

Hayden, Mount, see Grand Teton.

Hayden National Forest, Carbon: established in 1906 as Sierra Madre; renamed in 1908 for Dr. Hayden; became part of Medicine Bow National Forest in 1929; now known as Hayden Division.

Hayden Valley, YNP: named for Dr. Ferdinand Hayden, leader of the USGS expeditions of 1871, 1872, and 1878, to study geology, zoology, and make maps. Indians called him "man who picks up stones running."

Haynes Mountains, 8,000, YNP: named for Frank J. Haynes, pioneer park photographer; came with the Schwatka expedition in the winter of 1886-87; travel and weather were so bad that most members stopped, but four, including Haynes, went on; they wandered for days without food, and almost lost their lives. Haynes was a concessioner in the park for 40 years.

Hay Pass, 11,160, Fremont, Sublette: named for John Hay, Rock Springs banker; he used this pass when pasturing sheep on the Wind River Reservation.

Haystack Butte, Uinta: shaped like a haystack. In 1857 twenty-five Mormon scouts outwitted soldiers of Johnston's army by marching in various formations around this butte all day. They changed horses and clothing, producing a false show of strength; this delayed the march of the soldiers.

Hazard Point, Laramie: now known as Colorado Junction, where the UP railroad takes off the main line for Fort Collins, Colorado. The first train over this line came into Cheyenne in 1877.

Hazel Park, Johnson: see Hazelton Peak.

Hazelton, Johnson: named by Tom Smith for his daughter Hazel.

Hazelton Peak, 10,545, Johnson: named by Tom J. Smith, pioneer rancher, for his daughter Hazel; the peak was on his ranch.

Healy, Johnson: named for the Healy ranch.

Heart Lake, YNP: named prior to 1870 for an old hunter, Chat Hunney. The lake is heart-shaped and so changed spelling.

Heart River, YNP: outlet of Heart Lake.

Heart Mountains, 8,113, Park: a landmark noted by John Colter on his lonely 1807 trek; named by Indians for its heart shape; the name was used on Lewis and Clark maps of 1808 and 1810; from Cody the top of the mountain looked like the face of a reclining Indian.

Heart Mountains Relocation Center, Park: 465 tarpaper barracks were erected here to house 11,000 Japanese, evacuated from the Pacific coast area during World War II despite the fact that two-thirds of them were American citizens; many were loyal; they were not welcomed in Wyoming. During their stay until the end of the war, they farmed 1,800 acres of virgin land, brought in irrigation water, raised crops, and supplied seasonal labor away from camp. Wyoming benefited by their presence.

Heather Peak, Carbon: named for James Heather, lumberman and prospector.

Heber Reservoir, Uinta: now known as Austin Reservoir.

Hecht Creek, Albany: named about 1900 for Rye Hecht, rancher.

Hecla, Laramie: copper mining district in the 1880s; once a copper smelter and brick kiln were here; no buildings are here now.

Hedges Peak, 9,700, YNP: named by USGS in 1895 for Cornelius Hedges, member of Washburn's 1870 expedition; Hedges proposed the idea of making a national park out of this unusual region; he wrote many articles to further its creation.

Hedrick Lake and Point, Teton: named for Charles Hedrick who thought he could raise beavers; it cost too much to fence them in, so he gave up the idea.

Hedrick Spring, Teton: named for Charles Hedrick who built a homestead cabin here. He grew a beard to cover up a scar on his face he received in a hand-to-hand encounter with a grizzly bear when he was 15; was a mail carrier, and a good story teller.

Heebeecheeche Lake, Fremont: named for an influential Shoshone chief.

Held Creek, Albany: named in the 1890s for Ed Held, rancher.

Helen, Mount, 13,600, Fremont, Sublette: named for Helen, wife of an official with the Department of Interior in 1901.

94

Hell Creek, Albany, Carbon: named about 1910 for a terrible road along the creek.

Hell Gap, Goshen: known locally as Vincent Canyon for a homesteader here. When archeologists found traces of some of the oldest houses on the continent here—circles of post holes that marked sites of round huts, estimated to have been built more than 10,000 years ago, they named the site of their camp Hell Gap. This name appeared on an old Fort Laramie map, and probably was named for a fierce skirmish between Indians and whites, that took place in the early days in this gap.

Archeologists worked here four summers unearthing layers of artifacts and bones of the Paleo-Indians.

Hell on Wheels: name given first to Cheyenne, and then to other end-of-the-rail towns along the UP railroad in the 1880s—rip-snorting boom towns with swarms of gamblers, land speculators, claim jumpers, and camp followers who were looking for trouble, and easily found it.

Hells Half Acre, Natrona: a 320-acre chasm, dropping from the flat prairie into eroded badland towers, spires, and caverns; many fantastic shapes.

This area was once known as Devils Kitchen. Casper merchants wanted to attract more people by the wonders of the country, and had pictures taken of it. They ordered thousands of colored post cards of Devils Kitchen printed. When the post cards came back, the name printed under the picture was Hells Half Acre. The cards were used, and the name established.

It is now a public park leased by Natrona County to private operators.

Hematite, Goshen: discontinued post office named for iron ore.

Hemmert Creek, Lincoln: a family name of early settlers.

Hemingway, Natrona: railroad siding for loading livestock; named for Ambrose Hemingway, surveyor, rancher, and attorney.

Henderson Peak, 13,100, Sublette: named for Kenneth A. Henderson, mountain climber and author of *A Handbook of American Mountaineering*; he climbed many peaks here.

Henke, Albany: discontinued post office for Rudolph Henke, postmaster.

Henry Lake, Sweetwater: named for fur trader Andrew Henry who built a trading post here.

Henrys Fork River, Sweetwater, Uinta: named by Ashley for his partner, Major Andrew Henry.

Hering Lake, YNP: named by USGS in 1878 for Rudolph Hering, topographer for Hayden Survey.

Hermit Creek, Fremont: named for an old man who lived here alone for years.

Hermosa, Albany: a railroad station named for the view to the west; Spanish word for beautiful is "hermosa."

Herron Creek, YNP: named for Rudolph Herron, topographer.

Hesse Mountain, 10,399, Johnson: named for F. G. S. Hesse, Englishman who founded one of the oldest and largest cattle ranches in Wyoming, the 28 Ranch in 1882.

Hewes Creek, Sheridan: named for E. A. Hewes, early homesteader. Later, the name was changed to Columbus Creek for Columbus Ellery, a popular cowboy of the O Z Cattle Company.

Hibbard Flats, Teton: named for Tim Hibbard, a trapper here in 1865.

Hickey Mountain, Uinta: named for the nearby Hickey ranch.

Hidden Corral Basin, Teton: rustlers' hideout in the early days; can be entered only by a stream. Famous in *The Virginian*.

Hidden Dome Oil Field, Washakie: so named for oil drilling near here in 1912; this field not found until 1917.

Hidden Falls, YNP: in Cascade Canyon, where Cascade Creek plunges 250 feet over a glacial bench.

Hidden Tepee Creek, Sheridan: named for the many tepee poles still standing in a hidden canyon when the white men first came to the Big Horn Mountains.

Hidden Treasure Gulch, Carbon: named for a hidden treasure in the area.

Hidden Water Creek, Sheridan: so named because water disappears into the ground; causes much trouble in coal mines.

Hideout, Sheridan: a man hid here with a bunch of sheep.

Hidivide, Campbell: discontinued post office; named by J. A. Kohlruss, postmaster, because it was on a high divide.

Higby, Sheridan: named for Mr. Higby who, with Horace C. Alger, mined the first coal near Sheridan for commercial purposes. Later Higby sold his interest to C. N. Deitz, by which name the mine is known.

Hiland, Natrona: village; highest point on Chicago and Northwestern railroad in Wyoming; once known as Poison Creek Station, also as Wolton.

Hilight, Campbell: discontinued post office; railroad station; located higher than the surrounding country.

Hilliard, Uinta: railroad station for Reuben T. Hilliard, homesteader and one of the early conductors on the railroad. Once 36 brick kilns were erected here, shaped like beehives, to produce charcoal from logs which were floated in flumes miles down from Mill City. Charcoal was used to fire the smelters, but coke proved better, and the use of charcoal fell off. The project was known as "Sloan's Folly."

Hillmont, Sublette: discontinued post office named for its location on a hill.

Hillsdale, Laramie: town named for engineer Lathrop Hills, who on June 11, 1867, was leading a survey party for railroad construction. Near the present site of Hillsdale, they were attacked by Indians, and Hills was killed. His companions routed the Indians, and reached Camp Collins.

A marker in his memory was erected at Hillsdale in 1973.

Hinshaw Creek, Uinta: named for the Hinshaw ranch.

Hoback, Teton: discontinued post office; named for the river.

Hoback Basin and Canyon, Lincoln, Teton: named for the Hoback River. At the head of Hoback Canyon Dr. Marcus Whitman is credited with delivering the first Protestant sermon in the Rocky Mountain region, here on August 23, 1835.

Hoback Peak, 10,864, Lincoln, Sublette: named for the Hoback River.

Hoback River, Lincoln, Sublette, Teton: named by W. P. Hunt in 1811 for John Hoback, trapper and guide for Hunt's party in this region.

Hobbs Lake and Park, Sublette: named for William Hobbes, prospector and homesteader; spelling of the name was changed.

Hobbs Peak, 11,671, Fremont: named for William Hobbes who explored the Wind River Range, and made the third ascent of Fremont Peak.

Hobo Rock, Sheridan: the McShane Tie Company had a million-dollar investment in flumes and equipment to float ties out of the Big Horn Mountains. In 1890s men wishing to work for the company walked up a trail from Ranchester to the headquarters in the mountains. So named because it was a long walk; these men, or "hobos" often spent a night in a cave under this large rock.

Hockaday-Liggett Stage and Mail Route: seeking to get mail through from east to west, in 1851 John M. Hockaday and William Liggett started a semi-monthly stage service from St. Louis, Missouri to Salt Lake City, Utah; the trip took 21 days. They sold out to Russell, Majors and Waddell in 1858.

Hodges Peak, 11,130, Sublette: probably named by the Bannon Douglas survey party of 1905 for one of its members.

Hogadon Ski Basin, Natrona: named for John C. Hogadon, who took up a mining claim on Casper Mountain in 1889. This modern ski area, opened in 1959, has three ski lifts and a Constam T-bar lift on Casper Mountain and a Swiss-type chalet. A Kristi packer is used to form loose snow.

Hogadon Trail, Natrona: named for John C. Hogadon; a shortcut from Casper to Eadsville.

Hog Park, Carbon: two versions of name; for numerous ground hogs in the area; for Hog, a half-breed freighter in the early days.

Hog Park Stage Station, Carbon: usually called Half-Way Station as it was not actually located at Hog Park; once called Olson for the boss of Carbon Timber Company at Hog Park.

Hog Ranch, Converse: across the Platte River from Fort Fetterman; a dance and gambling resort opened in 1882, and closed in 1886; named for the greed of gamblers who fleeced anyone they could get to play with them; there was also other entertainment.

Hole-in-the-Wall, Johnson: a wall of red hills parallels the Big Horn Mountains for 50 miles. Buffalo Creek flows between them and cuts a rugged and picturesque canyon, a perfect hideout for outlaws and thieves. The canyon can be entered from the east through a gap, making an entrance easily defended by a few men. At the west end many trails make fine escapes.

Alfred Smith filed on a homestead here in 1895, but relinquished it in the early 1890s. A joking cowboy, Smith was registering with a friend at the Occidental Hotel in Buffalo. Asked to give an address, he wrote

"Hole-in-the-Wall," thus naming a place that became famous. Butch Cassidy and Flat Nose George "Kid" Curry operated from here, stealing and hiding livestock. Train robbers also hid here.

Another version of the name is that Frewens, a rich Englishman who located and ranched on the Powder River in 1878, may have named it for a London locale known as Hole-in-the-Wall. Mostly BLM land now; elk range; good fishing.

Holly Lake, Teton: hiking trail as high as 9,400 feet altitude; scenic views, wild flowers, birds.

Holmes, Albany: discontinued post office established in 1899; moved to Keystone in 1903; named for Avery T. Holmes, who lived in Laramie, but owned an interest in the Rambler mine.

Holmes Caves, Teton: a small entrance in a big sink leads to caves of tremendous underground size; not completely explored; discovered in 1898 by Edwin B. Holmes, John H. Holland, and Neil Matheson.

Holmes, Mount, 10,336, YNP: named by Henry Gannett for W. H. Holmes, artist and geologist of the Hayden surveys.

Holt, Hot Springs: discontinued post office named for Horatio Holt.

Holy City, Park: named for sculptures high on the ridge north of Wyoming 20 on the way from Cody to the east entrance of Yellowstone National Park. They look like the silhouette of a city.

Home on the Range, Fremont: see Jeffrey City.

Honey Combs, Washakie: odd pillars and grotesque shapes caused by the erosion of Slick Creek.

Honeymoon Island, Teton: site of the famous honeymoon in Owen Wister's *The Virginian*.

Hoodoo Basin, YNP: A lava flow overlain by travertine. Erratic boulders were left by a melting glacier, and eroded into weird and fantastic shapes, including the figure of an old woman with a shawl over her head about 60 feet high; a wide variety of human and beastly forms. Adam Miller discovered it in 1880, and named it Hoodoo or Goblin Land. It can be reached by trails.

Hooker, Mount, 12,504, Fremont, Sublette: named for Sir Joseph Dalton Hooker, author, who in 1877 accompanied Dr. Asa Gray on a scientific tour through Colorado, Wyoming, Utah, and California.

Hornaday, Mount, 10,036, YNP: named for Dr. William T. Hornaday, former director of the New York Zoological Gardens.

Horner Site, Park: in 1939 Jimmy Allen was hunting arrowheads; he found bison bones and ancient artifacts near the mouth of Sage Creek. Archeologists set up "diggings" here in 1948, and named the site for the woman who owned the land. Carbon-14 readings dated the bones, tools, and weapons at about 7,000 years old.

Horse Creek, Laramie: village; once a stage station on the Cheyenne-Deadwood route; in 1883 a bridge washed out when the creek was at flood stage, causing much trouble.

Horse Creek, Natrona: once a Pony Express station. In 1824 Edward Rose was guide and interpreter for a large party of hunters under Jedediah

Smith and Thomas Fitzpatrick. Rose was a squaw man, having married a Crow woman. He was greatly admired by the Crows for his courage and daring. Once he clubbed some Blackfeet Indians (called Blackfeet because they wore black moccasins) to death, and earned the Crow name Che-ku-kaats, "man who kills five." Treacherous Rose betrayed his white hunting party to Crows, who stole the horses owned by whites at this creek; hence the name.

Horse Creek, Sublette: named by Ashley in 1824 when Indians stole Thomas Fitzpatrick's horse here.

Horse Creek Diversion Dam, Laramie: completed in 1923 for irrigation; named for Horse Creek, on which wild horses once grazed.

Horse Thief Canyon, Sweetwater: rendezvous of outlaws who were suspected of horse stealing by early ranchers.

Horse Thief Trail, Teton: trail led across Jackson Hole in 1900s to a horse thief hideout at the head of Lava Creek.

Horseshoe Bend, Big Horn: launching ramp for boating on the Yellowtail Reservoir here.

Horseshoe Creek, Albany, Platte: named in 1878 by Jack Newell for a large horseshoe bend in the creek.

Horseshoe Hill, 8,200, YNP: resembles a horseshoe.

Horseshoe Stage Station, Platte: named for the creek on which it was located; established in 1861 as an important stage station, mail stop, and later telegraph station. Mark Twain and Buffalo Bill both stopped here in 1862; it was supervised for a time by Jack Slade, notorious dual personality.

In 1866 Portugee Phillips stopped here on his famous ride to telegraph the news of the Fetterman disaster to Fort Laramie; not satisfied that the message got through, he rode on. Sioux Indians led by Crazy Horse burned the station in 1868; settlers hid in a tunnel, and escaped death; now the site of Glendo.

Horsethief Canyon, Teton: John Wilson once found some branding irons here and imagined they belonged to horse thieves.

Horton, Weston: named for Fred Horton, pioneer doctor and surgeon; he had a post office in his home; discontinued. Dr. Horton came in 1890; near the ranch of Nels H. Smith, Cowboy Governor from 1939-1943.

Horton Gulch, Washakie: named for Billy Horton, a resident of Tensleep country for nearly 50 years.

Hot Springs County: created in 1911; organized in 1913 with Thermopolis as county seat; named for the hot springs at Thermopolis. Irrigated farming, livestock raising, and oil are its chief industries.

Hot Springs State Park, Hot Springs: one of the first state parks; along the Bighorn RR and around the natural hot springs at Thermopolis; these springs are used for their medicinal water, and for a recreational resort. They were ceded to Wyoming by Chief Washakie and his Shoshones in 1896, with the provision that some of the water was to be forever free for bath purposes. The tract of land contains 55,000 acres; it was part of the Shoshone Reservation set aside by the United States government in a treaty with Chief Washakie in 1868.

An annual pageant "Gift of the Waters" portrays the history of the gift. The hot springs, centuries old, have built terraces of minerals deposited by the cooling waters. Buffalo wander in the park.

Housetop Mountain, 10,553, Teton: has the appearance of a housetop.

Houston Creek, Crook: named for George Houston, a hunter who sold meat to miners in the Black Hills; he gambled and drank; was shot by his partner Cole on this creek, and buried here under a pile of rocks.

Howard, Weston: discontinued post office named for Howard Osborne, son of Bert Osborne, postmaster.

Howell Mountain, 10,000, Park: named for Billy Howell, early dude rancher who is buried on the mountain.

Howell's Dam, Weston: on the land of Bernard Howell; good fishing.

Hoyt Peak, 10,506, Park: named for John W. Hoyt, who as governor of Wyoming Territory made a trip through Yellowstone National Park in 1881.

Hoyt Stage Station, Laramie: named for stock tender and stage driver Hoyt, who always carried a long driver's whip with him.

Hubert, Platte: 1887 post office named for Hubert Teschemacher, rancher; discontinued.

Huckleberry Mountain, 9,700, Teton: named for its abundant cover of huckleberries. This was one of the hangouts of elk tusk poachers, who lived here in earth-covered shelters; they used gun silencers in hunting. A pair of elk tusks brought from $10 to $100 as charms and emblems of BPOE in the 1890s.

Gangs slaughtered hundreds of elk, and left carcasses lying; they sold the teeth. The first state hunter licensing system began in 1899. In 1904 D. C. Nowlin began strong law enforcement; BPOE members stopped buying elk tusks, and the racket was over.

Hudson, Fremont: when first started about 1905, it was called "Alta," an Indian word meaning swift water; it was renamed for John G. Hudson, owner of the land on which the town was located. Hudson was a rancher and legislator, instrumental in bringing in the railroad. The town Hudson is a trading center for Indians, coal miners, and oil field workers. It was a big coal mining town about 1912.

Hudson Valley, Goshen and Platte: named for Noal Hudson, an old-timer who once owned a tame buffalo bull named Jumbo.

Hugo, Mount, Fremont: named for Hugo Limber, a Shoshone.

Hulett, Crook: post office established in 1886; named for Lewis M. Hulett, first postmaster; located in lumbering, wheat and livestock raising area.

Humphreys, Mount, 10,965, YNP: named for Gen. A. A. Humphreys by Capt. J. W. Barlow in 1871. Gen. Humphreys was then Chief of Engineers, United States Army.

Hunt Mountain, 10,775, Teton: named for Wilson Price Hunt, leader of the Astorians in 1811.

Huntley, Goshen: town named for Huntley, a civil engineer on the Union Pacific railroad.

Hunton's Creek, Converse, Platte: named for John A. Hunton, who once owned the original Carey ranch in 1867; he supplied wood to Fort Fetterman from 1871-1881; he wrote about his experiences in a diary, later edited by L. G. Flannery and published as *Hunton's Diary*.

Hunt's Pass, Teton: named for Wilson Price Hunt (1811-1900), explorer who crossed what is now Wyoming in 1811. His party attempted to cross the Snake River in boats made of elk skins stretched across willow branches; the result was almost disaster for the party that lost part of their supplies; they recovered the horses they had abandoned and went westward over the mountain pass; the name was changed to Teton Pass in 1900.

Hurlbut Creek, Sheridan: named for Edmund Hurlbut, prospector who barely escaped hanging by a group of disappointed gold-seekers who believed he had misinformed them about gold on this creek.

Hurricane Mesa, 11,064, Park: a level stretch of prairie between the North and South forks of Crandall Creek; named by early settlers for the strong winds sweeping over it.

Hurricane Pass, Teton: a thin fence of rock that separates the head of two canyons, and gets the full force of the wind.

Huson, Sheridan: discontinued post office named for Edward W. Huson.

Huston Park, Carbon: named for Al Huston who had a hunter's cabin there in the early days.

Hutton and Hutton Lake, Albany: named for Charles Hutton, a rancher in 1860 on the plains before the coming of the railroad; he was a freighter for Edward Creighton while the latter was building the telegraph line in Albany County.

Hutton Lake Migratory Bird Refuge, Albany: established in 1929; named for Charles Hutton.

Hyattville, Big Horn: when the town was first established in 1886, it was called Paintrock for Indian pictographs on a nearby cliff. Samuel Hyatt started a store and the first post office, and the town was renamed for him. When the store was destroyed by fire in 1900, Sam Hyatt became a rancher.

Asa Shinn Mercer was also a pioneer settler here. He made himself famous by taking two shiploads of young women around Cape Horn in the 1860s for matrimonial purposes on the West Coast; finished with this enterprise, he came to Wyoming to settle.

I

Ice Cave, Natrona: on Bates Creek; a cave that holds ice.

Ice Slough and Creek, Fremont: ice to a depth of 18 inches was once found here under heavy grass. Pioneers refrigerated their meat here; ice can still be found under a two- or three-foot quagmire of swampy growth and evil-tasting water.

Ice Springs, Fremont: a Pony Express station; named for thick ice in winter.

Icecream Cone, 12,300, Teton: a mountain that resembles an ice cream cone; first ascended by F. Ayres in 1923.

Illco, Natrona: discontinued post office; from a trade name.

Illinois Creek, Albany: W. H. Holliday had a lumber mill here in the 1880s, and named the creek for his native state.

Illinois Pass, 11,750, Sublette: named by climbers from Chicago.

Image, 10,700, Teton: named for its reflection in Hanging Lake.

Independence Rock, Natrona: several versions of the name: in 1824 Broken-Hand Fitzpatrick was coming down the Sweetwater River with a large buffalo-hide canoe full of his winter's catch of furs. Swollen waters wrecked his canoe here on July 4th; he cached the furs, and named Independence Rock.

Others claim that Capt. Bonneville camped here in 1832, and named this granite monolith Independence Rock because it stands alone and independent on the prairie, covering more than 25 acres. Some say Gen. Ashley spent July 4, 1825 here, and named it.

In 1840 Father DeSmet christened it "Register of the Desert" because hundreds of emigrants carved their names on it. On July 4, 1862, twenty members of a passing wagon train held the first Masonic meeting in what is now Wyoming here. They loaded old wagon hubs with gunpowder, and placed them in crevices of the rock. When the powder exploded, it sounded like heavy artillery. Once a town of considerable size was here, but there is not a timber left today.

Over 5,000 names were carved on Independence Rock by travelers on the Oregon Trail more than a hundred years ago; some of them are still readable. Wagon tracks are still visible in the rocks to the southwest of Independence Rock within walking distance of Wyoming 220. The huge turtle-shaped rock is of igneous origin, consisting of feldspar that shows marks of glacial action. It is a tourist stop today.

Index Creek, Park: named for Index Peak.

Index Peak, 11,343, Park: once called Finger Peak; approached from the north, this forested ridge looks like a closed hand, with the index finger extended upward; named by the Hayden expedition in the 1870s; of volcanic origin.

Indian Creek, Albany: got its name from an Indian massacre on the Fetterman Trail in the 1870s.

Indian Hill, Laramie: discontinued post office near a large hill that once was a meeting place of Indians.

Indian Paintbrush Canyon, Teton: named for Castilleja linariaefolia, Indian paintbrush; the genus was named for Domingo Catillejo, a Spanish botanist; it was adopted as the state flower in 1917. The scarlet or orange-yellow colors of this plant are bracts; the flowers are very conspicuous. They splash the mountains with color, but will not transplant into gardens.

Indian Pass, 12,130, Fremont: too steep and rough for horses. Indians used to have a trail through this pass that they built up with rocks, but snow slides have wiped it out; forest rangers now mark trails in wilderness

102

and primitive areas with piles of small rocks on top of larger rocks; these piles are called "sitting ducks."

Indian Powwow Cavern, Washakie: vast cavern in high, red cliffs where Indians met for shelter or powwow; ancient figures are carved on the walls and ceilings; the cave has acoustic properties.

Inez, Converse: railroad station for Inez Richards, daughter of DeForest Richards, rancher and Governor of Wyoming from 1899-1903.

Ingleside, Laramie: limestone quarry which provides material for sugar refineries in Wyoming and Colorado; operated by Ingleside Limestone Quarry Company. A gravel pit is nearby.

Inkwell Springs, YNP: color is due to deposits of manganese oxide.

Innominate, 12,700, Big Horn, Johnson: the second main summit of Black Tooth Peak; named by the Willcox climbing party because of its similarity to Innominate Crack in England.

Inspiration Point, YNP: on the left bank of the Yellowstone River, one and a half miles below the Lower Falls; the view from here of Grand Canyon of the Yellowstone River, and of the falls is most inspirational; tourists can look 800 feet down into the canyon at cascading water. The canyon is aflame with color, like a rainbow fallen from the sky.

Inter-Ocean Hotel, Laramie: this famous hotel in Cheyenne was built in 1875 by Barney L. Ford, a noted black caterer; it was a social center for years; starting place of Cheyenne-Deadwood stage route.

President U. S. Grant stopped here in 1875. It was a temporary White House in 1903, when President Theodore Roosevelt stayed here for three days. It was the first hotel in the United States to have electric lights; it was gutted by fire on a sub-zero night in 1916.

Invasion Gulch, Johnson: a dry, boulder-strewn gulch that sheltered the Johnson County defenders during their siege of the T A Ranch during the Johnson County War.

Inyan Kara Creek, Crook: discontinued post office; named for Inyan Kara Mountain.

Inyan Kara Mountain, Crook: Indian name meaning "stone-made." Gen. George A. Custer carved his name on top of this mountain in 1874 on his way to the Black Hills. The first country church in Wyoming was built at its base by Methodists in 1891.

Ione Lake, Albany: named in 1860 for the Ione Land and Cattle Company.

Iowa Center, Goshen: so named because homesteaders here came from Iowa.

Iowa Column, 11,550, Fremont: named for Iowa mountaineers who were climbing in this region.

Iowa Flats, Platte: people from Iowa homesteaded here from 1909-1910.

Irma Hotel, Park: this famous hotel in Cody was built in 1902 by Buffalo Bill Cody, and named for his daughter Irma Cody Garlow. Its fireplace was built of stones from many countries. Western paintings by Remington hung on its walls. Its hand-carved, cherrywood bar was imported from Europe, and used by noblemen, freighters, and cowboys. It is still an operating hotel and is on the National Register of Historic Places.

Irma Lake and Irma Flat, Park: named for Irma Cody Garlow.

Iron Creek, Weston: named by Dud Meeks in the early days for its coloring by ferrous oxide. Iron Town, a ghost town, was on this creek.

Iron Mountain, Laramie: railroad station and post office; the station was abandoned in 1921; named for a nearby mountain of iron ore. This station was the northern end of the Goodnight Texas Cattle Trail, and the location of sheep and cattle fights from 1900-1902.

Tom Horn, a killer hired by cattlemen, always put two rocks under his victims' heads, so his employers would know who did the deed. In 1902 Tom Horn killed 13-year-old Willie Nickell instead of his father, who was a sheepman of Iron Mountain, and boasted about it when drunk; Tom Horn was convicted and hanged.

The Bar Circle ranch ranged 10,000 head of cattle in the vicinity of Iron Mountain in the days of the open range.

Irontown, Weston: a settlement on Iron Creek, named for the mineral in the water; it later became Merino, and finally Upton.

Irvine, Converse: railroad station for Billy Irvine, rancher, who organized the Ogallala Land and Cattle Company in the 1880s.

Isa Lake, YNP: both fickle and impartial in that it sends water to both the Atlantic and Pacific oceans; named in 1893 for Isabel Jelke of Cincinnati, Ohio, by a Northen Pacific railroad official.

Isabel Mount, Lincoln: named for Isabel Juel, wife of sheepman.

Ishawooa Cone, Creek, Mesa, and Pass, Park: a Shoshone name meaning "lying warm." The mesa, 11,840 feet in elevation, is a grassy table land. The pass, with an elevation of 9,870, is a natural passageway from the headwaters of the Shoshone River to the headwaters of the Yellowstone.

The mountain is famous for a snow patch which in spring is in the shape of a rearing horse. Old-timers say that when the horse's head with the reins shows up, high water has passed its mark.

Island Park, Sweetwater: an island in Green River at the town of Green River, where John Wesley Powell launched his boats for his historic exploration of the Green and Colorado rivers on May 24, 1869. His second expedition started from here May 22, 1871.

Islay, Laramie: railroad station and post office in 1887; named by Donald McPhee, rancher, for his native Scotland home on the Isle of Islay; many early Scottish settlers here. The post office was moved in 1931 and renamed Federal; now discontinued.

J

Jack Creek, Carbon: named for Jack Watkins, a desperado who had a cabin on the creek.

Jack Creek, Park: named for Jack Wiggins, an early trapper.

Jackalope Swimming Pool, Converse: uses water from a natural warm spring; named for that rare animal that looks like a jackrabbit with the horns of a deer; its habitat is Converse County.

Jackass Pass, 10,800, Fremont, Sublette; named by early trappers who claimed that only a jackass could be driven through it; an old Indian trail.

Jackson, Teton: town named for Jackson Hole; platted in 1897 by Mrs. Robert E. Miller who bought this sagebrush swale from John Simpson. Jackson became nationally known in 1920, when all city officials elected were women; it still has many log buildings, boardwalks, and western shops; the town caters to tourists and winter sports fans. Its motto is, "Last of old West; best of new." Now a year-round tourist center. Winter activities include skiing, snowmobiling, skating, cutter racing and ice fishing.

Jackson Canyon, Natrona: named for William J. Jackson, pioneer explorer.

Jackson Creek, Sheridan: named for W. E. Jackson, Superintendent of the Bighorn National Forest from 1897-1910.

Jackson Hole, Teton: in the language of fur trappers a "hole" was a valley protected by mountains, and usually named for the trapper who frequented the place. William Sublette in 1829 named this valley for his partner, David E. Jackson. The name "Jackson's Hole" has been simplified to Jackson Hole; it is surrounded by the Grand Tetons, the Wind River Range, and the Gros Ventre Mountains.

The world's largest elk herd winters here; 7,000 to 10,000 animals are fed baled hay. Cutter races settle the old bet "my horse is faster than yours." This is a fast growing sport with few rules.

Jackson Hole is ski country with steep mountains. America's first 63-person aerial tramway has been installed; also three double chairlifts. A chairlift to the top of Snow King Mountain runs all year for tourists who crowd this wonderland of beauty. In summer tourists enjoy boating, fishing, and hiking.

Jackson Hole Airport, Teton: only commercial airport in a national park. When it was started, Mayor Harry Clissold of Jackson went to the area, wet his finger to determine wind direction, and stepped off 6,000 feet for the runway which is still used. There is controversy now about lengthening the runway to accommodate large jet planes. Conservationists claim sonic booms and jet engine noise will disturb wildlife and also the wilderness atmosphere for tourists in the region. Only small turbo planes can land now.

Jackson Hole Museum, Teton: has many relics of the region's history, including Indian pottery and arrowheads found around Jackson Lake; the famous Lawrence collection of Western Americana gathered for more than 40 years by W. C. "Slim" Lawrence; world record trophy heads of elk and deer; and a huge grizzly bear skull.

Jackson Hole National Monument, Teton: see Grand Teton National Park.

Jackson Lake, Teton: named for Jackson Hole; was carved out by glaciers of last ice age, and held in by moraines deposited as glaciers melted; appears on explorer Clark's early map as Lake Biddle, honoring Nicholas Biddle, who published the Lewis and Clark papers in 1809; later it was misprinted on maps as Lake Riddle. Trapper Joe Meek called it Lewis Lake; it was also called Teton Lake, but finally took its name from the valley.

Jackson Lake was enlarged by a dam in 1911, which washed out; a second dam was finished in 1916; this supplies irrigation and recreation. Jackson Lake has good fishing, including large Mackinaw trout; it also furnishes sailboating, water skiing, and winter sports under the snow-dusted towers of the Tetons. Good hiking and horse trails lead from the lake.

Jackson Lake Lodge, Teton: exotic lodge built by Laurance Rockefeller, so all tourists can enjoy the Tetons framed in its windows. On this locale, Laurance and his father, John D., used to sit and eat their lunch while thrilling to the beauty of the valley and mountains. The lodge is a non-profit project; many log cabins near it also accommodate visitors.

Jade Lake, Teton: lies high in the Tetons, surrounded by steep cliffs covered with evergreens, whose reflection gives the water a beautiful, green color.

Jade is now the official stone of Wyoming; the law making it so was passed by the 1967 legislature. There are two types of jade: nephrite, a metamorphic mineral with a fibrous structure, and jadite, with a crystalline structure. Jade ranges in color from white through shades of green to jet black. It usually has a rind coating that may be red, saddle-brown, or white. It is found over a wide area in the central part of the state, mostly around Jeffrey City.

Chinese philosopher Confucius said, "It is not because jade is rare that it is so highly valued. It is because ever since olden days wise men have seen in jade the different values. It is soft to the touch, smooth and shining like kindness. It is hard, fine and strong like intelligence. Its edges seem sharp but do not cut, like justice; it hangs down to the ground like humility; when struck, it gives a clear ringing sound, like music. The stains in it which are not hidden and which add to its beauty are like truthfuless; its brightness is like heaven; while its firm substance born of the mountains and the waters is like the earth it came from."

Jagger Creek and Peak, 11,237, Park: rough, brushy topography in Sunlight basin.

Jakey's Fork, Fremont: Capt. Torrey and James K. Morse used this country as summer range, and built a corral near the mouth of the creek in the 1870s. "J. K.'s Fork" became Jakey's Fork. Another version is that a school was held here in a blacksmith shop from 1909-1910; the school and creek were named for Jake K. Moore, old-time trader and cowman.

Jakey's Fork Bridge, Fremont: there is a monument here on the grave of Jimmy Burroughs, cowboy foreman, who in 1895 was roping a steer, got tangled in the rope, and was dragged by his horse through the sage. Jimmy Lannigan made a five-hour ride to Fort Washakie for a doctor, but when he got back Burroughs was dead.

James Lake, Albany: named in the 1860s for James, a surveyor on the Laramie Plains; originally it was known as Seven Mile Lake for a creek of that name.

106

Janis, Goshen: named for Nicholas Janis, an Indian; it was located on the Platte River a mile west of the Nebraska state line; it was the site of Red Cloud Indian agency in 1871; it was moved to Crawford, Nebraska, in 1874. Janis stayed and cared for the buildings until they were sold in 1880. Janis went to Washington, D.C. with Chief Red Cloud in 1872 as an interpreter.

Jay Em, Goshen: inland town named for cattle brand of Jim Moore, Pony Express rider, who used his initials for a brand when he became a rancher in 1869. He was killed when he was thrown from a hay wagon in a runaway. The brand passed through several hands until secured by the Harris brothers who founded and named the town.

Hargraves was a Goshen County post office established in 1899 by "Uncle" Jack Hargraves, who clashed with the postal inspector when he called. "Uncle" Jack told the inspector to pack his post office (all supplies went into a large, wooden box) and get out, which he did. Ranchers then applied for a post office at the Jay Em ranch. Lake Harris brought the mail from Rawhide Buttes station free in 1909. The store and post office were moved from the ranch to the present site of Jay Em in 1915.

Jean Lakes, Sublette: named by Bill Hobbs, an old-timer at Pinedale, for Jean Redick. The Redicks owned a summer home on Fremont Lake; Hobbs was their friend.

Jedediah Smith, Mount, 10,615, Teton: named for Jedediah S. Smith, trapper, who, with William Sublette and David E. Jackson, bought the Rocky Mountain Fur Company in 1826 from Gen. Ashley. Smith wrote a journal of his adventures, describing the Indians and early life; he was an explorer, devout Christian, and a shrewd businessman.

Jefferson River, YNP: named for President Thomas Jefferson.

Jeffrey City, Fremont: once called "Home on the Range," but renamed for its promoter, Dr. Charles W. Jeffrey, a Rawlins physician and philanthropist; it is a company town for Western Nuclear Company, which processes more than 30 million dollars worth of uranium here annually.

Bob Adams started operating the first uranium mill in Wyoming here in 1957; the ore came from Crooks Gap and from Gas Hills. Uranium concentrate or "yellow cake" is shipped elsewhere for further refining.

Jeffrey City is in the center of the jade area. When Bert Rhoads started hunting jade in 1936, people thought him crazy. Verla Rhoads found a piece weighing 3,366 pounds in 1943; this is believed to be the largest single chunk of jade in the world. Only a small part was sticking out of the sand when Verla spotted this treasure.

Alan Branham, a Lander grocer, found the next largest piece, 2,410 pounds, and sold it to James L. Kraft, the cheese manufacturer who donated it to the Chicago Museum of Natural History. In 1945 Rhoads found a piece sticking out of the snow on Crooks Mountain. In the spring he went back, and found 42 pieces weighing 7,000 pounds. He had to hire a bulldozer to build a road; it cost him $700 to get his find to Lander.

Wyoming jade is the finest in the world; good quality jade is worth from $50 to $100 an ounce at the present time, and is now hard to find. It is now wanted in China, where supply is almost exhausted. One ounce of good jade will yield about $500 worth of jewelry. Jade was formed by an unknown process of heat and pressure from mineral deep in the earth, and heaved up when mountains were formed.

Jelm, Albany: named for E. C. Gillem. A corruption of his name is Jelm. He had a contract with the railroad to furnish ties in the 1860s. Another version: Scandinavian miners named it after "hjelm," helmet. See Cummins City.

Jelm Mountain, 9,665, Albany: named for E. C. Gillem, who cut ties here; a fire lookout station is here now.

Jenks, Laramie: discontinued post office; named for Mrs. Ada Jenks, postmaster in 1890.

Jenney's Stockade, Weston: named for Walter P. Jenney, geologist, who in 1875 left Cheyenne with 75 wagons and two ambulances to build a fort and supply station in the Black Hills by order of the Secretary of Interior. He had a military escort with Colonel R. I. Dodge as commander.

This fort became a relay station on the Cheyenne-Deadwood stage route; later it became part of the LAK ranch. When the old stockade was torn down, the Newcastle Chamber of Commece salvaged logs and lumber and rebuilt it as their office building; some of the original portholes are still left. This was the first outpost of white men in the Black Hills area; now it is a National Historic Site.

Jenny Lake, Teton: named for an Indian woman, Jenny, wife of Beaver Dick Leigh, who was a guide for the first Hayden expedition in 1871. The lake is glacier-formed. Now it has become a tourist center with modern comforts in log cabins, nature trails. All climbers in this region must register at the Jenny Lake Ranger Station.

Jensen Ridge, Teton: ascended in 1938 by B. Jensen and two companions.

Jepps Canyon, Carbon: named for Jepp Peterson, pioneer rancher.

Jeralee Peak, 12,700, Fremont: named by the first ascending party of C. Goetze and B. Underwood in 1960.

Jim Bridger Power Plant, Sweetwater: currently under construction by Pacific Power and Light Company in Nine Mile Draw; it will be in operation in several years producing 1,600,000 kilowatts of power for the Pacific Northwest, Idaho, and Wyoming. It will burn coal mined on the site; the water is piped from Green River.

Jim Creek, Albany: named in the 1880s for Jim, a miner.

Jim Smith Creek and Peak, Park: named for Jim Smith, an early rancher. One night there was an all-night party at the Smith ranch with freighters and cowboys; all available whiskey was consumed. In the morning MacGonigal went outside, and noticed that Index Peak had broken off during the night, and was shorter than Pilot Peak. Not being sure of himself or his eyes, he went back in, ate breakfast, and said nothing.

Smith went outside and saw the same thing, but he wasn't sure of what he saw, so he, too, said nothing about it. For several days neither friend mentioned it, but finally Smith could stand it no longer, and asked MacGonigal what he saw. Their suspicions were confirmed; a chunk had slid off Index Peak—it wasn't a hangover of DTs; it was the truth.

Jireh, Niobrara: town founded in 1908 by about 20 families who came from Ohio and Iowa to take up 160-acre homesteads and desert claims on the prairie; by 1910 more than 200 families had arrived.

108

The town grew with the addition of a blacksmith shop, lumber yard, real estate office, and newspaper; smoking, drinking, and dancing were forbidden; it was a cultural center with higher education and music, promoted by Jireh College; name from the Biblical Jehovah Jireh, meaning "the Lord will provide." Now it has gone back to bare prairie land, where only those who know where to look can find a foundation stone.

Jireh College, Niobrara: the first junior college in Wyoming; opened in 1910 in a large building, with 40 students registered; liberal arts, theology, commerce, music, and art were taught; board and room was $5 a week, tuition $15.

Christian Churches, now Congregational, helped build the three-story college building, and helped support it. An experimental farm was operated in connection with the college. John B. Kendrick, later governor and U.S. senator, came in a buggy to give a commencement address in 1915.

Drought drove away the homesteaders; the conditions following World War I ended the college, which had its last graduation in 1920.

Jock Draw, Albany: named about 1890 for Nick Jock, a consumptive who died here.

Joe Emge Gulch, Washakie: named for Joe Emge, killed in the Spring Creek raid of 1909, when cattlemen attacked sheepherders and their flocks.

Joe Yant or Soda Lake, Natrona: a wild bird and duck refuge for Joe Yant, retired refinery worker, who created it; an oil pipe break in the spring of 1973 covered lake with oily sludge killing hundreds of birds.

John Cherry Trail, Teton: a secret trail through the Gros Ventre Mountains known to few persons; described by John "Cherry," pioneer, whose real name was not known.

John Day's River, Lincoln: named for John Day, a member of the Astorian expedition under Wilson Price Hunt of 1811-1812.

John D. Rockefeller, Jr. Memorial Parkway, Teton: dedicated August 25, 1972; connects Yellowstone and Teton national parks; 82 miles long; contains 2,000 acres; made as a tribute to a great philanthropist and conservationist who saved the scenic area south of the Grand Tetons from commercial enterprises.

Johnson County: created in 1875 as Pease County; then it included what is now Sheridan, Big Horn, Washakie, and Hot Springs counties; named for Dr. E. L. Pease of Uinta County.

The name was changed in 1879 to Johnson County for E. P. Johnson, Cheyenne attorney; later the other counties were split off. Johnson County was not organized until 1881.

The county has had a tempestuous history, with Indian fights over the Bozeman road and forts, and later the Johnson County War. Now it is ranching and dude ranching country with increased oil and coal mining industries. Buffalo is the county seat.

Johnson County War, Johnson: in the spring of 1892 the small ranchers and homesteaders in the county prepared for an early spring roundup for branding cattle, in defiance of dates and regulations of organized big cattlemen, who were fighting the loss of free public grazing land and some rustling.

The large stock owners hired gunmen from Texas, loaded them with military supplies on a train, and came to Casper, marching north to Johnson County like an invading army. At the K C ranch they besieged and killed Nick Ray and Nate Champion. Messengers spread the word through Johnson County; Sheriff Red Angus swore in 100 deputies, and, with armed citizens, surrounded the gunmen entrenched at the T A ranch.

Colonel Van Horn from Fort McKinney came to the rescue of the cattlemen, who were taken to Cheyenne, and held there in jail at the expense of Johnson County. When Johnson County was not able to pay this expense, the armed invaders were released without trial.

Johnson Mountain, Platte: named for Osgood Johnson, a homesteader here and later a Wheatland farmer.

Johnson Reservoir, Natrona: built by Henry Johnson, rancher; very popular fishing area.

Johnstown, Natrona: a soda mining camp in 1892; the name was changed to Berthaton by Barns for his daughter Bertha in 1896.

Jojo Creek and Mountain, 12,540, Park: two early settlers here were named Joseph, so the creek and mountain were called Jojo.

Jones Creek, Hot Springs: named for Jones, an early settler.

Jones Creek and Pass, 9,600, YNP: named for Capt. W. A. Jones in 1873, in command of the first party to cross the Absaroka Range.

Jordan, Big Horn: discontinued post office named for Henry Jordan, a flour mill owner in 1897.

Jordan, Laramie: railroad siding originally called Shultz Spur in 1877 for a sawmill owner; the name was changed to Jordan about 1900 for John L. Jordan, rancher.

Joseph Peak, 10,494, YNP: named by the USGS in 1885 for Chief Joseph, the famous Nez Perce Indian chief.

Josh's Butte, Park: named for Josh Doane, an early settler who claimed he had been surrounded by Indians at this butte; to make his story better, Josh shot his own coat full of holes.

Joss House, Uinta: this Chinese house in Evanston in the 1880s was one of three in the United States. On Chinese New Year, about February 10, thousands of miners came here to worship and celebrate with firecrackers.

The Joss House was elaborate with hand-carved panels, embroidered draperies, and a teakwood altar on which a joss stick burned before an idol. After the labor troubles of 1885, the Chinese were driven from the neighborhood. The house burned in 1922.

K

K C Ranch, Johnson: see Johnson County War.

Kagorah Lake, Fremont: named for a Shoshone who helped build one of the earliest irrigation ditches on the reservation in 1886.

Kaiser Divide, Crook: named for the Kaiser family, pioneers.

Kanda, Sweetwater: railroad station named for Kanda, the manager of a Chinese store at Rock Springs.

Kane, Big Horn: discontinued post office; it was a railroad station named for Riley Kane, a cowboy, one of the first settlers in Bighorn basin, and foreman for the Mason and Lovell outfit.

When the community first started, the only water available for house use was brought in tank cars on the railroad from Warren, Montana, and stored in a cistern, from which residents got their water in pails or milk cans.

When Kane was a post office in 1895, on the M L ranch, mail was brought from Billings, Montana, on horseback 100 miles. In 1906 the post office was moved to the railroad. Kane is now covered by the waters of Yellowtail Dam.

Kane Bridge, Big Horn: named for Riley Kane, cowboy; it is also a launching ramp for boating on Yellowtail Reservoir.

Kaycee, Johnson: named for the K C brand owned in 1884 by Peters and Alston; it was a cowman's town, established in 1900. Near here in 1860 missionaries from the German Lutheran Church in Iowa established an Indian mission to instruct the Crows. When the Sioux took over the territory, one missionary was slain and the others fled.

Kearny, Johnson: discontinued post office named for Fort Phil Kearny.

Kearny Creek and Lake, Johnson: named for Fort Phil Kearny.

Keeline, Niobrara: named for George A. Keeline, the owner of the 4 J ranch; south of here are Spanish Diggings, a prehistoric site.

Keenan City, Teton: a mining town in 1876; Lt. Doane and his starving men came here, got food, and saved their lives; it is now a ghost town.

Keeney Cut-off, western Wyoming: named for Jonathan Keeney, a hunting companion of Jim Bridger; he was present when Rev. Whitman removed an arrow from Bridger's back.

Keets Creek, Weston: named for Henry Keets, an early cattleman.

Kelly, Teton: named for Bill Kelly, a rancher and sawmill owner in 1909; the town was originally Grovont, but the name was changed because another post office had the same name.

In 1925 the end of Sheep Mountain above Kelly broke loose, dammed Gros Ventre River, and formed Slide Lake; there were estimated 50,000,000 tons of earth, rocks, and trees moved in the slide.

In the spring of 1927 the dam broke. Forest Ranger C. E. Dibble cut fences to free livestock, and rushed to warn people in Kelly. They had 15 minutes to get to higher ground, where they watched an 8-foot wall of water sweep away the town; only the church and schoolhouse on higher elevations were left. Six persons lost their lives. The site is now a tourist attraction and ghost town.

Kelly's Park, Platte: used to be a dance hall and recreation area on the Platte River; no longer exists; see Fairbanks.

Kemmerer, Lincoln: county seat; started in 1897 by P. J. Quearly who named it for M. S. Kemmerer, who became president of Kemmerer Coal

Company; it is the center of a large coal mining and stock raising district. Near here you can fish with a pick and shovel for fossilized fish more than 45 million years old. The City Museum has pioneer relics, natural and mineral objects.

James Cash Penney opened a store here in 1902 in a small room on a muddy main street. With his policy of the Golden Rule, J. C. Penney has enlarged his chain of stores to more than 1,700; they are in every state. The mother store in Kemmerer is still serving customers.

Kendall, Sublette: discontinued post office named for August Kendall, a banker, stockman, and head of a tie camp that operated here; now it is a guard station of the Forest Service. The first supervisor's office for Bridger National Forest was once located here, now at Kemmerer.

Kendall Dam, Sublette: named for Kendall.

Kendall Warm Springs, Sublette: year-round 85-degree temperature; these springs have unique dace or small minnows mottled green, called Kendall dace.

Kendrick, Campbell: railroad stop for U.S. Senator John B. Kendrick; see Kendrick Park.

Kendrick Park, Sheridan: named for U.S. Senator John B. Kendrick who drove cattle up the Texas Trail and became a rancher in Sheridan County. In the early days most cowboys bought socks, 12 pairs for $1, and when they got dirty, they were thrown away. John Kendrick washed and mended his socks, saved his money, and finally became full owner of the O W ranch with its 200,000-acre spread near Sheridan. He became governor of Wyoming from 1915-1917, and U.S. Senator from 1917 to 1933.

The Park in Sheridan, named in his honor, contains a zoo with many native animals.

KendrickProject, Carbon, Natrona: was first known as Casper-Alcova Project; it was renamed in 1937 for Senator Kendrick who worked for conservation and the development of natural resources. Dams under this project built for the control of the North Platte River are: Alcova, Pathfinder, Kortes, Seminoe, and Casper Canal.

Kennaday Peak, 10,805, Carbon: named for Jack Kennaday, forest ranger; a lookout station is on the peak.

Kenny Lakes, Sublette: named by the Bannon Douglas survey party of 1905 for one of their members.

Kenyon Creek, Albany: named for Kenyon who lived here in the 1880s.

Kepler Cascades, YNP: spectacular falls named by Col. Norris in 1881 for Kepler Hoyt, son of territorial governor John W. Hoyt.

Kershner Hill, Big Horn: named for Kershner, an 1887 pioneer.

Kerwin, Park: a ghost town now, the old mining town was founded in 1885 by Willam Kerwin who made a small gold strike here; a snow slide in 1907 wiped away the town.

Kester Draw, Hot Springs: named for homesteader Kester who lived here. He got in a shooting scrape with another homesteader over some goods taken from his cabin; as a result he had a delicate operation performed in Thermopolis, and a silver plate put in his head; he lived.

112

Ketchum Buttes, Carbon: named for Jim Ketchum, homesteader.

Keyhole Reservoir, Crook: named for shape, completed in 1952; 9,418 acre-feet; good fishing, boating, water sports, and camping; a state park. Fish here are walleye, perch, channel catfish, and bluegill trout.

Keystone, Albany: a post office was established here in 1885 in a mining district; the mine was abandoned in 1892, followed by a lumbering boom; named for the Keystone Mine, which was named for Keystone Ranch, which was named by Galusha Grow, who came from Pennsylvania, the Keystone state.

Killion, Crook: discontinued post office that was established in 1886 at the road ranch of Mrs. Louisa Killion; she also operated a toll bridge across Inyan Kara Creek, the only crossing at this time.

Mrs. Killion, according to Crook County records, has the distinction of obtaining two divorces on the same day; one from Reed, and one from Killion. She drowned in the Belle Fourche River when it was at flood stage in 1896; by then she was Mrs. Conrey; the Calamity Jane of Crook County.

Killpecker Creek, Sweetwater: a salty name from the early days, probably pertaining to the water's effect on men.

Kilpatrick Creek, Crook: the creek waters are so strong medicinally that the creek was called Kilpatrick.

Kingman Canyon Pass, 7,230, YNP: name given to Glen Creek Canyon for Capt. D. C. Kingman, of the U.S. Army, who built the first road through the canyon from 1884-1885; the view from here is of unsurpassed beauty.

Kinnear, Fremont: post office and valley named for N. B. Kinnear, a rancher and civil engineer. Irene Kinnear was a pioneer school teacher on the Wind River Reservation; Jim Baker was one of her grandfathers.

Kinnie River, Sweetwater: named for Kinnie, an early rancher.

Kinnikinnic Lake, Teton: high under Grand Teton; often called Surprise Lake; named for plant.

Kirby, Hot Spring: post office and railroad station for Kris Kirby, Texas cowboy and first settler here on the Bridger Trail about 1878.

Kirby Creek, Draw, and Oil Field, Hot Springs: named for Kris Kirby. The Hole-in-the-Wall gang once had a rendezvous on Kirby Creek.

Kirkland Lake and Mountain, Fremont: named for A. R. Kirkland, rancher.

Kirtley, Niobrara: discontinued post office named for Emma Kirtley, postmaster. Mr. and Mrs. S. L. Kirtley came here in 1891 in a covered wagon from an Oregon community; originally it was known as Pleasant Ridge.

Kirwin, Park: a mining town founded in 1885 by William Kirwin. prospector, who made a small gold strike. The company drilled here for copper and molybdenum with a diamond drill; the town of about 2,000 became a ghost town. A giant snow slide in 1907 wiped away the remaining buildings.

Amelia Earhart also staked a mining claim here; wanted to build a house and retire here in land of vast distances and snow-capped peaks where the air and water were crystal clear. Three rounds of her log house were up, when she was reported lost in her flight over the Pacific in 1937. She was the first woman to cross the Atlantic in a plane in 1928; she crossed solo in 1932 in 13 hours and 30 minutes, setting a new record.

Kisinger Lakes, Fremont: named for a pioneer by that name.

Kitty Creek, Park: named for Kitty Chatfield, wife of Frank Chatfield. They were ambitious pioneers from Oregon who milked cows in Sunlight basin in 1885, and sold butter in Cooke City, Montana. They moved in a mowing machine, piece by piece, on pack saddles; prospected for gold in their spare time; whip-sawed lumber to build flumes and sluices for their placer mining. Kitty was wounded in her arm with a shotgun blast, and died in Cody in 1909.

Kiwanis Spring, Albany: picnic facilities in Telephone Canyon; spring has dried up.

Kleenburn, Sheridan: when a coal syndicate bought the coal camps north of Sheridan in 1920, they offered a prize in their Chicago office for a new name. Kleenburn, describing the coal of the region, won; however, old name of Carneyville was also used; the post office at Kleenburn was discontinued in 1933. It is now revived ghost town.

Kleer Creek, Albany: named for Kleer who lived here about 1900.

Klondike, Johnson: Frank Jones, a hunter at Fort McKinney, went to Alaska during the gold rush, and returned with a moderate fortune to live on a ranch with his wife's folks. He had the nickname "Klondike," which became the name of the post office; it was discontinued.

Klondike Canyon, Johnson: deep, rugged canyon in Big Horn Mountains; it boasts good hiking and fishing.

Klondike Lake and Peak, 13,100, Fremont: located in glacier land; named for the Alaska region by the Department of Interior.

Klondike Lake and Peak, Johnson: named for "Klondike" Jones.

Klondyke, Johnson: post office named for Klondyke Jones.

Knife Point Mountains, 13,007, Sublette: named for the sharpness of the ridge, probably by the USGS party in 1906.

Knight, Uinta: railroad station named for Judge Jesse Knight, an early ranch owner, who showed railroad engineers how to change the line to avoid the steep grade of Aspen Hills; suggested the feasibility of the present Aspen tunnel. He brought the first trees to Evanston and planted them after his son had picked a blade of grass, and asked if it were a tree.

Kooi, Sheridan: a mining town named for Peter Kooi, owner of the mine until it was sold to the Peabody Syndicate in 1920.

Kortes Reservoir, Carbon: named for the nearby Kortes Ranch; started in 1946 and completed in 1951; only 83 acre-feet of water, a height that permits great generation of electric power; dedicated in 1950 by President Harry Truman; a special automobile license was made for him.

Kosine Draw, Sheridan: named for Kosine, rancher.

Koven, Mount Theodore, 13,200, Fremont, Sublette: named for Theodore G. Koven, who made many first ascents in the Wind River Range; he lost his life on Mt. McKinley in 1932.

114

Kyle, Carbon: named for Kyle, oilman.

Kyle Oil Camp, Carbon: named for Kyle who had the original government lease on land here, and brought in the first oil well.

L

LAK Ranch, Weston: named for the brand of R. C. Lake (L), Samuel W. Allenton (A), and C. A. King (K); Chicago bankers and cattlemen who were the first to raise purebred Herefords in the region. J. C. Spencer bought out their interests in 1895; he sold to an Ohio Company in 1914; recreational area. See Jenney's Stockade.

LaBarge, Lincoln: named for LaBarge Creek.

LaBarge Creek, Lincoln, Sublette: named by Gen. Ashley in 1824 for Capt. Joseph LaBarge, a distinguished Missouri River pilot who started coming to the Wyoming Indian country when he was 16.

LaBarge Oil Field, Lincoln: named for LaBarge Creek; marked with flat-topped buttes; when the oil boom was on in 1920s, optimists called the town Tulsa, for the Oklahoma oil city; in 1935 when the boom had collapsed, the field took the name of a nearby creek.

LaBelle, Crook: post office on the Belle Fourche River. Jacob L. Kaufman, "Jew Jake," was the first postmaster in 1888. Patrons ducked under a 2x4, and sorted out their own mail, piled on a table in the corner of the store. When a postal inspector saw this, he moved the post office to Sundance.

LaBonte, Converse: a Mormon station, a stage station, and a Pony Express station; it was called Camp Marshall in 1883; named for LaBonte, a trapper and trader who frequented the region in the 1830s. LaBonte stage station was built in 1863; Overland stages changed horses here; it was closed in 1869. LaBonte is believed killed by Ute Indians about 1840 in Utah.

LaBonte Canyon and Creek, Albany, Converse: named for LaBonte, he was a member of the Richard Woolston expedition of 1838.

Laddie Creek, Big Horn: a corruption of Lettie Creek, for Lettie Kieth, who made the first garden in Bighorn basin.

Ladd Peak, 12,900, Sublette: named for noted mountaineer Dr. William S. Ladd, who ascended it in 1921. Dr. Ladd was president of American Alpine Club from 1929-1931; founder and donor of its clubhouse in New York City; friend of mankind. He took the aged Alaskan sourdough guide, Andy Taylor, into his Hudson River home.

LaGrange, Goshen: named for Kale LaGrange, rancher; incorporated in 1889; coldest town in Goshen County.

Lake Alice, Lincoln: named for Alice, the wife of a discoverer of a copper mine here; the mine was worked for a few years.

Lake Cameahwait, Goshen: named for Chief Cameahwait, a Shoshone.

Lake Christine, Johnson: named for Christine Fordyce of Tepee Lodge.

Lake Creek, Albany, Carbon: a branch of Douglas Creek; so named because it has a small lake at this source.

Lake Creek, Teton: originates in Phelps Lake, hence the name.

Lake DeSmet, Johnson: named for Father Pierre Jean DeSmet, who saw it in 1840 as he trekked westward with a party of fur trappers. The lake is surrounded by treeless hills, and springs suddenly into view, a huge, sparkling gem.

Lake DeSmet is very deep, and lies over masses of coal; some claim that sea monsters, survivors of prehistoric monsters, inhabit its depths, and rise to view at night. Indians thought it the home of evil spirits. The lake has good fishing, boating, and water skiing; there is an airfield here for landing planes.

Vast industrial power plants and strip coal mining will change the lake and surrounding scenic areas.

Lake Elsie, Big Horn: named for Elsa Spear Byron, a Sheridan author and historian; it was stocked with trout by the Spear family in 1923; they had a dude camp nearby.

Lake Hattie, Albany: named for Hattie Phillips.

Lake Helen, Big Horn: named for Helen Chatfield; located in the Cloud Peak Primitive Area.

Lake Ione, Albany: once a huge lake, but now a hay meadow; named in the 1860s for the Ione Investment Company, controlled by Ione, an Englishman.

Lake Leigh, Teton: named for "Beaver Dick" Leigh, trapper and guide for the Hayden expedition. Leigh was called "Beaver Dick" for his resemblance to that toothy animal. The lake was formed by glaciers.

Lake Louise, Fremont: good fishing; golden trout.

Lake Marie, Albany: named for Mrs. Mary Bellamy by her husband Charles in 1879. Mary Bellany was Wyoming's first woman legislator; elected from Albany County in 1910. She worked for the protection of women's and children's rights. Lake Marie is in the Snowy Range; it lies in a recess among granite cliffs at the base of Medicine Bow Peak in an alpine setting.

Lake Marion, Big Horn: scenic lake on a trail in the Bighorn National Forest.

Lake Mead, Johnson: named for Elwood Mead, the first state engineer of Wyoming, and the father of reclamation in the state.

Lake Mondell, Weston: named for Frank W. Mondell, U.S. Representative from Wyoming from 1899-1923.

Lake Mountain, 9,750, Albany: takes its name from Lake Creek.

Lake Owen, Albany: named for William O. Owen, pioneer surveyor in the 1870s.

Lake Solitude, Big Horn: was named by F. E. Matthes, topographer. He wrote: "The Cloud Peak region was the first high mountain district I was called upon to map for the Geological Survey. When I beheld that lovely tranquil lake on Paintrock Creek, I broke my vow to abstain from naming any features of the country. I named it Lake Solitude. . . . It thrilled me because it renders so vividly the awesome grandeur and utter wildness of that boldly sculptured mountain country. Lake Solitude is one of the most beautiful mountain lakes in existence."

Because it is in a primitive area into which roads may not be built, Lake Solitude still lies tucked away in its deep wilderness. It can be reached by trails maintained by the Forest Service. Ranchers who graze this land must check their cattle on horseback.

Lake Solitude, Fremont: lies in the Glacier Primitive Area at the head of Glacier Canyon.

Lake Solitude, Teton: fills a glacial basin; it can be reached by trails; there is a magnificent view from here of the north side of the Tetons.

Lakeview, Goshen: discontinued post office; named for a little lake on one of the branches of Cherry Creek.

Lakota, Carbon: an old camp east of Benton; named for Lakota sand, an oil-bearing stratum.

Lamar Mountain and River, 10,560, YNP: named for L. Q. C. Lamar, Secretary of Interior in 1886. Buffalo can often be seen in the Lamar Valley.

Lamont, Carbon: named for James Lamont, rancher who installed one of the first windmills in the area.

Lamoreaux Meadows, Fremont: named for Jules Lamoreaux, early freighter and store owner at South Pass City in the 1870s, He had an Indian wife and a son named Willow. Legend says that after her baby is born, an Indian woman has the tepee flap opened, and names baby for the first thing she sees.

Lance Creek, Niobrara: name appears on 1860 map; was given creek because of black, or water ash which then grew along its banks. Indian used this wood to make lance and spear handles.

Lance Creek has the distinction of flowing near the site where the first dinosaur fossils were ever found in the United States. These limestone fossil beds have yielded some of the best Triceratops, three-horned monster, bones; also those of Trachodon, the duck-billed beast. Paleontologists believe that great herds of prehistoric animals made their home here, when swamps and lakes covered the land.

Lance Creek, Niobrara: an inland village which grew with the development of the oil field; named for Lance Creek.

Lance Creek Oil Field, Niobrara: Three wells in Cow Gulch heralded the Lance Creek activity in 1917; within a year 25 rigs were operating; freighting to this new field was heavy; used over the 30-mile rough road from Lusk Railroad.

A pipeline was started in 1919. Lance Creek exceeded the great Salt Creek field in oil production by 1939, producing more than seven million barrels that year; it led the state in oil production from 1939-45.

Lance Creek Stage Station, Niobrara: see May's Ranch.

Lander, Fremont: county seat; originally known as Push Root because warm spring winds seemed to push plants "up by their roots"; also Camp Brown, which see; renamed for Gen. F. W. Lander, who was sent by the government in 1857 to survey along the Oregon Trail and improve the roads; he established the Lander Cut-off.

B. F. Lowe was the first owner of land where Lander now is; he was a good friend of Gen. Lander, and so named the town for him in 1869. Main street was a natural Indian and game trail, also much traveled by trappers and explorers. Indians called it the alley of warm winds.

First commercial rodeo was held in Lander in 1863. It is the home of Albert "Stub" Farlow, prominent cowboy whose picture on bronco Deadman was the silhouette which Secretary of State Lester C. Hunt chose to adorn Wyoming auto license plates. Allen True, a Denver artist, made the design from a photograph. This Wyoming license plate of 1936 started a nation-wide trend to adorn license plates with something symbolic of the state they represent.

Chicago and Northwestern Railroad got to Lander in 1906; now discontinued. The State Training School for the mentally retarded is located here. A museum with Indian beadwork and many pioneer relics decorate the rooms of the Noble Hotel. Lander is noted for its annual one-shot antelope hunt and cutter races. The Interstate Association of Cutter Racing meets in Lander in January; more than 60 teams compete. Pioneer Museum spotlights relics and historical exhibits. Claims to be the most "unwindy" spot in Wyoming.

Paul Petzoldt's National Outdoor Leadership School is based in Lander, teaching mountain climbing and wilderness survival.

Lander Cut-off, Fremont, Lincoln, Sublette; named for Gen. F. W. Lander, who in the spring of 1858 paid Chief Washakie and his Shoshones for a right of way through their territory. He directed construction of a road, leaving the old Oregon Trail at Burnt Ranch, and going through Big Piney Pass and Smoot in Lincoln County; this shortened the trail by about 200 miles.

Lander, Mount, 12,623, Fremont: named for Gen. Lander.

Lander Peak, 10,456, Lincoln: named for Gen. Lander.

Langford Mountain, 10,600, YNP: named by Washburn party of 1870 for N. P. Langford, first superintendent of Yellowstone National Park. He made the first authentic sketch of Yellowstone Lake from the summit of this mountain.

Lankin Dome, Fremont: a rough, granite dome for August Lankin, early rancher who lived here.

Lannigan Lakes, Fremont: named for Edward and James Lannigan, ranchers.

LaPrele, Converse: a stage, telegraph, and Pony Express station on LaPrele Creek, for which it was named.

LaPrele Creek, Converse: named by early trappers for the scouring rush or horsetail grass, called prele by French, that grows on its banks. Ayres Natural Bridge arches over LaPrele Creek.

Prairie is a French name for meadows. Early trappers had no name for the wide, open spaces, and called them "prairies." English-speaking pioneers adopted the name.

118

LaPrele Dam, Converse: named for the creek; constructed in 1907-1908.

Laramie, Albany: county seat; called Gem City; named for the Laramie River; first record of a settlement here was in 1867; the first train on the Union Pacific Railroad arrived in 1868, and with it all the riff-raff that comes to the "end of the trail" town. Organized gangs terrorized citizens; vigilantes could not control dance halls, or stop gun battles. The Dakota Legislature dissolved local government, and placed Laramie under the jurisdiction of federal courts.

Under the suffrage act Judge J. H. Howe summoned women to serve on grand and petite juries in 1870. Six women jurors, first in the world, meted out justice, and helped restore law and order. Mrs. Mary Atkinson, appointed by Sheriff Boswell, was the first woman bailiff in the world, and served with both the grand and petite juries. British women congratulated the women of Laramie and of Wyoming on the triumph they had won for women of the world in emancipating them from political serfdom.

The right of Women Suffrage, was given to the women of Wyoming December 10, 1869, when Wyoming became a territory. At the first general election of September 6, 1870, Mrs. Elza Swain, age 70, became the first woman to vote in such an election; she lived in Laramie.

President Theodore Roosevelt was a visitor in Laramie in 1905; with an escort of friends he rode horseback to Cheyenne over Sherman Hill.

The University of Wyoming is located in Laramie; its geological museum has a skeleton of a Brontosaurus, the dinosaur; and a mammoth skull found near Rawlins. Monolith Portland cement plant produced more than a million barrels of cement yearly.

Laramie County: was created by Dakota Legislature in 1867; the first county in Wyoming; named for Jacques LaRamie, the trapper. Within a year Carter, Carbon, and Albany counties were formed, cutting Laramie County drastically in size. County was organized in 1886; county seat moved from Fort Sanders to Cheyenne.

The first territorial legislature, 1869, chose Cheyenne as state capital; legislature of 1886 authorized the construction of a building, a stately edifice of Rawlins sandstone with a golden dome.

Laramie County Community College opened in 1969 on a large campus; has vocational and technical training plus regular courses; enrollment growth has been rapid.

Laramie, Hahn's Peak and Pacific Railroad, Albany: built across Laramie Plain to Centennial, and south into Colorado by 1907.

Laramie Peak, 10,274, Albany: named for Laramie River; rises more than a mile above the surrounding land; is visible for more than a hundred miles to south, east, and north; was a landmark for emigrants on the Oregon Trail. Weather can be predicted by clouds clustering around its peak.

A microwave station was installed on top of the peak in 1962. Helicopters carried in the equipment to install the towers.

Laramie Plains, Albany: these grass-rich plains lie at a high altitude, surrounded by mountains. A trader turned his oxen loose here in a winter storm in 1863, and left them to die; in the spring he found them fattened on the short, oily western grass that cures where it grows into nourishing feed. These plains are crossed by main lines of east-west travel today, as they were a century ago.

Laramie Range, Albany, Laramie, Natrona, Platte: once called the Black Hills; named for Laramie River; Laramie Peak is the highest point.

Laramie River, also Little, and North Laramie rivers: Albany, Goshen, Platte: named for Jacques LaRamie or LaRamee, French-Canadian trapper killed by Arapahoes on that river in 1818 or 1819 according to Jim Bridger. LaRamie was known as an honest and sincere man, well-liked by most Indians.

Francis Parkman, author, lived with Sioux Indians on the Laramie River for 17 days in 1846; he ate puppy with them; was bothered with dysentery; but was determined to stay and hunt buffalo with them, which he did.

W. G. Bullock and B. B. Mills of Fort Laramie brought 250 cows and several bulls to the Laramie River region in 1868; this was the first permanent herd of range cattle, and marked a new era; ranching on free range boomed until the big "die-off" of 1886-87; blizzards raged all winter; no chinook came to melt the crusted snow; great piles of dead cattle and a few staggering skeletons were found in the spring; end of another era. In 1887 cowboys started riding mowing machines and hay rakes; homesteaders built fences, and put up windmills.

Lariat, Sheridan: railroad station named for a cowboy's lariat.

Latham, Sweetwater: once a stage station; now a railroad station; named for Dr. Latham, surgeon of the Union Pacific Railroad.

Lathrop, George, Monument, Niobrara: a monument dedicated to all stage drivers, the astronauts of the 1870s and 1880s. The monument is over the grave of George Lathrop, first and last driver of the Cheyenne-Deadwood stage; near the site of Running Water Station, established in 1876.

George Lathrop, a most reliable driver, had as his cherished possession a whip with a 20-foot lash; the whip stock was covered with solid silver ferrules for a length of two feet. One spring in 1886 at 2 a.m. in a howling blizzard, with the mercury at 35 degrees below zero, the rear axle of the swaying coach snapped in two. Lathrop left his passengers bundled in buffalo robes and hay and rode 12 miles to Rawhide Buttes station for help. A passenger who rode with him said, "The horse I rode bareback was gray in color, and I never did get all the white hairs out of my black trousers."

Laughing Pig, Park: volcanic rock weathered to the appearance of a laughing pig on scenic road from Cody to Yellowstone National Park.

Lava Mountain, 10,400, Fremont: named for its reddish color.

Lavoye, Natrona: oil field ghost town for Louis Lavoye, homesteader of land here. Thriving town in 1924 when the Ohio Oil Company gave everyone a 30-day notice to move. More than 1,000 resisted; the marshall arrived with eviction papers. Buildings were jacked up on wheels and moved a few miles to a new Lavoye; for six months moving buildings were scattered over the prairie.

Lawver, Campbell: discontinued post office named for Lawver, homesteader.

Leather Pool, YNP: originally lined with brown algae; since 1959 it has been a clear, blue pool; in Lower Geyser Basin.

120

LeClair Ditch, Fremont: named for Edmond LeClair, foreman of constructon company; his father was an interpreter for Chief Washakie; his grandfather, Louis LeClair, married a Shoshone woman.

Ledogar Flats, Crook: named for Jake Ledogar.

Lee City, Park: old mining camp about 1890 at the head of Sunlight Creek; all gone now.

Lee Creek, Washakie: named for Lord Guilalee, English sportsman; once a favorite hunting ground for Indians. Many arrowheads are found here.

Lee Mountain, Albany: named for Charles Lee, early rancher.

Leeds Creek, Fremont: named for Abe Leeds, packer and guide about 1891. He led the first party of surveyors establishing section lines north of Dubois.

Leek Canyon, Teton: named for Stephen Leek, homesteader in 1889, guide, rancher, and author connected with the Forest Service. His lectures and famous photographs brought the first national attention to the starving elk herds in Jackson Hole.

LeHardy's Rapids, YNP: named for Paul LeHardy, topographer for Capt. Jones in 1873.

Leidy Mountain, 10,317, Teton: geologically much older than Tetons. Mount Leidy highlands are plateaus much broken by erosion and heavily timbered; summit ridges are bare; there are gravel beds of ancient streams; named for Prof. Joseph Leidy, anatomist on Hayden Survey.

Leigh Canyon, Creek, and Lake, Teton: named for Richard Leigh, "Beaver Dick," Hayden guide and Jackson Hole pioneer. Leigh Lake was glacier-formed. A 4.6-mile trail for hiking is maintained here by the Forest Service.

Leigh Creek, Washakie: named for Gilbert Leigh; see Leigh Peak.

Leigh Monument Peak, 7,500, Washakie: named for Gilbert Leigh, Englishman who was killed in a fall from the cliff in 1884. He lived on a ranch near Tensleep, and made frequent trips to the peak. One day his horse returned riderless; buzzards led searchers to his body in a tree at the foot of the cliff.

Leiter, Sheridan: post office for Joseph Leiter who was connected with the irrigation project of Lake DeSmet.

Lemonade Lake, YNP: named for its yellow-green water.

Lenore, Fremont: discontinued post office named for Lenore, daughter of W. T. Judkins, first postmaster and rancher.

LeRoy, Uinta: discontinued post office; railroad station named for LeRoy, a section foreman in the 1870s.

Leslie, Albany: discontinued post office named for Dr. Swigart's daughter Leslie.

Lester, Mount, 12,325, Sublette: named for Lester Faler, pioneer packer.

Leucite Hills, Carbon: volcanic rocks formed in little, conical peaks; named for their mineral leucite content, a fine potash-rich silicate.

Leverette, Niobrara: discontinued post office named by postmaster Paul Miller for a town in France, Leverette, where his brother was killed in World War I.

Levitt Slide, Uinta: a sharp incline out of Bridger Valley into Cottonwood Creek region. This opening was made by Daniel Levitt for dragging timber down into the valley.

Lewis Lake, Albany: in the Snowy Range; named for Lewis, a miner.

Lewis Lake, Falls, and River, YNP: named for Meriwether Lewis of the Lewis and Clark expedition of 1804-06. They did not enter what is now Wyoming, but in passing to the north, they named several rivers that rise in Wyoming. They have several geographic features named for them.

Lewiston, Fremont: camp first called Strawberry Creek, where this gold vein was located; renamed when a Mr. Lewis came from Denver, and erected a stamp mill here with his investors' money. Prospectors panned for gold on Strawberry Creek long after other creeks were abandoned.

Lewiston Lakes, Fremont: named for Mr. Lewis, gold mining promoter.

Libby Creek, Albany: named for George Libby, prospector in the 1870s. The name was on the map before John Maraden came, so it was not named for his sister Elzabeth.

Libby Flats, Albany: named for Libby Creek; from these heights water (1) can flow west into Platte River via French or Brush creeks, and make a big loop around Casper Mountain; after traveling more than 500 miles, it may be joined by water (2) that fell only a foot farther north on Libby Flats, and flowed 200 miles via Libby Creek and Laramie River to meet (1) in the Platte River.

Lick Creek, Sheridan: deer and elk lick for mineral salts in the canyon through which the creek flows.

Lightning Creek, Converse, Niobrara: named for violent lightning storms. On this creek in 1903 the last armed engagement between Sioux Indians and white men was fought. Eagle Feather and a group of Indians from Pine Ridge Reservation in South Dakota had a written permit from Major John R. Brennan, Indian agent, allowing them to hunt in Wyoming. They had traveled through Weston and Converse counties, shooting deer, antelope, and sage hens. Their women and children were with them on a happy hunt.

Sheriff Miller from Newcastle with a posse of stockmen pursued the Indians, overtaking them at Lightning Creek in Converse County; the site is now in Niobrara County. The Indians, feeling they were within their rights, resisted arrest. In the ensuing battle, Sheriff Miller, his deputy, and several Indians were killed, while the rest fled back to the reservation. At a hearing held later in Douglas, the Indians were released for lack of evidence that they had committed any crime.

Lightning Flat, Crook: discontinued post office; railroad station named for flats on which lightning storms occur.

Lily Lake, Teton: full of large water lilies that are hardy even though the lake freezes solid in winter.

Linch, Johnson: village named for the Linch family. Oil wells were drilled here in 1947.

122

Lincoln County: created in 1911; organized in 1913 with Kemmerer as county seat; named for Abraham Lincoln, 16th President of United States. Robert T. Lincoln wrote to those instrumental in naming the county: "I am much gratified to learn that a large county in the State of Wyoming has been named in honor of my father. As his son, I greatly appreciate so distinguished a mark of estimation in which his memory is held."

Lincoln County contains the very fertile Star Valley, famous for its dairy and agricultural products.

Lincoln Highway, US 30 across southern Wyoming; so named because it was authorized in 1912, the centennial anniversary of the birth of Abraham Lincoln.

Near the summit of Sherman Hill on the Lincoln Highway is an impressive, bronze bust of Lincoln, 12½ feet tall, resting on a 30-foot granite base. This statue is the dream and work of Robert I. Russin, art professor at the University of Wyoming. It was financed by Dr. Charles W. Jeffrey of Rawlins. A transcontinental railroad, binding the country together, was one of Abraham Lincoln's ambitions; it is especially fitting that his statue should stand here so close to Union Pacific tracks.

The inscription on the monument are the words of Lincoln: "We must think anew and act anew." Looking out over the beauty of Wyoming, Lincoln's sad, craggy face seems to be asking, "Why should there not be patient confidence in the ultimate justice of the people? Is there any better or equal hope in the world?"

Lincoln Ridge with Lincoln Point, 11,100, Fremont: a vast rugged ridge of volcanic origin; part of Absaroka Mountains; named for Abraham Lincoln.

Lindbergh, Laramie: discontinued post office first known as Salem; renamed for Charles A. Lindbergh, who made his solo flight to Paris in 1927; now a railroad station.

Linden, Crook: discontinued post office; established in 1888 at the road ranch of Edgar C. Wakeman. His wife chose this name because of the beauty of the locality.

Lingle, Goshen: named for Hiram Lingle, a great promoter of the valley and its agriculture; irrigated crops are raised here.

Lingle is across the Platte River from the site of the Grattan Massacre of 1854. This started 35 years of warfare on the plains.

Lion Geyser, YNP: its bursts of steam sound like a lion's roar.

Lion Rock, Teton: a rock on the Red Hill of Gros Ventre Mountains resembles a lion lying down.

Lionkol, Sweetwater: discontinued post office; highway junction and railroad station; the name is a condensation of Lion Coal Company.

Lisa's Fort, Teton: named for Manuel Lisa, trapper.

Little America, Sweetwater: in the 1890s a young sheepherder, lost in a wild Wyoming blizzard, made a promise to himself that if he ever got back to a warm fire and out of the 40-degrees-below-zero cold, he would build a shelter for all in the middle of this desert.

S. M. Covey did survive, and, thinking of Admiral Byrd's Little America in Antarctica, named his first building Little America in 1932. This store was relocated with Highway 30 in 1950, and has grown into a sprawling complex of gasoline pumps, shops, restaurants, and motels. Each year it is visited by more than a million people, three times the population of Wyoming. A promise fulfilled has become a very profitable dream.

Little Bear, Laramie: stage station on Cheyenne-Deadwood Trail; discontinued post office; named for Little Bear Creek.

Little Brooklyn Lake, Albany; named for the Brooklyn Mine about 1900.

Little Goose Creek, Johnson, Sheridan: named for the great numbers of wild geese that once stopped here. It was in this region that Calamity Jane, Martha Jane Canary, the rough and tender-hearted bullwhacker of the frontier, claimed she received her name.

She was riding scout with the troops when they tangled with Indians. She saw Captain Egan fall from his horse. After killing an Indian, Calamity threw Capt. Egan in front of her on the horse, and rode to safety. The captain, back at the post, said, "I name you Calamity Jane, heroine of the plains."

Little Medicine, Albany: discontinued post office named for Little Medicine River, which got its name from Indians for the wood that grew along its banks which was good for making bows and arrows.

Little Missouri River, Crook: rises in this county. Indian name was Wakpa Chan Shoka, heavily wooded river; named for the Missouri River into which it flows in western North Dakota. Missouri is the name of an Indian tribe.

Little Mountain, 9,200, Sweetwater: highest point in the county; a road leads to the summit of this pleasant, pine-wooded peak.

Little Piney Creek, Sheridan: named for the pines through which it flows; a very picturesque part of the Big Horn Mountains.

Little Powder, Campbell: discontinued post office on the present site of the Elmore Ranch.

Little Quadrant Mountain, 10,216, YNP: named for its shape; north and west slopes have curved surfaces, resembling a sphere.

Little Rock Creek, Park: named for an Indian scout, Little Rock, who was killed there.

Little Sandy Crossing, Fremont: an emigrant campsite as well as stage and Pony Express station in the 1860s. From here emigrants struck out across arid land to Big Sandy. The trip from here to Green River was a very dry 35 miles, often made in the cool of the night; this trek across the desert usually ended with empty water casks and with a wild scramble for the river.

Little Scotland, Fremont: named for a settler from Scotland.

Little Snake River, Carbon: named for its numerous turns and bends; flows back and forth into Colorado and Wyoming several times.

Little's Peak, 10,710, Teton: name comes from old Forest Service maps. This is a high point on the divide between Leigh and South Leigh creeks. USGS station was established here by the Bannon party in 1898.

124

Lizzard Head Peak, 12,842, Fremont: named by the survey party of 1877 for its shape. One of the party thought it should be named blizzard because of the number of snow squalls that formed here.

Loch Leven Lake, Fremont: named for species of trout planted here in the early 1930s; 18 acres in size.

Lockett, Converse: railroad station named for Lockett brothers.

Lodgepole Creek, Park: when the Nez Perce Indians fled, they left many tepee poles here.

Logging Creek, Sheridan: Shane Tie Company used this Creek to float logs to the Tongue River during timbering operations there.

London Flats, Goshen: named for John London, post trader at Fort Laramie, who owned considerable property there.

Lone Tree Pass, Albany: when Gen. Grenville Dodge, engineer for the Union Pacific railroad, was scouting in 1865 west of present Cheyenne for a route for the railroad to cross the big hill, he and his party were chased by Indians, and they found a pass out. It was marked by a lone pine growing out of a granite boulder; later, the pass was named Evans Pass. This much photographed tree is now protected from vandalism by a fence.

Lonetree, Uinta: stage stop; discontinued post office; marked by a lone, but majestic, pine tree, which was a landmark for pioneers; named in 1872 when Mr. and Mrs. Hoops arrived by ox team with a small herd of cattle.

Long Draw, Albany: named in 1890 by a roundup cook, Harvey, who walked the draw, and that evening told the boys, "It was the d--- longest draw I ever seed."

Lookout, Albany: discontinued post office; railroad station named in 1868 by railroad officials, because it was a high point from which they could see a great distance in all directions.

Lorey, Carbon: a road ranch on the Rawlins-Lander stage route; Mrs. McLaughlin soon closed down; the following verse explains why:
    There was an old woman who lived at Lorey,
    She built a Post Office and thought it would pay.
    She fed a tramp,
    And cancelled a stamp,
    And that was the business for the day.

Lost Cabin, Fremont: village built in the 1900s by John Broderick Okie; he came to Wyoming penniless; started as a cowboy and became a sheepherder; he started collecting property; eventually his vast holdings of land, livestock, and a chain of general stores made him a millionaire.

He built a castle-like mansion on Bad Water Creek; it was called "Big Tepee" by Indians who had never seen such a house. Okie built the whole village around his home, calling it Lost Cabin for the Lost Cabin Mine. He hired Japanese gardeners to produce green lawns and flowers; peacocks strutted in the yard; a greenhouse furnished flowers for his elaborate entertaining.

While the rest of Wyoming was lit with kerosene lamps, Lost Cabin gleamed with carbide lights. The first story of his mansion was of native stone; the second story of lumber freighted in by wagons. A veranda encircled most of the house, which had a grand hallway. Okie drowned while shooting ducks in a nearby reservoir.

Lost Cabin, sagging with age, is now a ranch. The main road used to go past Lost Cabin, over Birdseye Pass to the Bighorn Basin. After a highway was blasted through Wind River Canyon, this road was abandoned.

Lost Cabin Mine: since the mine has never been found, there are versions of it being in Fremont, Johnson, and Natrona counties. Before the Civil War, a party of Swedes found gold somewhere in the Big Horn Mountains and built a cabin there; attacked by Indians, all but two were killed. These two came to Fort Laramie, and asked the sutler there to keep some baking powder cans for them; these contained about $7,000 in coarse gold; in the spring they left with their gold and were never heard of again; another version is that one Swede staggered in with the gold and died before he could tell where the cabin was.

Another story is that Albert Hulburt came in 1849, built a raft, and floated down the Bighorn River; he found a rich vein of gold, built a cabin, and fled from Indians without leaving any landmarks. Later he took a group back, and they wandered all summer without finding the cabin or gold; when they wanted to kill Hulburt for fooling them, he fled the second time.

Yet another story is that men from Kentucky were shown by Indians where the gold was; they built a cabin, but never told where it was when they came to Fort Laramie for supplies.

Lost Creek, Fremont, Sweetwater: Minnie McCormick, a widow with several children to support, found yellow crystals along this creek one day in the 1930s; thinking them uranium, she sent samples to Madame Curie in Paris, who confirmed it. Mrs. McCormick could find no one to finance the mining, and her find lay untouched for years, hence name of creek.

Lost Ecstacy Lake, Sheridan: named for the novel *Lost Ecstacy*, written by Mary Roberts Rinehart in the Big Horn Mountains.

Lost Lake, Albany: so named because it is hard to find.

Lost Soldier Creek, Lake, and Oil Field, Carbon: soldiers from Fort Fred Steele in 1880 heard of a place in the hills, where whiskey was being made. They failed to find the whiskey and got lost in a snow storm; only one soldier returned; the other two died, although a fruitless search was made for them.

Lost Springs, Converse: village named for a stream that sinks out of sight in places and then reappears; smallest incorporated town with a post office in the United States.

Louis Lake, Fremont: pronounced Louie; Big Mountain Country Lodge is here; fishing, skiing, accommodations.

Louisiana Territory: in 1682 explorer LaSalle took possession of western lands drained by the Mississippi River for France, and named them Louisiana for King Louis XIV. Under President Jefferson in 1803 the United States bought Louisiana for $15,000,000, or less than 2½ cents per acre. This purchase included more than two-thirds of present Wyoming, which has been in eight territories: Louisiana, Missouri, Nebraska, Dakota, Oregon, Washington, Idaho, and Utah. The land west of the Continental Divide was a part of New Spain or Mexico.

Lovell, Big Horn: town began in 1900 in a log cabin store of Nathan Thaxton on the banks of the Stinking Water, now the Shoshone River.

Mormons came to the region in 1901; the town was moved to the road ranch of Ira Water. When the railroad came, it was moved to a railroad site. Lots were laid out and priced high; in the night residents led by Bishop Jolley moved the post office, newspaper, real state office, and other buildings to cheaper land, where Lovell now stands; named for Henry T. Lovell, a rancher who came in 1880.

A glass factory was started in Lovell in 1920; Belgian workers hand-crafted glass from silica sand; the building burned in 1928; a brick and tile plant soon opened. Big Horn Academy started in 1909; it was moved to Cowley in 1910 and became a high school there in 1920. Lovell is now a town of roses; it has a sugar beet factory and gypsum plant. Cutter races are a winter sport.

Lovers Lane, Teton: a scenic spot at the mouth of Teton Canyon.

Luce, Park: discontinued post office named for Maud G. Luce, postmaster.

Lucerne, Hot Springs: named by railroad officials for one of the principal crops in the region; luzerne is the French word for alfalfa.

Luman Creek, Albany: named for Luman, a trapper, who was fatally chewed by a bear in 1890. He dragged himself to Fort Laramie; before he died, he said he had gold buried in this creek; it has never been found.

Lunch Lake, Teton: where John D. Rockefeller and his son Laurance often ate their lunch, while feasting their eyes on the beauty of the Tetons, and planning for the preservation of the natural surroundings.

Lusk, Niobrara: in 1880 McHenry, a prospector, started mining a hill he called Silver Cliff. A large stone barn northwest of the hill, constructed by Jack Madden, squatter, was their camp site.

Miners, living in tents, 1885, worked the hill for gold, silver, copper, and the first uranium in Wyoming; a large mill was constructed, and considerable ore mined. Then finances from the New York Company failed to come; miners were paid in worthless checks; angry, they hung the owner of the mine in effigy, and the project ended. Machinery was torn down in 1898, and shipped to New Mexico.

Cheyenne-Deadwood stage started and established a station at the stone barn, called Running Water, one of the early names for the Niobrara River, near which the barn was located.

When the Fremont, Elkhorn, and Missouri Valley railroad came through in 1886, land for a station and town was given by Frank Lusk, rancher. The settlements known as Silver Cliff, Running Water, and New Rochelle—for Albert Rochelle—became Lusk.

In 1880s Lusk was at the crossing of the Cheyenne-Deadwood stage route, and the Texas Trail, on which thousands of cattle were driven from Texas to Wyoming and Montana from 1876-97. Today it is the county seat of Niobrara County, formed in 1911; it is at the crossing of Highways 85 and 20. A museum houses an old stagecoach and other relics of early days. Residents of Niobrara County enacted the pageant "Legend of Rawhide Buttes" for many years. See Rawhide Buttes.

Luther, Laramie: see Burns.

Lyman, Uinta: named for Francis M. W. Lyman, an apostle of the Mormon Church in 1898; originally called Owen for Owen Woodruff, who with Lyman started the town. An agricultural experiment station is here.

Lynch, Laramie: railroad siding named for P. J. Lynch, a Union Pacific railroad official.

Lyons, Fremont: discontinued post office named for Lyons, pioneer. It was settled in 1880 by ranchers and farmers and had a good school.

Lysite, Fremont: named for Jim Lysaght, prospector and miner; killed with his companion David by Indians in 1876 on Lysite Mountain. Spelling of the name was changed with usage.

A large wool warehouse was built here by John Broderick Okie of Lost Cabin. With a keen business sense, he filled the warehouse with wool in the spring, and shipped later, when prices went up.

Lysite Creek, Fremont, Hot Springs: named for Jim Lysaght.

Lysite Mountain, Fremont: named for Jim Lysaght; yellowish and blue-grey sand shales covered with heavy mantles of pebbles are now called lysite.

Lytle Hill, Crook: named for J. Lytle, pioneer.

M

M W Lake, Weston: named for the M W ranch on which the lake is located.

Mable Lake, Johnson: named for Mable Sage.

Macfarlane, Platte: discontinued post office; railroad station named for John or William Macfarlane, pioneers who drove cattle from Oregon.

MacKenzie Reservoir, Sheridan: named for Fort MacKenzie.

Macquette Creek, Park: named for Uncle George Macquette, one of the first settlers in Bighorn Basin.

Madden, Fremont: railroad station named for William Madden, sheepman and ex-senator.

Madison Junction, YNP: named for the Madison River; by a campfire here in 1870, members of the Washburn party decided that the natural features of what is now Yellowstone National Park were too magnificent and too valuable for personal exploitation; the idea of creating a national park was conceived here.

Madison Lake, Plateau, and River, YNP: River was named by Lewis and Clark, 1804-06 expedition, for James Madison, noted statesman, and later fourth President of the United States.

Maggie's Nipples, Carbon: two sharp-pointed hills named by cowboys for Maggie Baggs.

Mahoney Dome, Carbon: an oil dome located by John Mahoney and his son Frank. The first gas well here, which came in about 1920, provided Rawlins with gas for many years. The first oil well in 1930 had such a crooked hole it could not be used. In 1938 Sinclair Oil drilled the structure, and started oil production.

Mahoney Gap, Natrona: named for Timothy Mahoney, pioneer sheepman.

Mahoney Lakes, Carbon: named for John Mahoney; member of the cavalry at Fort Fred Steele for four years, worked on the railroad, and became a sheepherder; he learned the sheep business and became a prominent livestock man.

Mallo Canyon, Weston: named for Henry Mallo, early settler and land owner. Land purchased in 1935 by Walter Schoonmaker and given to Weston County for a recreation area. Large log lodge and log cabins were then built. Girl Scouts, church groups and 4-H clubs from several counties meet here.

Mammoth Glacier, Sublette: one of the large glaciers surrounding Gannett Peak.

Mammoth Hot Springs, YNP: sometimes called Capitol Hill. Here stood the buildings of old Fort Yellowstone, when the park was under the supervision of the War Department. First settlement began here in 1871 in two log cabins. In 1884 a hotel accommodated 800 guests, coming to bathe in the therapeutic waters of the springs.

Color in built-up terraces of travertine around the springs of flowing water is due to algae growth that reflects sunshine through a film of warm water. Richly decorated and beaded pipe-organ formations present a spectacle of unusual beauty.

Haynes started a photographic shop here in 1884; a stage company began in 1898 bringing in guests; 20,151 tourists and persons seeking medical relief came in horse-drawn vehicles in 1915.

Mammoth Kill site, Carbon: the drag line of an oil company snagged an ancient rib bone here in 1960. Scientists excavated for months uncovering the huge skeleton of a mammoth that once stood 11 feet high; he lived 12,000 years ago (Carbon 14 dating).

The mammoth had been trapped by prehistoric hunters in a bog; Clovis-type stone knives, scrapers, and stone tools were left where the hunters had feasted on the meat. The skull of the mammoth is now in the geological museum at the University of Wyoming. Leaves and plant pollen were also preserved in this ancient bog.

Manassa, Laramie: discontinued post office named for Jean Manassa.

Mandel, Albany: stage station on Rock Creek in 1863; moved because of Indians to the Little Laramie River; was on the Overland Trail until coming of the Union Pacific railroad in 1868; named for Phillip Mandel, one of the earliest settlers here and owner of stage station.

Mandel, Sheridan: discontinued post office for Mandel, postmaster. J. D. Loucks bought the land and post office building for $50 in 1882; he plotted the town of Sheridan on a piece of brown wrapping paper and named it for his Civil War commander, Gen. Philip H. Sheridan.

Manderson, Big Horn: first called Alamo; renamed in 1889 by railroad officials for Manderson, chief counsel for Burlington railroad.

Man-eater Canyon, Converse: Sheriff Malcolm Campbell caught Alfred Packer here and arrested him in 1883. Packer was convicted in Colorado for killing and eating five of his prospector companions in Colorado.

Mantz Creek, Albany: named in 1892 for Mack Mantz, rancher.

Manville, Niobrara: named for H. S. Manville, organizer of the Converse Cattle Company in the 1880s.

Marbleton, Sublette: founded by Charles P. Budd in 1912; there are six distinct types of log houses in the village; it served as an outfitting post for packers into mountain regions; it was later abandoned; named for A. H. Marble of Cheyenne.

Marcum, Sheridan: named for L. W. Markham, homesteader on top of Big Horn Mountains before the national forest was created; spelling of his name was changed.

Marguette, Big Horn: discontinued post office named for George Marguette.

Marie Lake, Albany: named for Mary Bellamy

Mariposa Lake, YNP: on Two Ocean plateau; named for the mariposa lily.

Marms Lake, Sublette: two lakes, close together, were dubbed Dad's and Marm's by fishermen.

Marna, Sublette: discontinued post office named by Mrs. Grace Snyder for a Nebraska town from which she came.

Marquette, Park: discontinued post office named for George Marquette, early French explorer; the place was covered in 1910 by the waters of Shoshone Reservoir.

Marshall, Albany: discontinued post office named for W. E. Marshall, postmaster.

Marston, Sweetwater: railroad station named for John Marston, master mechanic for the railroad at North Platte, Nebraska.

Marston Creek and Mountain, 11,321, Park: named for Charles Marston, rancher in the 1880s; he was also a guide for parties in Yellowstone National Park.

Martin's Cove, Natrona: see Devils Gate.

Mary Bay, YNP: named by H. W. Elliot, Hayden Survey, in 1871 for Miss Mary Force.

Mary Cooper Creek, Albany: named for Mary Cooper, homesteader.

Mary Lake and Mary Mountain, 8,500, YNP: named in 1873 by a tourist party for Mary Clark, member of the party.

Marysvale, Teton: ranch post office in 1892 named for the first postmaster, Mrs. Mary White. When Mrs. John Simpson became postmaster in 1896, she moved the post office to her ranch, land on which Jackson now stands; she then changed the name to Jackson for Jackson Hole.

Mason, Sublette: discontinued post office that was named in 1903 by postmaster C. Y. Phillips for his son Mason.

Massacre Hill, Sheridan: site of Fetterman fight in 1866; see Fort Phil Kearny.

Mather Peak, 2,410, Big Horn, Johnson: shaped like a four-leaf clover; named for Kirtley Mather, a member of USGS.

130

Maude Noble Cabin, Teton: erected in 1917; preserved to commemorate a meeting here in 1923, when Jackson Hole residents presented to Horace Albright, Supt. of Yellowstone National Park, a plan for setting aside a portion of Jackson Hole as a national recreation area. After many years of disagreements between Jackson Hole residents and government officials, this was finally accomplished in Grand Teton National Park.

Maverick Butte and Oil Field, Natrona: named for unbranded horses and cattle, known as mavericks, that once roamed here.

Maxon, Sweetwater: discontinued post office named for William Maxon.

Mayoworth, Johnnson: discontinued post office named by the first postmaster in 1890 for her daughter May, and her husband William Worthington.

May's Ranch, Niobrara: stage station on the Cheyenne-Deadwood route in 1877; located on Lance Creek; Jim May was stock tender and station keeper. This area was a popular place for holdups; Boone May rode shotgun on stages to protect them from road agents.

Maysdort, Campbell: discontinued post office; railroad station named for Mrs. May Downing, postmaster.

Maysville, Goshen: mining district in Rawhide Buttes that was of brief duration; named for Ed Mays, blacksmith.

McBroom Creek, Goshen, Platte: named for John McBroom who built a cabin here in the 1850s, where the immigrant road crossed the creek. It is now called Broom Creek.

McCarthy Canyon, Carbon: named for William McCarthy who came in the 1870s.

McCartney Cave, YNP: named for James McCartney who built a log cabin near Mammoth Hot Springs in 1871; it was large enough to serve as a hotel.

   When Nez Perce Indians passed by, McCartney and a friend hid in a sink hole not far from the present museum at Mammoth; this became known as McCartney Cave.

McClellan Gulch, Washakie: named for McClellan, pioneer.

McClintock Peak, 11,005, Teton: named for Frank McClintock, 10 years old, who with his father Henry made the first ascent of this peak in 1931. Frank was the youngest mountain climber to climb any of the Tetons.

McCormick Creek, Sheridan: named for John McCormick, rancher in the 1880s.

McCullock Peak, Park: named for Pete McCullock, early trapper, guide, and rancher.

McDonald, Big Horn: discontinued post office named for Alex McDonald.

McDougall Pass and Peak, Lincoln: named for Duncan McDougall, member of Pacific Fur Company in 1812.

McFadden, Carbon: railroad station and oil camp, first called Ohio City, but changed to McFayden for a prominent member of the oil company; the spelling of the name was changed by the Post Office Department. Oil was discovered here about 1917.

McFarlane Creek, Albany: named for John McFarlane, rancher. Emigrants were ferried across the creek when it was too high for fording.

McGill, Albany: discontinued post office named for Thomas A. McGill, rancher.

McGinnis Creek and Pass, Goshen: named for John McGinnis. He ran a road house in 1879 near the pass on the Cheyenne-Deadwood stage route, was arrested for selling liquor without a license, and was suspected of cattle stealing. On the way to Cheyenne, Ben Morrison, a law officer, took McGinnis ahead of the others, and claimed to have shot him to prevent his escape. Some claim this was the beginning of bitter range wars between cattlemen, rustlers, and homesteaders.

McIntosh Peak, Natrona: named for Willam McIntosh, rancher; a peak in the Rattlesnake Mountains.

McKinley, Converse: railroad station named for President William McKinley.

McKinnon, Sweetwater: named for Archibald McKinnon, Mormon official in Utah and father of twenty-two children.

McPhees Crossing, Laramie: named for the McPhee family; Islay, a discontinued post office, was here.

McTurk Draw, Fremont: named for Scotsman McTurk who ran sheep here in 1877.

Mead, Carbon: discontinued post office named for Alice L. Mead.

Meade Creek, Sheridan: named for Elwood Meade, member of USGS and first territorial engineer in Wyoming.

Meadow, Laramie: discontinued post office, originally on Carey Ranch on Horse Creek completely surrounded by meadows of alfalfa; moved several times.

Meadow Creek, Natrona: homesteaders of the 1890s thought this a beautiful meadow in which to live. When a big flood in August 1895 struck the tents in which people lived, they hurried to grab quilts and get to higher ground. Mrs. Nuby and her three children drowned. Their bodies were caught in piles of driftwood.

Meadowdale, Platte: discontinued post office named for its location in a meadow.

Meadowlark Reservoir, Big Horn: named for the state bird, chosen by the legislature in 1927. Its cheery song "Spring o' the year, spring o' the year" is a welcome spring sound in every county of the state.

Meadowlark Ski Area, Washakie: winter sports area in the Big Horn Mountains.

Meads, Carbon: railroad station named for Mead's Cut on the railroad between Saratoga and Encampment.

Meandel, Johnson: discontinued post office named for George Meandel.

Medicine Bow, Carbon: once a stage station; it has a picturesque stone hotel named *The Virginian* after the principal character of a novel by Owen Wister; the village was named for the Medicine Bow Mountains.

Medicine Bow Mountain Range, Albany, Carbon: name of Indian derivation. Indians came to these mountains for ash wood to make bows and arrows. At these gatherings they held ceremonial dances to cure diseases. Both the dances and the ash were "good medicine."

The name appears on Fremont's map of 1842. The range stands at elevations from 9,500 to 10,000 feet; most of it is heavily covered with evergreens.

Medicine Bow National Forest, Albany, Carbon, Converse: several divisions totaling 1,398,288 acres of mountain forest land; established in 1907; enlarged in 1935; also includes the Laramie Mountains.

Medicine Bow Peak, Albany, Carbon: a fire lookout station on this peak was the first in area, but has been abandoned because it was in the clouds much of the time.

In 1955 a United Airlines plane crashed into the peak, killing all 3 passengers and three crew members. Much of the plane wreckage fell on talus slopes, where it is buried. These are now called Disaster Wall.

Medicine Bow River, Carbon: like Medicine Bow Mountain, named for the ash that grew here; good bows and arrows—good medicine.

Medicine Butte, Uinta: named by Indians because of the great variety of herbs and roots they found on its slopes and used for medicine.

Also called Fremont's Monument; his party of explorers built a stone monument on top of it. Now each climber is supposed to add a stone in memory of Fremont. From its summit on a clear day one can see the Tetons 150 miles to the north.

Medicine Lodge Creek, Big Horn: Indian camp here, where they made "medicine" in dance ceremonies and wintered by warm waters that never froze. The site at the fork of Medicine Lodge and Dry Fork creeks has yielded artifacts radio-carbon dated 8000 B.C. to 300 A.D. Crow and Shoshone tribes stayed here in historic times.

Medicine Mountain, 10,000, Big Horn: on top of this mountain is located the famous, prehistoric Medicine Wheel, from which the mountain takes its name.

Medicine Tree, refers to a tree trunk into which horn or horns of Big Horn sheep have grown; specimens are in Jackson, Cody, Dubois, and Casper museums. Indians revered the Big Horn sheep. They placed a skull in the branched crotch of pine trees, six or seven feet above the ground; the tree was always on a high trail. As Indians passed, they left offerings of beads, shells, or other ornaments to show their superstitious veneration. Trees grew around the horns over many years. Modern Indians have no knowledge of the custom. Only five such trees have been found in Wyoming.

Medicine Wheel, Big Horn: Indian name for a place where they made "medicine" by worshipping. This almost perfect circle of stones, well sunken in the ground, is 70 feet in diameter; it has 28 spokes radiating from a central stone cairn. Six stone cairns are spaced around the circle, all facing the rising sun.

An ancient Sheepeater squaw claimed her people built it to worship; the 28 spokes were for tribes of her race. She remembered when Red Eagle, the chief, stood in the hub of the stones; worshippers chanted their songs, while young girls danced up and down the spokes; ceremonies were held before the fall hunt and again with the opening of buds in spring. This may be a fable; Indians claim to know nothing of its origin.

The Medicine Wheel was discovered by white men in the 1880s. It has been so molested by souvenir hunters that it is now fenced. A road was graded to it in 1935; there is an excellent view of Big Horn basin from here. It is a national historic landmark.

Wood found in the excavation of cairn six was dated about 1760 by Carbon 14 reading. See Great Arrow.

Medina Lake and Mountain, 11,541, Sublette: named for Joe Medina, a Spanish Basque. He was one of the earliest sheep foremen; he worked for the Hay Creek Company of Rock Springs.

Meeboer Lake, Albany: named for Joseph L. Meeboer, rancher.

Meek Mountain, 10,677, Teton: named for Joseph L. Meek, trapper in the region about 1830.

Meeteetse, Park: post office here in 1881 was one of the earliest settlements in the Bighorn basin; it was named for Meeteetse Creek. John W. Deane read thrilling stories of the West as a child in the East. He ran away from home at 15, helped drive longhorns up the Texas Trail, spent five months in an Indian village on Lodgepole Creek, was a mail carrier from 1877-84, and became mayor of Meeteetse. The village was moved to the Greybull River in 1893.

Meeteetse Creek, Park: a Shoshone Indian name meaning "meeting place," or place of rest. The distance was determined by the pronuciation of the word. If the syllables were long and drawn out, the place was far away; if said in short, clipped fashion, the place was close by.

Megeath, Sweetwater: For G. W. Megeath, president of Megeath Coal Company in the 1890s.

Meiers Crag, 12,700, Fremont: named for M. Meier, who with C. F. Darling made the first ascent of the crag in 1950.

Meldrum Mountain, 9,552, YNP: for John John W. Meldrum, U.S. Commissioner from 1894-1935.

Memorial Trail, Park: horse and foot trail to Clayton Gulch and Memorial Marker past Black Water Lodge, and to Clayton Mountain fire lookout station. In this vicinity 15 men lost their lives fighting the Black Water forest fire in 1937.

Menor's Ferry, Teton: in 1892 William Menor settled on the west bank of the Snake River; for more than 25 years he operated a homemade flat-bottom ferry, until the Snake River bridge was built in 1927. The present bridge was built in 1958.

In 1949 Laurance Rockefeller financed the restoration of the old ferry boat, which had been left upside down since 1927. Now tourists are given rides on this boat, which is guided by a cable. The diagonal crossing uses the swift waters of the river for power; located near Moose.

Menter Hill, Albany: named for Menter, owner of this hill before 1900.

Mercedes, Coverse: see Glenrock.

Meriden, Laramie: post office and store established in 1889 on Horse Creek. Named by Jessie Dunhame, first postmaster, for Meriden, Connecticut, her former home.

134

Merino, Weston: first called Irontown; became the terminus of the Burlington railroad and was renamed Merino for the breed of sheep shipped from here; now it is called Upton. Large sheep-shearing pens were built near town.

Merna, Sublette: discontinued post office; named by Mrs. Grace Snyder, first postmaster, for her home town, Merna, Nebraska.

Merrill, Uinta: this extinct town was once the county seat of Uinta county; it was chosen that by territorial governor Campbell when the county was formed. At the general election a year later Merrill lost the race for county seat to Evanston by one vote. It was named for Merrill, the commander at Fort Bridger at that time.

Merritt's Crossing, Hot Springs: where Gen. Wesley Merritt, with his cavalry and Shoshone Indian scouts, forded the Bighorn River in 1877 in pursuit of Chief Joseph and his Nez Perce Indians; the location is now below present Diversion Dam.

When Merritt's force was crossing the Owl Creek Mountains, they hitched 16 mules to a six-mule supply wagon, and all the men who could, crowded around the wagon to push on it. Other men held ropes fastened to the wagon on each side to keep it from upsetting. More trouble was had going down than up; the wagons, though rough-locked, ran away and upset, scattering their loads, as if they had been fired from a shotgun, hence the expression "we shot-gunned the hill."

Metzler, Fremont: discontinued post office named for Metzler, promoter of irrigation in the area.

Mexican Flats, Carbon: named for Joe Gonzales and his two brothers who homesteaded west of Dad; they were Mexicans. Joe and one of his brothers are buried on their homesteads. Wooden crosses mark their graves on a sandy hill, covered with greasewood, cactus, and old Indian campsites; it is a bleak and desolate area.

Middleton, Hot Springs: discontinued post office named in 1895 by Col. Cliney for Middleton, Ireland, where he was born. The colonel came with the United States Army to fight Indians in 1877. He became a rancher in Owl Creek country.

Midway, Sublette: discontinued post office that was midway between Fontenelle and Big Piney.

Midway Dome, Natrona: an oil field midway between Big Muddy and Salt Creek oil fields.

Midwest, Natrona: first called Shannon Camp when oil was hauled out with string teams to Casper in 1898; it took a week for the round trip in good weather; two weeks on snowy or muddy roads; Salt Creek was crossed 17 times; 16 horses pulled three tanks or about 50 barrels of crude oil. Team drivers hated the trucks that finally took away their business. When a truck mired down in the mud and had to be pulled out with horses, teamsters were triumphantly happy.

Midwest: main station of Midwest Oil Company in the Salt Creek Oil Field; it was the first place in the nation to have a football game played at night under electric lights in 1925.

Milford, Fremont: Altman built a sawmill here at a good crossing of the north fork of the Popo Agie in the early days; nothing is left now.

Milky Creek, Lake, and Ridge, Fremont: light-colored soil around the edge of the water gives milky appearance.

Millbrook, Albany: discontinued ranch post office; railroad station named in 1903 by Col. J. Bell for his ranch, Millbrook. The ranch took its name because of a sawmill on Mill Creek.

Millburne, Uinta: discontinued post office; railroad station; named for a grist mill run by John Wade in a clearing caused by fire; it was the first flour mill in the valley.

Mill City, Uinta: named for a sawmill at the mouth of Fish Creek; it was a company town. Lumber and logs were sent down to Hilliard by a flume; it took two hours, if no jam occurred. The sawmill soon moved down to Hilliard, and only logs were sent down the flume.

Mill Creek, Uinta: named for a sawmill erected in the early days by William S. Sloan, who built a flume to float out lumber and logs.

Miller, Natrona: discontinued post office named for U. S. Miller, postmaster here for many years.

Miller Butte, Teton: named for Robert E. Miller. Mrs. Miller was the mayor of Jackson in 1920, with an all woman town council. Mr. Miller started the first bank in Jackson in 1914.

Miller Creek, Crook: named for Miller, a horse wrangler who went out before daylight to gather up horses and was killed by Indians. He was a member of the Montana expedition of 1876, headed for gold in the Black Hills. He was buried on this creek.

Miller Creek, YNP: named for Adam Miller, discoverer of Soda Butte and Clark's Fork mines. In 1870 he fled down this creek escaping from Indians.

Miller Lake and River, Uinta: see Bear Lake and River.

Millersburg, Platte: In March 1888 Taylor Miller learned from Frenchy Cazaubon, a peddler, where he had picked up the pretty green stones he gave his wife. The stones were rich in copper. Miller filed a mining claim and started mining. His ranch became a mining settlement, Millersburg, and a small fortune in copper ore was taken out by prospectors; the place is now a forgotten ghost town.

Millersville, Uinta: stage and Pony Express station named for Miller, a stage driver.

Millis, Uinta: railroad station named for J. W. Millis, conductor on the Union Pacific railroad in the 1870s.

Mills, Natrona: suburb of Casper; named for James, William, and Thomas Mills, who plotted the Mills-Baker addition to Casper in 1919; James Mills was a railroad conductor.

Mills Branch, Laramie: a creek named for Abe Mills who settled here in 1875. In 1884 the main road from Cheyenne to Horse Creek followed the railroad for 18 miles east of Cheyenne, then turned north to Mills Branch, and down it to Horse Creek.

On Mills Branch in 1876 Alex and Charles Perry met Ed Stemler, a young man with a trapping outfit, and an old violin. He lived with them for five years as a welcome guest. Ed played the violin left-handed with the neck up, fingering it with his right hand. He was a very good musician.

Mineral Hill, Crook: old mining ghost town has the wreck of a large stamp mill.

Miner's Delight, Fremont: a nest of gold camps near South Pass City in 1868; so named because miners expected the "diggin' " to be rich in gold; the mines did not turn out so rich after all; it was renamed Hamilton City.

Minersville, Uinta: early settlement, now extinct; residents came from Coalville, Utah, and named new home in memory of the place in Utah, where they were miners.

Minick Basin, Hot Springs: during the range war, a sheepman, Minick, took his sheep into what cattlemen maintained was their country to winter. His camp was raided, his sheep killed. Minick, wounded, was left to die by the cattlemen.

Minnies Gap, Sweetwater: on the homestead of Minnie Crouse Rasmussen.

Minturn, Campbell: a Burlington railroad gravel pit east of Gillette; named for John Minturn, pioneer rancher.

Missouri Buttes, Crook: named for the Little Missouri River, which see. These four buttes are of igneous rock of the same formation as Devils Tower; one of them is higher than Devils Tower. They can easily be climbed, but crumblng rock approaches are treacherous.

Missouri Valley, Natrona: homesteaders here in 1907 wanted a post office; since most of them were from Missouri, they sent in the name Missouri Valley. They never got the post office, but did name the locality.

Misty Moon Lake, Big Horn: the lake is half-moon in shape when seen from above; misty clouds often hang over it; it is located in the Cloud Peak Primitive Area.

Mitchell Peak, 12,482, Fremont, Sublette: named for Finis Mitchell who loves the Wind River Range. He says, "Only God can place such beauty before man's eyes." He has taken over 35,000 pictures, and made more than 128 ascents of Wind River peaks. He has traveled in excess of 7,679 miles on foot in his backpacking jaunts into these mountains, and stocked 314 lakes with fish. He is an expert fisherman and mountaineer.

Moccasin Creek and Lake, Fremont: named for the lake's shape—like a moccasin; excellent fishing; the creek is named for the lake.

Model, Sheridan: a coal camp on an electric railway.

Mohawk Creek, Sheridan: for the Mohawk Mine at the head of the stream.

Molly Islands, YNP: in Yellowstone Lake; named by USGS for Molly, wife of Henry Gannett. These rocky islands are nesting grounds for pelicans, gulls, and cormorants.

Molly's Fork, Goshen: named for Molly Saffle or Saffel, daughter of a settler who came in 1882. She was known as the prettiest girl here. Many cowboys rode by her home, hoping to get a glimpse of her at this road house on the Cheyenne-Deadwood stage route.

Another story is that a woman, Molly, lived on the fork and cooked for wood choppers in the 1850s.

Mona, Crook: discontinued post office. Mrs. Eliza Mortimer, first postmaster, asked neighbors to help choose a name. Mrs. Bob Watson was then reading a novel in which Mona was the leading character, so that name was chosen.

Monaco Camp, Park: site of Buffalo Bill's last big game hunt. Albert I, Prince of Monaco, was a member of the party.

Monarch, Sheridan: discontinued post office; railroad station; named for nearby coal mine. Named for monarch, ruler, or best of coals.

Monday Creek, Albany: named for George Monday.

Mondell, Weston: discontinued post office named for Frank Mondell, who found out about coal at Cambria and helped with its development, was mayor of Newcastle from 1890-95, was a Wyoming Congressman for 20 years and sponsored the 640-acre homestead act. His home in Newcastle was a castle on a hill with rooms decorated with marble and ivory and hung with crystal chandeliers.

Moneta, Fremont: originally known as Big Springs; renamed Monta for Italian word for "coin"; another version says it is an Indian word meaning "running water"; yet another version says it was named for an Iowa village. It is located near Castle Gardens.

Montana Lake, Crook: named by members of a Montana expedition coming to mine Black Hills gold; see Miller Creek.

Monton's Spur, Converse: named for nearby Monton ranch.

Monument Creek, Natrona: named for a monument of granite erected here for hunters murdered by their guide here in 1888. S. Morris Waln and C. H. Strong of Pennslvania were hunting and prospecting with Thomas O'Brien as cook and guide. Their bodies were found by cowboys near an old campfire. O'Brien was later tried and sentenced in Colorado for horse stealing, but not for this suspected murder.

Monument Hill, Hot Springs: near Thermopolis is a hill that a Miss Avery climbed to build a monument, in gratitude for the restoration of her health by bathing in the hot springs; others have followed her example, and have added travertine from the springs to monuments already there.

Monument Hill, Park: stone cairn built on top of it by sheepherders.

Moorcroft, Crook: railroad came in 1891; the general store was a tent in 1893; it became a large shipping point in the 1890s. Now it is the site of the Black Hills Bentonite Company. Bentonite is gooey mud with a thousand uses; when wet it swells to 15 times its dry bulk; its principal use is in drilling oil wells and it is also used as a cosmetic base, in toothpaste, paper, plastics, and much more.

There are three versions of how Moorcroft was named: named for Alexander Moorcroft, first white man to build his cabin in this vicinity in defiance of Indians. Stocks Miller was the first postmaster in 1889, and named it for his English estate, Moorcroft Acres. Dr. Moocroft came here to vacation and hunt in the 1890s.

"Big Bill" Thompson, mayor of Chicago, once punched cows here.

Moore, Albany: discontinued post office named for Thomas Edwin Moore, first postmaster.

Moore, Platte: James and Mike Moore ran a post office here in 1884.

138

Moore Hill, Natrona: named for J. W. Moore who owned a ranch at the base of the hill.

Moore's Gulch, Albany: named for Moore who prospected for gold in the 1880s.

Moose, Teton: headquarters of Grand Teton National Park; has a museum specializing in the western fur trade; it is the site of the Church of the Transfiguration, a log chapel with the Tetons framed by a window in back of the altar. Margaret Murie, author of *Two in the Far North* and *Wapiti Wilderness* lives here. The museum exhibits life of early settlers and fur traders.

The village is named for moose, who are frequent visitors. The moose, largest antlered animal that ever lived on earth, sheds its antlers annually, and grows a new set, larger and heavier, each year. In spite of its size, a moose can run swiftly and silently. It is a strong swimmer, staying in water part of the summer to avoid flies. It eats willows and water plants, ducking its head under water as long as a minute to gather choice bites.

Moran, Teton: the old town was dismantled and moved in 1959, as it was too close to Jackson Lake Dam; named for Mount Moran which was named for Thomas Moran, an English artist who accompanied the USGS expedition under Hayden to the Yellowstone National Park region in 1871. Moran's panoramic picture of the Grand Canyon of the Yellowstone was purchased by Congress for $10,000, and hangs in Washington, D.C. His paintings are on display in park museums.

Moran Bay, Teton: first named Spirit Bay by Lt. Doane's party in 1870 because of resounding echoes there; renamed for Thomas Moran.

Moran Junction, Canyon, and Mountain, 12,594, Teton: named for artist Thomas Moran. On Mount Moran is the wreckage of a DC-3 near Skillet Glacier. It crashed in a blizzard in 1950; 24 were killed.

More's Gulch, Albany: named for miner, More, who discovered gold here in 1868.

Mormon Canyon, Converse: here in 1855 Mormons dug the first irrigation ditch in Wyoming to water crops and gardens for their Deer Creek way station located west of present Glenrock. Later it became an Indian agency, military post, Pony Express and telegraph station.

Mormon Creek, Park: a favorite camping place of Latter Day Saints.

Mormon Dam, Park: below Powell; first dam in this district, as Mormons started irrigation in Bighorn basin.

Mormon Ferry, Natrona: in 1847 a ferry boat was built at the direction of Brigham Young to cross the Platte River near present Casper. It was made of two large cottonwood canoes, fastened together with cross pieces, and covered with slabs; it was large enough so oxen or teams did not need to be unhitched from wagons. Nine Mormons stayed to operate the ferry; it was used until Louis Guinard built a bridge 1858-59.

Mormon Row, Teton: a small settlement of Mormons was here near Blacktail Butte.

Morning Glory Pool, YNP: a thermal spring of deepest blue, cupped like a morning glory. At one time its beauty was completely destroyed by tourists filling it with pop bottle caps.

Morrison Beds, Crook: named for Clinton Morrison; a triangular basin north of Alladin in the curve of the Belle Fourche River, where dinosaur and reptile fossils have been found.

Morrison Park, Albany: named for Clinton Morrison who in 1890 owned part of the park.

Morris Ranch, Park: discontinued post office named for Mary J. Morris.

Morrissey, Weston: discontinued post office; named for Morrissey, early rancher. Once vivid lights were reported tumbling here in the Ghost Light area. Motorists drove their cars off the graded road to avoid hitting them.

Morse, Campbell: discontinued post office named for Wayne Morse, rancher.

Mortar Geyser, YNP: named by Haynes, photographer for President Chester A. Arthur's party in 1883, because its eruptions sounded like mortar explosions.

Mortenson Lake, Albany: named for rancher Mortenson.

Morton, Fremont: post office named for Joy and Paul Morton, directors of Morton Salt Company; a man who homesteaded land here was a friend of the Mortons, and suggested their name.

Moskee, Crook: discontinued post office; 1925; first called Laviere, but caused a mixup with other post offices' names. The Post Office Department asked for a new name. It was a railroad station. The name was suggested by a cowboy for the Chinese word "moche," anything goes; spelling was changed. The Homestake Mine of Lead, South Dakota, had a sawmill here from 1920-40; only a huge sawdust pile is left.

Moslander Reservoir, Uinta: on Moslander ranch—a pioneer family.

Mosquito Creek and Park: named for the many mosquitoes; the Fort Washakie Women's Club holds summer camp here for Indian girls.

Moss Agate Hill, Converse: named for its agate deposit.

Moss Lake, Fremont: named for sheepherder Moss who grazed his sheep here in the early days.

Mosyer Juncton, Lincoln: named for the Mosyer ranch; located where the Cumberland branch leaves the Oregon Short Line.

Mother Featherlegs Monument, Goshen: marks the site of the dugout and grave of Mrs. Shephard, called old Mother Featherlegs by cowboys because of long, red pantalettes she wore tied around her ankles. They fluttered briskly in the breezes, as she dashed about on horseback. She was a go-between for road agents and desperadoes and she kept stolen jewelry and money hidden in her dugout; this was a place of "entertainment" for travelers; rot-gut whiskey was served.

Mother Featherlegs was the mother of Tom and Bill Shephard, Louisiana outlaws after Civil War. Dick David, one of the gang, known as dangerous Dick, the Terrapin, used her place as a hangout.

Mrs. O. J. Demmon, wife of a rancher who lived nearby, found Mother Featherlegs shot to death; she had fallen while filling a pail at a spring. A monument was placed in 1964 to preserve a story spot in frontier history.

140

Mount Arter, Fremont: named for Arthur Robinson, Forest Service. A friend called him "Arter," hence the name.

Mountain Home, Albany: an old stage station in the mountains; now it is a summer resort.

Mountain View, Uinta: post office started in 1891; named for the ranch of Mrs. Groshon; located at the base of a succession of hills and mountains that rise like stair steps.

Mounts and Mountains, look under their names.

Moyer, Lincoln: name of a pioneer rancher.

Mule Creek Oil Field, Niobrara: named for Mule Creek which has a quicksand bottom in places. One day cowboys came along and found a pal with his head and chest sticking out of the muddy water.

"Here's a rope to save you," they shouted, throwing him a lasso.

"Don't bother about me," the man answered. "Just save my mule."

"Where is your mule?" they yelled back.

"I'm a'sittin' on him."

Oil was discovered on the homestead of Ed Morse in 1919; within two years more than 40 wells were producing good oil. By 1938 a small refinery was built; production has now dwindled.

Mummy Cave, Park: a cave along Highway 20 from Cody to Yellowstone National Park. Here in 1963 a human mummy was found that Carbon-14 dating showed to be more than 1,200 years old. He is dressed in a crumbling sheepskin and has long fingernails, well-worn teeth, a sloping forehead, and wild, black hair. The mummy was once on display at the Whitney Gallery of Western Arts in Cody.

Smithsonian archeologists excavated the cave; numbering and removing layer after layer of earth, which was sifted for artifacts: bone pipes, basketry, grinding stones, and fragments of wood and leather.

Munger Mountain, 8,385, Teton: named for Munger, a miner who prospected for gold at the foot of this mountain.

Murke, Laramie: named for Prof. Murke, chemist of Great Western Sugar Company, who located the immense limestone deposits here; limestone is used in refining sugar.

Murky Lake, Carbon: named for James Murky, pioneer.

Murphy Canyon, Albany: named for John Murphy, homesteader here before 1911.

Murphy Creek, Johnson: a cliff near the entrance into Hole-in-the-Wall country resembles a man's face; cowboys called the cliff "old man Murphy" and the creek below it Murphy Creek.

Murphy Gulch, Sheridan: named for pioneer Murphy.

Murphy Mine, Fremont: discovered in 1856 by John R. Murphy.

Murphy Peak, 10,874, Teton: namd for T. F. Murphy who built a cairn on top of the peak; he was a surveyor in the 1930s.

Murphy's Gulch, Fremont: named for Uncle John Murphy, prospector, miner, saloon keeper at South Pass in the gold rush days; later he sold apples on the streets of Lander.

Murray Hill, Sheridan: named for Bill Murray, contractor who had logged off most of the hill by 1895; he sent ties by flume to Rochester for the railroad.

Musembeah Peak, 12,593, Fremont: Shoshone name for big horn. Dr. William Cropper and Bill Dietschy in 1955 found the entire skeleton of a bighorn sheep only 100 feet below the summit of this peak.

Mush Creek, Weston: named for soft, white mushy mud in the creek.

Muskrat Creek, Goshen: has many small, deep holes in which muskrats once lived. In the early days there was a copper mining boom in Muskrat Canyon.

Myarrville, Fremont: discontinued post office for Myarr, pioneer.

Myers Crossing, Uinta: named for John Myers who settled here in 1860; he built a bridge across the Bear River and charged a toll; the stage route passed by his home, which was used by passengers as a rest stop. Myers started cattle ranching here.

Myers Reservoir, Uinta: on the John Myers ranch; used for irrigating hay fields; a sports group from Uinta County has developed a picnic area here; it also boasts good trout fishing.

N

Nameless Peak, 11,585, Teton: once called Woodring Peak for the first Superintendent of Yellowstone National Park; now it is called Mount Fryxell.

Names Hill, Lincoln: emigrants on the Oregon Trail stopped to carve their names here on the limestone; the earliest inscription is dated 1822; still legibile is "James Bridger, 1844." To the southeast of the hill is the site of Mormon Ferry, where emigrants crossed the Green River in a shortcut to Idaho; near LaBarge.

The first emigrant train to pass Names Hill was probably the Stevens party in 1844. It was a place of early communication; emigrants might leave a message here for someone following.

Narrows or the Grand Canyon of Snake River, Lincoln: the gorge is more than 3,000 feet deep, and less than 40 feet wide in places. The river is lashed to white foam by the speed of its fall; its roar can be heard for several miles. John Day saw these rapids in 1811 while scouting to see if Hunt's Astorians could descend to the Columbia River by boat.

Nash Fork, Albany: named for A. J. "Dad" Nash, miner in the 1880s.

Natrona County: created in 1888; organized in 1890 with Casper as the county seat; named for its natural deposits of trona—carbonate of soda; contains the most extensive oil fields in the state, with three major refineries at Casper; it is also livestock country.

There are mountain parks on Casper Mountain featuring skiing; fishing and recreation are at nearby Alcova and Pathfinder reservoirs; also good jade and rock hunting.

142

Needle Creek and Mountain, 12,130, Park: named for sharp peaks on the top of the mountain.

Needle Plunger Park, Park: see DeMaris Springs.

Needle Rock, Uinta: near an old Pony Express station; named for the rock form.

Needles, YNP: dramatic pinnacles that dominate lower Cache Creek.

Needles Creek, Uinta: water contains minerals that form needle-like deposits.

Neiber, Washakie: discontinued post office and railroad station named for Mary M. Neiber, first postmaster. An old Shoshone burial ground is nearby; Indians hold ceremonies here to honor their dead.

Nellis Creek, Albany, Carbon: named for Ed Nellis, pioneer.

Nelson Park, Albany: Andy Nelson grazed his sheep here for years.

Newcastle, Weston: county seat; established in 1889 as the terminus of the Burlington railroad; named by Joseph H. Hemingway, first Superintendent of the Cambria coal mines, for English coal port Newcastle-upon-Tyne. Tubb Town was moved to the present site of Newcastle with the coming of the railroad. It was the site of the first school in 1890, as well as the first theater.

The "Western Gateway to the Black Hills" is also the oil capital of northeastern Wyoming, with two refineries of the Sioux Oil Company; it is the center of lumbering and livestock country.

President Theodore Roosevelt visited here in 1903. The Anna Miller Museum houses historical items of pioneer and county interest.

In 1965 a wagon train of 30 covered wagons, more than 100 horses, and nearly 200 men, women, and children trekked from Newcastle to Fort Fetterman and the State Fair in Douglas, reliving pioneer days for a week of traveling and camping.

New Fork Creek and Park, Sublette: the source of the name is obvious; it has good campgrounds.

New Fork Lake, Sublette: named Lake DeMalia by early trappers for the sister of Fontenelle; it was renamed for the creek. It contains about 1,100 surface acres and has rainbow and Mackinaw trout.

New Haven, Crook: post office established in 1909; named by Harry Wilson, postmaster, for New Haven, Connecticut, home of his favorite ball team.

New Rochelle, Niobrara: named for Albert Rochelle, miner; the first silver pits were worked here in 1879; the enterprise failed; see Lusk.

Newton, Laramie: discontinued post office named for George W. Newton, postmaster.

New Wolton, Natrona: once it was the Poison Creek stage station; now it is called Hiland.

New York Pass, 11,450, Fremont, Sublette: used by a group of New York mountaineers in 1955.

Nez Perce Creek and Mountain, 11,900, Teton: an eye-catching summit once called Mitten Mountain; also called Howling Dog at one time; renamed for Nez Perce (pronounce Nez Purs) Indian tribe who once hunted here. It was their custom to pierce their noses to attach ornaments.

Nickell, Carbon: railroad siding named for P. Nickell, land owner.

Nigger Baby Springs and Creek, Goshen: first known as W. H. Creek for the brand of W. H. Bowen; a roundup place for cowboys, and a camping place for soldiers from Fort Laramie in early days. Once after soldiers left, according to legend, a Negro baby was found dead in the springs, hence the name.

Nigger Channel, Teton: a Negro blacksmith homesteaded here and made an irrigation ditch from the Gros Ventre River to water his land; the ditch became enlarged and formed a river channel.

Nigger John Creek, Sheridan: named for the first Negro citizen of the county, who developed a ranch along this creek; he lived in a dugout in bank of the creek.

Nightcap Bay, Teton: a small bay in Jackson Lake named by John D. Sargent, pioneer of 1887; brilliant and erratic, he claimed the bay was visited by an apparition—a man in a boat which appeared at midnight on a certain night each year.

Nine Mile Creek, Johnson: nine miles from old Fort Reno.

Niobrara County: Lusk, county seat; created in 1911 from the eastern part of Converse County; organized in 1913; named by Harry S. Snyder for the Niobrara River which rises west of Lusk.

Extensive dinosaur beds were discovered in the northern part of Niobrara County in 1889 (then Converse); skeletons of Triceratops, a three-horned monster, and duck-billed Trachodon were unearthed here, and taken to eastern museums. One of the oldest and finest mummy dinosaur specimens was found here in 1908 with skin partly preserved. It is now in the American Museum of Natural History in New York City. An estimated 300 million years ago Niobrara County was an ocean teeming with marine life, a paradise for dinosaurs that completely disappeared with a changing climate.

The Mesozoic age that produced dinosaurs also produced large trees and ferns, that were later buried in the earth's upheaval. Flora was pressed into coal. Animal remains decayed and made oil that accumulated in and between rock layers.

The Lance Creek Oil Field, where dinosaurs once roamed, became active in 1917; it exceeded all fields in Wyoming in production from 1939-45; new fields in the northern part of the county is still being developed. Livestock raising is also a major industry.

A recent development is irrigation from wells 400 or more feet deep, which can produce as much as 2,250 gallons of water per minute. In 1967 approximately 1,000 acres were irrigated by the automatic-moving sprinkler systems that "walk," or travel on wheels in a circle of land; a variety of crops were grown.

A museum in Lusk houses an old stagecoach that once traveled the Cheyenne-Deadwood route; it was donated by Russell Thorp. Many other relics of pioneer times are at the museum.

Niobrara River, Niobrara: rises west of Lusk; name taken from the Omaha-Ponca Indian name Ni (water) obthatha (spreading) ke (horizon-

144

tally); it was called Running Water by early settlers. The Cheyenne Indian name for the Niobrara River was Hisse yovi yoe—unexpected or surprise river. They came upon it suddenly on the prairie, as it is marked by few trees.

Nipple Mesa, 11,465, Park: named for shape.

Noble Cabin, Teton: see Maude Noble Cabin.

Node, Niobrara: post office and store named for cattle brand.

Norkok Butte and Creek, Fremont: named for a Shoshone official interpreter at the Indian agency. His name was Noikot, Black Hawk, but writers changed the spelling to Norkok.

Norris Geyser Basin, Pass, and Mountain, 9,936, YNP: named for Philatus W. Norris, Superintendent of Yellowstone National Park from 1877-82. He was the first to occupy the office at Mammoth Hot Springs, new park headquarters in 1879; it is the world's most volatile geyser basin; it has several new features and has grown in activity since the 1959 Hebgen earthquake.

North Absaroka Wilderness Area, Park: rugged and picturesque land with many big game animals; it contains 351,104 acres.

North American Lake, Albany: named for the nearby North American mine.

North Fork, Fremont: there was a village here in 1874; it had a good early school.

North Gap Lake, Albany: lies in a gap between Brown's Peak and Medicine Bow Peak; it is a deep lake; brook and golden trout are here, as well as lake trout.

North Platte, Natrona: once a Pony Express station named for the river.

North Platte River, Carbon, Converse, Goshen, Natrona, Platte: referred to in *Wyoming Place Names* as the Platte River; it rises in northern Colorado, flows north, makes a huge loop around the Laramie Range and Casper Mountain, and flows southeast into Nebraska.

The Indians called it Mini Nebrathka, spreading water. In 1739 The Mallet brothers, Frenchmen, named it "La Platte," broad and shallow.

Northwest Community College, Park: see Powell.

Notch Mountain, 10,950, Park: named for its peculiar configuration.

No Water Creek, Washakie: usually dry; once after a cloudburst the creek flooded Worland.

Nowlin Creek and Meadows, Teton: named for Dan Nowlin, early state game warden; it is a summer elk pasture.

Nowood, Washakie: early trading post named for the creek. In the 1890s and early 1900s twenty-horse string teams hauled wagon loads of baled wool from Noble and Bragg shearing pens to Casper.

Nowood Creek, Washakie: a cavalry detachment once camped here, wet and wind-driven; it gave the creek its name because they found no wood to build a fire and warm themselves.

Nugget, Lincoln: early prospectors claim to have found gold nuggets here.

Null, Big Horn: discontinued post office named for David A. Null, postmaster.

Nuttel, Converse: see Glenrock.

Nylon Peak, 12,350, Sublette: named by mountaineers H. Willits and W. Stewart, Jr., who climbed the peak in 1946; they used nylon rope, light and strong, then available for the first time. Nylon Peak is sometimes called Mount St. Michel.

Nystrom Mountain, 2,356, Fremont, Sublette: named in 1877 by F. M. Endlich, a Hayden Survey member, for the family of his fiance.

O

Oakley, Lincoln: town settled in 1899; named by Thomas Sneddon, superintendent of the coal mines here, for his birthplace, Oakley, Scotland. The post office was discontinued in 1942. The mine closed and houses moved away. Now it is a grazing area for sheep and tramping ground for bottle hunters.

Oakwood, Crook: discontinued post office; named for oak trees by Mrs. Charles Moore, postmaster; she was pleased to find them there.

Oberg Pass, Carbon: named for Oberg, rancher in the pass; it is on the old Cherokee Trail.

Observation Point, 4,750, Weston: above Newcastle; from here on a clear day Laramie Peak and the Big Horn Mountains are visible.

Observation Tower, Sheridan: located on the summit of Tunnel Hill; Pilot Hill and the sites of Wagon Box Fight and the Fetterman Massacre are visible from here.

Obsidian Cliff, YNP: named by Superintendent Norris in 1879; it is a cliff of black, obsidian glass; it was formed by rapid cooling of a great wave of lava. Indians came from as far as Ohio to secure this obsidian for spears and arrowheads; they thought it had magic; it also chipped nicely.

When the road was built around this cliff in 1878, men built fires and then dashed cold water on the hot obsidian to crack it. This is the only road in the world built on native glass.

Obsidian Creek and Lake, YNP: named for Obsidian Cliff.

Occidental Hotel, Johnson: in the new tent town of Buffalo in 1879, Charles E. Buell was preparing his meal in a tent on Clear Creek, when a party of miners with a large pack outfit rode up. They asked if he would board them a few days; they also asked him to keep the gold they had found in the Big Horns.

Buell dug a hole in the ground under his mattress and hid their gold; he cooked and fed the men. That made him decide to build a hotel of hewn logs; he named it for the popular Occidental Hotel in Dodge City, Kansas.

This was the popular place where Owen Wister's Virginian "got his man"; it served as a town hall, hospital, and court house when the country was being organized in 1881; it was torn down in the early 1900s.

Ocean Lake, Fremont: named for its size, 6,248 acre-feet; it is near

146

Riverton; the lake serves as a refuge and nesting ground for Canada geese; it is used for recreation and boasts crappie, sunfish and bass fishing.

Ocla, Fremont: railroad station; this is the Indian word for water.

Odyssey Peak, 12,053, Fremont, Sublette: first climbing party in 1949 wrote *Wind River Odyssey* describing the region; it has also been called Pyramid Peak.

Oeneis Mountain, 12,222, Sublette: a scientific group collected butterflies in barren areas below timberline; they found excellent specimens of the genus Oeneis and named the peak.

Ogden Creek, Crook: rises on the Chester Ogden ranch.

O'Haver Hill , Crook: named for George O'Haver, landowner.

Ohio City, Carbon: established in 1918 when the first oil well proved out; it was named for the oil company and renamed McFadden in 1920.

Ohlman, Sheridan: discontinued ranch post office named for George Ohlman; Parkman is now the post office.

Okie, Fremont: discontinued post office for T. B. Okie, postmaster.

Okies Thorn, 11,600, Teton: a thorn-like pinnacle named for Leigh Ortenburger, nicknamed "Okie" because he attended Oklahoma University. He wrote *A Climber's Guide to the Teton Range.*

Oil City, Natrona: named by S. A. Aggers who came from Oil City, Pennsylvania in the 1880s, and drilled for oil here.

Oil Creek, Uinta: this creek carries a natural seepage of oil.

Oil Creek, Weston: creek flows through red beds and dissolves iron; in pools and stagnant places, iron stays on top of the water; it looks and tastes like oil.

Oilton, Weston: railroad station for loading oil.

Old Baldy, 12,005, Carbon: highest peak in the county; it is bald on top.

Old Baldy, Carbon: name of sportsmen's paradise developed near Saratoga by George B. Stoner, radio and TV tycoon; it boasts golf courses, fishing streams, and other recreation. It was named by Stoner for a legendary bald eagle that lived for years on a nearby promontory.

Old Bedlam, Goshen: officers' quarters at Fort Laramie. Two versions of the name: "bedlam" is a type of sawed lumber from which it was built. Bedlam was a London lunatic asylum; many thought this famous building was so named because it was a madhouse of noise and confusion.

One of the greatest rides in recorded history ended here in December 1866, when Portugee Phillips arrived from Fort Phil Kearny with news of the Fetterman Massacre and the need for reinforcements. In a blizzard and sub-zero weather he rode 236 miles over unmarked prairie. The thoroughbred horse he rode, Grey Eagle, dropped dead in front of Old Bedlam.

Old Bedlam, which had sagged badly since the fort was abandoned in 1890, has been restored as part of the Fort Laramie National Monument.

Old Faithful, YNP: most famous of all geysers; named by Gen. H. D. Washburn in 1870 because of its regularity of eruption; a timepiece of the ages. About every 65 minutes, after terrific hissing and rumbling, large cauliflower-like masses of steam unfold like an atomic explosion, and rise hundreds of feet above the water column. An estimated ten thousand gallons of scalding water rises 175 feet on a windstill day, and stands for four minutes, unfurling like a white flag, with the evergreen-covered mountains in the background.

Geologists judge Old Faithful to be still in its youth; perhaps two or three hundred years old; it has never been known to miss an eruption. Lt. Doane called it "the most lovely inanimate object in existence."

Old Faithful Inn, YNP: near the geyser for which it is named; it is the largest structure of logs and boulders in the world; it soars more than 90 feet in the central lobby; built in 1903-04, it is fittingly rustic and enchanting for the wonderland in which it stands.

Old Maid's Draw, Albany: named for Miss Myrtle Dawson who lived here from 1910 to 1920.

Old Man's Washboard, Teton: a series of cascades on the Upper Gros Ventre River.

Old Soda Lake, Natrona: In 1955 the American Oil refinery was dumping 2,000,000 gallons of refinery effluent into the Platte River. Dr. C. C. Buchler, refinery manager, developed a 500-acre man-made pond, landlocked in a basin of nearby hills. Refinery wastes then flowed through a 23,000-foot pipe into a settling pond that became lifeless except for green algae. Overflow from this pond filled the larger lake that unexpectedly became a wildlife refuge for birds, ducks, and antelope. The water is brackish but palatable to birds and animals. Tall willows surround the pond; its evaporation equals intake.

Old Soldiers Creek, Albany: named in 1878 for soldiers from Fort Fetterman who were stationed here to protect freighters on the road to Fort Fetterman.

Old Woman Creek, Niobrara: Indian name; an old woman disappeared here and returned later as a harmless spirit to haunt hills and knolls and to dance in the moonlight on the rimrock above the creek.

O'Moara Spring, Fremont: named for Sam O'Moara, gold prospector.

Onion Meadows, Fremont: named for wild onions; once an old Indian trail went through here from Moccasin Lake to Grave Lake.

Ono, Johnson: discontinued post office; community of homesteaders met to choose a name for the post office; after each suggestion someone shouted "Oh no." Eventually, they all laughed and chose Ono.

Opal, Lincoln: two versions of the name: a sheepherder called his dog "o pal"; railroad conductors named the station Opal for tints of opal in the surrounding mountains. The first store here was in a tent; a large sheepshearing shed was put up here in 1919; it is a shipping point for livestock.

Open Door Peak, 11,100, Teton: a formation on the side of the peak looks like an open door from a distance.

Oregon Basin, Park: an old bull became weak and mean when cowboys were trailing Carter's cattle from Oregon into Bighorn basin in the early days; he was left here to die. Spring roundup found the bull in good health and utterly indifferent to his solitude; he was known as "the

148

Oregon bull"—his range was Oregon basin.

A venture to irrigate this region in 1908 failed because finances ran out before canals could be completed to bring in water from the South Fork of the Shoshone River.

Oregon Buttes, Sweetwater: a group of buttes rising out of the prairie; they are the sentinels of the South Pass region. On top of them are petrified algae, showing they were once raised from an inland sea that was probably filled with volcanic ash, which helped petrify the algae. They were named Oregon Buttes because they were near the Oregon Trail; they were a pioneer landmark. The Continental Divide splits here: the two parts surround the Great Divide basin or Red Desert; they join again in Colorado.

Oregon Short Line, Lincoln, Sweetwater: an extension of the Union Pacific railroad, beginning at Granger, running west, and joining the Utah and Northern; the name was adopted in 1897.

Oregon Trail: a path of least resistance for westbound emigrants following the North Platte and Sweetwater rivers and on through South Pass, branching into several routes; it was used from 1834 to 1868, the coming of the railroad.

In 1849 more than 35,000 gold seekers traveling with covered wagons drawn by oxen or horses used this route. Mormons seeking religious freedom followed it pushing handcarts. It was the path of Empire, filled with caravans, plodding through heat and blizzards, plagued with Indian attacks, broken wagons, sickness and death. There was no turning back.

Neihardt, Nebraska poet, describing the Oregon Trail also voiced the feelings of Indians:

"Were all the teeming regions of the dawn
Unpeopled now? What devastating need
Had set so many faces pale with greed,
Against the sunset?
. . . . They did but look
And whatsoever pleased them, that they took."

Orin Junction, Converse: named for Orin Hughitt, uncle of the president of the Chicago and Northwestern railroad. The Colorado and Southern railroad, which became part of the Burlington system, came from the south and joined the other railroad here in 1901; it is located at the junction of Highways 20 and 87, near the old LaBonte stage station and near Bridger's Crossing of the Platte River.

Orpha, Converse: discontinued post office named for Mrs. Orpha Grace Tracy, postmaster.

Osage, Weston: named for the oil regions of Oklahoma; Osage is an Indian name for "on top of the hill." The first oil well was drilled there in 1890; a gusher well drilled in 1920 changed the village from a flag stop on the railroad to a booming oil town with a refinery and a population of 1,500 in less than a year.

In the early days the post office was moved at night twice, until people began to wonder where they would find it next; a nearby ridge has oyster, clam, and turtle shells, as well as petrified fish now scattered on dry, sagey prairie.

Another version of the name is that railroad officials heard a homesick lady getting off the train exclaim happily after she had taken a deep breath, "O--o--h, sage"; then they named the station Osage.

Osborn Mountain, 11,905, Sublette: named for Robert L. Osborn, homesteader.

Oscelo, Carbon: a group of mining claims in the Ferris-Haggarty area known as the Oscelo group; it was probably named for a miner.

Oshoto, Crook: post office established in 1911; the neighbors met to discuss a possible name; the weather was bad, so Sam Rathburn, former Indian scout, suggested Oshoto, an Indian name for bad weather.

The first bentonite processing plant in the world was built at nearby Clay Spur; it is the stickiest, gooiest mud known; it will stick the wheels of a car tight against their fenders when wet. Processing consists of drying and powdering; it has a thousand uses.

Osmond, Lincoln: named for George Osmond, first president of the Star Valley Stake, a Mormon ward in 1901; it is a farming district.

Osprey Falls, YNP: named for the osprey hawk that feeds on fish.

Otto, Big Horn: named for Otto Franc who established the Pitchfork ranch, named for its brand. Otto lost the county seat fight to Basin by 38 votes, when Big Horn County was formed in 1896.

Ouzel Falls, Teton: named for the water ouzel, a bird that bobs in and out of water torrents, getting its food; it does not have webbed feet like most water-loving birds.

Overland, Albany: a railroad stop on the Hahn's Peak railroad; named for the Overland Trail.

Overland Trail: stretched from St. Louis, Missouri, across southern Wyoming and on to California; the name is obvious; Ben Holladay purchased the transportation and mail contract in 1862; he changed the route from the Oregon Trail to avoid Indians.

The Overland Trail entered Wyoming from Colorado near Virginia Dale Station, crossed the Laramie Plains, went over Bridger Pass, west to Fort Bridger, and on; it followed the old Cherokee Trail most of the way and became the main stage and emigrant route.

Overland Trail, Carbon: station on the Saratoga and Encampment railroad.

Owen, Albany: discontinued post office; it was named by John Merta, first postmaster, for William O. Owen, surveyor.

Owen, Platte: post office in 1887 named for Billy Owen, surveyor.

Owen Creek, Sheridan: named for J. Frank Owen, rancher here in 1881.

Owen, Mount, 12,922, Teton: named for William O. Owen, surveyor, who claimed to have made the first climb of Grand Teton with three companions in 1898. Mount Owen is the second highest summit in the Tetons—excellent for climbing.

Owens, Weston: named for John Owens, picturesque pioneer.

Owl Creek, Hot Springs, Park: named by Indians for the many owls living here; their name was Pa-pa-da; John D. Woodruff, adventurer, built the first cabin in Bighorn basin here in 1871; it had a dirt roof and floor.

150

Woodruff became a scout at Camp Brown. About 1876 he drove in 6,000 sheep from Oregon, and later some cattle. The cabin was ranch headquarters.

Owl Creek Mountains: on the boundary line between Hot Springs and Fremont counties; it was named for the creek. They are a branch of the Absaroka Mountains; their core is granite, covered with limestone and sandstone.

Oxbow Bend, Teton: the Snake River cut a new channel and left a quiet backwater with abundant plant food; it is ideal for ducks and Canada geese; pelicans pause here in their annual migration. Trumpeter swans, and even great blue herons nest on Cottonwood Island here.

Oyster Ridge, Lincoln, Uinta: there are outcroppings of oyster shells and other marine fossils in the sandstone here.

P

P K Creek, Sheridan: named for the P K ranch of the Patrick brothers.

Pabst Peak, 10,261, Fremont, Sublette: H. and C. Titcomb climbed the peak in 1901, and drank a bottle of Pabst beer on top, hence the name.

Pacific Creek, Teton: its water, some of which comes from Two Ocean Lake, flows to the Pacific Ocean via the Snake River.

Pacific Power and Light Company, Converse: also known as Dave Johnston's Power Plant; a huge, generating plant on the Platte River, it uses coal for power; thus shipping coal by wire hundreds of miles; it is located on the Pony Express and Oregon trails where a hundred years ago, horses' hooves furnished fastest power known.

The plant, with its 420,000 kilowatt capacity and its brilliant lights at night, is a landmark for aircraft and jets; it can be seen by pilots as far as one hundred miles away.

Pacific Springs, Fremont: a pleasant spot about three miles west of the Continental Divide, where westbound emigrants could relax, and for the first time, taste water flowing to the Pacific Ocean. The Sublette brothers discovered the springs in the 1820s.

A Pony Express and a stage station were located here. The Sublette Cut-off to Fort Hall, Idaho, left the main trail here. Marcus Whitman and H. H. Spalding and their brides paused here, July 4, 1836, with a Bible in one hand, and an American flag in the other. Dr. Whitman knelt and took possession of the land to the west as a "home of American mothers and the Church of Christ."

Pahaska Tepee, Park: built in 1901 by Buffalo Bill Cody as a hunting lodge where he entertained many distinguished guests. Pahaska was a Sioux Indian name for Buffalo Bill, meaning "long hair"; the Sioux made him a member of their tribe; it is now a campground and tourist lodge; it is in the National Register of Historic Places.

Paintbrush Canyon, Teton: named for the Indian Paintbrush, which was chosen as the Wyoming state flower in 1917. Dr. Grace

Raymond Hebard, University of Wyoming, hired a New York artist to paint the paintbrush, and promoted passage of the bill adopting it.

Painter, Park: discontinued ranch post office named for John R. Painter.

Paintrock Creek and Lakes, Big Horn: named by Indians who used clay of variegated colors found on the creek's banks for ceremonial and war paint.

Palisades, Park: rock sculptures north of US 20 on the scenic drive from Cody to Yellowstone National Park.

Palmer Canyon, Plate: named for William Palmer, homesteader in 1907.

Papoose Creek and Peak, 10,923, Park: also known as Indian Peak. Indians once considered this a favorite hunting ground.

Paradise Basin and Pass, Fremont: spectacular scenic country.

Paradise Canyon, Albany: named for Paradise, a rancher.

Parco, Carbon: railroad station called Grenville for Gen. Grenville Dodge, until it became an active oil refinery camp in 1923. Renamed Paco for Producers and Refiners Corporation, commonly known as P&R; it is now Sinclair for Sinclair Oil Company; this is a town for employees.

Park, Sheridan: discontinued post office; a reservoir for irrigating was built here in 1911; it is near a large park, an opening in the forest. Willis Spear built Spear O'Wigwam, a tourist lodge.

Park County: named because of its proximity to Yellowstone National Park; established in 1909, after having been part of Sweetwater, Fremont, and Big Horn counties; Cody is the county seat.

Ranching operations date back to the 1880s, when the first cattle were brought in. Irrigation led to farming; one area in Wyoming where fruit, especially apples, can be grown in protected valleys.

Oil and gas were discovered in 1912; now this is the second largest industry. A multimillion-dollar processing plant for gypsum is located at Himes. Lovell has a processing plant for bentonite. Lumbering, sugar beets, dude ranching, tourist trade, and winter sports are other sources of county income.

Parker, Laramie: discontinued post office named for Mrs. Julia Parker.

Parker Peak, 10,203, YNP: named for Rev. Samuel Parker; once it was a favorite campsite of Indians, because of its commanding view of all approaches.

Parkerton, Converse: an oil town on the edge of the Big Muddy Oil Field; named for Rev. Samuel Parker who in 1835 preached the first Protestant sermon in the Rocky Mountain region at a rendezvous of trappers, traders, and Indians at the head of Hoback Canyon.

Parkman, Sheridan: a railroad station in 1894 named by its officials for historian Francis Parkman who earlier had made a trip through the region. He wrote *The Oregon Trail*.

Park Run Creek, Albany: named for the park or clearing through which it runs.

Pass, Sheridan: discontinued post office named for a natural mountain pass on the Bozeman Trail; it was once a boom settlement in anticipation of the Burlington railroad coming its way. The population vanished when it was bypassed by the railroad, which went west to Parkman in 1894.

Pass Creek, Sheridan: flows through a natural mountain pass.

Passaic, Sheridan: discontinued post office in 1940; named by Mrs. Jim Jennings, postmaster, for her native town, Passaic, Missouri. She homesteaded in the fall of 1913 but did not get a cabin built; she lived in a tent all winter, even in sub-zero weather.

Pasup Creek, Fremont: on the Wind River Indian Reservation; it is an Indian name for "dry creek." Fuller's earth, used in refining oil, is found along this creek.

Pathfinder Canyon, Natrona: see Fiery Narrows.

Pathfinder Reservoir, Carbon, Natrona: named for John Charles Fremont, explorer of 1842, called "The Pathfinder." The dam was started in 1905; it is the oldest dam on the Platte River; supplies were hauled in by teams; grading was done with horses and scrapers. The foundation was hand-dug to bedrock; stones were hand-quarried. Wooden derricks with blocks and tackles placed the larger stones brought in by teams and wagons. Workmen and masons climbed down wooden ladders to build the foundation. The dam was completed in 1909; it was built in a deep granite canyon and is 218 feet high and 432 feet long; it can impound 1,016,000 acre-feet of water for power, irrigation and recreation.

Pat O'Hare Creek and Peak, Park: named for an Irishman, Pat O'Hare, trapper and rancher.

Patrick, Goshen: discontinued post office named for Edwin Patrick, postmaster.

Patten Creek, Platte: named for Patten, early squatter.

Pavillion, Fremont: town named for a large, nearby butte.

Pavillion Butte, Fremont: named by surveyors because its shape resembles a pavillion.

Pazeka Lake, Albany: has epsom salt content in the water; it was named in the 1880s for a commercial laxative, pazeka.

Pea Green Buttes, Big Horn: eroded into the shape of inverted bells, they are pea-green in color.

Peale Island, YNP: named for Dr. C. A. Peale, author of the report on thermal springs in Hayden's report of 1878; the island is at extreme south of Yellowstone Lake.

Pease County, named for Dr. E. L. Pease, representative from Uinta County in the first territorial legislature; it was created in 1875 and had few, if any, settlers; the name was changed to Johnson County in 1879 for E. P. Johnson, Cheyenne attorney.

Pechenpaugh, Sheridan: discontinued post office named for D. C. Pechenpaugh, Superintendent of the Burlington railroad.

Peckville, Natrona: oil camp near Midwest named for Rev. Oscar Peckenpaugh. The post office was in his home.

Pedestal Peak, 13,200, Fremont, Sublette: named for mushroom-shaped pedestals on its summit.

Pedro, Carbon: discontinued post office named for the mountains.

Pedro, Weston: a railroad siding named by Burlington officials in 1892. The first commercial shipment of bentonite was made from here; it was hauled by teams, and shoveled by hand into a boxcar; then it was sent to Denver and used in a medicinal mixture for congestion of lungs; it was called Denver Mud. Old-timers used bentonite to remove oil and dirt from their hands, and called it "native soap."

Pedro Mountains, Carbon: a granite range that rises precipitously from sandy desert land. A pygmy mummy was found here in 1932 by two prospectors; it was probably one of the "little people" of Sheepeaters.

Pelican Bay and Springs, YNP: named for Pelican Creek.

Pelican Creek, YNP: named by the Washburn party of 1870, who found abundant waterfowl life here, including white pelicans. The area is reached by a hiking tral; lots of wildlife.

Pelton Creek and Park, Albany: named for Clark Pelton, who took up a mining claim here in 1903.

Pemmican Pinnacle, 11,500, Teton: named for pemmican, a food made by Indians and trappers; dried meat was ground between stones and mixed with dried berries and buffalo tallow; stored in stomach pouches or rawhide bags.

Pendergraft Meadows and Peak, 10,599, Teton: named for O. A. "Slim" Pendergraft, an early game warden in the area.

Pennock Mountain, Carbon: named for Homer Pennock, pioneer, and first to explore Medicine Bow Range for minerals; also known as Wood Mountain and Cedar Mountain.

Peno Creek, Johnson, Sheridan: named for Peno, a Canadian trapper who shot and wounded a buffalo bull. The bull gored Peno's horse to death, and broke Peno's limb. He slept and woke to find a big bear standing over him; the bear had a sliver in its paw. Peno removed the sliver, and the bear guided him to a friendly Indian village.

Penrose, Park: town founded about 1904 by Mormons; named for Apostle Penrose. Industrious agriculturists, the Mormons developed irrigation in Bighorn basin.

Penrose Canyon, Park, and Peak, 12,443, Johnson: named for Penrose, who in the early days attempted to homestead in Penrose Park. Penrose valley has several lakes, and a beautiful waterfall.

Penta Geyser, YNP: water comes from five vents during eruptions.

Pepperville, Platte: crossroads store for Fred Pepper, owner.

Percy, Carbon: railroad station for Percy T. Browne, construction engineer who was killed by Indians; it is a timber-loading station; it once challenged Rawlins for the county seat. Old Percy is all moved away as homesteaders' homes. New Percy on the railroad is just a whistle stop.

Perdo, Carbon: once a post office at the end of the route from Leo.

Perrin, Fremont: discontinued post office named for Jack Perrin, rancher.

Petrie, Natrona: railroad station named for John Petrie, livestock agent for the Chicago and Northwestern railroad.

154

Petzoldt Caves and Ridge, Teton: named for Paul Petzoldt, one of Wyoming's most famous mountain climbers. He has climbed mountains from the Tetons to the Himalayas.

Pfeiffer Hill, Crook: named for homesteader Pfeiffer.

Phelps Lake, Teton: named for Phelps, a hunter and trapper who joined the Hayden survey party in 1872. The lake is oval-shaped and about three miles long. There is a nature trail for hiking from White Grass Ranger Station.

Phillips, Goshen: discontinued post office named for Johnny Phillips.

Phil Peco, Sweetwater: named for Phil Mass, first settler on Henry's Fork about 1857; he was a trapper for the American Fur Company. Pico is Spanish for peak. Phil Peco means Phil's Peak; the spelling was changed.

Philpott Canyon, Crook: named for early settler Philpott.

Philsmith Point, Teton: named for Phil Smith, one of Wyoming's famed mountain climbers who pioneered many first ascents in the Tetons.

Photo Pass, 11,400, Fremont, Sublette: named Photographic Pass by the Colorado Mountain Club in 1950; very scenic.

Pickett Creek, Park: named for Col. William D. Pickett.

Piedmont, Uinta: originally called Byrne for Moses Byrne, pioneer. Because of the likeness to Bryan, the name was changed to Piedmont meaning "at the foot of the mountains." Mrs. Byrne suggested the name Piedmont in memory of the Italian region where she once lived. Moses Byrne built five large charcoal kilns to produce charcoal for Utah smelters. Their ruins still stand. The Union Pacific railroad once had a roundhouse here.

Pierre River, Teton: named for Pierre Chouteau, Jr., of the Rocky Mountain Fur Company.

Pierre's Hole, Teton: Pierre, Iroquois Indian, noted friend of the white men, killed here by Blackfoot Indians.

Pilot Butte, 7,932, Sweetwater: famous landmark for pioneers; a pipe staircase now goes up the east side to the summit of the plateau; there is a panoramic view from the top.

Pilot Butte Reservoir, Fremont: named for a nearby butte that guided early travelers. The dam was completed in 1926; it holds 30,000 acre-feet of water for irrigation on the Riverton project; it is also used for power and recreation.

Pilot Hill, Sheridan: a sentinel back of Fort Phil Kearny; lookouts signaled from here when they saw emigrant trains or Indians.

Pilot Knob, Albany: a guide for early travelers; it appears on maps as early as 1885.

Pilot Knobs, Teton: see Teton Range.

Pilot Peak, 11,708, Park: outstanding landmark; it is a lava flow from an ancient volcano. Pilot is higher and sharper than its companion sentinel, Index, when viewed from the south and east. When seen from the north and west approach on Highway 212, they have traded profiles, and Pilot, to the south, seems lower and broader. Often there is confusion as to which is which.

Pine Bluffs, Laramie: named for stunted pines on nearby bluffs; first it was known as Rock Ranch, but the name was changed by railroad officials. In 1868 Pine Bluffs consisted of a tent, a slab shack with a stone chimney, and a square shed of canvas-covered poles; it became the largest cattle-shipping point on the Union Pacific railroad about 1884; it was on the Texas Trail.

Pine Grove Stage Station, Carbon: a home, or swing station where drivers and horses changed; it had meals and sleeping accommodations for passengers as well as a blacksmith shop. In 1865 Indians were desperately trying to stop traffic on the Overland Trail; the Army stationed five soldiers here to protect travelers' safety.

Pinedale, Sublette: first settler, a cattleman, in 1878; located on Pine Creek, it was named for the creek by Charles Peterson, postmaster, when the post office started in 1899; it is the incorporated town farthest from a railroad in Wyoming; it was made county seat of Sublette County in 1921.

Pinedale is headquarters for a ranger station, gateway to Bridger Wilderness Area, and a tourist town. The Green River Rendezvous is enacted here the second Sunday of every July, when trappers, traders, and Indians in authentic dress have their annual get-together. Cutter races are held here in winter.

Piney, Campbell: discontinued post office; named for Piney Creek.

Piney Creeks, Sublette: named by A. W. "Piney" Smith, first settler here in 1878.; his nickname was given because he lived among pines.

Pingora, 11,884, Fremont: a Shoshone word meaning "high, rocky, inaccessible peak or tower"; it is a good description of this vertical, granite chimney; the peak was climbed by O H. Bonney and Frank and Notsie Garnick, who named it, in 1940.

The evening before the climb, while camped at Lonesome Lake, Frank Garnick remarked, "I know some day some damn fool will climb it." The next day he and his two companions did climb it.

Pinnacle Mountain, 1,400, Park: has pinnacled ridges extending in all directions.

Pinnochio Pinnacle, 12,000, Teton: named for its profile as seen from Bonney Pinnacle to the south.

Pinyon Peak, 9,705, Teton: named for pinyon pine on it.

Pioneer Hollow, Uinta: a narrow valley followed by pioneers bound for Utah; now it is followed by the railroad.

Pipe Organ Ridge, 12,200, Fremont, Sublette: named for its impressive, fluted appearance by the first ascending party G. Bell and J. Sargeant in 1949; it has rotten rock for climbing.

Piper Buttes, Niobrara: named for William Piper, who built up a ranch here in the 1890s. He sent for a mail-order wife, an actress from Chicago; she was an excellent housekeeper and a good horsewoman; she rode side-saddle.

Pipersville, Sweetwater: discontinued post office named for John Piper, postmaster.

Pippin, Campbell: discontinued post office named for Arthur Pippin, postmaster.

Pisgah, Mount, 6,000, Weston: highest point in the county; resembles a huge molar, roots and all; named by Frank Mondell (his father was a minister) who found salt water on one side and sweet water on the other; he gave it the Biblical name of the mount from which God showed Moses the Promised Land.

Water from a little lake on top of Mount Pisgah was piped to Cambria, about three miles, in 1890.

Pitchfork, Park: discontinued post office; named for the creek.

Pitchfork Creek, Park: named for the Pitchfork ranch of Otto Franc; the ranch was named for Franc's brand.

Pitchfork Oil Field, Park: named for Pitchfork Creek.

Pitchstone Plateau, 8,700, YNP: the lava flows here are only thousands of years old; it represents the most recent volcanic action in the park and is located in its southwest corner.

Pixley, Lincoln: railroad siding named for Charles Pixley, rancher.

Pixley Creek, Lincoln: named for George and Theodore Pixley, settlers here about 1900.

Platinum, Albany: here in the 1920s prospectors found traces of platinum and grains of gold, silver, and copper; promoters imported mining machinery and bought the meadows at the foot of Centennial Ridge as a site for a city; the project failed; the land was seized for taxes in 1938; this property, once valued at more than $100,000, sold at auction for $7,000. The place is now abandoned.

Platte County: named for the Platte River; it was established in 1911 and organized in 1913 with Wheatland as the county seat. Mining, agriculture, and livestock-raising are its chief industries. Huge mines at Hartville and Sunrise produce iron ore that is shipped to Colorado for processing; marble is mined near Laramie Peak and crushed at a converted sugar beet mill.

Glendo Reservoir furnishes recreation in water sports, fishing, and camping. Jade has been found here, brought down the Platte River as float from jade fields in central Wyoming. Jade, one of the heaviest rocks, floats when frozen in ice.

Platte River: see North Platte River.

Platte River Bridge, Natrona: in the 1850s Louis Guinard built a toll bridge near present Casper to replace the Mormon ferry. The bridge was made of cedar logs resting on stone-filled cribs; it cost Guinard about $60,000. The bridge was later rebuilt by John Richeau, whose name pronounced in French sounds like Reshaw—so it was known as Reshaw Bridge.

Here the Battle of Red Buttes was fought, when 19 men of the 11th Kansas Cavalry were killed by Indians pushing piles of dirt before them. Caspar Collins was also killed near this bridge fighting Indians. Fort Caspar and present Casper are named for him.

Playground of the Gods, Park: weird and colorful rock formations along Highway 20 from Cody to Yellowstone National Park; it is composed of eroded lava.

Pleasant Valley School, Converse: also known as the Ed Smith

School; it is probably the first frame schoolhouse built in Wyoming and now is located near the Pioneer Museum on the State Fair Grounds at Douglas.

Plentycoos Creek and Peak, 10,937, Teton: named for Crow Chief Plentycoos; the name means many achievements, or plenty coups (coup is French for strike or blow). He was an outstanding member of his race, counting coups no less than 80 times for striking, or killing an enemy.

Chief Plentycoos led the Crow allies of Gen. Crook in the Battle of the Rosebud against Sioux Indians in 1876. He was the first of the Crow to take up farming and cattle-raising, after white men stopped the nomadic existence of his tribe.

Plont Stage and Pony Express Station, Fremont: operated by Frenchman Plont near the Tom Sun ranch. Jack Slade and his hirelings killed and buried two men near the station about 1862.

Plume, 11,600, Fremont, Sublette: a prominent pinnacle that juts out from the east face of War Bonnet Ridge like a plume or thumb.

Plunkett Oil Wells, Fremont: an Irishman, Plunkett, dug wells here.

Point of Rocks, Sweetwater: railroad station; it was once the old Almond Stage Station, famous in the time of the Pony Express; it was named for a sandstone ridge jutting out over Bitter Creek. Once this was the closest Union Pacific railroad station to South Pass City; stages ran there daily; now only stone ruins are left. The Jim Bridger Power Plant north of here started operating in 1974, with the first 500,000 kilowatt unit. Point of Rocks is now the place where a 7-mile spur of railroad takes off to the Jim Bridger plant.

Poison, Johnson: named by early cowboys.

Poison Basin, Carbon: livestock died here by thousands from selenium poisoning; they ate milk vetch which drew selenium from the ground. Selenium became valuable about 1940 as an ingredient in making glass; now it is extremely valuable for its electrical properties.

Poison Cave, YNP: the opening is only two feet across; deadly volcanic gases escape here and cause eyes to smart and water if a person bends over to look at the opening.

Poison Creek Stage Station, Natrona: once it was New Wolton; now the place is called Hiland.

Poison Spider Creek, Natrona: an early surveyor needed a new thread for his transit, went to a spider web to get it, was bitten, and died. Another version says a sheepherder was bitten here by a poisonous spider. Yet another says the water was poisonous to livestock.

Kit Carson found an oil seep by the creek; this oil, mixed with flour, was used by pioneers as axle grease.

Polecat Bench, Park: strata here are estimated to be 60 million years old; they contain fossils of small animals, crocodiles, and turtles; below these strata are dinosaur fossils, estimated to be 120 million years old.

Polecat Springs, Teton: water has an unpleasant odor due to minerals held in solution, so it was named for a polecat or skunk.

158

Pole Creek, Albany: named by Indians for excellent, straight tepee poles they could get here.

Pole Creek Ranch, Laramie: first regular stop on the Cheyenne-Deadwood stage route; in 1876 Schwartze built a two-story hotel here and served meals; he could stable 50 head of horses.

Pole Mountain Recreation Area, Albany: this mountain was named by Indians for its good tepee poles; the area also is known as Vedauwoo, Indian for "earth-born"; it is a very scenic area with rocks, trees, and flowers. The area swarmed with tie cutters in 1867; ties floated down the creek to where it was crossed by the Union Pacific railroad; this was the first timber industry in state.

Pollock, Albany: discontinued post office named for Homer W. Pollock, rancher.

Pollux Peak, 11,067, Park, YNP: named for a Greek character.

Pomeroy Basin, Lincoln: named for the Pomeroy family.

Pony Express Route: started in 1860 by Russell, Majors, and Waddell for rapid transit of the mail to the west coast; 504 miles of the 1,919-mile route were in Wyoming, which had the longest mileage of the eight states through which the Pony Express passed.

Riders started from St. Joseph, Missouri, and Sacramento, California, at the same time on April 3, 1860, with mail pouches on the back of saddles; they passed each other near South Pass; the trip took 10 days, used 500 fast horses, usually mustangs, 200 riders, and 190 relay stations spaced about 70 miles apart. The keeper at the station had a fresh horse ready; two minutes were allowed for a rider to change the mail pouches and horse.

Each rider received an inscribed Bible and took an oath not to drink, use profane language, or fight. These riders lived dangerously, suffering the hardships of winds and blizzards; they often died swiftly at the hands of Indians.

The charge for mail was $5 per ounce. In the 16 months the company operated the Pony Express, it lost $200,000 on the venture, and went bankrupt. This dramatic service stopped in October 1861, when a trans-continental telegraph line was joined by east and west crews at Salt Lake City.

The fastest news carried by the Pony Express was of Lincoln's inauguration in 7 days and 17 hours. The Pony Express was re-run in 1960, with a large crowd of spectators watching the passing of the east and west riders near South Pass City.

Poor, Carbon: discontinued post office on Big Creek named for "Old Billy Poor," pioneer settler.

Popo Agie Primitive Area, Fremont: a roadless tract of 70,000 acres of wilderness beauty in Shoshone National Forest. Wilderness, once invaded with roads, lumbering, and mining, can never be restored.

Millions of future tourists, longing to see unspoiled nature, will make primitive and wilderness areas of Wyoming one of the principal future assets of the state.

Popo Agie River, Fremont: pronounced Po-po-zha; Crow Indian name for "head water"; called Wan-ze-Gara by Shoshone Indians, its source is high in the mountains. Another version is that it is an Indian name for wild rye grass, which was tied in bundles, and used on the sides of wikiup shelters to shed water.

The rendezvous of trappers, traders, and Indians were held here from 1824-40, with lots of drinking, gambling, and brawling. Trappers spent their year's catch in a few days; then, with a few supplies, they went back to months of solitude getting more furs.

Porcupine Creek, Big Horn: trail leads to Devils Canyon, with campsites and fishing.

Porter Creek, Albany: named for Charles and Lew Porter, who ran a sawmill here in the 1880s.

Portuguese Houses, Johnson: old trading buildings of hewn logs; it was one of the state's earliest settlements and was erected about 1828 by Antonio Mateo, a Portuguese trader, on the Powder River; first trading post in Wyoming. Jim Bridger said this trading post was once besieged by Indians for 40 days, and successfully resisted; it fell into disuse about 1840.

Portugee Phillips: see Fort Phil Kearny.

Pothole Country, Teton: knob-and-kettle topography formed by melting of ice masses imbedded in morainal debris; potholes fill with water at times; this used to be good bear-hunting country.

Poverty Flat, Uinta: settled by Polson and sons from Sweden and other pioneers. Their struggle to make a living gave it the name.

Poverty Flats, Converse: an old tent town near Fort Fetterman in 1886; the old cemetery still remains; it is located 1½ miles northwest of Douglas.

Powder River, Campbell, Johnson, Natrona: named for dark, fine soil resembling gunpowder found along its banks in places; it is said to be "a mile long, an inch deep, and runs uphill"; it is also said that "its water is too thick to drink, and too thin to plow." In sign language, Indians rubbed dirt between their fingers, and let it fall to denote Powder River. This is one of the few rivers in the world that flows directly north.

The rallying cry "Powder River; Let 'er Buck" was heard around the world, after Wyoming men first used it in France in 1917, when leaping out of trenches to attack the enemy. It became the battle cry of an entire division in Argonne. Frenchmen shouted "Poudre Riviere!"

Bill Schultz, a cowboy, first uttered the cry "Powder River! Let 'er buck!" in a cowboy drinking spree in Casper, after driving 1,600 steers and dry cows from Riverton to Casper. Many of the cowboys did not know the country, and were told by "wise" ones to saddle their swimming horses to cross the Powder River.

When they got to the river, it was dry, with only water holes for the thirsty cattle. When the cowboys reached Casper, they celebrated with a drinking spree. Schultz paid for a round of drinks and uttered the cry, which grew in popularity. A Powder River cowboy never tries to keep his horse from pitching, but just "Let 'er Buck!" The Wyoming National Guard carried this slogan on its emblem for many years.

Powder River, Natrona: village named for the Powder River.

Powder River Pass, 9,666, Sheridan: highest elevation on Highway 16; it goes through granite peaks.

Powell, Park: established in the 1890s as Camp Colter by the Department of the Interior as headquarters for the Shoshone reclamation project; it was renamed for Major John Wesley Powell, first engineer of the reclamation project, which was the result of his foresight, energy, and planning; this became a fine irrigation district, with staples sold through the Big Horn Cooperative Marketing Association. The state has an experiment station here specializing in irrigation.

Northwestern Community College, a junior college, was established at Powell in 1946; the cultural center of Bighorn basin, it offers training in vocational and graphic arts as well as regular college courses.

Pow-wow Cavern, Washakie: a huge cave where Indians once met to smoke and pow-wow; the walls and ceiling are decorated with petroglyphs of ancient origin.

Prairie Center, Goshen: named for its location, the prairie.

Prairie Creek, Campbell: rambles over lots of prairie.

Pratt, Goshen: a cattle-shipping station; named for Col. H. J. Pratt of the Pratt and Ferris Cattle Company.

Pratt's Peak, Converse: also Buck's Peak; named for Buck Pratt, a prospector with long, grey whiskers; he had one ear bitten off by a horse.

Pratts Soda Lakes, Natrona: sodium lakes owned by William Pratt; a railroad siding near Evansville loaded this sodium.

Preacher Creek, Albany: named for Gus Scott, an old southern preacher.

Preachers Rock, Big Horn: a large rock, on which someone painted with black paint, "Prepare to meet thy God"; the present road does not pass it.

Preachers Rock, Sheridan: landmark on an old mountain road to Big Goose Ranger Station.

Prospect Creek, Hot Springs: in the early days a prospector searched for minerals along its banks.

Prospect Gulch, Albany: named for the many prospectors' claims made there in the 1870s.

Prospectors Mountain, 11,231, Teton: named to commemorate the discovery of minerals northwest of here in pioneer times.

Prune Creek, Sheridan: rises high in the mountains above Sheridan and widens out in a morass of dark brown water resembling prune juice.

Pryor Gap and Mountain, Park: named for Sergeant Nathaniel Pryor, Corps of Discovery; it was named in the late 1800s.

Ptarmigan Mountain, 12,200, Park: for the birds which were common here in the early days; they have completely feathered feet.

Pulpit Rock, Sweetwater: also known as Table Rock; it is near Green River City. Brigham Young, Mormon leader, on the way to Salt Lake City in 1847, is said to have preached a sermon here.

Pumpkin Buttes, Campbell: named because their shape and color resemble pumpkins; three large, flat-topped mountains used as landmarks by early travelers and as a hideout by Big Nose George Parrot and his gang. Big Nose George was finally hanged by vigilantes at Rawlins, after he had tried to wreck and rob a Union Pacific train by pulling the spikes from the rails. A section boss discovered some loose rails and flagged the train down. The gang fled to Montana, where Big Nose George was finally caught.

Pumpkin Buttes were called Wa-ga-mu Paha by Sioux Indians; this means Gourd Hills; it was so named because of a tribal ceremony held here in which gourds were rattled. It was explored by Capt. W. F. Reynolds in 1859. The Bozeman Trail passed near the buttes. Portugee Phillips sighted them as a landmark during his famous ride.

The discovery of uranium in the Pumpkin Buttes area caused a flurry of excitement in the 1950s; stockmen resisted the invasion of prospectors staking claims, cutting fences, leaving gates open, and running over grasslands; only a few small mines were developed.

Punteney, Hot Springs: discontinued ranch post office named for V. D. Punteney, ranch owner.

Pylon Peak, 12,378, Fremont, Sublette: named by Iowa mountaineers because of two tremendous, pylon-like towers.

Q

Quadrant Mountain, 10,216, YNP: roughly resembles a segment of a sphere.

Quaking Aspen, Uinta: stage and Pony Express station.

Quealy, Lincoln: a coal camp established in 1910; named for Patrick John Quealy, general manager of the Kemmerer Coal Company.

Quealy Oil Field, Albany: named for P. J. Quealy, who owned the land on which the oil wells were drilled.

Quintet Mountain, 11,900, Fremont: named by five climbers who ascended its five peaks, and left cairns on all of them.

Quiver, Mount, 12,600, Fremont: named by climbers J. Toler and E. Fitzgerald in 1959, because the steep climb up boulder fields and across glaciers made them quiver.

R

Raderville, Natrona: discontinued post office named for Rader family, the first in the area to get an automobile and so the first to get mail. A community of families from Minnesota thought the post office should be named for them.

Ragan, Uinta: railroad station named for Charles Ragan, pioneer.

Ragged Top, Albany: outline as ragged as the teeth of a tiger.

Raid Lake and Peak, 12,532, Sublette: near the scene of conflict between cattlemen and sheepherders in 1903, when cowboys killed 1,200 sheep corralled here.

162

Rairden, Washakie: named for early settler, Dr. Rairden.

Ralston, Park: railroad siding named for saloonkeeper Ralston who had his business here.

Ralston Reservoir, Park: completed in 1908 for irrigation.

Rambler, Carbon: once a town for truckers and miners; it was named for the Doane-Rambler copper mine; not even a timber is left now.

Ramshead Lake, Teton: the skull of a mountain sheep was found here.

Ram's Horn Peak, Fremont: named for Ramshorn ranch and Camp Yellowstone, started by C. C. Moore at the mouth of the DuNoir River in 1907. The ranch was named for a ram's horn which was found there.

Ranch A, Crook: a Chicago millionaire, Moe Annenberg, built himself a "fishing shack," a log cabin with glass-lined bathrooms, bronze window frames, horsehide draperies, decorated with Indian beadwork; the cost in the Depression year of 1931 was $900,000. When it became the property of Peter Smith, son of Nels Smith, Governor of Wyoming from 1939-42, the value of the place was estimated at $3,000,000.

Former governor Nels Smith dug his own oil well with a shovel; he used a water pump powered with a washing machine motor. Oil seeps from sandstone into his small well, probably the world's only hand-dug oil well; it produces "sweet crude" at a 24-foot depth; it is so pure it does not need refining.

Ranchester, Sheridan: established in 1894 as a shipping point by the McShane Tie Company; it was named by Senator S. H. Hardin of the 04-Bar ranch; he was English and combined the word ranch with "chester," the English for a walled town, especially one founded by the Romans in Britain.

Near here is Connor Battlefield, where Major Gen. P. E. Connor surprised 700 Arapahoes under Chief Black Bear and destroyed about 250 lodges, killing women and children.

Randolph Peak, 9,200, Park: a pioneer character, Randolph, a game poacher, had a hideout on this peak.

Range Lake, Albany: see Brooklyn Lake.

Rattlesnake Mountains, Natrona: named for their feared and respected inhabitants, who give a "gentleman's warning" except in August, when they are shedding their skins. They can strike a distance of a foot, when cornered or stepped on, but prefer to run and hide.

Raven Creek, Weston: named for black birds in the bushes along the creek.

Rawhide Buttes Stage Station, Goshen: first building here in 1876 was burned by Indians; rebuilt in 1877, it became the home station for Russel Thorp, Sr., owner of the Cheyenne-Deadwood stage line. Stages came from Cheyenne, 116 miles, in 21 hours. Calamity Jane was one of the first travelers to the Black Hills on February 22, 1876. She and Wild Bill Hickok frequently rode the stage line.

Concord coaches carried nine passengers inside and up to 11 more on top. Rates from Cheyenne to Deadwood were $20 first class, $15 second class, and $10 third class. Sometimes third class had to get off and push the stage up hills or over hard spots. The first six months of 1877, 3,128 people used this stage line.

Gold was hauled back from Deadwood to the railroad at Cheyenne in heavy iron treasure boxes under the seats. Two armed guards rode "shotgun" to the right of the driver. There were numerous holdups by road agents. The old stagecoach is in the Lusk Museum.

Rawhide Creek and Buttes, Goshen: two versions of the name: it was the site of an early day fur trading post, where beaver pelts and buffalo hides were collected, pressed into bales; taken by horses to the Platte River, and shipped to St. Louis.

A legendary version is told in the dramatic "Legend of Rawhide" by Niobrara County citizens; a man traveling west with a wagon train vowed he would shoot the first Indian he saw. The next morning he shot an Indian maiden. Irate Indians attacked the train and the man gave himself up to save his sweetheart. He was skinned alive by Indians near the buttes, which were then called Rawhide.

These three buttes have many Indian campsites. They were the scene of early copper mining and sawmill operations.

Rawhide Springs, Goshen: old stage station and a nice camping place.

Rawlins, Carbon: county seat; Gen. John A. Rawlins was in command of troops protecting Gen. Grenville Dodge, when he was laying out the route for the Union Pacific railroad in 1868. The men were very thirsty, when Dodge discovered a spring.

Gen. Rawlins thought the water was so refreshing that he said "If anything is ever named after me, I want it to be a spring." Gen. Dodge replied, "We will name this Rawlins Spring." Later, he located a railroad division point near the spring and called it Rawlins. A county museum is now located here with pioneer relics, Indian artifacts, and geological specimens.

The state penitentiary was located at Rawlins by a legislative act of 1889. In early territorial days convicts were sent to the House of Correction at Detroit, Michigan. In 1872 a building for detention was completed in Laramie. This building burned and another was used, prisoners being under control of Albany County authorities until they were transferred to the new buildings completed at Rawlins in 1898. Prisoners now manufacture automobile license plates for the state and make historic signs.

Rawlins Red, Carbon: a red mineral from paint mines near Rawlins produces this famous paint; a carload of it was shipped in 1874 to paint the Brooklyn Bridge in New York; it is also used on section houses.

Ray Lake, Fremont: named for Capt. Ray who supervised the digging of a ditch from here in 1894 for irrigation; it also boasts fishing and boating.

Raymond, Big Horn: discontinued ranch post office named for C. W. Raymond.

Raynolds Peak, 10,905, Teton: named for Cpl. W. F. Raynolds, leader of an exploratory and geological expedition from 1859-60.

Recluse, Campbell: post office established in 1918 and so named because of the distance between the ranches and the post office.

Red Bird, Niobrara: discontinued post office and store for Red Bird, owner.

Red Butte, Weston: also known as Fanny's Peak; a spectacular red butte with a white limestone cap, it has long been a landmark; it is in red soil country with good wheat land. Legend says a girl, Fanny, leaped from the peak to escape Indians.

In the 1850s Sir George Gore of Ireland and 75 hunters slaughtered a large number of buffalo here, taking only their tongues. His friend, W. A. F. "Fritz" Williams mounted a large telescope on Red Butte to study the stars.

Red Buttes, Albany: railroad station named in 1868 for red soil and hills.

Red Buttes, Natrona: stage and Pony Express station; William Cody, a Pony express rider, made the longest nonstop ride from this station. Completing his own run of 116 miles between Red Buttes and Three Crossings, he found his relief rider killed by Indians. He galloped on to Rocky Ridge station—another 76 miles. He returned to his own beat to Red Buttes in record time.

Red Buttes Battle Site, Natrona: Sergeant Amos J. Custard, 11th Kansas Cavalry, on the way from Sweetwater station to Platte Bridge, camped here in 1865 near Willow Spring, although he knew of Indian danger. Indians attacked, pushing piles of dirt before them as breastworks, and killed all but three men who escaped to the river.

Red Cloud Indian Agency, Goshen: on the Platte River one mile west of the Nebraska-Wyoming state line; this agency was established in 1871 for the Oglala band of Sioux Indians. Three years later it was moved to Crawford, Nebraska. The buildings were sold and moved away in 1880. The agency was named for Chief Red Cloud; a post office here was called Little Moon.

Red Desert, Sweetwater: named for red soil; it contains the world's largest body of shifting sand and desert land—about 700 square miles of arid land in a rough square. It is mostly public land managed by the Bureau of Land Management; there is also Union Pacific land given them by the government when the railroad was being constructed. It is good sheep pasture in winter, as well as good wildlife habitat for antelope, elk and wild horses; the area contains important archeologic sites. More than 100 varieties of plants grow on the Red Desert, which has many good finds for rockhounds.

Red Desert, Sweetwater: railroad siding named for Red Desert, through which the Union Pacific railroad runs for a hundred miles.

Red Mountains, YNP: volcanic in origin; their porphyry is red in color; they are about 10,000 feet in altitude and timbered almost to the summits.

Red Rock Canyon, Fremont: between Lander and South Pass, it has breath-taking beauty, especially at sunset; this place inspired the following poem by the author of this book.

Wyoming Paradise

I am tired, said Jehovah,
And this is the seventh day.
My work is almost finished,
Why not leave it that way?

I will leave the unpolished mountains,
Bare hills of tinted stone;
These scraps of unused prairies,
Here with the dreams I have known.

I will scatter loose threads of rivers,
Drop seeds of enduring pine;
And use the grey of the sagebrush
To soften the bright sunshine.

The winds that I used for music . . .
I think I will turn them loose;
My paintbrushes though can stay here
Ready for future use.

On days when I grow weary
Of watching man's struggle and strife,
I will come back to this beauty
With its wild and primitive life.

Then I may paint a sunset,
Or carve a canyon from stone;
Yes, it is good to leave this . . .
One spot I can call my own.

Red Walls Reservoir, Johnson: named for Red Walls.

Red Wall, Johnson: see Hole-in-the-Wall.

Redbank, Washakie: named for red soil; here Governor W. A. Richards once had a ranch in Canyon Creek Canyon. See Big Trails.

Redman, Johnson: a community named for Indians who once considered this country their favorite hunting ground.

Reeds Rock, Albany: named for Silas Reed, first surveyor-general of Wyoming.

Reed's Stage Station, Fremont: named for Johnny Reed.

Reese Mountain, Albany: named about 1900 for rancher Reese.

Regan, Uinta: named for Regan, a squaw man who owned a ranch near Piedmont; he was an old-timer who liked to hunt and trap.

Register Cliff, Platte: site of Seth E. Ward trading post; thousands of emigrants carved their names here in the 1850s and later; the earliest date was 1842. Wheels of covered wagons on the Oregon Trail wore ruts four feet deep in sandstone near here; the trail is still visible.
  Messages for those to follow were also carved or written in axle grease

on cliff. Three generations left their marks here: T. H. Unthank, 1850; O. N. Unthank, 1869; O. A. Unthank, 1931. There is an Indian burial ground on the summit of the cliff.

Reliance, Sweetwater: town named for Reliance Coal Mines, which were named by Union Pacific railroad officials in the 1870s for their dependable coal.

Western Wyoming Community College was located here; now it has been moved to new campus south of Rock Springs.

Rendezvous Peak, 10,924, Teton: an aerial tram from Teton Village at the base to the top of the peak can carry 63 passengers; it operates all year. The tram rises 4,135 vertical feet in a length of 12,600 feet; it cost $2,000,000 to construct and was opened July 31, 1966. The peak offers sightseeing in summer, excellent skiing in winter. Skiers can flash down the longest vertical drop in the United States—4,135 feet. Dining and a souvenir building are on top of the peak.

Rendezvous Promontory, Sheridan: so named because from here Red Cloud and his Sioux chiefs had an unobstructed view of the surrounding country. Red Cloud got his name when he was young. He dashed on horseback across the Dakota prairies, with a scarlet blanket flying from his shoulders.

A great warrior, Red Cloud never lost an opportunity to kill white men who invaded and stole his lands. When other chiefs wanted to sign peace treaties, Red Cloud said, "No, No! I want war. The words of white men are written in water."

In more than 200 battles he fought against Generals Miles, Sheridan, Crook, and Terry, never giving up, even breaking out of the reservation to fight. He was finally given a two-story house on the Pine Ridge Indian Reservation in South Dakota. There he died in 1909.

Reno Hill, Johnson: discontinued post office named for General Jesse Lee Reno, soldier.

Rescue Creek, YNP: named by Washburn; this is the creek where Everts was lost and not found.

Reservoir Creek, Albany: carries reserve snow water from Laramie Peak.

Reservoir Lakes, Albany: four small lakes like reservoirs, one above the other.

Reshaw Bridge, Natrona: named for John Richeau or Richards, whose last name was pronounced in French to sound like Reshaw. He built the bridge over the Platte River near present Casper in 1851-53; 386 feet long, it was an important crossing on the Oregon Trail. The bridge has been reconstructed and a recreation park developed near it.

Reshaw Creek and Reshaw Hills, Platte: named for John Richeau, early mountain man and renegade.

Rex Lake and Rex Oil Field, Albany: named by Louis Coughlin in 1918 because the name Rex, meaning king, stirred his fancy.

Rhinehart Lake, Sheridan: for Mary Roberts Rhinehart, noted author who sat by this lake when she wrote *Lost Ecstasy*.

Rhoda Creek and Gulch, Sheridan: also called Slater Creek; named for Rhoda Slater, daughter of a homesteader in 1882.

Richards, Fremont: railroad station named for Richards Peak.

Richards Creek, Fremont: named for W. A. Richards, U.S. Indian Commissioner.

Richards Creek, Platte: named for DeForest Richards, homesteader.

Riddle Lake, YNP: named by R. Hering, topographer for Hayden Survey of 1872, because the lake is on a divide, and water from it flows to both Atlantic and Pacific oceans.

Rifle Pits Ridge, Crook: an expedition from Montana was headed for the Black Hills to prospect for gold in 1876, when they were harassed by Indians here, and dug pits for protection.

Rim Base, Uinta: named by trappers because an eastern wall of the basin makes the water flow east to Salt Lake.

Riner, Sweetwater: railroad station named for J. A. Riner, judge.

Ring Mountain, Albany: named for a growth of shrubs which form a perfect circle on the west side of the mountain.

Ringbone Lake, Sheridan: named by Bud Mead when he finished eating a round steak here.

Ringrose Draw, Albany: named for Fred Ringrose, rancher.

Riverdale, Crooks: discontinued post office; named by William T. Hazelton, postmaster in 1881, for the topography.

Riverside, Carbon: rendezvous for bartering between white men and red in 1851. During a blizzard a party of mountain men went to the rescue of snow-trapped Indians near here, and received in pay their choice of Sioux maidens.

Later Doggett had a way station and post office here known as Doggett. With the copper strike, a village grew in the 1890s and chose the name Riverside, as it was on the Encampment River. A 40-room hotel burned, and another was built. When the copper boom ended, the town faded. Now it is a village for tourists.

Riverton, Fremont: the town was platted and planned before a building was erected in 1906; it was first named Wadsworth for H. E. Wadsworth, Indian agent at Fort Washakie. Residents renamed it Riverton because four rivers converge about a mile from town.

Riverton is located on land ceded from the Wind River Indian Reservation; it was developed into an irrigation project and opened to white settlement. So eager were the first settlers, that they were evicted by the cavalry from Fort Washakie. A group from Lander "jumped" their abandoned claims. Original claimants marched back with rifles to reclaim their plots, pulling up the Lander stakes.

Days of dust and drought followed; many wanted to "give the land back to the Indians." Eventually water wells were drilled, homes built, and sagebrush fields grew green with irrigated beets and alfalfa. A uranium boom in the Gas Hills, about 35 miles to the east, made for the rapid growth of the town. Mills now process yellow cake in Riverton.

In 1960 a lady mayor, Mrs. Willa Corbitt, was elected; so effective was her government that she was re-elected several times. After 15 years of planning, Central Wyoming Community College started its building program in Riverton in 1967 and opened in 1968; it has vocational courses,

168

computer science and adult education in addition to regular college work.

Roaring Fork Creek, Albany: named in 1880 by Jack Newell for waterfalls in the creek.

Roaring Mountain, 8,000, YNP: named by USGS for the sound of rushing steam escaping constantly from vents near the summit of the mountain. Geyser comes from the Icelandic word "geysa," meaning to gush. A geyser is a deep fissure filled with water; internal heat in the earth raises the water temperature; steam forms under pressure, and drives a column of water and steam upward.

Robbers Roost Creek, Niobrara, Weston: named for Robbers Roost Stage Station.

Robbers Roost Stage Station, Niobrara: also known as Burnt Station. The crossing of the Cheyenne River here, with its steep banks lined with timber and brush, was an ideal place for outlaws to wait and ambush stagecoaches, hence the name. The station was burned by Indians in 1878 and never rebuilt.

Roberts Mission, Fremont: a school on the Wind River Indian Reservation founded by Rev. John Roberts, who came to the reservation in 1883 to be a missionary for the Episcopal Church. He was a friend and teacher of the Indians for more than 40 years; he buried Sacajawea in a nearby cemetery and translated part of the Bible into both Shoshone and Arapahoe languages.

Roberts Mountain, 12,767, Fremont: named for Rev. John Roberts.

Robertson, Uinta: first agricultural settlement in Bridger valley; it was named for John "Uncle Jack" Robertson, trapper and squaw man in 1834.

Robin Lake, Big Horn: named by Spears in 1931 for Senator Robinson of Arkansas, a ranch guest who helped stock the lake with fish.

Robinson, Sweetwater: railroad station named for "Black Bill" Robinson who carried mail over the Medicine Bow Mountains in the 1870s.

Robinson Creek, Carbon: named for "Black Bill" Robinson.

Rochelle, Weston: discontinued post office named for Albert Rochelle, rancher. Mrs. Albert (Kathleen) Rochelle was elected state representative from Niobrara County in 1926.

Rochelle Hills, Weston: named for saline deposits in the vicinity.

Rock Creek, Albany: railroad station; the name is obvious. In the early days a stage from here ran to Miles City, Montana; it was a shipping point for freight and livestock to northern Wyoming. In 1883 the Union Pacific railroad shipped out 100 carloads of cattle every 24 hours; cattlemen waited their turn, sometimes, two weeks in the fall season.

Bentonite was first produced for sale here by William Taylor in 1888. It was called bentonite because it occurs in the Fort Benton formation. Pioneers used it for grease on axles, Indians for soap. Now Wyoming is the leading bentonite-producing state, processing more than half of all used in the United States.

Rock Eagle, Goshen: discontinued post office; the name is obvious.

Rock of Ages, Teton: A good spire for climbing; it will last a long time.

Rock River, Albany: when the Union Pacific railroad changed its route in 1901, officials changed the name of the station from Rock Creek to Rock River. When Henry Ford's ten-millionth car cavalcade on its coast-to-coast swing stopped to stage a parade in Rock River, an old stagecoach was put in the parade. It used to run via Fort Fetterman and Fort McKinney to Junction City, Montana; it was pierced by bandit bullet holes. Four horses pulled it in the parade.

Rock Springs, Sweetwater: a Pony Express rider in 1861, detouring to avoid Indians, discovered the springs for which the town was named. A stage station was built here—a stone cabin and bridge—in 1866 by Archie and Duncan Blair; good water was a rarity in this section of the country.

When the town was settled, houses were built anywhere and in any direction, mostly along paths leading to coal mines; vast bituminous coal fields were here, excellent for railroad consumption and distribution; it started in 1868.

The population became as mixed and confusing as the streets. Italians, Greeks, Russians, Finns, Irish, Chinese, and Negroes mingled as miners of coal. Chinese, brought in by the Union Pacific railroad as strike breakers in the mines, were attacked by others in the labor riots of 1885. Thirty Chinese were killed, many driven out; others opened cafes and laundries.

The famous Butch Cassidy once worked in a butcher shop in Rock Springs when he was 18 years old, hence the name "Butch."

Rock Springs is now such a rapidly expanding city with workers from the trona mines and oil fields, builders of the Jim Bridger power plant, coal miners, and tourists from Flaming Gorge Recreation Area, that lodging even for one night is hard to find. Blairtown was the original rail station in 1868 and is now a suburb. Acres of mobile homes surround Rock Springs.

Western Wyoming College, on its new campus west of Rock Springs, has an extensive program including technical training and adult vocational classes.

Rockchuck Peak, 11,150, Teton: named for hardy animals that live under rocks.

Rockdale, Carbon: see Arlington.

Rockwood, Sheridan: post office and headquarters of the McShane Tie Plant or Big Horn Timber Company in the 1900s. The sawmill was up here in the mountains so steep that ties traveled from a sorting pond down the Tongue River—a distance of ten miles—in nine minutes through wooden flumes filled with water to Ranchester. The buildings at Rockwood were burned in the forest fire of 1898 and rebuilt.

Rocky Ford, Crook: discontinued post office at the site of an historic road ranch on the trail from Sundance to Spearfish, South Dakota. There was an excellent rock bottom ford on Rocky Ford Creek here; it was the camping place of Col. Joseph T. Reynolds in 1876.

Rocky Mountains: first called Missouri, Mexican, Shining, Snowy, and Stony mountains. French trappers called them Montagnes Rocheuses, or Mountains Rocky. The central Rockies lie in Wyoming and include the Wyoming, Snake River, Wind River, Teton, Gros Ventre, and Big Horn ranges.

The Rocky Mountains, mostly granite, were thrust up in one of the most tremendous uplifts in the earth's history, known as the Laramide Revolution, which occurred about 75 million years ago. Great faulting took place; level sea bottoms were broken and stood on edge; mountains surged upward; smoke and volcanic ashes exploded over the plains for centuries. Then glaciers came to sculpt and erode the lava flows and granite heights.

The Rocky Mountains are not one great wall of rugged country, but are broken in several places by high plains, as at South Pass. Some ranges extend into the plains as peninsulas do into oceans; prairies and high plains form bays among high, rocky ridges.

Rocky Ridge, Fremont: Pony Express, stage and telegraph station on the Oregon Trail; the land was so rugged that Mormons, pulling and pushing handcarts, had to detour around the ridge for which the station was named; it was also known as St. Mary's stage station; built by Russell, Majors, and Waddell in 1859, it was burned by Indians in 1865, and telegraph wires were cut; the station was rebuilt, but nothing remains today.

Rockypoint, Campbell: post office, store and filling station were named for their location.

Rogers Canyon, Albany: named for Oscar Rogers, early day carpenter, who brought wood from his ranch to Laramie.

Rolling Thunder Mountain, 10,902, Teton: named for clouds that gather and thunder that rolls and echoes down the canyons.

Rongis, Fremont: old stage stop and discontinued post office named by Eli Signor, manager, in 1888; Rongis is his name spelled backward.

Roosevelt Meadows, Lincoln: named by an admirer of Teddy Roosevelt.

"Rough Riders," the Second U.S. Volunteer Cavalry under Col. J. L. Torrey, was organized at Fort D. A. Russell in 1898. These Wyoming cowboys and ranchers were expert horsemen mobilized for the Spanish-American War. Their name was usurped and attributed to Teddy Roosevelt after the Wyoming unit was deployed.

Teddy Roosevelt campaigned in Wyoming in 1900 and visited here again in May 1903 when he rode from Laramie to Cheyenne with an escort of noted men, including Senator F. E. Warren; the ride took seven hours on horseback. Roosevelt was greeted with a 21-gun salute at Fort D. A. Russell.

Rosie's Ridge, 7,900, Teton: named for Rudolph Rosencrans, first forest ranger at Black Rock ranger station, which he built of hand-hewn logs in 1904. He made many valuable maps of the region.

Ross, Converse: discontinued post office established in 1882 by James Ross.

Ross Lakes, Fremont: named for Nellie Taylor Ross, Governor of Wyoming from 1925-27; she was the first woman to become governor of a state and was a strong advocate of equality and prohibition. She proposed enactment of a statute that would make it as great a crime to buy liquor as to sell it. Mrs. Ross was appointed Director of the U.S. Mint in 1933.

Rothwell, Hot Springs: discontinued post office established in 1883 by Henry Rothwell at the Padlock ranch on Owl Creek.

Rotten Thumb, 11,653, Teton: named for its thumb-like appearance from Mount Moran's summit and the rotten nature of its rock.

Roughlock Hill, Johnson: in the early days a log had to be put through the spokes of the wheels to keep them from turning in order to brake a wagon going down this hill.

Rowland Pass, YNP: named for R. B. Rowland, who, with park superintendent Norris and Adam Miller, explored this area in 1878. Once a primitive road crossed the pass, but this has long been abandoned.

Roxson, Niobrara: discontinued ranch post office named for Roxie Hanson, postmaster; it combines the first and last halves of her name.

Rozet, Campbell: village established in the 1890s; it was probably named for the many nearby wild roses (Spanish for small rose is roseta). It has a picturesque hall built of cinder stones in a Spanish design. Rozar in Spanish means "to graze"—another possible meaning.

Rudefeha, Carbon: see Ferris-Haggarty mine.

Running Water Stage Station, Niobrara: named for the Niobrara River which was once called Running Water. The first station built here was burned by Indians almost as soon as it was finished. Jack Madden built a large stone barn in 1876, which was used as a station. Nothing is left of the barn now. See Lusk.

Rupe Hill, Crook: named for William E. Rupe, pioneer.

Rush Creek, Albany: named for a thick growth of rushes on the banks.

Russell Peak, 9,169, Park: named for Mr. Russell.

Rustic Geyser, YNP: so named because it is surrounded by a cordon of logs, placed by early trappers; it is now beautifully coated with a heavy deposit of geyserite.

Ryan Park, Carbon: named for Barton Thomas Ryan, who ran a sawmill here when the Union Pacific railroad was being built; it has an excellent ski area in the Medicine Bow Mountains.

Ryckman, Uinta: railroad camp named for James H. Ryckman, notary in Uinta County in 1889.

S

S K Mountain, Lincoln: named for the S K horse brand of Plunkett, Roche and Company.

Sacagawea, Mount, 13,607, Fremont, Sublette: named for the famous girl guide of the Lewis and Clark Expedition from 1804-06; a Shoshone, she had been stolen by Mandan Indians and taken to present North Dakota; her husband Charbonneau won her gambling. Lewis and Clark hired him, so that Sacajawea could guide them westward. Carrying her two-month-old son Baptiste on her back, she led, remembering the way.

Sacajawea's name translated "boat launcher"; explaining it, Charbonneau waved his arms; the explorers, misunderstanding, called her "Bird Woman." Back with her people, the Shoshones, she obtained horses and fresh provisions for the expedition to continue westward. Without her wisdom, fortitude, and ability to make friends with the Indians, the expedition would have failed. She taught the men how to live in the wilderness, nursed them back to health, when sick, with herbs, and saved their records, when a canoe overturned.

Sacajawea died at Fort Washakie in 1884 at the age of 96. She is buried with her son Baptiste and her nephew Bazil in a Shoshone cemetery in the land of her fathers.

> First of all the women leaders,
> First to make her name a legend
> In the history of Wyoming,
> First to lead with dauntless courage,
> First to blaze the unknown pathways,
> Was that fearless Indian maiden . . .
> Sacajawea!
>
> When the white men sought a leader
> For their expedition westward
> Through the land of hostile red men,
> Through the deserts and the forests,
> Through the drought and through the blizzards,
> Wisely they sought out this maiden . . .
> Sacajawea!
>
> On her back a son she carried,
> While she led them ever westward,
> Keen of eye and long of memory,
> Safely over unmarked prairies,
> Safely over mountain passes,
> Daughter of a brave Shoshone . . .
> Sacajawea!
>
> When the men grew gaunt with hunger
> She would find them roots and berries;
> When they met defiant Indians,
> She, a woman, spoke for friendship;
> When they were engulfed by rapids,
> Swimming, she saved all their records . . .
> Sacajawea!
>
> Now within her native valley,
> Close to her beloved mountains,
> In the land of the Shoshone,
> She is sleeping; renowned leader
> Of explorers, Clark and Lewis;
> First of all Wyoming's daughters . . .
> Sacajawea!
>   (By author)

Saddleback Hills, Carbon: this mountain, named for its shape, covered seven coal mines near Carbon; the mines lasted a long time, until miners and the railroad moved to Hanna; Carbon became a ghost town.

Saddle Mountain, 10,670, YNP: a massive peak that appears as a saddle.

Saddle String, Johnson: discontinued post office named for saddle strings by which the cowboys tied their extra coat and mail behind the saddle.

Sage, Lincoln: railroad station named for sage on the prairies; there is open pit mining for phosphate rock here.

Sage Creek, Niobrara: Fort Hat Creek was built here by mistake, instead of on Hat Creek in Nebraska. The first stage station was burned by Indians; the second building of logs had a tunnel leading down to Sage Creek to supply water in case of Indian attack; Indians and road agents made the country to the north very dangerous for the Cheyenne-Deadwood stage line.

Sage Creek Stage Station, Carbon: named for the creek. In 1861 the log station was built with an adobe roof and fireplace. Indians were fighting mad at the white men's intrusion into their lands and attacked the station in 1863 without success.

Saint Joe, Big Horn: named for Joe Brown, early rancher; it was once a post office, then a community name.

St. John Mountain, 11,412, Teton: named for Orestes St. John, geologist in 1877 with Hayden survey. The face of the mountain fell off in 1933; rolling and bouncing, huge rocks shook the valley below.

St. Lawrence Basin, Creek, and Ridge, Fremont: named for prospector Harold St. Lawrence who hunted gold here; no one knows what became of him.

St. Mary's Stage Station, Fremont: also known as Rocky Ridge Station; built in 1859 by Russell, Majors and Waddell; burned by Indians in 1865 while the five men garrisoned there hid in an abandoned well. The station was rebuilt, but all is gone now, except such relics as melted glass and square-cut nails.

St. Michaels Mission, Fremont: in 1910 the Arapahoes asked for a church and industrial school. Under the leadership of the Rev. John Roberts, the Episcopal Church built a school of locally made bricks. It was named for Michael White Hawk, a pupil of the Rev. Roberts who helped him translate the Bible into Arapahoe.

St. Stephens, Fremont: a Catholic school for Arapahoes started in 1888 named for St. Stephen of the Bible; known for its beautiful gardens and flowers, the site was once a camping ground of the Arapahoes, and was known as Camp of Black Coal, an Arapahoe chief.

Salem, Laramie: discontinued post office first known as Myra; it was renamed Lindbergh for Charles A. Lindbergh, after he flew across the Atlantic Ocean in 1927. Now only a grain elevator is here.

A group of Swedish immigrants homesteaded here in 1862. They given 160 acres for 5 years residence, or they could commute in six months and pay the government $1.25 an acre. The settlers were farmers growing grains, corn, and potatoes; this was the first dry farming in the state.

Salt Creek, Weston: one-third water, one-third alkali, and one-third salt. Salt was mined here in the 1880s. There were 70 salt springs on a ½-acre area. Two evaporating furnaces were erected to dry the salt, which was sold in Deadwood for livestock.

174

Salt Creek Oil Field, Natrona: named for Salt Creek. Oil seeps here in 1880 were used to grease wagon axles. Phillip Shannon drilled the first well here in 1888 to a depth of 80 feet, producing 60 barrels per day. His cable-drilling equipment and other supplies were freighted from Laramie with 16-horse string teams. Wooden derricks, "carpenter rigs," marked each producing well.

Shannon organized the Pennsylvania Oil and Gas Company and hauled out his first crude oil in horse-drawn tanks; it was used by the railroad as a lubricant without straining; it sold for $10 a barrel. He built the first small refinery in Casper in 1895.

In 1908 the first big gusher was brought in; Salt Creek became one of the big oil fields in Wyoming; in 1911 it was producing less than 200,000 barrels; it hit its peak in the 1920s with more than 35 million barrels yearly. When production tapered off, it was brought back by water-injection techniques.

Salt River, Lincoln: named for the salt ledges and saline springs on it. the Snake Indians called it "To-sa carnel," white lodges, for extinct mineral springs.

Salt River Range, 10,000 to 11,000, Sublette: named for the river to the west of it.

Salt Wells, Sweetwater: stage and Pony Express station; the water was salty and brackish. Emigrants dug three wells trying to get good water; it is now a railroad station.

Sam Kent Lake, Fremont: also known as Sonnicant Lake; it is located in the Glacier Primitive Area.

Sand Creek, Albany: named for a bed of quicksand along its banks.

Sand Creek, Crook: named for the sandy bottom. The first flour mill in the region was built here by Dan Toomey; it used water power. Vice-President Theodore Roosevelt visited his cousin John Boyden, rancher, here several times in the 1890s; they went fishing on Sand Creek.

The U.S. government fish genetic laboratory conducts research here; a state park is located on Sand Creek; it boasts good fishing.

Sand Creek Sphinx, Albany: a wind-weathered sandstone form.

Sand Dunes, Sweetwater: world's largest shifting sand dune area; dune-buggy races are held here; it is a good hunting ground for Indian artifacts.

Sand Point, Platte: trading post established by Seth E. Ward in the 1840s near Registe Cliff, which was first called Sand Point; it became a stage and Pony Express station on the Oregon Trail.

Sanders, Albany: railroad station named for Fort Sanders.

Saratoga, Carbon: town started in 1878 by Fenimore Chatterton, post trader at Fort Steele; it was named for Saratoga Hot Springs, New York. Indians called it "Place of Magic Water," and swarmed there during a smallpox epidemic, hoping for relief which they did not find; most of them died. The railroad came in 1907.

Swimming in its warm, mineral waters makes Saratoga a popular resort town; it also boasts hunting, fishing, and skiing.

Saratoga and Encampment Railroad, Carbon: a branch line of the Union Pacific railroad, leaving the main line at Walcott; it reached Encampment in 1908.

Saratoga Hot Springs State Park, Carbon: the state has set aside hot mineral springs for free bathing and for treatment of rheumatism and similar ills. Old-timers called them "Indian Bath Tubs."

Before the area became a state park, Cadwell, who homesteaded there, had a bathhouse with wooden tubs. He filled the tubs with warm spring water using a windlass and turntable powered by a black horse named Nig.

The springs are now dammed into pools for swimming, wading, or just sitting.

Satanka, Albany: a railroad siding named by Union Pacific railroad officials for a Japanese section foreman in 1902.

Sauerkraut Lake, Sublette: after an extended trip, a camping party stopped here; all they had left to eat was sauerkraut and fish they caught.

Savageton, Campbell: discontinued post office named for Bailey Savage, early postmaster and storekeeper.

Savery, Carbon: village named for Savery Creek.

Savery Creek, Carbon: named for Savery, a trapper in Jim Bridger's time.

Savery-Pot Hook Project, Carbon: named for Savery Creek. The project is partly in Colorado; about 16,000 acres in Wyoming are improved by irrigation—6,000 acres are new lands; it is located along the Little Snake River.

Sawmill Canyon, Platte: see Slade Canyon.

Sawmill Geyser, YNP: the water spins and resembles revolving sawblades.

Sawtooth Mountain, Albany: named for its series of small peaks which resemble sawteeth.

Sayles Creek, Johnson: named for Frank Sales, pioneer.

Scab Creek, Sublette: a bull lost here by a rancher was found at the head of this creek; he was infected with scabies.

Schiestler Peak, 11,668, Sublette: named for Felix Schiestler, an early sheepman living on Little Sandy.

Schoolbook Glacier, Teton: named because, like a textbook, it displays all glacier features in miniature—bergschrund, crevasses, severed ice blocks, morainal rock debris, and a turquoise lake, colored from rock flour held in suspension.

Schurz Mountain, 11,139, YNP: named by USGS of 1895 for Carl Schurz, Secretary of Interior from 1877-81.

Scotch Plunge, Hot Springs: outdoor swimming pool near Thermopolis; bathers bring their own swimming suits.

Scout's Peak, Washakie: overlooks the valley and town of Washakie like a scout.

Seaman Hills, Niobrara: named for Samuel Seaman, rancher at the

176

foot of the hills. Laramie Peak, the Black Hills, and the Big Horn Mountains can be seen from the top of these hills on a clear day.

Seeds-ke-dee Project, Lincoln, Sweetwater: an irrigation project on both sides of the Green River between LaBarge and Green River City; water is supplied by Fontenelle Dam; it provides a wildlife refuge for migratory birds with nesting ponds, as well as feed and resting stations. The Green River was called Seeds-ke-dee or Sage Hen River by Indians.

Seely, Crook: village named for John D. Seely.

Segnup Creek, Fremont: Shoshone name for "muddy."

Seminoe Mountains, 7,000-8,066, Carbon: granite peaks with rich iron ore deposits, yet unworked; named for Basil Cimineau Lajeunesse, French trapper who was a guide for Gen. Fremont in the Wind River Mountains in 1842. He warned Fremont, "We will eat mules," meaning Fremont's men would starve if they went on west. Fremont went on, and they did eat mules.

In 1858 Lajeunesse established a trading post on the Oregon Trail above Devils Gate. He was married to an Indian woman, Cimineau, whose name he added to his own; from the English pronunciation and spelling comes Seminoe.

Seminoe Reservoir, Carbon: named for the Seminoe Mountains; built in a deep gorge of the Platte River, it was started in 1936 and completed in 1939; it can store 1,020,000 acre-feet of water. It is part of the Kendrick Project for control of the Platte River and provides power, irrigation, and recreation; Seminoe State Park here boasts good fishing, boating, and hiking; it is located in a sand dune area.

Separation, Carbon: railroad station named for Separation Flats.

Separation Flats, Lake, Peak, and River, Carbon: peak or ridge, 10,037, is very narrow and plunges steeply down 3,000 feet on both the north and south sides, separating the flats below. There is a remarkable view from the top of the ridge.

Sepulcher Mountain, 9,652, YNP: named for a tomb-like rock on its northwest slopes; the rock has a prominent foot stone and a head stone. The mountain is composed of breccia.

Sessions Mountain, Uinta: named for Byron Sessions, Mormon pioneer.

Seven Brothers Lakes, Johnson: seven lakes so close together, they are like brothers; located in the Cloud Peak Primitive Area, it boasts good fishing.

Seven Brothers Peak, 12,640, Johnson: named for Seven Brothers Lakes; it probably has never been climbed.

Seven Mile Creek, Albany, Carbon: named in the old trail days because it was seven miles from Rockdale station to the Overland route.

Seven Mile Lakes, Albany: three lakes seven miles southwest of Laramie on an old country road; it was a landmark in the 1880s for measuring the distance to Laramie.

Shangri-la, Fremont: a choice fishing spot deep in Dinwoody Canyon; like its Himalayan namesake, it is hard to reach—takes two hours of scrambling through rugged rocks.

177

Shangri-la Ski Run, Park: in Rock Creek Canyon above Mirror Lake; the name means Utopia, a beautiful place that nears perfection.

Shannon, Natrona: discontinued post office named for the Shannon Oil Field.

Shannon Lake, Natrona: created to provide water to produce electricity to pump the Shannon Oil Field; the dam on Salt Creek is 40 feet high and 960 feet long.

Shannon Oil Field, Natrona: named for Phillip M. Shannon, who filed claims here in 1889 and was president of the Pennsylvania Oil and Gas Company; it is part of the Salt Creek Oil Field.

Shannon Pass, 11,100, Sublette: named for Harmon Shannon, forest ranger.

Shanton, Albany: named for Capt. John Shanton of Roosevelt's "Rough Riders"; he was chief of police in Panama at one time.

Sharp Nose Draw, Fremont: named for the Arapahoe chief Sharp Nose, one of the signers of the agreement of 1896, when Indians transferred 64,000 acres of land, including the hot springs at Thermopolis to the government.

Shawnee, Converse: village named for the Indian tribe; the name means "southern"; it was given tribe that migrated west from Savannah River, Georgia.

Shawnee Basin, Carbon: named for the Indian tribe; sub-bituminous coal is found here; it has a greater moisture content than bituminous.

Sheep Creek, Albany: named in the 1880s by Mack Mantz for mountain sheep at its head.

Sheep Creek, Johnson, Sheridan: named by an old prospector in 1887, who found the region teeming with wild game. He shot a bighorn sheep here, hence the name. He did not see a white man or a habitation here at that time.

Sheep Mountain, 9,583, Albany: named for wild sheep that lived here in the early days; the last one was taken out about 1904.

Sheep Mountain, Sheridan: rocks on the side of the mountain look like sheep.

Sheep Mountain, 11,190, Teton: also known as Sleeping Indian, whom it resembles as seen on the road to Kelly.

Sheep Mountain Federal Game Refuge, Albany: established in 1931; it was named for Sheep Mountain, which it includes.

Sheepeaters Canyon, YNP: named for a tribe of early Indians, the Sheepeaters, who dwelled in caves and mountain canyons in the eighteenth century to avoid destruction by more belligerent Plains Indians.

The Absaroka Mountains were their favorite hunting grounds. They used large dogs, now extinct, as pack animals; they built rock pens in which they captured bighorn sheep for slaughter; this was their chief food, hence the name. One of these pens is still standing far up in Dinwoody Canyon. One of their last tribes, with Togwotee as chief and medicine man, joined the Shoshones.

178

The Sheepeaters are believed to have built the Medicine Wheel on top of the Big Horn Mountains; they lived among the cliffs and clouds and carved pictographs of their life with obsidian rocks from the present Yellowstone National Park, their main stomping ground.

Sheffield Island, in Colter Bay, Teton: named for Ben Sheffield, early dude rancher.

Sheldon, Crook: discontinued post office named for Otis Sheldon, first postmaster.

Sheldon Creek, Albany: named for the Sheldon family who lived here in 1880.

Shell, Big Horn: village named for Shell Creek; this is in scenic country; there is a ski course in the nearby mountains.

Shell Creek, Big Horn: two versions of the name: probably named for numerous fossil shells on its banks; it appears as Shell Creek on Irving's map of 1837, and on Colton's map of 1869. Cowboys claim it was named for Dick Shell who picked the village site.

Shell Creek Falls, Big Horn: Shell Creek tumbles 75 feet to make these beautiful falls in Shell Canyon.

Shell Creek Valley, Big Horn: Jacob Rech planted the first handful of beans here in Bighorn basin in 1890; they were small navy beans that did so well, he teamed up with Dave Null to grow them commercially; they were flailed out by hand. When the railroad came to Manderson in 1906, the first carload of beans was shipped out.

Sheridan, Sheridan: county seat; Jim Mason, trapper, erected the first building here in 1978. Harry Mandel converted a dirt-roofed cabin into a store and post office in 1881. Mandel sold out to Jim Loucks for $50 in 1882. One evening Loucks walked to top of the hill where the courthouse now stands. He watched the sun set behind the Big Horns, shedding a golden glow over the valley and decided it would be a lovely place for a town. He went back to his cabin and plotted the town on brown wrapping paper, naming it Sheridan for his commander of Civil War fame, General Philip Sheridan.

Sheridan is the lowest town in Wyoming, with an altitude of 3,745 feet; it is a rancher's town with slow growth; the first state fair, "Wyoming Industrial Convention," was held here in 1903. In 1892 the Burlington railroad reached Sheridan. Rich nearby coal fields developed and the town grew rapidly.

Sheridan Flouring Mills, a modern plant processing hundreds of carloads of wheat each year, started with the Denio Milling Company in 1919. Before that, several local mills were run with water power. The State Training School for Girls was established here in 1926. the Veterans Administration's mental hospital, old Fort Mackenzie, in also located here.

Kendrick Park was named for U.S Senator John B. Kendrick, pioneer stockman who drove cattle up the Texas Trail. He was governor of Wyoming from 1915-17, and U.S. Senator from 1917-33. The park has a zoo with native wildlife, as well as monkeys and lions. An experiment station specializing in dry land problems of crops and livestock is also located at Sheridan.

Sheridan All American Indian Days, Sheridan: originated in 1952, Indians from all over America, more than 40 tribes, gather at Sheridan each August in authentic regalia to relive old Indian dances, games, and customs for better relationship among the tribes and between Indians and whites.

Miss Indian America is chosen for her poise, Indian leadership, and ability. Indian arts and crafts are displayed, and may be purchased.

Sheridan College, Sheridan: founded in 1948 with a two-year program in general education and professional training, the school now has more than 400 students attending; it also has evening classes for adults; it is located in a picturesque setting at the foot of the Big Horn Mountains. Dental training is a specialty.

Sheridan County: created in 1888 with John Loucks, then representative from Johnson County, sponsoring the bill, and suggesting the name Sheridan, from its principal city; it was taken from northern part of Johnson County.

Livestock, oil, coal, timber, and dude ranching are its main industries. A state-operated Bird Farm is located here; the county has vast reserves of coal.

Sheridan Creek, Fremont: the first timber drive was down this creek in 1906 by Jim Stewart and a crew of Indians. The creek was named for Gen. Philip Sheridan, who was here on his trip with President Chester A. Arthur in 1883.

Sheridan Inn, Sheridan: lavish hotel opened in 1898, built by the Burlington railroad and Sheridan Land Company as a showplace and social center, and operated by the Buffalo Bill Hotel Company. Buffalo Bill recruited acts for his Wild West Show from its vast, encircling porch. The first electric lights in Sheridan were powered by a steam boiler used here in 1893.

The Sheridan County Historical Society made a great effort in 1966-67 to save the famous old building from being razed for the erection of a modern business on its site. In 1967 they reopened the bar, which was made in England and freighted overland in the 1890s. Present at the gala reopening were Fred Garlow of Cody, grandson of Buffalo Bill, and Betty Canary, columnist and great niece of Martha Jane "Calamity Jane" Canary.

This is the first time in history that a historical society operated under a liquor license. The Burlington railroad offered tours from Sheridan to Clearmont in old, wooden passenger cars. The inn was finally purchased and saved from destruction by Mrs. Neltje King.

Sheridan, Mount, 10,308, YNP: extinct volcano named by Gen. J. W. Barlow, leader of a military expedition in 1871 for Gen. Philip Sheridan, who so vigorously supported all efforts to preserve Yellowstone National Park and its natural wonders.

A zigzag trail for horseback riders and hikers leads to its summit, where, on a clear day, 471 peaks are visible within a radius of 200 miles.

Sheridan Pass, Fremont: used in 1883 by the presidential cavalcade of President Chester A. Arthur on his way to Yellowstone National Park; named for Gen. Philip Sheridan who conducted the party. President Arthur was more interested in fishing than in scenery.

180

Sherman, Albany: a town on the Union Pacific railroad established in 1867; it was then the headquarters of the railroad building westward and had a huge windmill and water tank, a five-stall roundhouse and turntable, two section houses, and 25 log buildings.

Now only a graveyard marks the site, which was between the present Lincoln Highway and the Ames Monument. The town was named for Sherman Pass, and was the highest point on the Union Pacific railroad at 8,235 feet. In 1902 the railroad bed was moved about three miles to the southeast.

Sherman Hill and Pass, Albany: a relatively flat summit in the Laramie Range, through which the Union Pacific railroad and Lincoln Highway pass; discovered by Grenville Dodge, surveyor, when he was chased by Indians in 1865; Dodge named the pass for his Civil War general, W. T. Sherman.

Sherman Mountains, Albany: a small range named for Sherman Pass.

Shirley Basin, Carbon: named for the Shirley Mountains; this was once a wet, sub-tropical country; once many tree trunks and pieces of grey-brown petrified wood from forests that grew here about 50 million years ago lay scattered over the ground.

The basin has vast open pits where uranium-rich ore was extracted; huge machines moved five tons of overburden to get one ton of ore. Extracted by five huge processing mills, it had to be reprocessed and enriched.

Two fifths of all uranium in the United States now comes from Wyoming, which has 40 percent of all reserves in the nation.

Shirley Mountains, Carbon: a granite range named for John Shirley, a freighter who once hauled supplies to ranchers in this region with teams and wagons. His route took him into these mountains to homes of Finnlanders who had homesteaded there. Thus, when John headed for the hills, folks said he was going to Shirley's Mountains.

Shorty, Campbell: named for Shorty Turley, old-timer.

Shoshone Canyon and River, Park: the river was first known as "Stinking Water"; named by John Colter in 1807 for its bad odor from sulphur springs near Cody, it is on Clark's map of 1814. At the demand of citizens for a less descriptive name, the Wyoming legislature changed the name to Shoshone, for the Indian tribe, in 1902.

Shoshone translates "abundance of grass," or grass lodge people; they are also known as Snakes from their in-and-out or serpentine motion, used in weaving grass into shelters.

The Shoshone River Bridge west of Cody on Highways 14 and 20 is the highest crossing in the state, 100 feet high and 594 feet long. Beyond the bridge are three tunnels, including one of the longest tunnels in the world—3,203 feet long; it has forced ventilation and overhead lighting. These tunnels improved a once-hazardous road down this narrow canyon.

Shoshone Creek, Geyser Basin, Lake, YNP: named for the Shoshone Indians.

Shoshone Indian Reservation, Fremont: see Wind River Indian Reservation.

181

Shoshone Lake, Fremont: named for the Shoshone Indians; there is a good hiking trail here.

Shoshone Lake Pickets, 10,850, Fremont: three sharp pinnacles that stand like soldiers west of Shoshone Lake.

Shoshone National Forest, Fremont, Hot Springs, Park: contains part of the first national forest in the United States; known then as Yellowstone Timberland Reserve, it was set aside by President Benjamin Harrison in 1891 to protect timber on the public domain; it was enlarged and renamed Shoshone for the Indian tribe in 1945. Now it contains 2,458,644 acres and is one of the largest national forests.

Shoshone National Monument, Park: see Spirit Mountain Caverns.

Shoshone Plateau, 11,260, Park: remnants of a petrified forest are here; it provides grazing grounds for elk, deer, and mountain sheep. There is an excellent view of the Tetons and the Wind River Range from here on a clear day.

Shoshone Reservoir, Park: see Buffalo Bill Dam.

Shoshoni, Fremont: town named for the Shoshone Indians; the name has several spellings. The Shoshone Indians agreed to open part of their reservation to homesteaders in 1905; the opening date was August 15, 1906. The Chicago and Northwestern railroad platted the townsite of Shoshoni in the summer of 1904. Hopefuls numbering 10,559 registered for the right to draw for 1,600 homesteads. A wild, lawless tent town grew overnight as the railroad was being built. In July 1906 the militia was called in from Douglas to restore order. Building materials were hauled in by teams and wagons. The town suffered big fires in 1907 and 1908.

Shoshoni is located in good sheep raising country. Nearby are large rock beds, where a great variety of rocks, tumbled by ancient waters, are now on high, dry plains.

Shrap, Natrona: discontinued post office named for Robert H. Shrap, postmaster.

Shurtliff, Uinta: named for Shurtliff, once postmaster at Fort Bridger.

Sibley Lake and Reservoir, Sheridan: named by Gen. Crook for General Sibley.

Sibley Peak, Platte: named by Jack Slade because it resembled in shape an army tent, used in the Civil War, which was invented by Gen. Sibley; it is near the old Horseshoe stage station, where Slade was once caretaker. A stagecoach carrying about $30,000 was robbed near here; the loot was never found; some say it is buried on or near Sibley Peak. The shape of this peak has now been destroyed by highway construction.

Sibylee, Platte: discontinued post office and railroad station named for Sybil, early rancher; the name was spelled several ways, but finally changed to Sibylee by A. Trabing, mail carrier.

Siebolt Creek, Albany: named for Frank Siebolt, landowner.

Sierra Madre Mountains, Carbon: name is Spanish for "mother range"; this land was once part of Mexico. Copper was discovered here in 1906; the Ferris-Haggarty mine and others developed, 14 towns sprang up, and more than 5,000 miners and prospectors moved into the region. An aerial tramway 16 miles long was built over the mountains to transport copper ore to the smelter at Encampment. The boom ended about 1908 with the decline in the price of copper. Collectors of bottles that purple in the sun now dig in the sites of old towns.

Signal Cliff, Washakie: Crow scouts watched from here for smoke signals in the Big Horn Mountains and relayed them to tribesmen in the basin. Indians controlled puffs of smoke with blankets or hides and conveyed messages about buffalo herds or enemy movements.

Signal Hill, Lincoln: served as a lookout in the early days of Mormon travel, who signaled when unannounced parties were entering the valley.

Signal Mountain, Teton: in 1891 Robert R. Hamilton became lost while hunting in this vicinity. His companions, searching in all directions, agreed that whoever found him first, would build a signal fire on top of this mountain, hence the name. After seven days his body was found in the Snake River. The mountain was denuded by a forest fire in 1879; a fire lookout station was then built on top of it.

Signal Peak, Platte: on its summit Indians built signal fires to call distant bands to hunt or to war.

Signal Point, YNP: a point on the east shore of Yellowstone Lake that was used by early explorers to signal messages to others of the party.

Signor Reservoir and Ridge, Fremont: named for Signor Eli, early storekeeper.

Silver City, Albany: two men once thought they had a silver prospect on a mountainside north of Centennial. They built a cabin that was known as Silver City. All is gone now, as was the hope of the prospectors.

Silver Cliff, Niobrara: see Lusk.

Silver Crown Hills, Laramie: a gold and silver mining boom was here in 1885. The prospect holes were "salted." Professor Wilbur C. Knight, University of Wyoming, exposed the fraud before Cheyenne businessmen lost their money.

Silver Lake, Carbon: named for silver discovered in adjacent mountains.

Silver Run Lake and Creek, Albany: named for silver that silted into the creek's waters.

Silver Springs, Goshen: named for a ledge of silver-bearing rock above the springs; owned in the early days by O. J. Demmon, rancher.

Silver Tip Creek, Albany: named for a silver-tip bear that Jack Newell killed here in 1878.

Simpson's Hollow, Sweetwater: named for Capt. Lew Simpson, who was in command of a wagon train freighting supplies to Col. Johnston's army that was fighting the Mormons.

The wagon train was surrounded here in 1857 by the Mormon Utah Militia under Orin Lee and ordered to surrender, which they did. The Mormons burned 75 supply wagons and took the oxen. They left Simpson and his men one wagon; he was thus forced to spend the winter at Fort Bridger and did not enter Utah until June 1858.

Sinclair, Carbon: a town for employees of the oil company. In 1923 it was called Parco; it was renamed when the refineries were acquired by the Sinclair Oil Company in 1934.

Sinks, Fremont: where the Little Popo Agie River disappears into underground caverns and emerges in a waterfall several hundred yards below; there, a deep pool of swirling water is home for huge trout which rise to catch food tossed to them by people on an observation platform above the pool.

An Indian legend is that an Indian maiden grew up near and loved this river. She fell in love with a member of another tribe; her father told the lover to go back to his people, but the girl and her lover eloped; the angry chief followed them, almost catching them. But a cavern opened and sucked in the lovers and the river.

Sinks Canyon, Fremont: cut by the Little Popo Agie River; it gets its name from the Sinks in the river; it is a picturesque area and boasts skiing in the winter.

Sisters Hill, Johnson: named for two Sisters, the name of pioneer brothers.

Sisters Hills, Sheridan: three prominent peaks close together.

Sitting Camel Rock, Albany: named for its shape, a tantalizing rock for climbers, where ropes and pitons are needed on crumbly sandstone.

Six Mile Creek, Goshen: so named because it is six miles long.

Six Mile Creek, Sheridan: six miles from Dayton.

Six Mile Ranch, Goshen: a Cheyenne-Deadwood route stage station with a bloody history; an infamous roadhouse in the 1860s; women who lived at this "hog ranch" went about in soldier clothes. They were very resentful when some befrilled rivals stopped off en route to the Black Hills in 1876.

Sixty-Six Mountain, Goshen: a huge mountain or ridge on which 66 emigrants were massacred by Indians in the early 1860s; it is near the Oregon Trail and the Nebraska state line. One man, Ed Stemler, escaped because the Indians were superstitious of his red hair. Stemler later established a ranch near the mountain.

Skillet Glacier, Teton: a skillet-shaped glacier between the two summits of Mount Mora.

Skull Creek, Crook: named by Geneal Custer's scout Reynolds for buffalo skulls left here by the Gore expedition of 1854.

Skull Creek, Park: a number of human skulls were found here, probably from a battle with Indians.

Skull Creek, Weston: named by early settlers because of many buffalo skulls they found here bleaching in the sun.

Skull Creek Oil Field, Weston: named for Skull Creek.

Slack, Sheridan: discontinued ranch post office named for Col. Slack, army officer; it was a stopping place on Bozeman Trail.

Slade Canyon, Platte: also known as Sawmill Canyon; it was called Slade Canyon because of old chimneys left standing here, believed by some

184

to have marked the rendezvous of Slade and his outlaw gang, who robbed stagecoaches and freighters in the 1860s. Slade, a vicious gunman, cut off his victims' ears and carried them in his vest pocket. No caches of gold or jewelry have ever been found in the canyon.

Another version of the origin of the chimneys is that they were too solidly built to have been put up by outlaws; that they are the remains of cabins erected by sawmill workers.

Slate Creek, Teton: flows through slate rock.

Slater, Carbon: village on the Wyoming-Colorado state line named for William Slater, who came here in 1871 with Robert Dixon; they were the first cattlemen here.

Slater, Platte: named for homesteader Ellis Slater.

Slater, Sheridan: discontinued post office named for Slater, early homesteader on Rhoda Creek, sometimes called Slater Creek. Rhoda was Slater's daughter.

Slater Flats, Platte: named for homesteader Ellis Slater.

Sleeping Giant Mountain, Park: named for its size and shape; there is good skiing here.

Sleeping Indian Mountain, 11,196, Teton: appears like the head of a huge Indian lying on his back when viewed from the road to Kelly.

Sleeping Ledge, Fremont: a red sandstone cliff covered with Indian petroglyphs, mostly of animal design; it is located in the Dinwoody area.

Slick Creek, Washakie: named for Slick Nard who attempted to rob a traveling sheep shearer of $700. Nard shot the man in the arm, but the shearer whipped up his team and outran the robber to Thermopolis.

Slick Mountain, Albany: named for its appearance. It is solid rock, steep, and appears to be polished.

Slide Lake, Teton: in June 1925 the end of Sheep Mountain in Gros Ventre Range, wet with heavy rains, broke loose; a secton of earth, estimated at 50,000,000 tons, slid 1½ miles into Gros Ventre Canyon in less than three minutes; it pushed more than 300 feet up the opposite canyon wall and settled back, forming an earth dam which created Slide Lake.

In 1927 Slide Lake, overflowing with spring floods, washed out the dam. An eight-foot wall of water destroyed the town of Kelly and took six lives.

Sliding Hill, YNP: a foothill of Sepulcher Mountain keeps breaking away and sliding down into the river where it is carried away.

Sloans Lake, Laramie: located in Cheyenne: named for Mathias Sloan, one of the earliest settlers, who had a dairy ranch near the lake. For years his son, John, was Cheyenne's only milkman. Mathias Sloan was one of the survivors of the Wagon Box fight near Fort Phil Kearny.

Slough Creek, YNP: in 1867 Hubbel went ahead of his prospecting party and reported back that he had found "a slough." When the party arrived at the creek, they found a rushing torrent and called it Slough Creek as a joke.

Smith Creek, Sheridan: named for David A. Smith who built his squatter's cabin at the mouth of this creek in 1878 or 1879; it was once called Hereford Creek for the cattle that grazed there.

Smith Gulch, Fremont: named for George Smith who came to South Pass in 1868.

Smith North Creek, Albany: named for Smith and North, tie-cutters in railroad construction days.

Smith's Fork, Lincoln, Uinta: named for Jedediah S. Smith, who drew accurate maps for the Ashley party; he was the first white man to explore this stream. Smith was a devout Christian with a trapper's rifle and a friend of Jim Bridger.

Smith's Station, Uinta: a squaw man, Tilford Kutz, built a log hut here in 1873, and had a ferry to take passengers across Black's Fork.

Smoot, Lincoln: this village, settled in 1891, was called Cottonwood; it was renamed for Senator Reed Smoot of Utah, an apostle of the Mormon Church.

Snake River, Lincoln, Teton: the first white men known to have seen the Snake River were the explorers Lewis and Clark in 1805. Clark named it Lewis River, and thus it appears on early maps.

Trappers named rivers to suit themselves, and they called the Snake "la maudite riviere enragee," the accursed mad river. Wilson Price Hunt and the returning Robert Stuart and party in 1812 accepted the name Mad River because of the difficult passage over its cascades and falls.

Later it was named Snake River for the Snake or Shoshone Indian tribes who lived here. The Indian name for it was Yam-pah-pa, the name of a root that grew along its banks. The Shoshones were called Snakes because the sign language for them was a serpentine movement of the hand, suggesting the weaving of grass, with which they made their lodges.

Snake River Range, 6,000-9,863, Lincoln, Teton: mostly limestone, sandstone, and shale; it was named for the Snake River.

Sniffle, Mount, 11,962, Park: throws long afternoon shadows over the abandoned site that Amelia Earhart chose for her log cabin in 1935, before her tragic flight over the Pacific Ocean, where she was lost July 2, 1937. The community has erected a stone memorial with a bronze plaque here in her memory.

Snow King Mountain, 6,237, Teton: once known as Kelly's Hill for Bill Kelly, rancher; it was renamed Snow King because of the excellent skiing; it has a drop of 4,135 feet in ski trail, with a ski lodge at the base and lunch room on the summit. The cable tow started in 1939. A ski lift now runs all year to give tourists a magnificent view of the Tetons and Jackson Hole from its summit.

Snowshoe Canyon, Carbon: a pair of snowshoes was once found hanging here.

Snowy Range, 8,500-11,500, Albany: so named because snow is perpetually on some slopes of the mountains, which appear white most of the year. The University of Wyoming Science Summer Camp is held here every summer; it started in 1922 and offers courses and field trips in botany, geology, zoology, and conservation.

Snowy Range is a recreation area in summer with fishing, camping, and hiking. The winter sports area has skiing, toboggan runs, and slalom courses. The ski area on Barrett Ridge was developed in 1938 by the Forest Service.

186

Snyder, Natrona: discontinued post office named for Ora Snyder, first postmaster.

Soda Butte, YNP: a travertine mound of an almost extinct hot spring; the water has the taste of soda.

Soda Butte Creek, YNP: named for Soda Butte. Canyons of the creek show sedimentary rocks, formed as mud and ooze in ancient seas, before the Rocky Mountains and the whole state of Wyoming were lifted in the Laramide Revolution.

Soda Lake, Natrona: see Joe Yant Lake.

Sodergreen Lake, Albany: an artificial lake made by Oscar Sodergreen in 1886. It provides trout fishing and boating.

Sodium, Natrona: a railroad station named for nearby deposits of natron or sodium.

Soldier Creek, Albany, Carbon: a company of soldiers from Fort Sanders camped here to protect railroad construction workers from Indians in 1868.

Soldier Creek, Sheridan: two versions of the name: Frank Grouard, noted scout, led 25 soldiers along this creek to escape after a skirmish with Indians.

The creek was practically dry until in 1883-84 a cattle company built a ditch to irrigate, draining the surplus into this creek. Some soldiers tried to cross it with a loaded wagon drawn by mules; rescuers were giving their attention to the mules who were about to drown. The commanding officer shouted, "Don't mind the mules. Save the soldiers!"

Soldier Meadows, YNP: near Mammoth Hot Springs where soldiers were stationed in 1917, when Yellowstone National Park was under army administration.

Soldiers and Sailors Home, Johnson: Fort McKinney was given to the State of Wyoming in 1903; the Soldiers and Sailors Home in Cheyenne was then transferred to Buffalo.

Soldiers' Creek, Crook, Weston: Gen. George A. Custer and his soldiers camped on this creek in 1874. Horatio N. Ross, miner with the expedition, discovered gold on French Creek, east of present Custer, on July 30, 1874.

News of the discovery of gold was carried to Cheyenne by scout Charlie Reynolds, and the government found it impossible to keep gold seekers out of this land which had been pledged in treaties to the Indians.

Solfatara Creek and Plateau, YNP: named for volcanic vents that spout up hot and sulphurous gases.

Somber Hill, 9,430, Albany: named by USGS because there are no adjacent hills or mountains; from the lookout tower on top, one can see far into Colorado and over Medicine Bow Peaks.

Sonnicant Lake, Fremont: also known as Sam Kant Lake or Samkant Lake; probably named for a Sam Kant.

Soukup, Campbell: discontinued post office named for Martha Soukup, postmaster.

South Absaroka Wilderness Area, Hot Springs, Park: contains 483,130 acres, U.S. Highway 14 and 20 running west from Cody to Yellowstone National Park is a narrow strip of land between the North and South Absaroka Wilderness areas. Roads may not be built in wilderness areas. The area was named for the Absaroka Mountains.

South Bend Stage Station, Lincoln: also a Pony Express and telegraph station; it was built of stone in 1850.

South Fork, Shoshone River, Park: here was the famous home ranch of Buffalo Bill, known as the T E ranch.

South Mountain, Albany: so named because it is south of Laramie Peak.

South Pass, 7,526, Fremont: an open strip of high country at the southern tip of the Wind River Range; it is a break in the Continental Divide. Robert Stuart and his party of returning Astorians crossed here October 22, 1812, unaware of their important discovery to transcontinental travel.

The pass has been used by Indians for centuries; it was named South Pass because it is farther south than other mountain passes; the name was attributed to Jedediah Smith, or Thomas Fitzpatrick who used the pass in 1824. In 1832 Capt. Benjamin Bonneville led a party with 20 mule- and horse-drawn wagons through the pass; this was the first time for wagons. Ashley had drawn a cannon through in 1827.

Gold was first discovered here in 1842. From then until 1867 groups went to "work" the region. The big boom came in 1867 with good discoveries like the Carissa Lode, Miners Delight, and Burr mines; 5,000 people flooded the area; steam-powered stamp mills were installed by 1869. Although more than $6,000,000 in gold was dredged from the hills, the gold strike was short-lived. Miners by the 1870s were drifting to coal fields along the Union Pacific railroad for a more dependable livelihood.

On the hills once panned for gold new wealth has been found. U.S. Steel strip mined here for taconite, a low-grade iron ore, and produced more than one million tons of agglomerate annually. Trucks carrying 45 tons of ore took it to crushers where it was crushed and recrushed; then it was refined by a settling process. Wet ore was then mixed with bentonite as a binder, rolled into balls, and dried by furnaces. Iron balls were shipped to Provo, Utah, for further processing.

South Pass City, Fremont: in 1866 a group of prospectors, discharged soldiers from Fort Bridger, made their camp on the site that a year later became South Pass City. With the gold strike, it grew rapidly and flourished until miners left in the 1870s; it was an Overland Stage station, a Pony Express station, and a telegraph station. Martha Jane "Calamity Jane" Canary worked here during the gold rush.

Esther Hobart Morris, a dynamic citizen of South Pass City, held her famous tea party at her home here in 1868. She had both candidates for the legislature, Col. Wm. H. Bright, Democrat, and H. G. Nickerson, Republican, pledge that if elected, they would work for woman suffrage. Col. Bright was elected, kept his promise, and introduced the bill giving women of Wyoming full rights of franchise.

The bill became law, earning for Wyoming the title "Equality State." Mrs. Morris became the first woman justice of the peace in the world. She handed down just decisions in this turbulent mining town. A statue of

188

Esther Morris, representing Wyoming, is in Statuary Hall, Washington, D.C.

South Pass City is still one of the most romantic towns in Wyoming, with its old false-front buildings. A museum here has treasures in western and Wyoming history. The town is now being restored as a historical center.

Spalding Peak, 12,200, Teton: named for Bishop Frank S. Spalding, who led the second ascent of Grand Teton in 1898.

Spanish Diggings, Goshen, Niobrara, Platte: discovered in 1879 by A. A. Spaugh, cowboy, who thought Spaniards had dug here for gold. He misnamed them Spanish Diggings. The main mines, with pits 30 feet deep dug into solid quartzite with stone tools, are in Platte County. Villages, marked by tepee rings of stones, are scattered over an area 10 by 40 miles. Quartzite was carried to these villages from the pits for chipping into crude tools.

Scientists who investigated the mines declared them prehistoric diggings; probably 10,000 years old; dated by the slow-growing lichens on mined rocks; this was the first organized industry in Wyoming.

Men from the Smithsonian Institute, Washington, D.C., walked hand to hand picking up all good artifacts, mostly digging tools, scrapers, and spears. Caches of crude tools of this distinctive lavender and golden quartzite have been found as far east as Ohio and Indiana, indicating the trade and travel of prehistoric people.

Spanish Mountains, Teton: name given by early explorers to the Gros Ventre Range.

Spanish River, see Green River.

Sparhawk Lake, Natrona: named for Frank Sparhawk, pioneer forest ranger.

Spear Lake, Big Horn: named for Willis Spear, pioneer. He made trails into this region and stocked 21 lakes with fish; many trails from Spear Lake lead to scenic points and good fishing spots.

Specimen Ridge, 8,700, YNP: named prior to 1870 because of petrified forests here and the great variety of minerals and semi-precious stones. Yellowstone River has cut deep, revealing 27 petrified forests that grew one on top of another.

These forests, unique in the world, record the history of incomparable eons of time. For each of the forests, soil formed by erosion of rocks and seeds sprouted and grew into huge Sequoia trees, which were buried by volcanic ashes and lava. Then the cycle started again with the forming of soil. It is estimated by scientists that the last forest was buried about 40 million years ago.

Trees were redwood, sycamore, hickory, oak, magnolia, walnut, and pine. Jim Bridger once said, "Yessiree, thar's miles o' peetrefied trees, and on 'em trees are peetrefied birds a'singin' peetrefied songs."

There are petrifactions and imprints of leaves of plants that do not grow above an elevation of 3,000 feet—evidence that Specimen Ridge with its forests both growing and petrified was lifted upward thousands of feet during its formation.

Speck Pinnacle, 12,700, Fremont: named for Dr. John F. Speck who led the first ascent of this pinnacle with other Iowa mountaineers in 1948.

Spence, Big Horn: discontinued post office and railroad station named for Spence, pioneer.

Spence Dome Oil Field, Big Horn: named for Spence, landowner.

Spencer, Niobrara: discontinued ranch post office named for Mrs. Nelson W. Spence, postmaster.

Spencer, Weston: railroad station named for J. C. Spencer, once owner of the L A K ranch.

Spider Peak, 12,200, Fremont: a flat-topped plug, nearly vertical on all sides; it was named by D. Dornan for the numerous, hairy, brown spiders, as big as a nickel, that he found there. He ascended the peak in 1960.

Spirit Bay in Jackson Lake, Teton: named by Doane party in 1870 for tremendous echoes and re-echoes; it is probably now Moran Bay.

Spirit Mountain Caverns, Park: first known as Frost Caves. Ned Frost discovered them one frosty morning in November 1908. His hounds were pursuing a bobcat that had disappeared into the side of Cedar Mountain west of Cody, and he found the entrance.

Frost discovered the caves decorated with sparkling crystals, stalactites, and stalagmites. There were many openings, and vast underground ramifications. Only about 9 miles have been explored. The caverns are open to visitors, but not fully developed; they were designated the Shoshone National Monument.

Indians saw steam coming from the caves, and thought it was the breath of a spirit that dwelled inside the mountain, so they called it Spirit Mountain.

Split Rock, Albany: a rocky precipice named for its appearance; it has cracked in two, and the two halves settled apart.

Split Rock, Natrona: a huge split in a granite peak of the Rattlesnake Range; it is a landmark that can be seen for almost one hundred miles to the east and west. East of it on the Oregon Trail was a stage station on the Sweetwater River.

Here in 1862 the traditionally friendly Shoshones went on the warpath; taking white freighters by surprise, they stole all their horses and mules. The Indians commanded a Negro cook to prepare a meal for them; when he did not understand, they killed him, and helped themselves to his larder, still not breaking the claim of their leader Chief Washakie, that his people never killed a white man.

Sponge Geyser, YNP: named for the appearance of its cone.

Sportsman Ridge, 10,200, Teton: probably named by hunters.

Spotted Horse, Campbell: discontinued post office and filling station named for the Cheyenne Indian chief, Spotted Horse.

Spread Creek, Teton: named for its many tributaries.

Spring Creek, Albany: a railroad station named for Spring Creek, which is so named because it originates in springs.

Spring Creek Canyon, Washakie: cave high in a bank produced artifacts used about the time of Mesa Verde, 200 A.D. Those found included atlatls and wooden darts with sinew binding still painted with red pigment; the find was discovered and worked by Jake Frison, once a rancher here; he is now head of the Department of Anthropology, University of Wyoming.

Spring Creek Raid, Washakie: this last, great, armed conflict between sheepmen and cattlemen took place in 1909. Cattlemen, wanting the free range for themselves, claimed that sheep polluted the water and damaged grass so that cattle would not graze after them. They drew lines and warned sheepmen to stay out of the ranges they claimed for themselves, although they were on public domain.

Joe Emge, once a cattleman, and Joe Allemand brought 5,000 sheep into the area claimed by cattlemen along Spring Creek. Twenty armed and masked men surrounded the sheep camp one spring night and killed the owners and a herder; they cremated the bodies in the sheep wagons and clubbed sheep to death, or "rimrocked" them by driving them over cliffs; this was known as the Tensleep Raid.

The National Woolgrowers appropriated $20,000 for prosecution; jurors and law officers were threatened; one witness committed suicide, leaving a note incriminating several prominent ranchers. But a "deal" was made, and punishments were very light; those imprisoned were pardoned in a few years.

Springer, Goshen: discontinued post office named for Mr. Springer, irrigation promoter.

Springer Reservoir, Goshen: named for Mr. Springer, promoter of Springer Irrigation Company, which successfully operated a large acreage.

Spring Valley, Uinta: discontinued post office and railroad station named for Spring Valley, Utah. The village prospered in 1899. Finns built a hall for social meetings and erected a steam bathhouse. Residents enjoyed schottisching and waltzing in the public dance pavillion. This coal town had only a brief duration of six years.

Spurgin's Beaver Slide, YNP: named for Capt. W. F. Spurgin who built the first road across Yellowstone National Park; it was used in the memorable pursuit of the Nez Perce Indians in 1877.

Squaretop Mountain, 11,679, Sublette: named for its dramatic shape and steep granite walls; it is the most photographed of all the Wind River peaks; stands 3,713 feet above upper Green River Lake in the Bridger Wilderness; it was once called Roosevelt Butte.

Squaw Canyon, Albany: a squaw lived here in the 1880s; she mined and sold coal to the ranchers.

Squaw Creek and Flat, Lincoln: a hunting party of Idaho Blackfeet Indians camped on this creek in the 1890s. One brave surprised a grizzly bear eating service berries. The bear badly mangled and killed the Indian, who was buried here.

Every year at the same season his squaw came from her Idaho reservation to mourn at his grave; several times she was accompanied by their daughter. When she grew wrinkled and feeble, the squaw came on horseback. Finally, she ceased to come. She had joined her chief in the happy hunting grounds.

Squaw Mountain, Albany: this peak resembles a squaw wrapped in a blanket.

Squaw Mountain, Carbon: when Indians fought buffalo hunters, they hid their squaws on this mountain.

Squaw Mountain, Platte: rock formation on the mountain has the appearance of an Indian squaw with a blanket over her head. Indians regarded this as a sign from the Great Spirit. When the chiefs went forth to battle, they left their women and children on this mountain under the guardianship of the squaw.

Squaw Hollow, Sweetwater: campground and facilities on Flaming Gorge Reservoir.

Stager Canyon, Carbon: named for nearby Overland stage station.

Stagner Flats, Ridge, and Mountain, Hot Springs: named for Speed Stagner, a Missourian who married a squaw and was adopted into the Shoshone tribe.

Stambaugh Creek, Fremont: named for Lt. Charles B. Stambaugh who led his men into an Indian ambush on this creek in 1870 and was killed.

Stambaugh Peak, Fremont: see Atlantic Peak.

Standard Peak, 11,900, Park: the 11th standard parallel crosses a shoulder of this mountain.

Stansbury, Sweetwater: early coal town named for Captain Howard Stansbury who led a survey party for a railroad route in 1849.

Star Valley, Lincoln: name was given this lovely mountain vale by Apostle Moses Thatcher, Mormon, in 1870. As he stood on a knoll, he said, "I hereby name this valley Star Valley because it is the star of all valleys."
    The first creamery was built in the early 1890s, starting a new industry. Ernest Brog freighted out the first three 800-pound tubs of cheese to a railroad station in Idaho by teams in sub-zero weather in 1927. The cheese was packed in hay to keep it from freezing while traveling. At night men kept a ring of fire surrounding the cheese. The trip took five days and the cheese sold on the market in Portland, Oregon, for 28 cents a pound.

Static Peak and Pass, 11,294, Teton: this peak, first climbed in 1934, was named for static electricity that tingled climbers' bodies.

Stauffer, Sweetwater: named for Stauffer Chemical Company which has a multi-million-dollar mining and processing plant for trona or soda ash. This chemical gold is refined and used in the manufacture of glass, soap, detergents, textiles, plastics, rubber, and many other products. Natural gas is largely used for power.

Steamboat Geyser, YNP: named by Dr. Ferdinand Hayden in 1878. The geyser erupts with a deafening roar like a jet engine; scalding water flies upward to nearly 400 feet for three minutes; the geyser is so named because water splatters at an angle in a pulsating, paddlewheel fashion.

Steamboat Mountain, Sweetwater: named for its size and shape; this is a wildlife habitat for horses and elk.

Steamboat Point, Sheridan: a prominent limestone formation resembling a steamboat.

Steamboat Rock, 11,300, Fremont: named for its shape, this formation is a mile long.

192

Steele Creek, Johnson: named for Jim and Lewis Steele, cowboys who built a cabin at the head of this creek.

Stephen, Converse: named for Stephen Arnold Douglas; the post office here was called Orpha.

Stevenson Island, YNP: in Yellowstone Lake; it was named by Dr. Hayden in 1871 for James Stevenson, explorer with the USGS, who built the first boat for white man travel on lake.

Stevenson Mountain, 10,352, YNP: named for James Stevenson, director of the Hayden surveys in the Tetons.

Stewart, Goshen: discontinued post office named for L. M. Stewart.

Stewart Draw, Teton: named for Henry Stewart, rancher. The Stewart ranger station was once here; it was built of logs in 1910. The Beaver Creek campgrounds are here now.

Stewart Peak and Point, Sublette: a peak named for William D. Stewart, fur trader who spent several years here.

Stinkingwater Peak, 11,597, Park: in the Sunlight mining region with many old mines and trails; this peak was named for the Stinking Water River.

Stinking Water River, Park: named by John Colter in 1807 for its bad smell of sulphur; it was officially renamed Shoshone River in 1902.

Stockade Beaver Creek, Weston: named for the stockade erected by Walter P. Jenney here in 1875 to protect those making a mineral survey in the Black Hills for the government. A recreation camp was developed here much later.

Stockade Lake, Park: once called Leg Lake, it lies high on the Beartooth Plateau; it was renamed because of the Beartooth stockade. Its ruins were discovered in 1891 by cowboy Benjamin Greenough, "Pack Saddle Ben." Circular walls of the old stockade were of heavy logs, with holes cut through them for rifle ports; it commanded a good view on all sides.

Story, Sheridan: two versions of the name: named for Nelson Story, who got rich in the Montana gold fields, went to Texas, bought cattle, and drove the first trail herd by the Texas Trail through Buffalo in 1866. Col. Carrington at Fort Phil Kearny forbade him to continue north into Montana because of Indian danger. One dark night Story rounded up his 3,000 steers and fighting cowboys and took off; the soldiers could not leave the fort unprotected to follow him. He reached Montana after one skirmish, with all wagons and steer herd intact.

Another version is that Story was named after Charles P. Story, a pioneer newspaperman in Sheridan. It is now a summer resort town in the Big Horn Mountains, with fishing, hiking, and relaxing; it also boasts a state bird farm and fish hatchery.

Storm Point, 10,040, Teton: so named because this point receives the full force of southwest winds; it is a popular peak for climbing and has a fine view of the Tetons from the summit.

Stove Draw, Albany: a mountain draw in which an old stove sat in the 1880s.

193

Stratified Primitive Area, Fremont: contains 202,000 acres. A famous petrified forest is up Frontier Creek, seven miles from the beginning of the primitive area; that forest, millions of years old, is exposed by erosion; this is a fine hike with exotic mountain scenery.

The Wilderness Act passed by Congress in 1964 protects these primitive and wilderness areas from roads. Their future use is to be studied in public hearings; Congressional action is required to change their status. Grazing is permitted where it is already established.

These primitive and wilderness areas hold a great future source of wealth for Wyoming. Increasing population pressure will bring thousands of tourists to seek the brief reprieve of vacations spent in primitive surroundings for relaxation and relief. Tourist dollars are now the third major source of Wyoming income.

String Lake, Teton: once known as Beaver Dick Lake; it was renamed because it lies in a narrow, winding depression, possibly an old river bed, connecting Leigh and Jenny lakes; it has a four-hour loop trail for hikes.

Stroner, Crook: discontinued post office; was on the ranch of John F. Stroner.

Strong, Big Horn: discontinued post office named for Frank Strong.

Stroud Peak, 12,200, Sublette: its black, triangular shape can be seen from Green River Lake; named for William J. "Rocky Mountain Bill" Stroud, a Rock Springs man who always wore the same suit and hat, whether conducting business, visiting friends, or climbing mountains. He took many fine photographs of mountain scenes, was a friend to all, and carried candy for children in his dusty pockets.

Strouds, Natrona: railroad station named for Joshua Strouds, homesteader; it was established in 1884.

Strouss Hill, 8,170, Natrona: named for John Strouss, rancher.

Stump Creek, Lincoln: named for Stump, who, with White, dipped salt water from a spring above Auburn, put it in vats, and boiled the water off with wood fires. Then they hauled the salt west to sell to Idaho ranchers.

There were salt mines nearby, where blocks of salt could be cut for livestock use.

Sturgeon Creek, Albany: named in 1896 for William Sturgeon, rancher.

Stygian Caves, YNP: named because they are infernal and deadly; poisonous and suffocating gases rise from their openings, killing any small bird or animal that ventures near.

Sublet, Lincoln: discontinued post office and old mining camp; this is the post office spelling of Sublette.

Sublette County: named by Perry W. Jenkins who introduced the bill in the legislature for forming the county in 1921; it was named for William L. Sublette, fur trader and trapper mainly in the Wind River Mountains. In 1834 he formed a partnership with Robert Campbell and established a trading post on the Laramie River, which became Fort Laramie. There were five Sublette brothers, Andrew, Milton, Pinkney, Solomon, and William.

194

William Sublette was the first dude wrangler in Wyoming; in 1833 he received $500 from Capt. William Stewart, wealthy Scotsman, for letting him trek along with the Sublette party. In 1843 the first group of 20 dudes was gathered by Stewart in St. Louis, outfitted and guided by Sublette, and spent the summer hunting and exploring in the Wind River Mountains. He had 20 wranglers and attended the Green River rendezvous.

Big Piney and Pinedale were in the contest for the county seat of Sublette County; Pinedale won by a small majority. Some of the most spectacular mountain country in the state is in Sublette County; 80 percent of the land is under federal jurisdiction; livestock raising, dude ranching, and packing into mountains are the region's main industries; it is a sportsman's paradise.

Sublette Cut-off, Lincoln, Sublette, Sweetwater: originally known as Greenwood's Cut-off; this is a branch of the Oregon Trail which left the main trail six miles southeast of Dry Sandy crossing; it went west to Bear River where it met the trail coming from Fort Bridger; 53 miles were saved—precious miles in the days of covered-wagon travel; it was not popular because it led through a 30-mile waterless stretch. Often it was traveled at night to save thirsty animals. The trail was first used by the Sublette brothers in the 1820s.

Sublette Peak, 11,100, Teton: near Togwotee Pass with a superb view of the Wind River Range, Gros Ventres, and Tetons; it was named for William Sublette, who was in Jackson Hole many times.

Sudden Lake, Teton: another name for Slide Lake, which see.

Sugar Loaf, Albany: peak of solid granite; it sparkles in the sun like sugar.

Suggs, Sheridan: a railroad terminal and camp town in 1891 named for Suggs, rancher; the name was changed by Burlington railroad officials to Arvada in 1892.

Suicide Lake, Sublette: Lake formed by mountain slide; it was named by Finis Mitchell in 1952 when he was trapped by the slide. He tried to climb out on a tree; the tree broke and he fell, landing on his knapsack. He escaped serious injury and crawled out over rocky boulders.

Sulphur Springs, Carbon: stage station built on the new route in 1863; it was a sandstone building with a sod roof and was guarded by Kansas volunteers who dug rifle pits in nearby bluffs to guard the mail and the station; these depressions can still be seen. The station was named for the strong odor emanating from nearby water flows.

Summit Inn, 8,836, Albany: highest point on the Lincoln Highway.

Sun, Natrona: discontinued post office named for Tom Sun, pioneer rancher who built the first cabin here in the 1870s; once it was known as Devil's Gate; the Indians burned it and Sun rebuilt; it was a favorite stopping place of Ezra Meeker.

Soldiers from Rawlins once became lost in the region, and came to the Tom Sun ranch. They didn't discover the door was open, and took a window out to get into the cabin for food. Sun said, "Men lacking sense enough to enter another's house through an unlocked door would get lost anywhere."

This place, one of the oldest and most historic ranches in Wyoming, still serves as ranch headquarters.

195

Sunbeam Peak, 13,400, Fremont: named by Phil D. Smith in 1946, because it catches the early sunshine.

Sundance, Crook: county seat; established in 1879 by Albert Hoge as a supply station for cattle ranches; it takes its name from Sundance Mountain, under which it nestles. Its romantic old courthouse was dedicated in 1887 and outlasted three roofs; it was torn down when new courthouse, dedicated in 1968, was erected.

Sundance has cold drinking water coming from a spring under Sundance Mountain. Lumbering and livestock raising are the chief industries in the area.

A buffalo jump near here was excavated by the University of Wyoming team; the site was used about 800 A.D. to 1600 A.D. for communal hunting.

Sundance Creek, Crook: named for Sundance Mountain; the banks are bright with wild roses in the summer.

Sundance Formation, sandstone formation with red, green, and grey shale that lies over the Chugwater formation over most of the state.

Sundance Mountain, Crook: known as "Temple of the Sioux"; here they held a colorful, prayerful ceremony, a dance in worship of the sun every year. Similar sundances were held by other tribes; they probably originated with plains Indians early in the eighteenth century.

A large center pole was erected with a buffalo head on top of it. Usually 12 shorter poles were placed in a circle around the center pole, which was known as the medicine pole. Men fasted and danced for three days inside these poles, blowing on eagle-bone whistles. Once they threaded rawhide thongs through their chest flesh, and danced until the thongs tore out; this cruel form has long been discontinued.

Women squatted on the sides and beat on skin drums while the men danced; medicine men chanted. Sick were brought to the lodge for cures. Bodies of the dancers were painted by medicine men. Each morning the dancers faced the sun and stared at it all day while dancing. A big fire took the place of the sun at night. On the fourth day the dancers faced the rising sun and prayed. Then they rested and feasted. Each tribe had its own variations of its sundance.

The rock of Sundance Mountain is mostly porphyry, which produces a bell-like musical sound when the rocks are struck together.

Sundance Pinnacle, 11,081, Sublette: named for the annual ceremony of plains Indian tribes—a pageant of mythical sacrifice and healing. Shoshone tribes dance four days and nights; this is a sacred occasion to them, not a tourist attraction, so they do not announce the time of the dance to the public.

Sunlight Basin, Creek, and Peak, 11,922, Park: prospectors in the early days were lost in a fog here and wandered for hours. Suddenly the sun broke through the fog. They looked down on the creek's basin and saw it flooded with sunlight, hence the name.

Sunrise, Platte: site of a town located in 1881 by Landon, post trader at Fort Laramie; it was named by Lt. Eaton who, with some miners, was inspecting copper deposits above Eureka Canyon. The place gave them a fine view of the sunrise, for which they named it.

The town was established in 1903; mining of vast resources of low-grade

196

iron ore started in 1898 and produced one-half million tons a year; it was converted from open pit to underground mining in 1941. See Chicago Mine and Hartville.

Sunset Lake, YNP: a large lake with a beautifully colored basin.

Superior, Sweetwater: coal mining town named for Superior Coal Company which mined superior coal. It became almost a ghost town in 1970; now it is booming with the growth from the Jim Bridger Power Plant worker influx.

Supply, Lincoln: an old emigrant post office and store.

Surprise Lake, Teton: on Amphitheater trail; this is a beautiful surprise.

Surveyor Park, Sublette: a USGS survey camp was here in 1906; a trail here leads through the famous "knotty pine" forest; knotty growth is caused by mistletoe or parasite attacks on trees; the wood is used for decorative purposes. Mary Faler, woman packer, once had a tourist lodge here; she guided and packed visitors into the wilderness areas.

Survey Peak, 9,277, Teton: hydrographic divide near the summit; there are arrowhead chippings along old trails.

Susie, Lincoln: railroad station and coal camp named for Susan Quealy, wife of Pat Quealy.

Sussex, Johnson: discontinued post office on a ranch; it was named by the rancher's wife, Mrs. H. W. Davis, who came from Sussex County, Delaware.

Swan, Carbon: discontinued post office named by Guy Nichols, first postmaster, for William Franklin Swan, rancher.

Swan, Platte: railroad station named for the Swan Cattle Company. The firm was organized in 1883 by Alexander H. Swan, Englishman; the firm was financed from London and Edinburgh, Scotland; in its heyday it claimed land on both sides of the Laramie River for 130 miles; its herds ranged from Ogallala, Nebraska, to Fort Steele—more than 300 miles.

In the early 1880s the company bought 540,423 acres from the Union Pacific railroad for $1 an acre. The federal government had given the railroad the odd-numbered sections of land on each side of the railroad out for a distance of 20 miles as a grant to encourage its building. In 1883 the Swan Cattle Company imported 400 Hereford bulls from England.

After the hard winter of 1886-87, the firm went into receivership, reorganized in 1888, and regained part of the range but badly cramped by homesteaders and their barbed wire fences. In 1924 the British owners sold out, and the last of the great, foreign-owned spreads in Wyoming was gone. Swan founded the Wyoming Hereford ranch. The old headquarters east of Chugwater is now an historical landmark.

Swan Lake, YNP: named in 1879 by P. W. Norris, first explorer of this region, for trumpeter swans. In 1932 a national survey showed only 69 trumpeter swans alive in the United States. Under protection, the swans are making a slow increase in numbers. These large, graceful birds mate for life and nest on top of muskrat and beaver houses.

Swan Lake Flats, YNP: 900 different flowers bloom here, including the Rocky Mountain fringed gentian. This gentian has unofficially been known as the Yellowstone National Park flower since 1926; it is of fine texture—deep blue in color; it was named for King Gentius, ruler of Illyria some 2000 years ago. He used a bitter tonic from gentians to check malaria in his army.

Sweetwater Agate Beds, Fremont: these polished, water-formed jewels with dendrite inclusions have eroded out of the granite of Rattle-snake Mountains; they have been tumbled and polished by water and once lay scattered by the thousands under sagebrush on dry prairies. They are not so plentiful now, as rockhounds have picked up most of them. They fluoresce green under a black light because of the uranium they contain; they are hunted at night with this light. The beds are east of Jeffrey City near the Sweetwater River.

Sweetwater County: created by Dakota legislature in 1867 as Carter County; it was renamed by the Wyoming Territorial legislature for the Sweetwater River in 1869; South Pass City was county seat until 1873, when it was moved to Green River City; the northern part of the county was cut off when Fremont County was created in 1884.

Sweetwater County now contains 10,495 square miles and is the largest county in Wyoming—larger than seven states; it has a great variety of scenery from the shifting sands of the Red Desert to pineclad mountains, from sagebrush mesas to the blue water of recreation lakes.

It is estimated there are twelve billion tons of coal reserves in the county; the largest, Rock Springs Coal Field, covers 3,000 square miles. The first gas well was drilled in 1922, the first oil well in 1928; there are great reserves in these fields. Mining and refinement of soda ash from trona mines are now the principal industries. There are several multi-million-dollar processing plants; more than 950,000 tons are produced yearly. Soda ash is used in production of glass, soaps, detergents, plastics, and rubber.

Firms in the county produce more soda ash from mining and refining trona than is produced in the rest of the world; trona formed in a huge prehistoric lake that became briny and shrunk in size; then it was flooded again with fresh water that produced a shale covering. The first trona mine opened in 1947. This sodium carbonate was discovered in 1896.

Flaming Gorge Recreation Area is now bringing thousands of tourists to Sweetwater County; the lake has 300 miles of shoreline, and is 90 miles long; boating, water-skiing, fishing, and camping are favorite sports.

Look Slow
Dedicated to Sweetwater County
You say you don't see much! Not anything at all?
That's jest because you want to see it all at once.
Out here there's room and time to take it kinda slow.
We don't pile houses up, or even crowd the grass.
You look too quick. Look slow. It's miles out to them hills.
Jest let your eyes drift up along their curves until
You catch those vague blue shapes that blend into the sky;
Them's mountains, ma'am, and if you traveled all one day
You'd get to see 'em good. They're bigger than New York.
I know; I bin there once. Too much of everything.
The lights—too bright. You can't hear anything but noise.

I bet you never heard the meadowlarks greet you.
"It's a beautiful morning," they say. A herd of antelope
Is grazin' there jest off the road. Did you see 'em?
No, they don't advertise. They hide by blendin' with
The sage. Out here you jest discover things yourself.

You reckon you must go. Well, watch the shadows shift
And deepen as them mountains come in view. Jest think
How long it took a pine to grow right outa rocks.
That gold down in them draws is cottonwood. It's fall,
In foothills quaking asp are turning russet now.

And stop fer half an hour at sunset time and walk
Out in them hills. Jest stand and let the twilight come
To you, and watch the softness of them colors spread
Across the open sky. There's lots to see out here.
Wyoming's like great music, ma'am; you have to learn
To love its moods, and listen for the melody.
So long!
                              Poem by author.

Sweetwater River, Fremont, Natrona: said to have been named by
Gen. William H. Ashley in 1823, because the water tasted sweet to his
trappers after the bitter alkali water they had been drinking. French
trappers called it Eau Sucree, sugar water.
    There is also the story that a mule carrying a load of sugar fell into the
river, giving it the name Sweetwater.

Sweetwater Rocks, Fremont: a range of granite rocks paralleling
the Sweetwater River; it contains large feldspar and mica crystals.

Sweetwater Station, Natrona: a stage and Pony Express station, as
well as a military post for the protection of emigrants near Independence
Rock and the Sweetwater River crossing on the Oregon Trail.

Swift Canyon and Creek, Lincoln: a unique spring that gushes
ice-cold water at intervals of about 18 minutes and then completely stops;
it forms a creek and a canyon. As water ceases to flow from the spring, air
enters the cavern and is expelled as water again flows; it is called the
spring that breathes.

Sybille Creek, Albany, Platte: quoting from General John Fremont:
"We came in view of Fort Platte, a post belonging to Messrs. Sybille,
Adams and Company at junction of Laramie and Platte Rivers"; pro-
nounced Se-bill. The creek was named for this French trapper and trader,
Sybille, in the 1830s.

Sybille Game and Fish Experimental Unit, Albany: a
3,081-acre tract in mountainous country used as a wild animal refuge and
research center by Wyoming Game and Fish Department. Elk, bighorn
sheep, deer, and buffalo may be seen here along Highway 34.

Symmetry Spire, 10,546, Teton: named in 1929 on the first ascent for
its slender and symmetric shape; it is a popular peak for climbers. Routes
vary from easy to very difficult. Six climbers lost their lives on the peak in
1971 in several accidents.

T

T A Creek, Johnson: named for the T A ranch.

T A Ranch, Johnson: owned by Dr. Harris; this was the final battleground in the Johnson County War, which see.

T B Mountains, Albany: brand of Trabing brothers, early ranchers.

Table Mountain, Albany: named for its flat-topped appearance.

Table Mountain, 11,101, Teton: ascended in 1872 by photographer William H. Jackson, his assistant, and a mule, Molly, loaded with equipment for taking and processing glass photoplates. Jackson wanted a perfect viewpoint for taking a picture of Grand Teton from the west.

They climbed over piles of loose rocks and debris for nine days to the summit of Table Mountain to get the picture, which is unsurpassed to this day.

Table Rock, Sweetwater: railroad station. Table Rock is also known as "Pulpit Rock"; this is where Brigham Young delivered a sermon to Mormons on the way to Utah in 1847.

Nearby are Diamond Mesa and Ruby Gulch, which were "salted" in 1876 with precious stones by two prospectors. They took interested persons, blindfolded, to see the great discovery and fleeced such men as Horace Greeley, the Rothschilds, and Tiffany out of more than $500,000 for mine promotion, before a cook picked up, from an ant hill, a diamond that showed marks of a lapidary's tool.

Rubies and diamonds were planted in ant hills, as well as garnets, sapphires, emeralds, and amethysts; it is impossible to find all these gems in one locale, under natural conditions.

Tabor Mountain, Sweetwater: named for U.S. Senator "Buckskin Joe" Tabor of Colorado.

Taft Ranch, Fremont: near here, southeast of Lander, the first oil well in Wyoming was drilled.

Taggart Lake, Teton: named for W. R. Taggart, member of Hayden Survey in 1872. He was also with Capt. W. F. Raynolds and the Army Engineers exploring Jackson Hole in 1860. There is a nature hiking trail along the lake and Beaver Creek; it also leads to Bradley Lake.

Taggart Meadows, Carbon: named for Pete Taggart, tender at Crooks Creek station, an early freighting stop.

Taminah Lake, Teton: from Shoshone word meaning "spring." It is still spring above timberline, when summer or fall has come to Jackson Hole.

Tangled Creek, YNP: hot water flows in many interlacing channels.

Tantalus Creek, YNP: named for the Greek God Tantalus, son of Hades; it drains Vixen Geyser.

Tapman Mountain, Big Horn: named for pioneer Tapman; he made a saddle from a tree stump and bolted a buffalo horn to it.

Tappan Creek, Fremont: named for Jim Tappan. He and Abe Leeds were guides and wranglers for dudes in the Upper Wind River country in the 1890s. Leeds Creek was named for Abe Leeds, surveyor, who helped establish section lines here.

Tar Springs, Fremont: Osborne Russell, trapper, on the way to the rendezvous in 1837 described this oil spring near present Lander. He said trappers stopped here, and set fire to oil around the spring, enjoying the dense column of black smoke it produced.

Tardy and Old Tardy Geysers, YNP: irregular in eruptions.

Targhee National Forest, Lincoln, Teton: named for Chief Targhee of the Bannocks, who was reported killed by Crows in 1871. Targhee National Forest extends into Wyoming from Idaho. The headquarters are in St. Anthony, Idaho.

Tatman Mountain, Big Horn: named for J. J. Tatman, rancher, and one of the first settlers in Bighorn basin.

Taylorville, Niobrara: discontinued post office on Lightning Creek; named for Merritt L. Taylor, postmaster in the 1890s. Taylor, a scout, trapper, and rancher, once eluded Indians by walking backwards in the mud of the creek.

Teapot, Natrona: oil town named for Teapot Rock.

Teapot Dome, Natrona: an oil field named for Teapot Rock; it was made a Naval Reserve under President William H. Taft and closed to private exploitation. In the administration of President Warren G. Harding the reserve was transferred from Navy Department to Department of Interior. Albert B. Fall, Secretary of Interior, then leased the Teapot Dome Oil Field to Sinclair Oil Company without competitive bids.

Then the tempest in the teapot really brewed! Fall and Harry F. Sinclair both were convicted and imprisoned. The Supreme Court invalidated the lease. The reserve was returned to the control of the Navy in 1928.

Teapot Rock, Natrona: a huge, rounded rock that once had a teapot spout and handle. A fierce wind crumbled the handle away in 1962. This eroded sandstone is 75 feet high. The spout of the teapot is now crumbling away.

Teckla, Campbell: discontinued post office named for Mrs. Teckla Putman, postmaster for many years.

Teewinot Mountain, 12,317, Teton: Shoshone name that was once applied to entire Teton Range, it means "many pinnacles." Osborne Russell says the Shoshones also called the Tetons "Hoary-headed Fathers."

Teewinot Mountain, which dominates the view from Jenny Lake, was first ascended in 1929 by F. Fryxell and Phil Smith.

Telephone Canyon, Albany: named in 1882 when telephone line was built through the canyon; it was one of the earliest lines in Wyoming.

Telephone Lakes, Albany: two small lakes in the Snowy Range. Judge M. C. Brown had a telephone installed in his mining camp about 1900; this was a novelty in the region, and it gave the mine and nearby lakes their name.

Temple Peak, 13,249, Sublette: named for its shape; it was used as a topographical station in Hayden Surveys; the peak was first ascended in 1877.

Ten Mile, Carbon: ten miles from the junction of Highways 12, 130, and 230.

Ten Mile Station, Goshen: a road ranch on the Cheyenne-Deadwood route; it was ten miles north of Fort Laramie; coaches stopped here only when necessary.

Tensleep, Washakie: village named for the Indian method of reckoning time; the site was ten days travel or "ten sleeps" from Fort Laramie; it was also ten sleeps from Yellowstone National Park and from the Indian agency at Stillwater, Montana. Once called Sackett Fork for Col. Sackett, the army engineer who in 1867 mapped the area.

The early post office here was run by Martha Bull, a teetotaler, who sold candy and nicknacks. A salesman sold her some Rock N' Rye cough syrup; all the cowboys in the vicinity soon developed bad coughs; the good syrup in the bright bottles didn't last long.

A buffalo herd was started in 1974 at Cal Hampton's Mahogany Butte ranch near Tensleep. Buffalo can stand cold winters better than cattle.

Girl Scout National Center West is located west of Tensleep in a wilderness site which stresses outdoor education and wildlife appreciation.

Tensleep Canyon and Creek, Big Horn, Washakie: named for an old Indian camp site "ten sleeps" from several important points. The drive through this canyon, now on Highway 16, is very picturesque; the canyon was once almost inaccessible.

Tensleep Raid, Washakie: see Spring Creek Raid.

Tepee Glacier and Pilla, Teton: named for Theodore Tepee, who fell here, and rolled to his death after ascending Grand Teton in 1925. He was the first to die climbing Grand Teton.

The glacier is really a snowfield, as it almost melts away in the summer. The pillar is a spear of red granite on the south slope of Grand Teton.

Terhune, Crook: discontinued post office named for Bertha Terhune, first postmaster.

Terry Lakes, Fremont: named for Captain Terry, former army officer and rancher.

Teton County: named for Teton Range; created in 1921 from northern part of Lincoln County, whose county seat, Kemmerer, was too far away. Teton County did not have a population of 3,000, or a property valuation of $5,000,000 at that time, as required by law, so it was created by a special act and organized in 1923 with Jackson as county seat.

Teton Creek, Teton: named for the Teton Range.

Teton National Forest, Fremont, Lincoln, Sublette, Teton: named for the Teton Range; it was carved out of the Yellowstone Timber Reserve in 1897 and officially given the name of Teton National Forest in 1907.

Federal elk and wildlife is located in Teton National Forest. Timber cutting, livestock grazing, conservation, and recreation are practiced, so that the greatest benefits, both economic and social, may be derived; its headquarters are in Jackson.

Teton Pass, 8,431, Teton: first known as Hunt's Pass, which see. In 1885 Robert Miller horse-packed a disassembled wagon over this pass. Later it took 11 days of hard labor to get wagons over this historic hump

202

that trappers had long traveled to the rendezvous in Pierre's Hole, now Teton Basin, in Idaho.

The first automobile, a Hupmobile, went through the pass in 1914. An auto now on a modern highway can go over in one hour; it boasts magnificent scenery and there is skiing from November to May.

Teton Range, 8,000 to 13,766, Teton: probably the first name applied to the Tetons was "Pilot Knobs" by Wilson Price Hunt in 1811. Alexander Ross, who visited the area in 1824, gives a clue to the first use of "Trois Tetons," (French name meaning three teats). He claims this name was first given to smaller buttes near the Crater of the Moon, which more closely resemble female breasts. French trappers had named these Idaho buttes, and then in their wanderings applied the name "Les Trois Tetons" to the more spectacular Wyoming mountains. Indians called them Tee-win-ot, three pinnacles.

The Tetons, unrelieved by foothills, rise abruptly 7,000 feet above the floor of Jackson Hole, and spiral majestically into the sky. Their bases are robed in forests of pines and silver spruce; their summits are glistening rocks covered with glaciers creating awe-inspiring beauty. William H. Jackson took the first pictures of them in 1872. They are the most photographed mountains in the world.

The Tetons were formed by a bursting of the earth's crust or a fault 40 miles long, breaking abruptly up on the east side, hinged, and more sloping on the west. Scientists think they are about three million years old, formed of granite and crystalline rock from deep within the earth. They have been carved and polished by glaciers of three ice ages, which left valleys and alpine lakes to reflect their grandeur. Grand Teton is the Matterhorn of America.

Teton River, Teton: once called Pierre's River for Vieux Pierre, Iroquois Indian scout in 1924 for the Hudson's Bay Fur Company; it was renamed Teton for the Teton Range.

Teton Village, Teton: it boasts new ski headquarters with chalets, lodgings, restaurants, and a romantic clock tower. An aerial tram, capacity 63 passengers, rises from here to the top of Rendezvous Peak, 10,924 feet; it runs all year.

Teton Wilderness Area, Park, Teton: 563,500 acres set aside by the United States Forest Service in 1934, which preserves virgin splendor with no roads, no buildings. This is wonderful pack country for those seeking escape from civilization to fish and relax. The area includes the headwaters of the Yellowstone and Snake rivers separated by the Continental Divide.

Tevay, Johnson: discontinued ranch post office named for Ed Tevay.

Texas Annexation, Albany, Carbon: Texas and its territory was admitted to the Union as a state in 1845; the northernmost area became part of Albany and Carbon counties.

Texas Trail or Trails, Laramie, Goshen, Niobrara, Weston, Crook: following the Civil War there were too many cattle in Texas. Large herds of these Texas longhorns were driven north to shipping points on railroads and to replace the vanishing buffalo on the prairies of Colorado, Nebraska, Wyoming, and Montana.

John B. Kendrick, late U.S. Senator from Wyoming, drove cattle up the

203

Texas Trail. In 1879 he traveled more than 400 miles between Fort Worth, Texas, and Running Water (now Lusk), Wyoming, without seeing a single habitation or a wire fence.

The trails entered Wyoming at Cheyenne and Pine Bluffs and went north past Torrington, Lusk, and Moorcroft and into Montana from 1866-97.

Thayer Junction, Sweetwater: junction from the main line of the Union Pacific railroad to Superior; it was named for Thayer, a pioneer living here.

Thayne, Lincoln: established in 1889 and named for Henry Thayne, first postmaster and merchant. This is the home of the Swiss Cheese Company, which produces more than three million pounds of cheese annually; it is the world's largest cheese factory.

Theresa, Converse: discontinued post office named for Theresa Henry, daughter of rancher.

Thermopolis, Hot Springs: after the U.S. government treaty with the Indians and cession of part of the Wind River Indian Reservation, land around the natural hot springs was opened for settlement. In 1897 the townsite of Thermopolis was platted.

Dr. Julius A. Schuelke selected the name: a combination of thermae (Latin for hot baths or springs) and polis (Greek for city), making Thermopolis. A settlement of people from six miles away on Owl Creek then moved to the new town. That site is since known as Old Town.

When Hot Springs County was organized in 1913, Thermopolis was chosen as the county seat. Since the mineral waters of the springs have great medicinal value, the town grew rapidly. These are the world's largest hot springs; 18,600,000 gallons of water at 135 degrees Fahrenheit pour out every 24 hours, forming beautiful terraces of travertine, brilliantly colored with algae. A boardwalk leads through these terraces.

In accordance with the wish of Chief Washakie, part of the water is available for free baths. Washakie Fountain is a monument to this great friend of white men. "Gift of the Waters" is a pageant portraying the history of the Shoshone Indians and of the region; it is enacted annually. The Shoshone name for hot springs is Bah-Bui-Wana, Smoking Water.

Gottsche Rehabilitation Center, a state bathhouse, and Hot Springs State Park with buffalo are all located at Thermopolis, A pioneer museum has a stagecoach, trapper displays, and antique organs.

Thimble Peak, 12,300, Sublette: sticks up like a thimble among larger peaks.

Thomas Fork, Lincoln: originally Thompson's Fork, it was named for David Thompson, a member of Ashley's trapper brigade of the 1820s; the name has been shortened to Thomas Fork.

Thompson's Mountain, Pass, and Plateau, 9,749, Lincoln, Sublette: named for David Thompson, an astronomer and surveyor, who was also a member of William Ashley's fur expeditions of the 1820s.

Thor Peak, 12,018, Teton: named for Thor, god of thunder; this is a peak for climbers; it is located back of Mount Moran.

Thorofare Buttes and Creek, 11,417, Park, Teton, YNP: named for Thorofare Plateau.

Thorofare Mountain, 12,053, Park, Teton, YNP: named for Thorofare Plateau.

Thorofare Plateau, 11,800, Park, Teton, YNP: a tremendous plateau in elk and moose country so named because it is a thoroughfare for thousands of big game animals in their annual migrations. Indians described it as the "passing of the great herds."

The plateau is dissected by many creeks. Petrified wood can be found near Castle and Hidden creeks.

Three Crossings, Fremont: a stage, Pony Express, and telegraph station on the Oregon Trail, which crossed the Sweetwater River three times within a short distance.

Here Buffalo Bill, Pony Express rider, found his relief killed; he rode on to Rocky Ridge and back to Red Buttes, the start of his run, a distance of 322 miles in 21 hours, a feat unequaled in recorded history.

When the station was burned by Indians, it was replaced by one of stone with a log stockade and a lookout.

The transcontinental telegraph line which passed through here was joined with one from the west coast at Salt Lake City. The first message flashed across the country October 24, 1861. This meant the end of the Pony Express. Indians puzzled over "talking wires"; they hated them and often tore them down and burned poles. Buffalo enjoyed rubbing on the poles. It was hard and dangerous work to maintain those lines in the early days.

Three Forks, Park, Sublette: the main Green River is formed here by the junction of Wells Creek, Trail Creek, and the center fork of the Green River. Located high in the Wind River Range, this area boasts excellent fishing.

Three Mile, Goshen: road ranch three miles downriver from Fort Laramie; a large store, blacksmith shop, ice house, billiard hall, and sod corral, 100 feet square and 12 feet high, were erected here; it had eight two-room cottages occupied by women.

A sign above the door of the store read "Pay today and trust tomorrow." The place was on the Cheyenne-Deadwood stage route; good meals were served for 50 cents.

Three Patches, Sweetwater: named for three patches of aspen trees near the crest of Aspen Mountain, 8,680, a high spot in the immediate area. It is a favorite picnic spot.

Threetown, Carbon: railroad station; mining districts at Hanna were called One Town, Two Town, and Three Town; the station was named for Three Town.

Thunderhead, Converse: a rock formation like a huge head; it is located in the Medicine Bow National Forest a few miles south of Douglas; this is scenic country with hiking trails, good fishing, and rock hunting.

Tie City and Tie City Pass, Albany: a large tie camp during the construction of the Union Pacific railroad and after its completion; ties, poles, and wood were cut here and delivered to the railroad; located in Telephone Canyon, once this town had ten cabins and a saloon; there is no trace of its existence now.

Tie Down Flat and Tie Down Gulch, Washakie: named for "Tie

Down" Brady, named for his handiness in tying down stock and re-branding them to suit himself; he was shot by his partner while he was washing dishes; it took all the lumber in the country to make him a coffin.

Another version of the name says a horse thief was caught here; since there was not a tree from which to hang him, he was tied down to the ground with four stakes and left to die.

Highway 20 now crosses Tie Down Gulch within sight of the spot where this man was left to pay this painful penalty of death for stealing horses. It was considered a worse crime to steal a horse than a cow, because the horse owner might be left on foot, a long way from nowhere.

Tie Siding, Albany: village in timber country established in 1868; workers supplied ties to the railroad during construction days; this was also a supply center for ranches in the Red Buttes and Pole Mountain areas.

Tigee Lake, Fremont: named for Tigee, Shoshone chief.

Tiger Tower, 11,650, Fremont: a knife-edged ridge named for its difficult faces for climbers.

Timmoco Creek, Fremont: a Shoshone word meaning windy and blustery like a man, not calm like a woman.

Tin Cup Creek, Mine, and Mountain, Fremont: named for Tin Cup Springs in the creek, because one needed a tin cup to get a drink.

Tin Cup Creek and Canyon, Lincoln: first settlers on this creek near the present site of Freedom came in 1879 and used tin cups to drink from the creek. A road was built down the canyon, and Mormons used it, fleeing from a federal raid in Idaho.

Tinkcom, Big Horn: discontinued post office named for D. A. Tinkcom, postmaster.

Tipperary, Fremont: discontinued post office; named by an Irishman for the song Tipperary.

Tipperary Flat, Uinta: Irish settlement here chose name when the song, Tipperary, was at the height of its popularity.

Tipton, Sweetwater: railroad station named because it is on the summit of a hill. Harvey Logan and some of Butch Cassidy's Hole-in-the-Wall gang robbed a train here. They blew the safe and got less than $50 cash and three bags of coins which they thought were gold.

At the first opportunity after a successful getaway, they stopped to divide the loot according to their ironclad rules. This was so that in case of the killing or capture of any member, the others could escape with their share of loot.

After the Tipton robbery they stopped somewhere southeast of Rock Springs to divide. When they opened the sacks, they found only pennies. Logan let out a war whoop and said, "They can't make us take that kind of money!" In disgust he poured the pennies down a prairie dog hole.

Tisdale, Johnson: discontinued ranch post office named for David T. Tisdale, rancher.

Tisdale Divide and Gulch, Johnson: where John A. Tisdale, small rancher, was murdered and his team shot during the Johnson County War. He was not a rustler.

206

Titcomb Lakes and Needles, Sublette: named for Harold and Charles Titcomb, who made the second ascent of Fremont Peak in 1901; they spent the night under the rocks part way up.

Harold Titcomb was assistant superintendent of the Carissa gold mine at South Pass, a mine engineer, champion archer, and philanthropist.

Togwotee Pass, 9,658, Teton: pronounced To'go-te; named by Capt. William A. Jones, U.S. Corps of Engineers, in 1873; he was shown this pass by his Indian guide, Tog-we-tee, a Sheepeater and sub-chief under Washakie; the name was misspelled in the records.

Tog-we-tee means lance thrower or "exactly there" from an Indian game. An Indian threw a lance at a target about 50 yards away; then other Indians threw lances to see how close they could come to the first lance.

The first automobile chugged over this pass in 1916 along an old wagon road that followed Indian trails. A rodeo and barbecue marked the official opening of the road through the pass in 1921; there is a marvelous view of the Tetons from the pass.

Tollgate Butte or Rock, Sweetwater: in the early days Mormons cut a roadway here and charged a toll for its use.

Toltec, Albany: discontinued post office named by William Taylor, merchant at Rock Creek in 1884; he found some "workings" in a nearby hill; they reminded him of the Toltec Indian mines in Mexico, about which he had been reading.

Tomahawk Lake, Fremont: once an Indian hangout reached by trail from Fiddler Lake; there is good trout fishing here.

Tom Creek, Weston: an early settler, Bob Bennett, killed a wildcat here; to him all cats were Toms, so he called it Tom Creek.

Tongue River, Sheridan: from the Cheyenne Indian name for it, I-tan-i-ho, meaning tongue. A rock above Little Tongue River resembles a tongue. Indian sign language for the Tongue River was to touch finger to the tongue and then wave the hand, as if going away.

Top Notch Peak, 9,948, Teton: has a distinctive notch in the summit.

Torchlight Dome Oil Field, Big Horn: shallow oil wells were drilled here in 1905 and gas was struck; a gas well burned like a torch-light.

Torrey Creek, Lake, and Peak, 12,300, Fremont: named for Capt. Robert A. Torrey, commander at Fort Washakie. Later he became a prominent cattleman.

Torrington, Goshen: county seat named by William Gilbert Curtis, who established a post office at his ranch ½ mile west of the present town; he named it for Torrington, Connecticut, from which he came; people from there came from Torrington, England; it is said that there are only three Torringtons in the world.

In order to get a post office, Curtis had to carry mail twice a week from Fort Laramie without compensation. When the railroad came through, the post office was moved in 1900 to the location where the town of Torrington was platted. The old Oregon Trail was on the south side of the Platte River, the Mormon Trail on the north side.

Torrington is in an irrigated farming district; Holly Sugar Company plant is located here, as is St. Joseph's Orphanage for children. Southeast

University Center started here in 1948, an extension of the University of Wyoming; it became Goshen County Community College in 1956 and opened on a new campus with extensive buildings in 1968; now it is known as Eastern Wyoming College.

A state experiment farm is located at Torrington; it tests livestock feed and feeding, as well as irrigated farming methods.

Tosi Creek and Peak, 11,370, Teton: named for a Shoshone medicine man, Tosi, who hunted with author Owen Wister. Hunting lodges on the creek were built and operated by William S. Wells from 1897-1906; this was the first dude ranch in Wyoming.

Tower, Crook: discontinued post office named for Devils Tower by Lillie L. Marshall, first postmaster.

Tower Creek and Tower Junction, YNP: named for Tower Falls.

Tower Falls, YNP: a ribbon-like cascade of water that plunges 132 feet through eroded rocks that rise like towers; it was named in 1870 by the Washburn exploration party; it is located in a setting of primitive beauty.

Towner Lake, Albany: named for Ben Towner, miner here in the 1880s. Also it is known as Gregory Lake; Gregory was a miner here, too.

Trabing, Johnson: August and Charles Trabing established a road-house on Crazy Woman Creek in 1878; it was on the route from Cheyenne to Powder River military posts; it was the first store in what is now Johnson County; the goods were hauled in by ox teams on the Bozeman Trail. Trabing was an early social center.

Trabing Creek, Sheridan: named for August and Charles Trabing, freighters.

Trail Creek, Albany: named about 1880 for a wild animal trail leading from the creek to the mountains.

Trail Lake, Carbon: so named because it is on an old sheep trail.

Trapper Creek, Big Horn: trappers lived in dugouts here in the 1880s.

Traverse Peak, Teton: climbers must traverse from Bivouac Peak to reach it.

Tremain, Laramie: railroad station named for D. C. Tremain, first settler on Horse Creek in 1888.

Trident Plateau, 10,969, Park, YNP: three long, parallel ridges with precipitous north and south walls, rising abruptly more than 1,500 feet; it was named for shape.

Trigger Lake, Johnson: shaped like the trigger of a gun.

Trilobite Point, 10,000, YNP: famous for its fossils; trilobites are some of the earliest forms of marine life; the fossils show the division of the small body into three segments.

Trout Creek, Park: named for the many trout in the creek.

Trout Peak, 12,244, Park: named for Trout Creek, it is the highest and most eastern peak in the northern Absarokas.

Tubb Town, Weston: DeLoss Tubbs established a road ranch and store on Salt Creek in 1889. With the influx of the railroad builders, Tubb Town became a rambunctious burg with plenty of tootin' and shootin' for a brief time.

When Burlington railroad was surveyed where Newcastle now is, about two miles from Tubb Town, the buildings were all moved to the Newcastle site within 48 hours.

Tullis, Carbon: discontinued post office and railroad station named for Tullis, a retired postal inspector who was killed a few weeks after the post office was established .

Tulsa, Lincoln: during the oil boom of the 1920s optimists called the new village Tulsa, after Tulsa, Oklahoma, the oil town. After the boom collapsed, the village was renamed LaBarge for a nearby creek.

Tunnel Hill, Sheridan: so named because the waters of a creek are tunneled under the hill to irrigate farms beyond the hill.

Turner Creek, Weston: named for "Shorty" Turner, cowboy and early settler here.

Turnercrest, Campbell: discontinued post office named for George W. Turner, postmaster; it was located on top of a hill.

Turnerville, Lincoln: discontinued post office named for Turner, pioneer.

Turpin Creek and Meadows, Teton: named for Dick Turpin, honest and hot-headed trapper here in the 1880s; the ranch is now used as a starting point for pack trips into the Teton Wilderness Area.

Twenty-one Creek, Hot Springs: named by Col. Michael Sliney, Indian fighter in 1877. He crossed this creek 21 times with loaded wagons in a few hours of travel.

Twin Creeks, Uinta: in 1887 county officials didn't like the idea of women voting in this precinct. An "old rounder" turned some mice loose at the polling place; every feminine voter gathered up her skirts and fled home. The ingenuity of the wicked won the election.

Twin Lakes, YNP: small lakes holding hands through a stream; one is turquoise blue, the other emerald green; the story is told that one was bluer than the other, so the second one turned green with envy.

Two Bar Post Office, Platte: established in 1891 at Grant ranch and named for its brand.

Two Ocean Creek, Teton: the creek separates on the Continental Divide; one branch flows about 3,488 miles to the Atlantic Ocean via the Yellowstone, Missouri, and Mississippi rivers; the other fork flows about 1,353 miles to the Pacific Ocean via Pacific Creek and the Snake and Columbia rivers.

Two Ocean Lake, Teton: misnamed because it drains only to the Pacific Ocean via Pacific Creek and the Snake and Columbia rivers.

Two Ocean Pass, Teton: on the Continental Divide where Two Ocean Creek splits and flows to two oceans. Russell, here in 1835, described the splitting of the waters, and how trout could cross the divide here. Headwaters of the Atlantic and Pacific creeks are here.

In 1892 Theodore Roosevelt hunted elk here for ten days; he enjoyed visiting with Beaver Dick, a squaw man, who lived with his Indian wife and half-breed children in a skin tepee.

Two Ocean Plateau, 10,045, YNP: on top of the Continental Divide. One can see Yellowstone Lake to the north, Absaroka Range to the east, the Teton Range to the southwest, and the Wind River Range to the southeast.

Twogwotee Pass, Teton: name of Shoshone Indians who lived in the mountains. Chief Washakie named To-go-te and other chiefs to guide President Chester A. Arthur and his party to Yellowstone National Park in 1883.

Tygee Valley, Lincoln: named for Terghee, Bannock Indian chief; spelling was simplified.

Tyhe Peak, Fremont: named for a Shoshone medicine man, Tyhe.

U

Ucross, Sheridan: village named for the brand of the original owners of the land; the brand was a "U" with a cross under it; it was first called Cedar Rapids by a settler from Cedar Rapids, Iowa; the Post Office Department objected to this name, and suggested Charger. Local people sent in a second name, Ucross, for post office, which was accepted.

Uhl Hill, Teton: named for early homesteader Uhl.

Uinta County: Evanston is the county seat; it is named for the Uintah Mountains, a majestic mountain range in Utah to the south, visible from all parts of the county; this is the only east-west mountain range in the United States and is named for the Uintah Indians. It is the Indian word for "Land of Pines."

Uinta was the first new county created by the Wyoming territorial laws in 1869; it then extended the full width of the state. It was given its present boundaries in 1911, when Lincoln County was formed. Uinta is the smallest county in Wyoming, but almost twice as large as Rhode Island. It has no elevation lower than 6,000 feet, with cool summers and cold winters; it is quite arid.

The Union Pacific railroad with shops at Evanston gives major employment in the county; it is also tourist country with hunting, fishing, boating, and water skiing on the Sulphur Creek Reservoir. Livestock raising, dairying, and lumbering are the chief industries. A furniture factory has been started in Evanston.

Fort Bridger, one of the earliest settlements in the state, is now a state park, preserving its romantic history in museums and restored buildings, such as officers' quarters and Pony Express stables.

The first newspaper in Wyoming, the *Daily Telegraph*, was published here by Hiram Brundage in 1863; it was printed on one side of a 6½x10½-inch sheet. The first schoolhouse in the state was built here and is still standing.

GRANDMA SCHOOLHOUSE
Dedicated to Uinta County

Near the fort that once protected,
Stands a schoolhouse, old and small,
Almost ninety years she has weathered . . .
Great, great grandma of them all.

Grandma of the vast brick buildings
That now trace Wyoming's plains;
Grandma of the sand-stone structures
Where profoundest wisdom reigns.

Just one room, a pine board cabin,
Where the simple things were taught
To the first Wyoming children
While their dads explored and fought.

Braced against her stands the milk house,
Staunch companion through the years.
Grey and curling are her shingles;
In her ridge a curve appears.

Wrapped in shawl of russet color
(Once they say that it was red)
Grandma Schoolhouse sits a-dreaming
Of the trend that she has led.

Mae Urbanek

Ulm, Sheridan: railroad station named by a railroad builder for Ulm, Germany, where he was born.

Underhill Ridge, Teton: probably named for Bob and Marian Underhill. Mrs. Underhill is one of the great women mountain climbers of this generation. Bob Underhill has made many first ascents of American peaks. They both have climbed over many Wyoming hills.

Underwood, Laramie: discontinued ranch post office and railroad flag stop named for John J. Underwood.

Undsoeld's Needle, 11,500, Teton: named for William Undsoeld who first climbed it in 1952.

Union Pacific Railroad: across the entire southern part of Wyoming, with feeder lines running north into other counties. The Civil War brought out the necessity of uniting settlements along the Pacific Ocean with the rest of the country by means of a transcontinental railroad.

President Lincoln worked unceasingly to interest wealthy men in the project. Finally, with the aid of Congress in 1865, the building of the Union Pacific started west from Omaha, Nebraska. At the same time Central Pacific started east from Sacramento, California. The name Union Pacific comes from the purpose of uniting the Pacific population with the rest of the Union.

Union Pacific officials had difficulty deciding on the route; the mountains west of Denver would require costly tunnels; South Pass meant snow-blocked tracks in winter. Jim Bridger was called into consultation. Taking a piece of charcoal from the fire, he drew the mountains he knew so well and through them traced his suggested route, an old buffalo trail. This was the route the railroad followed. The vast coal beds of southern Wyoming were a necessary boon.

It was necessary to ship oak ties out from Pennsylvania for use on the treeless prairies. When timbered mountains were reached west of Cheyenne, large tie camps sprang up. Indians attacked surveying crews; teams and scrapers built grades. Many of the workers were Irishmen who called the railroad "U-Pay."

Money for construction ran low. Men like Oliver and Oakes Ames, Massachusetts manufacturers, with their financial help and drive for funds, kept the crews paid, and the work going on. Congress gave the railroad 20 sections of public lands for each mile of track, mineral rights included. These were odd-numbered sections lying in 20-mile strips on each side of the track.

This first transcontinental railroad in the United States brought about the development and settlement of Wyoming, as towns sprouted along the tracks; coal miners dug black treasure from the earth; homesteaders came with milk cows and chickens to replace the crews that laid the railroad tracks. Finally, on May 10, 1869, the two railroads met at Promontory, Utah, and a golden spike was driven, uniting a 1,848-mile stretch of rails. The iron horse took the place of oxen.

Railroads are the arteries of a country, uniting and feeding it—filling it with pulsing, throbbing activity.

The last Union Pacific passenger train passed through Wyoming May 1, 1971, after 104 years of service; Amtrack took over.

Union Pass, 9,210, Fremont, Sublette: Wilson Price Hunt, westbound in 1811, followed an Indian and game trail through this pass. Capt. Bonneville crossed it in 1833. Capt. William F. Raynolds, guided by Jim Bridger, crossed the pass in 1860; he named it Union because it unites two great watersheds: the Green River to the west, and the Wind River to the east.

Another version of the name is that Capt. Raynolds called it Union Pass and Union Peak, because he hoped that the threatening Civil War could be averted.

Union Peak, 11,400, Fremont, Sublette: named by Captain Raynolds.

University of Wyoming, Albany: only four-year college in Wyoming; it is located in Laramie. The university opened on September 6, 1887, with ex-governor Hoyt as president. Old Main, the only building, housed all classrooms and laboratories. The enrollment was 42 students; the campus was 17 acres in size.

The University of Wyoming has now grown to more than 35 large structures, made of native sandstone, on a 437-acre, beautifully landscaped and planted campus. From two graduates in 1891, after 75 years of expansion, there were 1,013 graduates in 1964. Students now attend from every state in the Union and more than 20 foreign countries, because of the excellent educational facilities and democratic atmosphere.

As a land grant college, the University of Wyoming also carries on extensive work through Agricultural Extension offices in the counties. Two-year junior colleges, connected with the university, are at Casper, Sheridan, Powell, Riverton, Rock Springs, and Torrington.

The university football team acquired the name "Cowboys" in 1891, two years before the first official game. A 220-pound cowpuncher, Fred Bush (ex-Havard), trotted on the field to play against Cheyenne. He had on a checkered shirt and Stetson hat. Someone yelled, "Look at the cowboy!" Many team members were ex-cowboys. The name stuck.

Upper Geyser Basin, YNP: on September 7, 1927, Col. Charles A. Lindbergh circled over this area in the Spirit of St. Louis. He was barnstorming the country after his historic trans-Atlantic flight in May.

Upton, Weston: first known as Irontown, because of its brackish water; the name was changed to Merino, a breed of sheep, when sheep raising became the chief industry in the area. When the Burlington railroad came, its officials named the town Upton for George S. Upton, one of their surveyors in 1902; it is now a large bentonite center with two processing plants, shipping out about 300 tons daily.

Urie, Uinta: village named for Nicholas Urie, homesteader.

Utah and Northern Railroad: see Oregon Short Line.

Uva, Platte: Col. W. G. Bullock, sutler's agent at Fort Laramie, started a ranch here in 1871; he was so bothered by Indians he moved to the Chugwater. Later a post office was established here (it is discontinued now) and named Uva by postmaster W. R. Ralson. Uva is Spanish for grape. There were many wild grape vines on the North Laramie River.

Another version of the name is that it was an old cattle brand. Uva was once a road ranch on the Oregon Trail. In the days of the open range the large Duck Bar cattle spread centered here; it was a cattle-shipping point. The Teschemacher brothers, rich Englishmen and cattle owners, lived here until, after involvement in the Johnson County War, they returned to their native country. The widow of John "Portugee" Phillips also made her home here.

V

V Bar V Ranch, Sublette: five miles northwest of Bondurant is the site where the Rev. Samuel Parker in 1835 preached the first Protestant sermon in Wyoming. In the middle of his remarks to trappers and Indians, a herd of buffalo appeared; every man took off with his horse and gun, leaving Rev. Parker to discourse to empty ground. However, the Rev. Parker joined the others in feasting on buffalo meat that night.

Vagner Lake, Carbon: named for Charles Vagner; he was with the Carbon Timber Company during its early logging operations here.

Valentine Geyser, YNP: first erupted on Valentine's Day 1902.

Valentine Lake, Creek, and Mountain, 11,147, Fremont: in Popo Agie Primitive Area; boasts golden trout.

Valhalla Canyon, Teton: named by J. Durrance and party when they camped here under Grand Teton; they considered this the most beautiful cliff-hung camp cirque in the Tetons. Valhalla is Old Norse and means an adorned hall or temple.

Valiate Lake, Fremont: a beautiful lake near the Continental Divide in the Wind River Range, named for Mrs. Valiate Decker, GP Bar ranch.

Valley, Park: old dude ranch with rustic buildings named about 1890 by James McLauglin, hunter and trapper for its location in the valley of the South Fork of the Shoshone River.

Van Dyke, Sweetwater: named for Van Dyke, landowner of coal claims near the station.

Van Kleeck, Goshen: discontinued post office named for Edward Van Kleeck.

Van Ortwick Hill, Albany: a steep, rugged ridge named in the 1880s for Gilbert Van Ortwick, rancher.

Van Tassell, Niobrara: village named for Schuyler Van Tassell, a pioneer rancher with large holdings. He did not want a town named for himself and ignored its railroad station; he continued to freight his supplies 150 miles from Cheyenne.

Ferdinand Branstetter Post No. 1 was started here in 1919, the first American Legion Post organized in the United States. Branstetter came to Van Tassell in 1914 and was the first to enlist from this community; he was also the first to be killed in trench warfare. Van Tassell is on the National Register of Historic Places.

Vaughn, Goshen: once a section house and beet dump named for Mr. Vaughn; nothing is here now.

Vedauwoo Glen, Albany: a favorite picnic spot in the rocks and evergreens east of Laramie; it is the Arapaho name for "earth-born"; the site was owned by Governor B. B. Brooks in the 1890s.

Mrs. Mabelle Land Dekay named her play depicting the birth of Wyoming "Vedauwoo"; later she named the picnic spot.

Vermillion Creek, Sweetwater: named by Gen. Fremont in 1842 for the red earth in the creek bottom.

Verona, Sheridan: a railroad station named by a railroad worker for a city in Italy.

Verse, Converse: discontinued post office named for "verse" in the county name.

Veteran, Goshen: village where practically all land was filed on by ex-servicemen who drew lots for the land in 1920.

Victoria, Carbon: near the southern boundary of the county; it was a stopping station used by sheepmen on the trail from West Fork; it was named for Victoria, Texas, by Mr. and Mrs. Roy Deming in 1890.

Virginia Cascade, YNP: named by E. Lamertine in 1886, foreman of government work here, for Virginia, the wife of the president of the Yellowstone National Park Association.

Viva Naughton Lake, Lincoln: made by damming up Hams Fork River in 1941; as part of the Kemmerer project for water, a large dam was built in 1962 by Utah Power and Light Company for power production; the lake also provides good fishing.

W

Wadsworth, Fremont: see Riverton.

Wagner Lake, Teton: named for Wagner, early trapper, who was killed by a stranger he befriended.

Wagner Prong Creek, Sheridan: named for Billy Wagner, early settler who served as county commissioner.

Wagon Box Fight Site, Sheridan: in 1867 a wood-cutting crew from Fort Phil Kearny used overturned wagon boxes as a fort for protection from Indians. Here Red Cloud and his warriors faced new breech-loading rifles for the first time; bravely they charged time after time, but were mowed down by unceasing fire. They were defeated and their losses were heavy; 32 men behind 14 wagon boxes stood off more than 3,000 Sioux for seven hours of continuous fighting.

Wagon Gulch, Fremont: named for wagons of emigrants who went up this gulch instead of past Stony Point.

Wahb Springs, YNP: named for author Ernest Thompson Seton's famous grizzly bear, Wahb, who roamed the Yellowstone area. Seton was an illustrator and writer of nature stories.

Walcott Junction, Carbon: here a branch line of the Union Pacific railroad leads to Saratoga and Encampment; it was named for Walcott, conductor between Cheyenne and Green River City.

During the copper mining development in the mountains near Encampment in the 1890s and early 1900s, more freight was handled at Walcott than at any other Union Pacific station between Omaha and Ogden, Utah; mine and smelter machinery, coal, coke, and building materials came in; copper ore and smelter products went out.

Walker Creek, Sheridan: named for Ben Walker who mined at the head of Wolf Creek and argued with Joseph O'Neil, rancher, over mine claims; he was shot and killed by O'Neil and buried near his cabin in 1884; the inquest was held near midnight by the light of a campfire.

Walker Mountain, Sheridan: named for Ben Walker who mined at the head of Wolf Creek; see Walker Creek.

Wall Rock Creek, Sheridan: named for beautiful wall of rocks near the mouth of the creek.

Wallow Lakes, Johnson: named for buffalo wallows, where these huge animals took their dirt baths.

Wallrock Creek, Albany: named in the 1870s for rock benches on both sides of the creek.

Waln, Big Horn: discontinued post office named for postmaster Waln.

Walsh, Sheridan: discontinued post office named for Edith Walsh, postmaster.

Walt Bailey Peak, 12,142, Sublette: named for Albert Walter Bailey, who founded the first classes in mountaineering at Casper College. As a graduating exercise these classes climbed Devils Tower in Crook County.

A popular and eminent mountaineer, Walt Bailey died of pneumonia in

1958 on Mount Alpamayo in Peru, South America. He had climbed many peaks in the Wind River Range.

Waltman, Natrona: village named by railroad officials for Waltman Walters, son of an early general manager of the Chicago and Northwestern railroad; it was once known as Keg Springs.

Walton, Natrona: in wool shipping area; originally called Wolton, the name was changed to Walton for easier pronunciation.

Wamsutter, Sweetwater: the original name was Washakie; this caused much confusion, because freight for Fort Washakie was often sent here; so the name was changed in 1884 or 1885 to Wamsutter, for a German bridge builder on the Union Pacific railroad.

Turritella agates are scattered over dry prairies south of Wamsutter. These agatized shells were once the homes of life in marshy flats or lakes here. "Turris" is Latin for tower; the tiny shells twist like miniature towers. Millions of shells are weathered out of their matrices. Turritella agates are excellent for sawing and polishing.

Wapiti Ranger Station, Park: built in 1903 in the Yellowstone Timberland Reserve, this is the oldest ranger station in the United States; now it is located in the Shoshone National Forest.

Wapiti is an Indian name for elk; this majestic animal is as tall as a horse, handsomely formed with a luxurious dark mane; the bull is armed with imposing antlers that are shed early each spring.

Wapiti Wilderness by Margaret Murie tells of life in Jackson Hole and in the mountains; it is about elk and other wildlife and is illustrated with pen-and-ink drawings by Olaus Murie. The Murie home is at Moose.

War Bonnet Ridge, 12,369, Fremont, Sublette: named by Orrin Bonney in 1940 because of towers or "feathers" on its wedge-like summit.

Ward, Crook: discontinued post office named for Felix Ward, postmaster.

Warm Springs, Platte: the spring has a temperature of 70 degrees and remains unfrozen in the coldest weather. It was called "Emigrant's Wash Tub" as many did their washing here when traveling in the early days.

Warpath Lookout Station, Sheridan: Indians used to climb and watch from here; they sent out smoke signals of warning or information. Later, whites watched from here for the smoke of forest fires.

Warren, Niobrara: discontinued ranch post office named for Francis E. Warren, governor and U.S. senator. Later, the post office was renamed Bridge, for the postmaster; again, it was renamed Bright for Joe Bright, postmaster.

Warren was on the ULA ranch, which was named for Eula Wulfjen, daughter of the owner. John B. Kendrick helped hew logs for the house, stables, and blacksmith shop here; he was foreman for years in the 1880s. Eula Wulfjen became Mrs. John B. Kendrick in 1891.

William Keating bought the ranch in the 1890s. It was located on Lance Creek. In 1895 Miss Houston, who taught school at the ranch, had a bad toothache. It was winter time; large stones were heated all night for foot warmers. Bundled up in a sled, the family left at 3 A.M. in sub-zero weather for Edgemont, South Dakota.

At noon they stopped to feed the team, built a big fire to reheat the

216

stones, and made coffee. They reached Edgemont at 8 P.M. and roused the dentist from his home. The Keating children got as big a thrill out of the trip, as children nowadays might get from flying to Hawaii.

Warren Air Force Base, Laramie: see Fort D. A. Russell.

Warren, Mount, 13,720, Fremont, Sublette: named for Francis E. Warren, stockman, first governor of Wyoming, and U.S. senator. It takes 8 hours of hard rock and ice climbing to ascend Mount Warren.

Warren Peaks, Crook: named for U.S. Senator Francis E. Warren who in 1892 introduced a bill in the U.S. Senate for the establishment of Devils Tower National Park; no action was taken on the proposal.

Warrior Ridge, 12,406, Fremont, Sublette: named by Orrin Bonney for its precipitous and unclimbed faces.

Wasatch, Uinta: an Indian name. In the winter of 1868-69 it was an end-of-track town on the Union Pacific railroad and was soon gone. This was the last "Hell-on-wheels" town in Wyoming.

Wasatch National Forest, Uinta: named for the Wasatch Mountains; its 46,722 acres extend into Wyoming from Utah, with headquarters at Salt Lake City, Utah. Wasatch is an Indian name.

Washakie County: Worland, county seat; it was created in 1911 and organized in 1913; the name was suggested by Senator Cross of Converse County for Chief Washakie, a Shoshone Indian and great warrior, a just ruler of his people, and the best Indian ally the white men ever had. The name Washakie means "rattler."

Chief Washakie made himself a distinctive rattle of tanned buffalo skin filled with rocks tied on the end of a stick; he used this rattle to lead his warriors in fights and to scare the enemies' horses. Chief Washakie had a good tenor voice and often sang, accompanying himself with his rawhide rattle, "wus-sik-he."

Washakie County is ideal farming and livestock country in the Bighorn Basin; it is surrounded on three sides by the scenic Big Horn Mountains. It was the prized hunting ground of Chief Washakie and is the only Wyoming county named for an Indian chief.

Jim Bridger had 22 geographic features in Wyoming named for him, Chief Washakie rates at least 11 place names, while Jacques LaRamie has only nine.

The Holly Sugar Corporation has had a factory at Worland since 1917; it can handle 1,350 tons of beets daily. There are ten producing oil fields in the county; many fishing and recreation areas are popular in the summer, with skiing in the winter at Meadowlark Ski Area.

Washakie Creek, Sublette: named for Chief Washakie, one of nature's noblemen, always an example of fearless rectitude. He loved to wear a wide-brimmed sombrero, adorned with a silver coffin plate, on which was engraved *Our Baby*. He did not rob a grave to get this, but traded a bow and arrow to a coffin dealer in Evanston for it. He thought it a fine ornament.

Washakie Lake, Fremont: named for Chief Washakie. President Chester A. Arthur once presented Chief Washakie with a silk stovepipe hat. He wore the hat adorned with feathers. Golden trout abound here.

Washakie, Mount, 12,524, Fremont, Sublette: named for Chief

Washakie. After allotting the Wind River Indian Reservation to Chief Washakie and his Shoshones in 1878, the United States government, in violation of their treaty, placed Arapahoes, enemies of the Shoshones, on the reservation, much to the displeasure of both tribes. When a Shoshone then greeted an Arapaho, if he ever did, he extended two fingers, keeping the other fingers clenched, a sign of distrust.

Chief Washakie's house was the largest one on the reservation; it was kept in repair by the government. However, most of the time, Chief Washakie and his family lived in a tepee. He said the house was "heap cold." He kept his favorite horse in the house.

Washakie National Forest, Fremont, Sublette: originally part of the Yellowstone Timber Land Reserve; in 1908 it became the Bonneville National Forest, which was divided in 1911 into Bridger and Washakie national forests. In 1945 Washakie National Forest became the Washakie Division of the Shoshone National Forest.

It was named for Chief Washakie who boasted that "no white man's scalp had ever decorated the door of his tepee." He was the only Indian ever buried with full military honors by the United States Army; this was in 1900.

Washakie Needles, 12,496, Hot Springs: two peaks at the head of Owl Creek; part of an intrusive dacite plug, it is more erosion-resistant than the surrounding rock. The surface at the top of the highest needle has a 30-foot flat area. There is a hole through this peak, a few feet below the top. It was called a needle and named for Chief Washakie.

He climbed this peak in his youth to "make medicine"; after three days without food or drink, he returned with a great vision and many eagle feathers. Capt. Jones of the U.S. Army Corps of Engineers led an expedition into this country in 1873 in the hopes of putting through a road. He climbed and named the Washakie Needles.

When in 1868 the U.S. Treaty Commission informed Chief Washakie they would define the boundaries of his reservation by latitude and longitude, he asked how they would do that.

"By the stars," one commissioner replied.

Washakie shook his head. "When I die I go up yonder," he said, pointing to the heavens. "But now we are on earth. We will mark out the area by rivers and mountains. They are on earth." The commissioners agreed with him; rivers and mountains are the boundary lines of the reservation.

A pass, a range, a trail, a park, and a hotel are also named for Chief Washakie.

Washam, Sweetwater: discontinued post office named for Mrs. Pauline Washam, postmaster.

Washburn, Mount, 10,243, YNP: named by Hayden in 1871 for Gen. Henry Dana Washburn, leader of the Washburn party of 1870. Gen. Washburn climbed this mountain alone to discover the direction of, and route to, Yellowstone Lake.

Mount Washburn stands aloof and serene; it is fairly easy to climb; it is accessible to automobiles over a one-way road up the south slope and down the north side. The mount is made up of layers of volcanic breccia; the view from its summit is a 100-mile panorama of snow-capped mountains, alpine lakes, and wooded canyons.

Washburn Range, YNP: originally known as Elephant's Back for its size and shape, it was renamed for Gen. Washburn. The range is made up of volcanic breccia thrown out by ancient craters and built up to a height of 6,000 feet; the wind and water have eroded valleys in the layered rocks; then vast lava flows occurred, filling some of the valleys; they were ground and polished by glaciers.

Watt, Johnson: named for Peter Watt, pioneer cattleman.

Wauneta, Laramie: discontinued post office named by H. B. Newman for Wauneta, a local girl.

Webb Lake, Albany: named for John Webb, early rancher here.

Wedding-of-Waters Cave, Hot Springs: in cliff near the spot where the Wind River becomes the Bighorn River. Here in 1959 George C. Frison found and excavated this cave, finding atlatls, darts, and chipped points dating back 4,000 years.

Welcome, Crook: discontinued post office named for Welcome Gulch, an old mining camp.

Welcome Gulch, Crook: prospectors who traveled here on foot from Spearfish, South Dakota, found gold. They named the gulch Welcome because the find at the end of their journey was welcome.

This was a center of mining activity for many years; rich gold seams and pockets were found. Grace Hawthorne, actress, financed the first company to operate here. Inter-ocean ore taken out of here, containing free gold, was given first prize at the World's Fair in Chicago in 1893.

Wellington, Washakie: a German settlement here in 1900. A. G. Rupp built a store and named the village after his son Wellington.

Wells, Sublette: discontinued post office and dude ranch named for William Wells, an early rancher who brought exploring and hunting parties into the region; he was editor of the *Pinedale Roundup* from 1907-09.

Wells, Uinta: discontinued post office named for William Wells, postmaster.

Wells Creek, Sublette: named for William Wells, rancher.

Wendover, Platte: a stage station on Cheyenne-Deadwood trail, a discontinued post office, and a railroad station.

West Thumb Bay, YNP: so named because Yellowstone Lake is roughly shaped like an open hand, with the thumb pointing west and fingers pointing south.

Weston County: Newcastle, county seat; named for John B. Weston, geologist and surveyor, who organized a pack outfit, and explored the canyons north of the present Newcastle for coal in 1887. He and Frank Mondell located rich anthracite deposits; the railroad came because of this coal; it reached and founded Newcastle in 1889.

Weston County was created in 1890; coal was mined at Cambria until 1929, with a peak development of 400,000 tons yearly. As early as 1891 shallow oil wells were drilled in the county; by 1962 there were 21 producing oil and gas fields. The Sioux Oil Company at Newcastle has one of the largest refineries in the state; livestock raising, lumbering, mining and processing bentonite are other industries.

In commemoration of Wyoming's 75th anniversary in 1965, an expedition of 33 covered wagons with 69 people in authentic old-time attire traveled from Weston County to the state fair in Douglas, a distance of about 110 miles in nine or ten days. They camped out, cooked over campfires, and slept under the stars. They took "sponge baths" and had a church service sitting on bales of hay. The wedding of Donna Holwell and Douglas Scott took place on the trip. Governor and Mrs. Clifford Hansen joined the trek part time.

Westvaco, Sweetwater: trona mining town of FMC Corporation; more than a million tons of trona were processed here yearly; it is a company name.

Whalen Canyon, Platte: named for Richard Whalen, freighter and early rancher.

Whalen Diversion Dam, near Goshen and Platte county line: built on the Platte River for irrigation and named for the canyon.

Wheatland, Platte: county seat; founded in 1894, it was first named Gilchrist for a rancher. When the town site was moved to Wheatland Flâts where irrigation was being developed, the name was changed to Wheatland. A camp nearer the mountains in 1885 was called Wheatfield. Wheatland Flats were named for their wheat fields. The first land was plowed here in 1885 by Bill Bodley with an ox team.

Wheatland once had one of the largest flour mills in Wyoming; it also had a sugar beet factory. These are now closed down. Marble, mined near Laramie Peak, is now processed for masonry and art work in the converted sugar beet factory. Strip-fallowed wheat has largely taken the place of irrigation.

Wheatland Reservoir, Albany: built in 1901-02 on the Laramie River under the Carey Act of the 1880s to bring water to arid lands and make farming possible. Johnny Gordon, a poet and fiddler known as the "Father of the Flats," first thought of storing water here and bringing it to Wheatland Flats.

A tunnel from Wheatland Reservoir carried water to Bluegrass and Sybille creeks and to the flats for irrigation. This was the first region irrigated under the Carey Act.

The reservoir broke in 1969, flooding the valley and causing extensive losses and damage. The reservoir and ditches are now restored.

Wheeler Flat, Albany: named for Wheeler, pioneer.

Wheeler Lake, Platte: named for Wheeler, a landowner here in the 1880s.

Whetstone Creek and Mountain, 9,600, Teton: named for the Whetstone Mining Company owned by Eastern capitalists; in 1896 tons of quicksilver and a sawmill were packed in here; a ferry was used to cross the Snake River; miners thought they could recover gold flour in the river with quicksilver. They failed in this as well as in finding the mother lode.

Another version of the name is that the company was named for the creek, which was named because a rock in the area resembled a whetstone.

Whiskey Creek and Mountain, Fremont: an old still and caches of whiskey were on the mountain before 1900; early settlers thought it cheaper to make whiskey than to buy it.

Charles Beck, a prohibitionist, developed a camp for Quaker boys and girls on this mountain; he tried in vain to have its name changed.

220

Whiskey Gap, Carbon: Major Farrell was in charge of moving the post office and stage station equipment from old Oregon Trail sites to the new station on the Overland Trail. He noticed some of his men were intoxicated. He ordered wagons searched and found a barrel of whiskey in a civilian wagon.

Farrell ordered the barrel smashed near a spring where they were camping. The whiskey poured over the ground and into the spring; soldiers ran with cups and pans to get what they could. Others stamped holes in the ground with the heels of their boots and lay on their stomachs to drink. One soldier said it was the finest spring water he had ever tasted. Farrell wrote in his record that it was fortunate the Indians did not attack that night.

Whiskey Peak, Carbon: named for Whiskey Gap.

Whistler Creek, Albany: named for Cliff Whistler, landowner here.

White Creek, Big Horn: named for Jim White, trapper, who was murdered on its banks in 1880 by two men who had wintered with him. They stole his team and wagon.

White Mountain, Sweetwater: scenic drive on top.

Whiting Spring, Platte: named for early school teacher, Whiting, who homesteaded here.

Whitman, Niobrara: discontinued post office on ranch named for E. R. Whitman, postmaster. Whitman was an authentic and colorful scout in "Legend of Rawhide," a Niobrara County production.

Whitney Gallery of Western Arts, Park: opened in Cody in 1959, it was named for Gertrude Vanderbilt Whitney, an artist who created and donated the statue of Buffalo Bill, which is near the museum.

This art gallery has the world's largest collection of Western American art, both paintings and sculptures; George Catlin's paintings of his historic trip up the Missouri River in 1832 are here; other artists represented are Alfred Jacob Miller, Frederic Remington, and Charles M. Russell.

Dr. Howard McCracken, authority and author on Western American art, is director. He started with bare walls and now has collected more than two million dollars' worth of Western art. The gallery is now too small for the vivid paintings that portray the history and development of the West.

BUFFALO BILL

Dedicated to Park County

I am riding to the mountains,
Riding westward on the trail;
Where adventure leads I follow,
Fair the day or fierce the gale.

All my friends rode on before me,
All the scouts that I once knew;
Buffalo have almost vanished;
Indians are meek and few.

I, Pahaska, ride forever,
On old Brigham, swift and wise,

Westward to unbranded mountains
Where the untamed eagle flies.

Mae Urbanek

Whoopup Canyon and Creek, Niobrara, Weston: named by cowboys because spring floods came a'whoopin' through; when dry, the creek bottom is paved with smooth, many-colored pebbles; it is lined with red walls in which are caves with petroglyphs that tell stories of ancient hunts.

Widdowfield, Carbon: named for Robert Widdowfield, deputy sheriff in Carbon County in 1878. He assisted in the arrest of George Parrot, "Big Nose George," and "Dutch Charlie," Union Pacific railroad bandits. Big Nose George was taken by a mob from a Rawlins prison and hanged to a telegraph pole.

Wiggins Fork Creek and Wiggins Peak, 12,160, Fremont: named for Jack Wiggins who homesteaded what is now Rocking Chair ranch, named for its brand. Wiggins packed surveyors into the country in 1900; it is claimed he gave them a quarter of beef so that they would name this creek after him; he wanted his name perpetuated in Wyoming.

Wiggins Fork Creek is famous for its petrified and agatized wood; there are perfect pieces of ancient wood preserved in agate of jewel-like quality.

Wigwams, 10,851, Teton: peaks named for their shapes as seen from the west.

Wilcox, Albany: an old Union Pacific railroad station named for Levi Wilcox, roadmaster on the railroad; he had a jewelry store in Laramie in the early days.

Near Wilcox in 1899 two men flagged down a train and ordered the engineer, whom they covered with revolvers, to cut off most of the train and, with engine, express, and baggage car, pull across the bridge and stop.

The bandits then dynamited the bridge and the express car and escaped with $60,000 in unsigned bank notes to Hole-in-the-Wall. Sheriff Hazen, Natrona County, pursued them with a posse. They shot and killed the sheriff and escaped to Montana. Butch Cassidy was credited with the robbery.

Wildcat, Campbell: discontinued post office named for Wildcat Creek, where wildcats once roamed.

Wilder, Johnson: discontinued post office named for E. S. Wilder, postmaster.

Wiley, Park: discontinued post office and ghost town named for Solon L. Wiley, who invested a personal fortune in taking water from the South Fork of the Shoshone River for his Wiley ditch to irrigate thousands of acres south and east of Cody. The project failed. The Oregon Basin Oil Field was discovered here later.

Williams Divide, Crook: named for homesteader Williams.

Willow Creek, Fremont: an overshot water wheel, 20 feet in diameter, was erected here below South Pass City in 1868 to mill gold from the Carissa Lode; the wheel stood until about 1910.

Willwood Diversion Dam, Park: completed in 1924 for irrigation and named for the district it irrigates.

222

Wilson, Teton: named for Elijah N. Wilson. He ran away from his Utah home as a child and lived with the Shoshone Indians in Wyoming; he was a Pony Express rider and a stagecoach driver; he established the first post office, store, and hotel in Wilson and was known as "Uncle Nick," especially to children, who gathered in his log cabin to hear him tell about his life with the Indians and how he helped five Mormon families over Teton Pass in 1889; they found food for their starving cattle in Jackson Hole.

On an old typewriter, pipe clenched between his teeth, Uncle Nick slowly pecked out the highlights of his life, full of Western expressions and "Uncle Nickisms." All his originality was lost when his manuscript was edited by Howard R. Driggs, college professor, and published as *Nick Wilson, Pioneer Boy among the Indians*.

Wilson is now a scenic outfitting point for pack trips.

Wilson Creek, Albany: named for Wilson, foreman of a sheep outfit about 1900.

Wilson Meadows, Fremont: named for Floyd Wilson, mountain climber; he had a camp here in 1946 for climbers.

Winchester, Washakie: discontinued post office named for R. S. Winchester, rancher and postmaster. When the railroad came through, Winchester objected to having his name on the boxcar that served as a station. So the railroad officials named the station Chatham.

Wind Creek, Weston: usually dry, but always windy here.

Wind River, Fremont: discontinued post office named for Wind River.

Wind River, Fremont: named by Indians for prevailing strong currents of wind coming down the river from the northwest, between the Shoshone and Wind River ranges.

The Wind River becomes the Bighorn River at the Wedding of the Waters in Wind River Canyon south of Thermopolis. There is no junction of rivers in this canyon. Probably this legendary Wedding of the Waters took place near Riverton, where the Popo Agie and Wind River join.

Wind River Canyon, Fremont, Hot Springs: a great cleft in the Owl Creek Mountains named for the Wind River; sheer cliffs 2,000 feet high line the canyon, revealing succeeding ages of geological history from Precambrian granite to Triassic Chugwater formations.

On one side of this 12-mile-long canyon, the Burlington railroad has carved and blasted a right-of-way; on the other side, Highways 20 and 789 follow the rushing course of the river. These highways were opened to travel in 1924.

Wind River Diversion Dam, Fremont: completed in 1923 for irrigation.

Wind River Indian Reservation, Fremont: the only Indian reservation in Wyoming; headquarters are at Fort Washakie; this land was allotted to Shoshones by the treaty of 1868, signed at Fort Bridger; the government bargained with Chief Washakie to get him and his Indians out of Bridger Valley so the railroad could go through.

In 1878 the United States government broke this treaty with a faithful and friendly Indian, Chief Washakie, and moved Arapaho onto the Shoshone Indian reservation. These two tribes were traditional enemies, and neither tribe was happy about the situation. Washakie gave his consent for the Arapaho to stay the winter of 1878-79 only; the government never moved them off. Eventually the Shoshones brought suit against the government for giving their land away and received more than $4,000,000 in damages; it was known as Tunnison money; George T. Tunnison was their lawyer.

In 1896 a section of the reservation, 55,000 acres, was ceded by the Shoshones to the government; this tract included the famous Hot Springs and Thermopolis area, and the land of the Riverton Project. The reservation now contains about two million acres. More than 2,000 Aprapaho live on the eastern part, more than 1,500 Shoshones on the western part; the two tribes leave each other strictly alone; they do have government councils that meet together.

The Arapaho now have a cooperative canning factory, supplied by their irrigated farming, as well as leathercraft and beadwork shops at Ethete. The Shoshone have slowly taken to farming, which they consider "women's work." They raise livestock.

White persons wishing to travel, fish, hunt, or climb mountains on the reservation must obtain a permit; fishing and hunting licenses can be bought from tribal game wardens. Both tribes hold separate sundances each year; the time is partly determined by the ripening of service berries. These pageants are based on mythical history, healing, and thanksgiving. Indians dance for three or four days and nights without food and water; see Sundance Mountain. The dates are not announced, as the Indians do not wish white spectators; however, whites are allowed to watch without cameras.

Wind River Peak, 13,499, Fremont, Sublette: formerly named Snow Peak, it was renamed for the Wind River Range and is the highest peak visible from the South Pass region; it was named by the Hayden Survey in 1877.

A report from F. M. Endlich, member of survey who climbed peak stated: "From the top a stone could be thrown eastward that would fall 2,000 feet before striking." The east face is steep; the west face is a grassy and granite slope. It is a favorite peak to climb.

Wind River Range, Fremont, Sublette, Teton: a continental backbone of granitic gneisses raised from deep in the earth by the upheaval of the Laramide Revolutions; it contains Gannett Peak, at 13,785 feet the highest point in Wyoming and the seven largest glaciers in the United States, Alaska excepted. Wilderness areas and the Wind River Indian Reservation protect 750,000 acres from roads and exploitation. The range ends in Togwotee Pass in the north and at South Pass in the south.

Capt. Benjamin Bonneville thoroughly explored the Wind River Range, making a complete circuit around it in the 1830s; he was the first to climb Gannett Peak, took complete notes, and drew maps. Washington Irving wrote from Bonneville's notes.

Windy Creek, Albany: named for Windy Peak.

Windy Peak, Albany: named by Jack Newell in 1878; he said all the wind in southeastern Wyoming was made up there.

Winegar Hole, Teton: 14,000 acres of meadow and swamp, located in the northwest corner of the county; it is bear, elk, and moose country with no maintained trails. Named after Willis Winegar, early Mormon freighter and hunter.

224

Winifred Peak, 12,700, Sublette: climbed in 1919 by A. C. Tate who named it for his daughter Winifred.

Winton, Sweetwater: discontinued post office and railroad station; a coal mining community, it was named for Winton Mageth or Meagath, original owner of the coal mine here.

Wisconsin Couloir and Pass, 11,550, Fremont, Sublette: named for Wisconsin climbers.

Wisconsin Creek and Gulch, Sheridan: named for a man from Wisconsin who lived here—George Ives, an errant highwayman and fancier of fine horses, which he raised; his place was a gang hangout in the early days.

Wise, Big Horn: discontinued post office named for George W. Wise.

Wister Draw, Teton: named for Owen Wister who had a cabin here.

Wister, Mount, 11,480, Teton: named for Owen Wister, author of *The Virginian*, a book that interested many people in Wyoming and depicted its wild, free life. Wister once maintained a summer home near here.

Wittombona Lake, Fremont: also called Hatchet Lake.

Wolf, Sheridan: post office named for Wolf Creek, where wolves once roamed. Here Howard Eaton started a dude ranch.

Wolf Creek Ranch, Sheridan: the first dude ranch in Wyoming. Mary Roberts Rhinehart spent summers here writing.

Wolf Range, Sheridan: known to oldtimers as the Panther Range; this small group of mountains southwest of Dayton was named for wolves.

Wolton, Natrona: discontinued post office named because in the early days this was a large shipping station for wool. Jack Clark was the station agent here in 1890, when it was known as Poison Creek Station.

In 1895 the Chicago and Northwestern railroad built a reservoir on Poison Creek as a watering place for livestock. At one time Wolton had one of the largest machine-shearing plants for sheep in the West. Buildings were made of logs hauled from the Big Horn Mountains, 40 miles away; wool was freighted to Casper on wagons.

In 1906 the road ranch moved to the railroad and the name was changed to Walton for easier pronunciation.

Woodring, Mount, 11,585, Teton: named for Sam T. Woodring, first superintendent of Grand Teton National Park; before that, he was chief ranger in Yellowstone National Park.

Woodrock, Sheridan: first it was a tie camp of the Burlington railroad; both wood and rock were found here; it was also known as McShane Tie Camp; when the tie lumber was exhausted, the plant was moved and renamed Rockwood.

Woodrow Wilson, Mount, 13,500, Fremont, Sublette: named by the Jones, Bessie, and Doll party of 1924, after one of them facetiously remarked, "It seems to have 14 points." President Woodrow Wilson made a speech to Congress in 1918, with 14 points to establish a "just and lasting peace."

Orrin Bonney, an authority on mountain climbing in Wyoming, believes with others that Mount Woodrow Wilson is the peak Gen. John Fremont climbed in 1842, rather than Fremont Peak. These mountain climbers are basing their opinions on detailed descriptions Gen. Fremont gave of the mountain he climbed and of its snowfields.

Woodruff, Uinta: named for Mormon apostle Woodruff, who settled here.

Woodruff Narrows Reservoir, Uinta: named for Mormon apostle Woodruff.

Woods Creek, Albany: named for Samuel Woods about 1880.

Woods Landing, Albany: it is said that no one, tired or hungry, who came to Samuel S. Woods's home, left without receiving all the comforts Mrs. Woods could give. In the 1880s Woods was a freighter on the route from Laramie to North Park, Colorado; later, and for many years, he was a sawmill owner. A community hall built here later attracted cowboys, lumberjacks, and Laramie college students to its dances on Saturday nights.

Woolsey Mountain, 13,000, Big Horn, Johnson: named by T. H. Rawles and W. B. and A. W. Willcox for Betty Woolsey's farther, whose death occurred tragically just before the first ascent of this peak.

Worland, Washakie: county seat; named for C. R. "Dad" Worland, who by 1903 had established a campsite on Bridger Trail by Fifteen Mile Creek; his camp grew into the town of Worland. The first school in 1904 was in a room partitioned off from the store; a schoolhouse was built in 1905; the Burlington railroad came in 1906.

Worland lies in rich farming and livestock feeding districts; the oldest sugar-processing mill in Wyoming is located here. The Boys Industrial Institute opened here in 1913. Oktoberfest, a pageant of old Germany, is held here the first weekend in October.

Eohippus, dawn horse only four feet high, roamed here and in Big Horn Basin 40 million years ago. Their fossilized remains have been found near Worland; it is a good area for rock hounds.

Worshipper, 10,900, Teton: named for its shape, like a church spire.

Worthen Dam, Fremont: where Lander gets its water supply.

Wright, Campbell: discontinued post office named for R. A. Wright, first postmaster and landowner; this coal mining town started in the 1970s.

Wyarno, Sheridan: post office and railroad station; see Arno.

Wylie, Park: discontinued post office named for Solon Wylie, builder of a canal to irrigate the Oregon Basin in 1908; see Oregon Basin. Wylie located his dam southeast of Cody on the Shoshone River, where a drop in height allowed a hydroelectric generator to produce 16,000 horsepower; he built a machine shop and lumber mill. The Wylie Company finally went broke.

Wyman, Albany: discontinued post office named for Charles Wyman, postmaster.

Wyman Gulch, Washakie: named for Morral Wyman, foreman of the old Bay State Cattle Company.

Wyncote, Goshen: E. B. Hudson and his wife, on a farm on Lucerne canal, were given a post office in 1903 with the coming of the Burlington railroad. The railroad officials set off a used passenger car for post office

226

use about three miles west of present Lingle. Several stores were started. H. D. Lingle offered free land to the railroad for its depot; this offer was accepted and Lingle was started. All of Wyncote moved to Lingle in 1909.

Wycolo, Albany: abandoned railroad station on Wyoming-Colorado state line.

Wyodak Coal Mine, Campbell: name from abbreviations of two states; mine operated by Homestake Mining Company of Lead, South Dakota; largest strip coal mine in the world; coal veins are 90 feet deep; started in 1920; has yielded more than one million tons of sub-bituminous coal.

Millions of years ago great swamps lush with ferns, sub-tropical plants, and trees grew here. This was the age of dinosaurs. A great climatic change took place; plants, trees, and dinosaurs were buried under thickening layers of mud, and perhaps volcanic ashes. Vegetation became coal and oil; later the Laramide revolution took place, and the whole mass rose; erosion had worn away part of the covering over the coal.

Wyoming, on July 10, 1890, Wyoming became the 44th state; for a history of the name, see Wyoming Territory. In 1889 at a special election a constitution was approved, and a delegation was sent to Congress asking for statehood. Opposition arose there against suffrage for women, the literacy requirement for voting, compulsory education, and the provision that aliens could own land. The 1880 census also showed a population of only 20,789 in Wyoming Territory; statehood required 60,000 residents.

Teritorial Representative Joseph M. Carey spoke so ardently for "Wyoming, young and enterprising," that statehood was granted. The census of 1890 showed a population of 62,555. December 10 is Wyoming Day; it commemorates the anniversary of woman suffrage, adopted December 10, 1889, by the territorial legislature.

Wyoming, 97,914 square miles, is now the ninth state in size; with a population of 328,591 in the 1970 census. Only Alaska of the fifty states has a smaller population. Great industrial growth has enlarged the population in recent years.

Pioneers with lofty imaginations and granite determinations settled Wyoming. Here life has an intangible quality, a challenge that cannot be put into words. It is known as the Equality State, the Cowboy State, and sometimes the Sagebrush State.

On Wyoming's fiftieth anniversary, Dr. Lester C. Hunt, later governor and U.S. senator, wrote: "The trapper, the explorer, the Pony Express rider and the cowboy may have passed over the hills, but the sunset against which the pioneers saw them silhouetted, still flames over Wyoming in scarlet and gold. Times may change, but the fundamental character of Wyoming will never change. There will always be the brightness of its sunshine, the pureness of its air, the music of its winds, the grandeur of its mountains, the inspiration of its forests, and the peace and security of its wide open spaces."

State motto: Cedant Arma Togae—Let arms yield to the gown, symbolizing the law.

Wyoming Central railroad, see Chicago and Northwestern railroad.

Wyoming Hereford Ranch, Laramie: was established on Crow Creek in 1882 by Frank and Morgan Swan who imported bulls from England; Prince Domino died in 1930 and has a memorial over his grave.

The ranch was once 60,000 acres in size; it has been in continual existence longer than any breeding ranch of major importance in North America.

Wyoming National Forest, Lincoln, Sublette: originally part of the Yellowstone National Forest, it was organized as the Wyoming National Forest in 1907; Bonneville National Forest was added in 1923; the name was changed to Bridger National Forest in 1941 to honor Jim Bridger.

Wyoming Peak, 11,363, Lincoln: highest peak in the Wyoming Range, it was first ascended in 1877 by A. D. Wilson of the Hayden surveys.

Wyoming Pioneer Museum, Converse: on state fair grounds; it features relics of the Indian wars, emigrant days, and agricultural development.

Wyoming Range, 10,000-11,363, Lincoln: first called the Bear River Range, it was renamed after the creation of Wyoming Territory in 1869.

Wyoming State Capitol, Laramie: located in Cheyenne; this building has been in use since 1888; it was made from sandstone from quarries near Rawlins and resembles the national Capitol in its classic lines; the east and west wings have been added. The senate chamber is in the west wing, the house of representatives in east wing.

Each chamber is decorated with four large murals depicting industry, pioneer life, law, and transportation; the murals are the work of Allen T. True. The ceiling of each chamber is stained glass, with the seal of the state in the center.

In the state seal a woman standing on a pedestal holds a banner bearing the words "Equal Rights"; beneath her on the pedestal is an eagle on a shield, which bears the number 44. On one side of the woman stands a man who represents ranchers and farmers; on the other side of her stands a man representing miners and oilmen.

Above the golden dome of the Capitol flies the state flag which was designed by Vena Keays of Buffalo and selected from 37 designs submitted in a contest conducted by the Daughters of the American Revolution in 1916. (Miss Keays is now Mrs. Keyes of Casper.)

Miss Keays, a graduate of the Art Institute in Chicago, wakened from sleep one night, with a clear and complete design in mind: the Great Seal of Wyoming centered in a white buffalo that once was monarch of the plains—white, the emblem of purity and uprightness; a blue field for the blue of Wyoming skies and mountains—symbolic of fidelty, justice, and virility; a red border representing the red men who knew and loved the land before the white men came to shed their blood conquering it. Miss Keays had the buffalo facing out to signify freedom; the only change made in her design was to face the buffalo toward the staff for better balance and proportion.

The Wyoming flag was officially adopted in 1917.

Wyoming state slogan: Stop roaming; try Wyoming; healthy, wealthy, growing Wyoming.

Wyoming State Fair, Converse: called "Wyoming Industrial Convention," the first Wyoming state fair was held in Sheridan in 1903. In 1904 Casper put on a larger show with automobile races, but became exhausted by its efforts.

228

The Chicago and Northwestern railroad then gave the land along the Platte River in Douglas in 1905, specifying that the fair be held for 25 consecutive years and be called "Wyoming State Fair." The state legislature has provided many fine buildings for this "show window" of Wyoming life and industry; youth activities and achievements are among the main features of the fair, held each year in August; livestock entries and sales, agricultural exhibits and contests, school displays, handiwork of homemakers, and arts and crafts, are also highlighted. The chief entertainment is a rodeo.

Wyoming State Historical Museum, Laramie: located in Cheyenne, this building preserves historical items, manuscripts, and pictures of Wyoming's past; Indian costumes fancy with bead and porcupine quill work; the canoe, *Mauritania*, that Jim Baker carved from a cottonwood tree; artifacts; pioneer relics. Any item of historic interest is collected and displayed here. Written records and newspapers are preserved on microfilm.

Wyoming Territory: created by an Act of Congress on July 25, 1868, it was first called Lincoln Territory. Senators had a lively debate on the name. Lincoln was discarded because no state or territory was then named for an individual. Cheyenne had several pronunciations; one senator thought Shoshone meant snake. Finally Senator James W. Nye of Nevada ended the debate by saying "Let's call it Wyoming."

Congressman James M. Ashley of Ohio in 1865 had introduced a bill creating a territory called Wyoming, the name coming from Wyoming valley in Pennsylvania, which was called Maughwauwama by the Leni Lanape Indians. Maughwauwama or Mecheweaming translated as "large plains," or "plains and mountains alternating." The simplified, English spelling became "Wyoming." Ashley's bill failed, but others were intorduced, until the territory was formed in 1868.

This territory had the same boundaries as the present state. Wyoming is unique in that it is the only state containing land from all four additions to the United States west of Mississippi River: Louisiana Purchase; Oregon Acquisition; Texas Annexation; and Mexican Cession.

Uinta was the first county created by Wyoming Territorial laws in 1869; Carter County, created by Dakota legislature in 1867, was renamed Sweetwater; Carbon, Albany, and Laramie counties already existed, created by Dakota legislature. All five counties extended the full width of the state.

The territorial government was organized and Governor John A. Campbell inaugurated April 5, 1869. He chose Cheyenne as a temporary capital. Gov. Campbell was appointed by President U. S. Grant.

Wyoming Western Railroad, Lincoln: see Oregon Short Line.

Wyopo, Fremont: three miles east of Lander, it was a crude oil loading station on an abandoned railroad.

Wyuta, Uinta: railroad station on the Wyoming-Utah border.

Y

Yampa River, Lincoln: old Indian name for Snake River. Yam-pah-pa was the name of a plant used for food, that grew in profusion along the river's banks. Another version of the name is that it was the Ute Indian word for "bear."

Yellowstone Canyon, YNP: see Grand Canyon of the Yellowstone.

Yellowstone Falls, YNP: rapids of the Yellowstone River whip white foam over a 109-foot precipice, making the Upper Falls. In the background is Chittenden Memorial bridge; the old bridge was built in 1903 and served until 1961, when a new one was constructed to span the Yellowstone River. The bridge was named to honor Captain Hiram Martin Chittenden, U.S. Corps of Engineers and author. He supervised construction of the first Fishing Bridge in 1901 and the Theodore Roosevelt Arch near Mammoth Hot Springs.

The Lower Falls drop 308 feet, twice as far as Niagara; they are in a setting of pristine beauty; the dramatic orchestration of cascading water can be heard for a mile. Uncle Tom's Trail, built by Thomas Richardson about 1902, was a dangerous path down the south wall of the Grand Canyon to the base of Lower Falls. It has been replaced with a stairway and a safe trail.

Yellowstone Forest Reserve, Fremont, Hot Springs, Park: created in 1902, it was the first reserve to be created. The reserve later became known as the Shoshone National Forest. See Yellowstone Timberland.

Yellowstone Lake, 7,741, YNP: named for the Yellowstone River, it is one of the largest high altitude lakes in the world—139 square miles in area, with a shoreline more than 100 miles. It is crudely shaped like an open hand; probably shaped by lava flows that left a depressed center, later deepened by glaciers.

Yellowstone Lake appears on explorer Clark's early map as Lake Eustis, named for William Eustis, Secretary of War in 1811. Clark discussed this lake with Colter, the first white man to see it in 1807-08. The lake was once drained by the Snake River ·that flows to the Pacific Ocean. A prehistoric terrestrial upheaval changed the drainage system, and sent its water to the Atlantic Ocean via the Yellowstone River. The lake is a remnant of a vast, prehistoric ocean that covered most of Wyoming. In 1907 a steamer was used on the lake.

Yellowstone Lake is the home ground of rare trumpeter swans, great blue herons, Canada geese, terns, and pelicans that resemble fleets of white boats on its cold, blue waters. The lake is prized for its trout fishing; no license is required. It also charms artists and dreamers with the anger of its sudden storms and the beauty of its sunsets.

Yellowstone National Park, named for the Yellowstone River. Its marvels were first seen by John Colter in 1807; it was conceived as a preservation of natural wonders by the Washburn, Landford, Doane Expedition of 1870. As members sat around a campfire discussing the wonders they had seen, Cornelius Hedges suggested keeping out private exploitation and preserving the area for all people for all time.

Yellowstone National Park was created by Congress in 1872 as the first and largest national park in the world. It is 3,472 square miles in size, nearly three times the size of Rhode Island. It is an amazing museum of volcanic activity: mountains formed by hot fires deep within the earth and then carved and polished by three ice ages; petrified forests stacked 27 deep in Specimen Ridge, revealing a history of incredible length.

More geysers than in all the rest of the world combined, about 3,000, play here, acting as safety valves for internal heat and pressure. Old Faithful is the queen of all geysers. Indians believed them evil spirits that dwelt in the earth; they shunned the present park, and offered sacrifices before daring to come for the obsidian so prized for making tools and arrowheads.

The first automobile entered the park in 1902, the second one in 1909, both from Montana. Automobiles were legally allowed in the park in 1915. There were more than 400,000 in 1972. Back in the 1900s officials were afraid "fire-engines" would scare wild game and fowl; these were only curious, running off a little way and coming back to see what was making all the noise. The only animals scared were horses drawing stagecoaches; they stood on their hind legs.

Yellowstone National Park is a wildlife paradise, where tourists can even get photographs of coyotes. There are more grizzly bears, a species almost extinct, here than any place in the world. They are not the black bears (these are also brown) that panhandle on roads and cause "bear jams." Grizzlies stay back in the wilderness and eat grass, berries, and rodents.

Rocky Mountain fringed gentian was chosen in 1926 as the Yellowstone National Park flower. Its name is derived from Gentius, King of Illyria, who discovered its medicinal value. There are more than 200 species of birds in the park.

Caught in the wild rush of tourists during summer months, it is difficult to think of Yellowstone National Park as a wilderness. The largest areas in the park are rarely touched by human feet; they lie in pristine loveliness only miles from the gleaming flow of automobiles. Trails for hikers and horseback riders are maintained by the park service and lead to a wonderland unknown to those tied down by seat belts, making an average of four or five hundred miles a day. Much of the beauty of Wyoming cannot be seen from an automobile. The Howard Eaton Trail circles for more than 150 miles.

The fascinating story of Yellowstone National Park is told in *Colter's Hell* by Grace Johnson; *Roadside Geology of Yellowstone Country*, by William Fritz tells of its geologic history, as does *Yellowstone—Its Underworld*, by C. Max Bauer; *Haynes Guide*, a paperback revised every year, is packed with information.

Yellowstone River, YNP: called by Indians Mi-tsi-a-da-zi, Yellow Rock River and named by early French explorers and trappers Roche Jaune, or rock yellow for the yellow soil and rocks of its canyon. Lewis and Clark, explorers, crossed this river in Montana in 1805 and officially used the translation Yellowstone in their reports.

Rising on Younts Peak and Two Ocean Pass, the Yellowstone River flows north northreast for 700 miles to join the Missouri. Although less than 100 miles run through Wyoming, its tributaries drain almost a third of the state.

Yellowstone Timberland Reserve, Park, Teton: first national forest created by President Benjamin Harrison in 1891 to protect timber on the public domain; the Teton Forest Reserve was carved out of it in 1897; it was enlarged by President Theodore Roosevelt in 1902 as the Yellowstone Forest Reserve; it was again enlarged and renamed the Shoshone National Forest in 1945.

Yellowtail Recreational Area, Big Horn: boating, fishing, skiing and picnicking are popular on water backed into the scenic Big Horn Canyon by the Yellowtail Dam in Montana; it was named for Yellowtail, Indian chief.

Yellowtail Reservoir, Big Horn: about 28½ miles of the 71-mile-long reservoir are within Wyoming. The dam in Montana was completed in 1965; it furnishes electric power.

Yoder, Goshen: named for Frank and Jess Yoder, who owned land where the village started.

Yosemite Peak, 9,980, Teton: so named because its east face resembles some of the giant formations in Yosemite Valley, California.

Younts Creek and Peak, 12,165, Park: named for Harry S. Younts, a packer for the Hayden Survey in 1878; he climbed the west spur of Grand Teton that year. In 1880 he was appointed gamekeeper of the Yellowstone National Park, thus becoming the first "ranger."

Z

Zenith, Teton: discontinued post office named for the height of its location.

Wyoming

Green of the pine, grey of the sage,
Mixed with the rocks crumbling with age;
Guarded by mountains touching the sky,
Blessed with a grandeur none can deny.

Mae Urbanek